PERFECTION IS
FINALLY
ATTAINED NOT
WHEN THERE IS
NO LONGER
ANYTHING TO
ADD, BUT
WHEN THERE IS
NO LONGER
ANYTHING TO
TAKE AWAY.

Antoine de Saint-Exupéry

CONTENTS:

This is a story based on actual events.
It has been modified to fit the comicbook format.

MADISON
SQUARE
GARDEN

1991

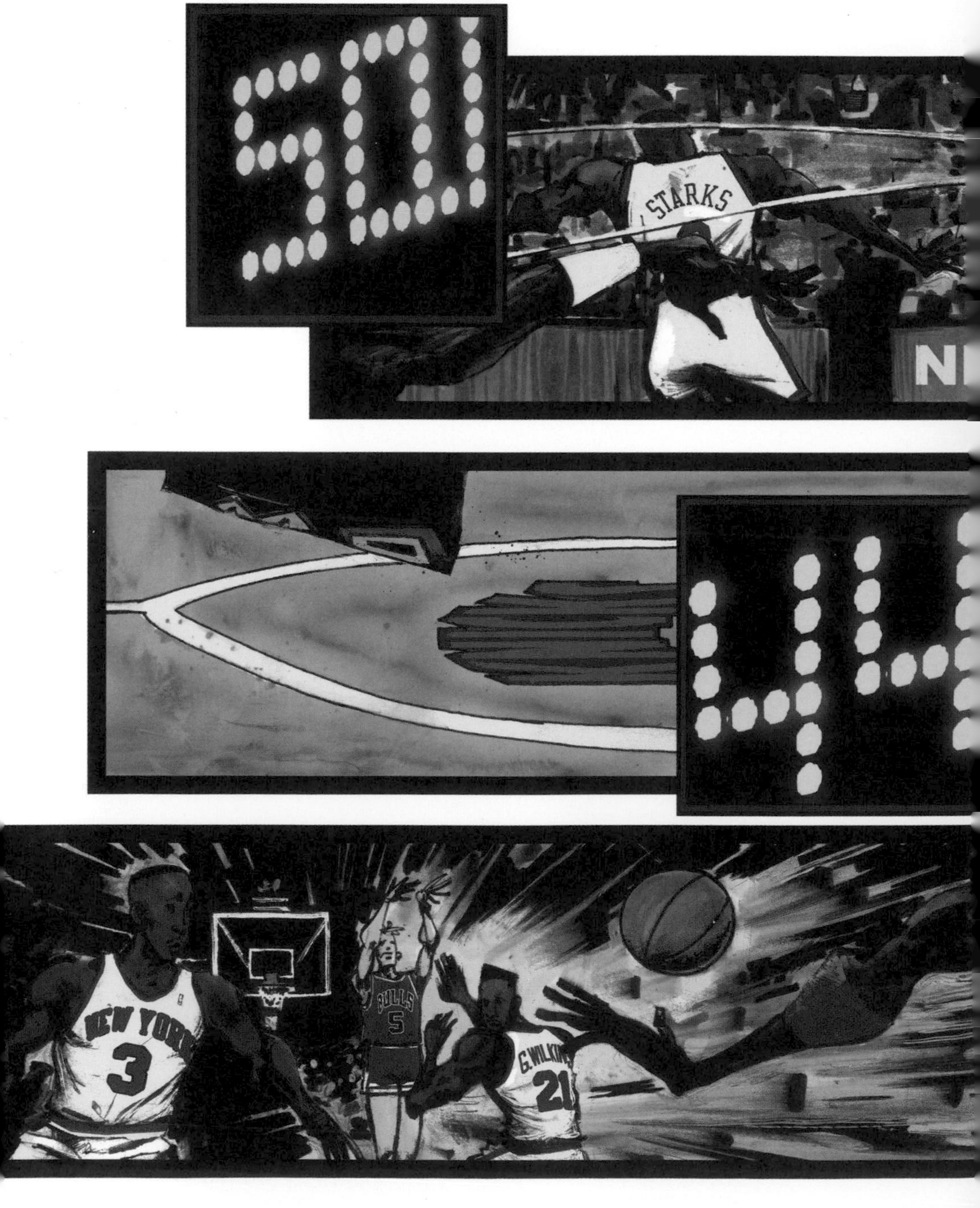
50
STARKS
NEW YORK
3
BULLS
5
21

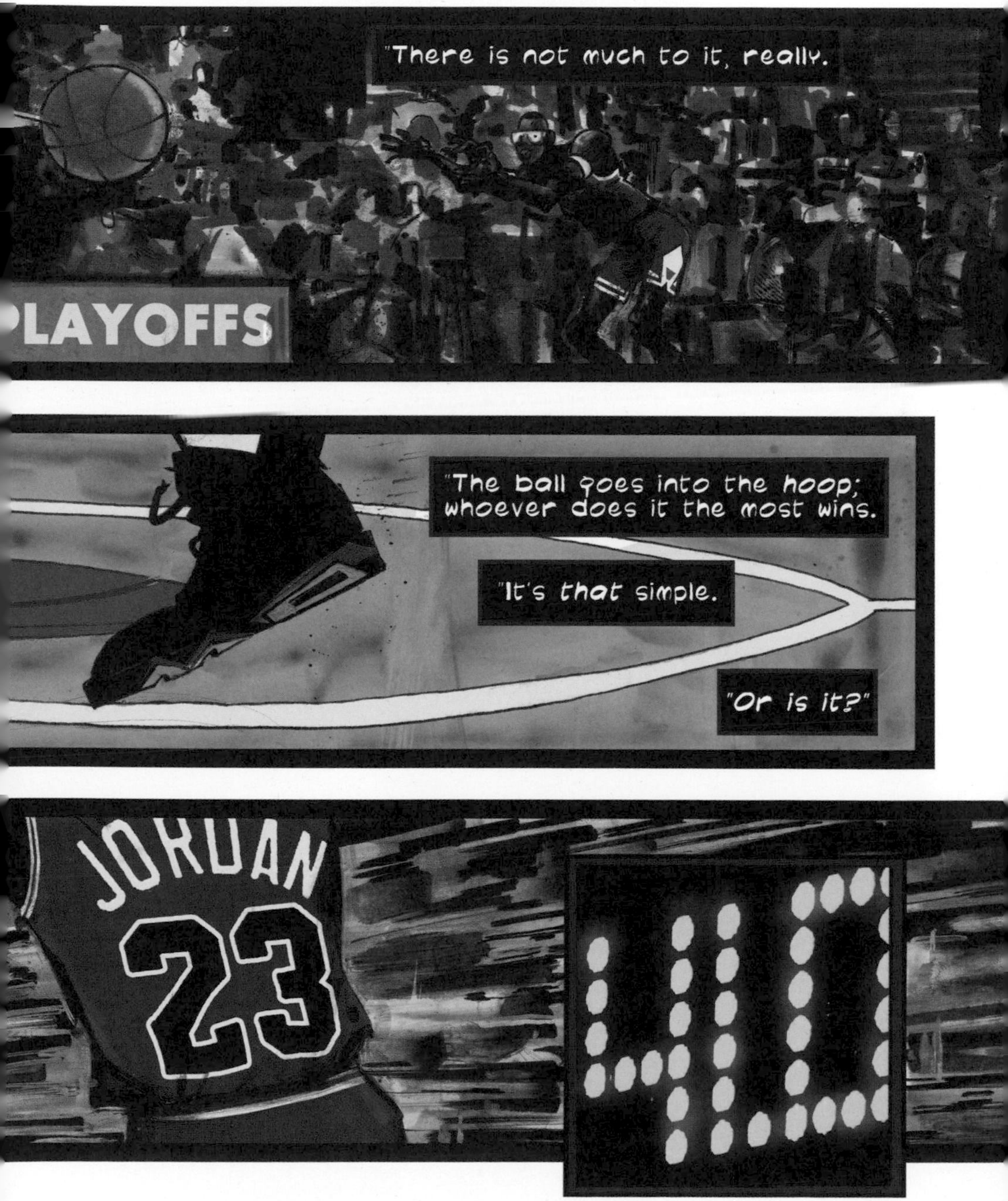
"There is not much to it, really.
PLAYOFFS
"The ball goes into the *hoop*; whoever does it the most wins.
"It's *that* simple.
"Or is it?"
JORDAN
23
40

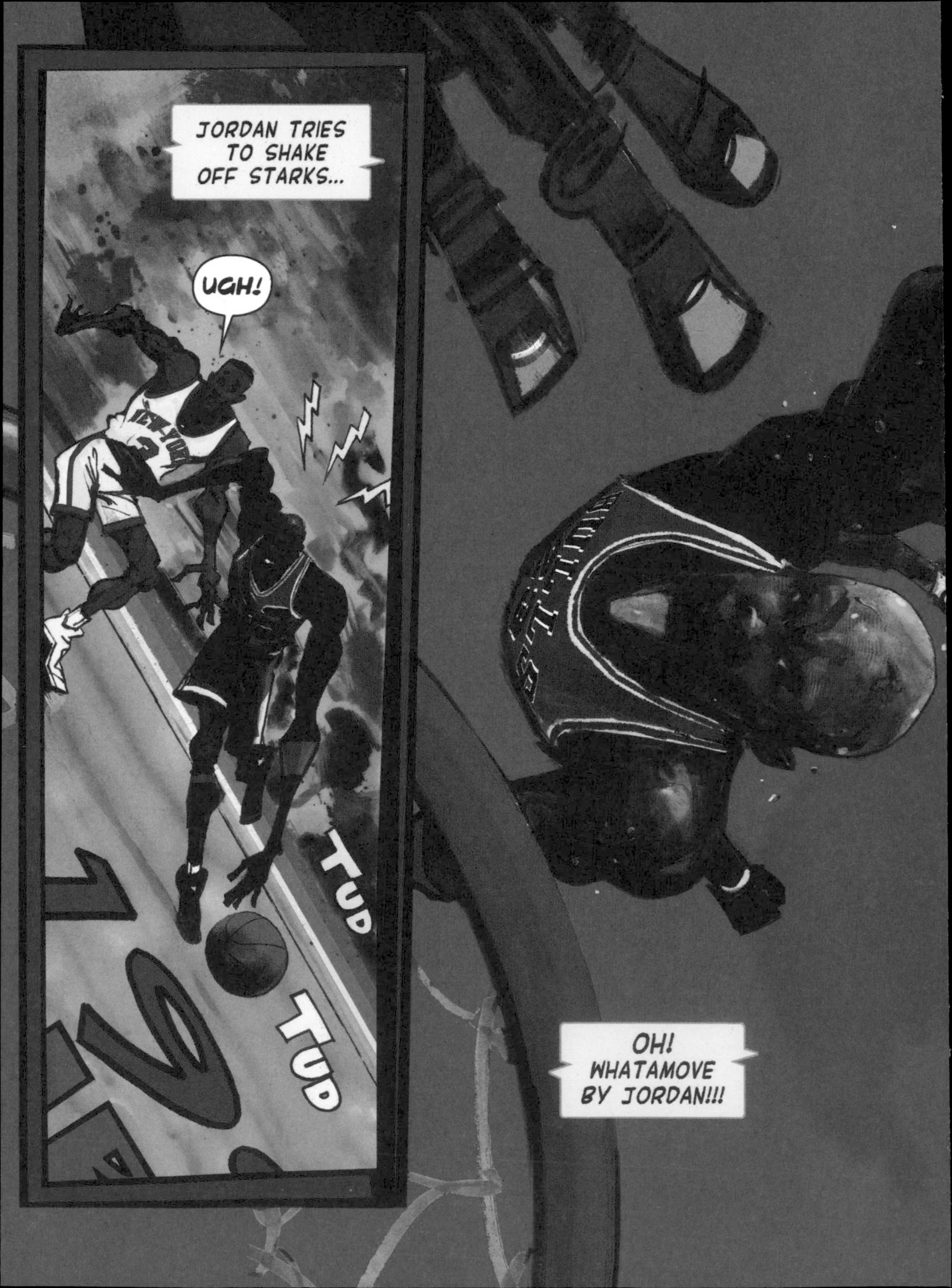
JORDAN TRIES TO SHAKE OFF STARKS...
UGH!
TUD
TUD
TUD
OH! WHATAMOVE BY JORDAN!!!

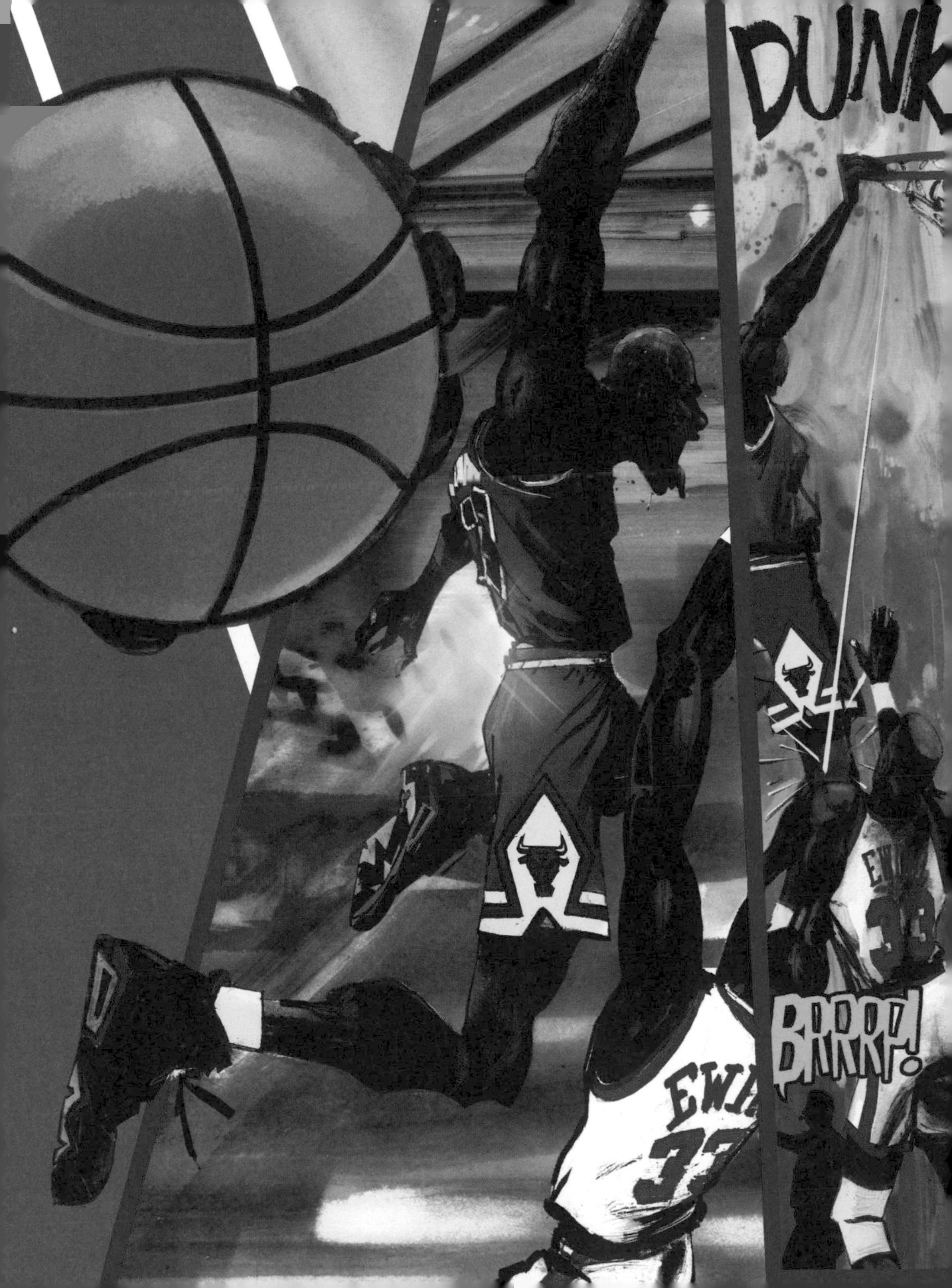
DUNK
BRRRP!

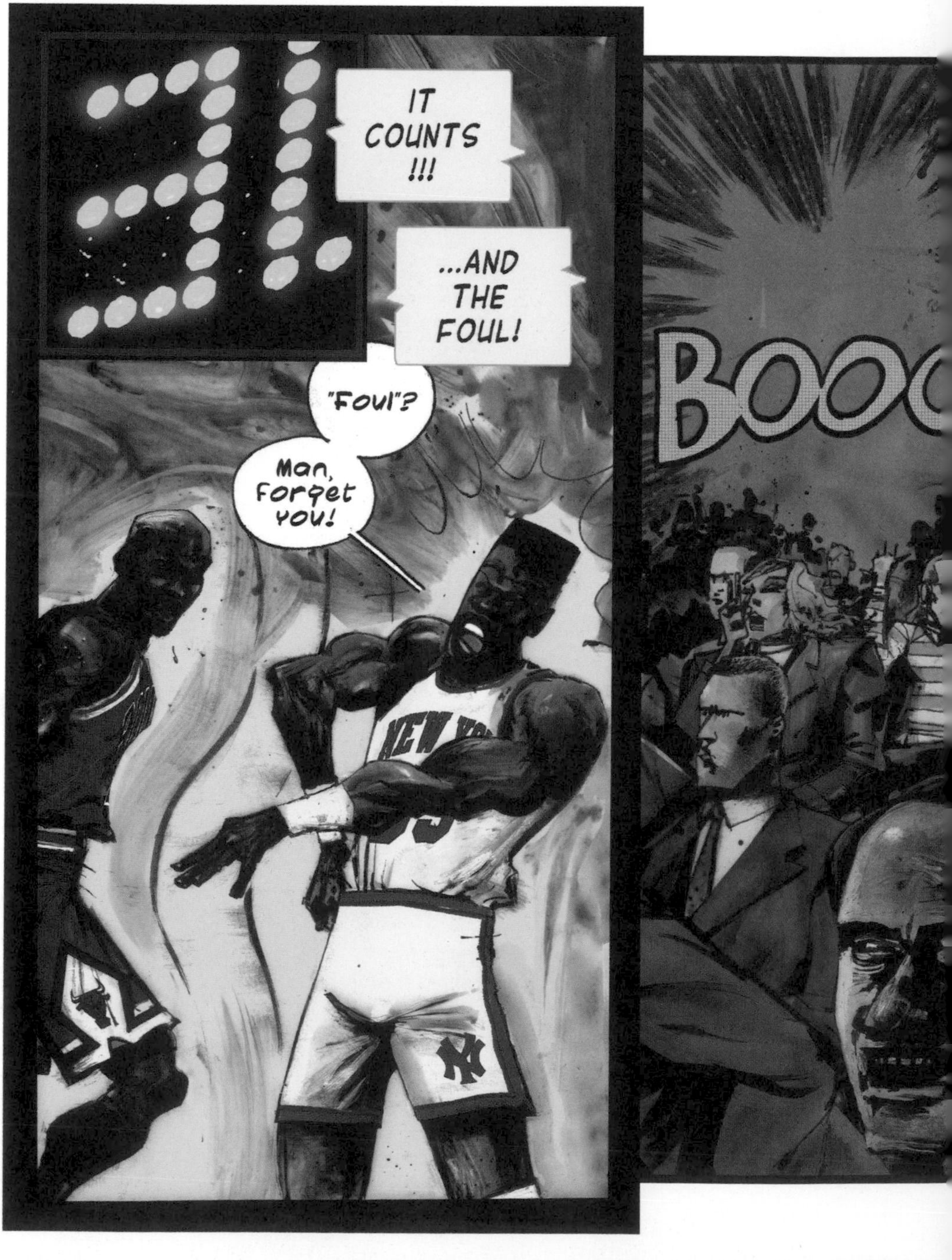
IT COUNTS !!!
...AND THE FOUL!
"Foul"?
Man, forget you!
NEW YO
BOOO

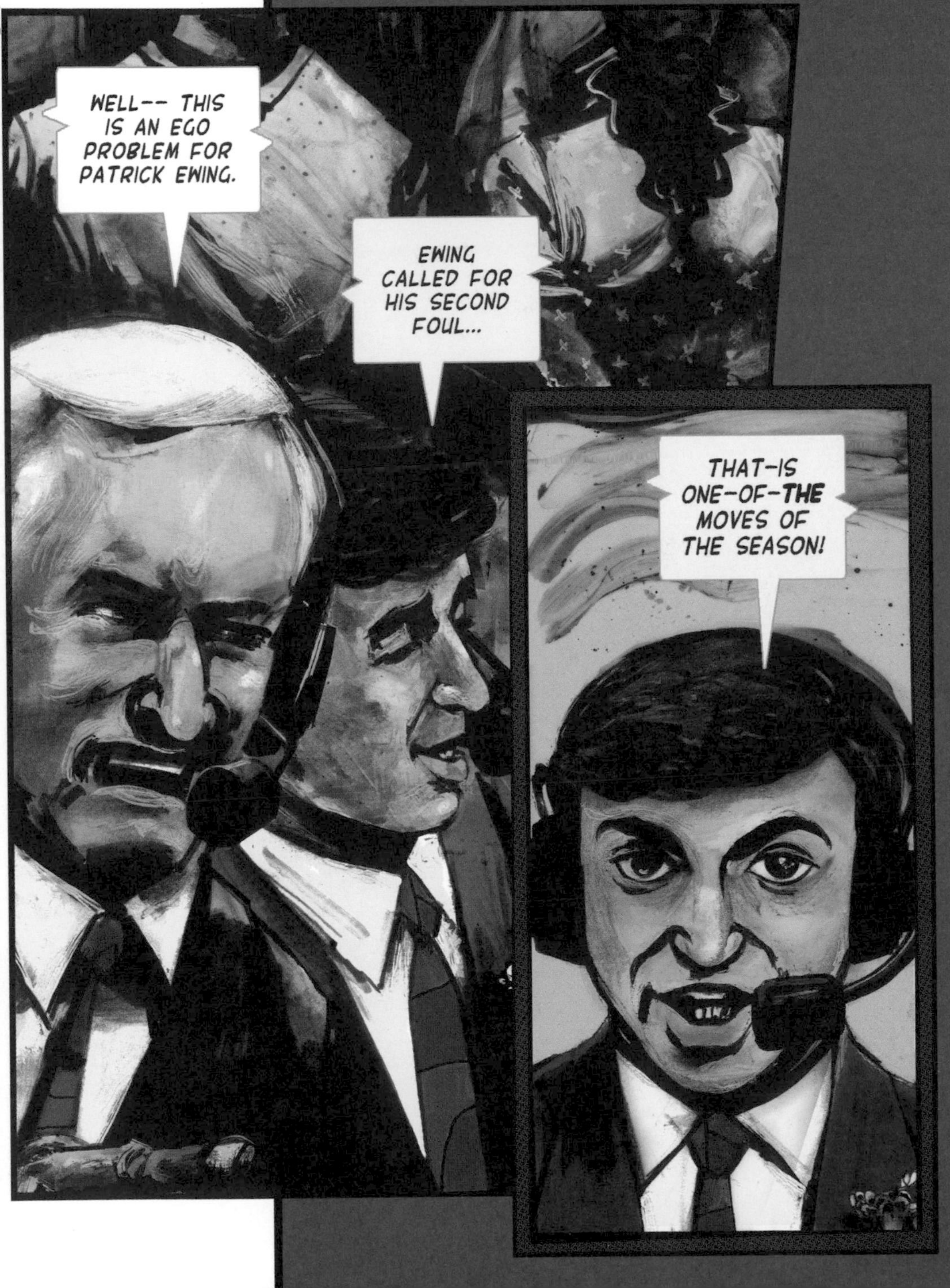
WELL-- THIS IS AN EGO PROBLEM FOR PATRICK EWING.
EWING CALLED FOR HIS SECOND FOUL...
THAT-IS ONE-OF-THE MOVES OF THE SEASON!

MICHAEL JORDAN
BULL ON PARADE

WRITTEN + DRAWN
by
WILFRED SANTIAGO

SEATTLE
Since 1976
www.fantagraphics.com

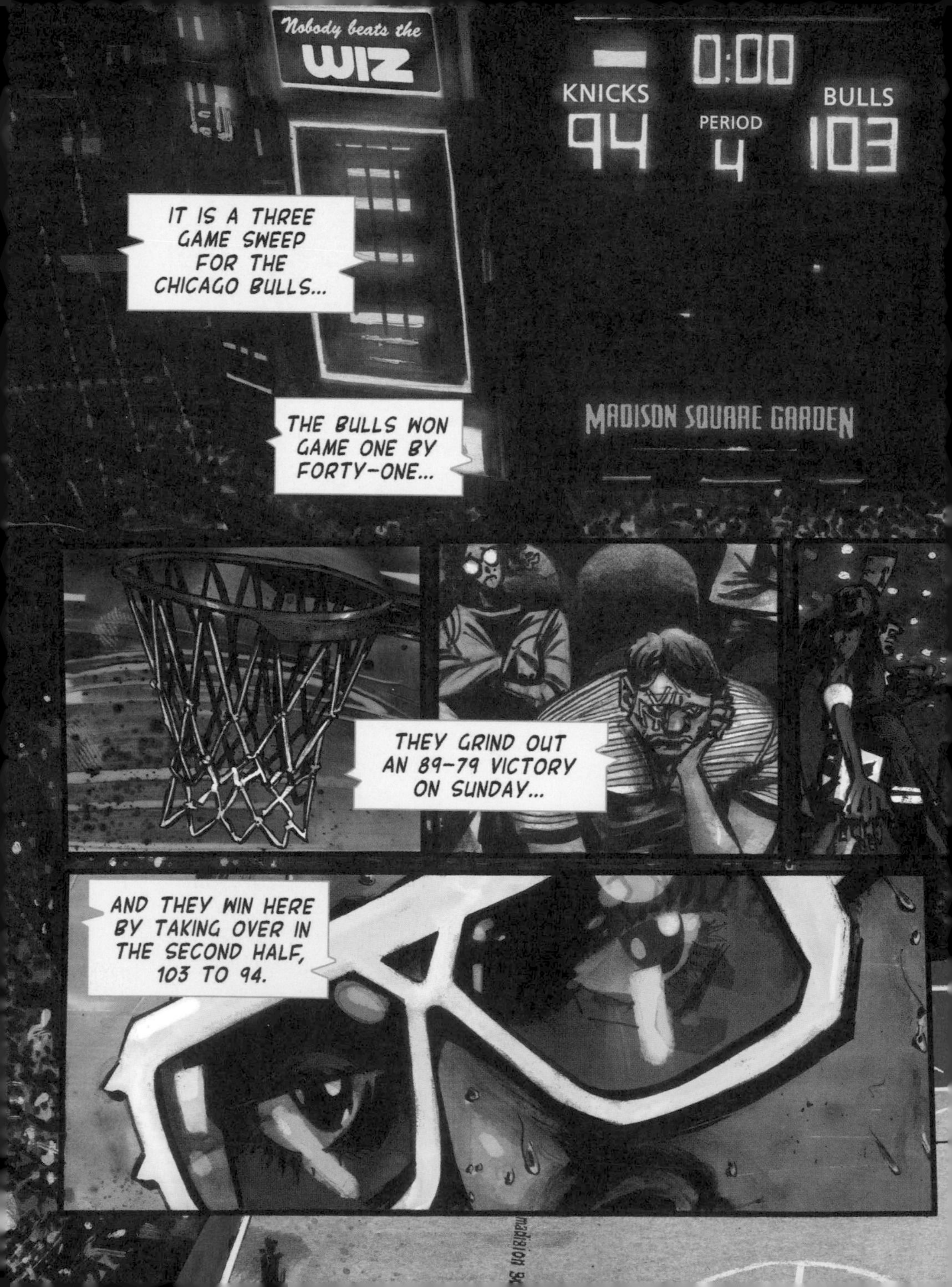
Nobody beats the WIZ
0:00
KNICKS 94
PERIOD 4
BULLS 103
IT IS A THREE GAME SWEEP FOR THE CHICAGO BULLS...
MADISON SQUARE GARDEN
THE BULLS WON GAME ONE BY FORTY-ONE...
THEY GRIND OUT AN 89-79 VICTORY ON SUNDAY...
AND THEY WIN HERE BY TAKING OVER IN THE SECOND HALF, 103 TO 94.

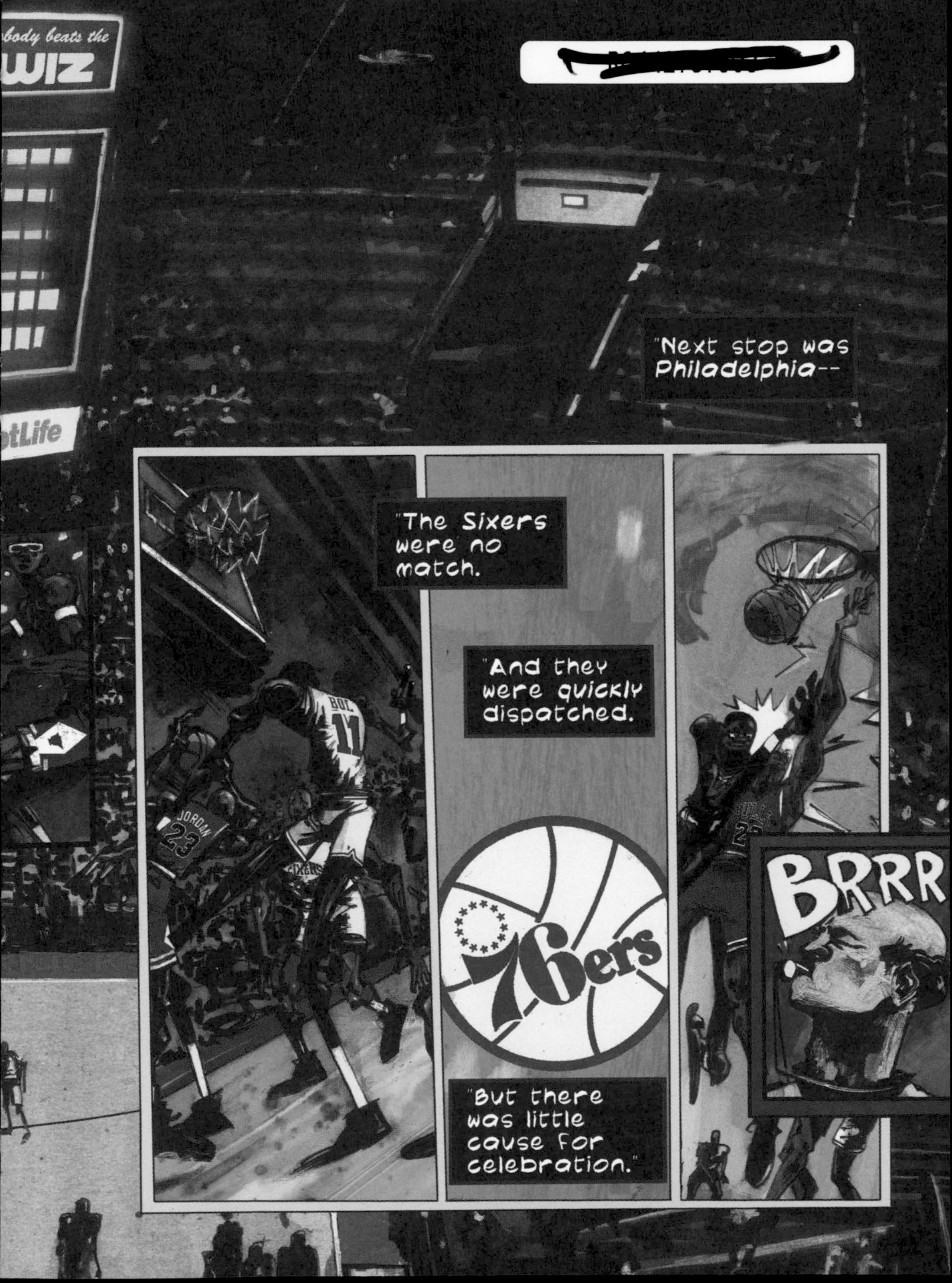
body beats the
WIZ
[redacted]
"Next stop was Philadelphia--
"The Sixers were no match.
BOL
11
JORDAN
23
"And they were quickly dispatched.
76ers
"But there was little cause for celebration."
BRRR

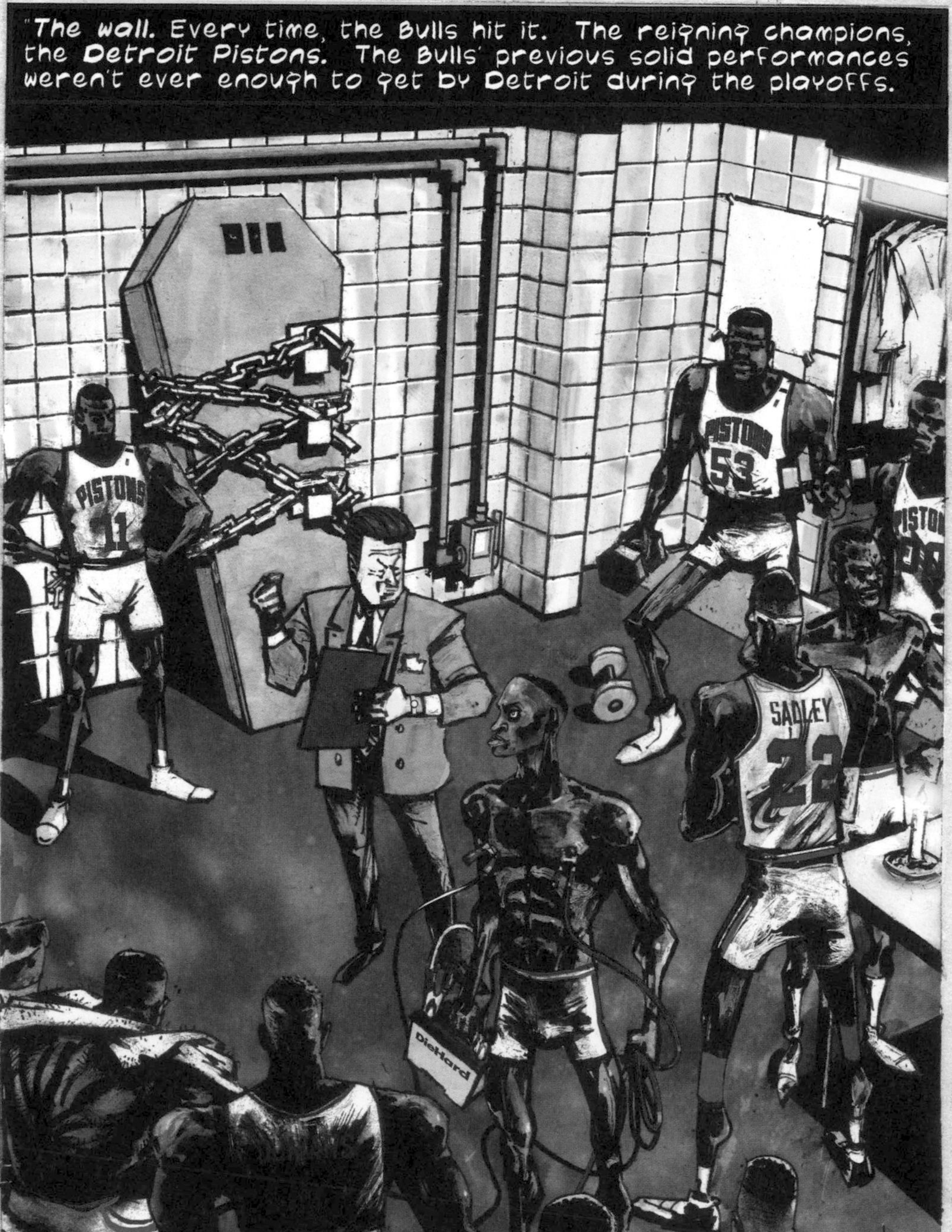
"The wall. Every time, the Bulls hit it. The reigning champions, the Detroit Pistons. The Bulls' previous solid performances weren't ever enough to get by Detroit during the playoffs.
PISTONS
11
PISTONS
53
PISTONS
SALLEY
22
DieHard

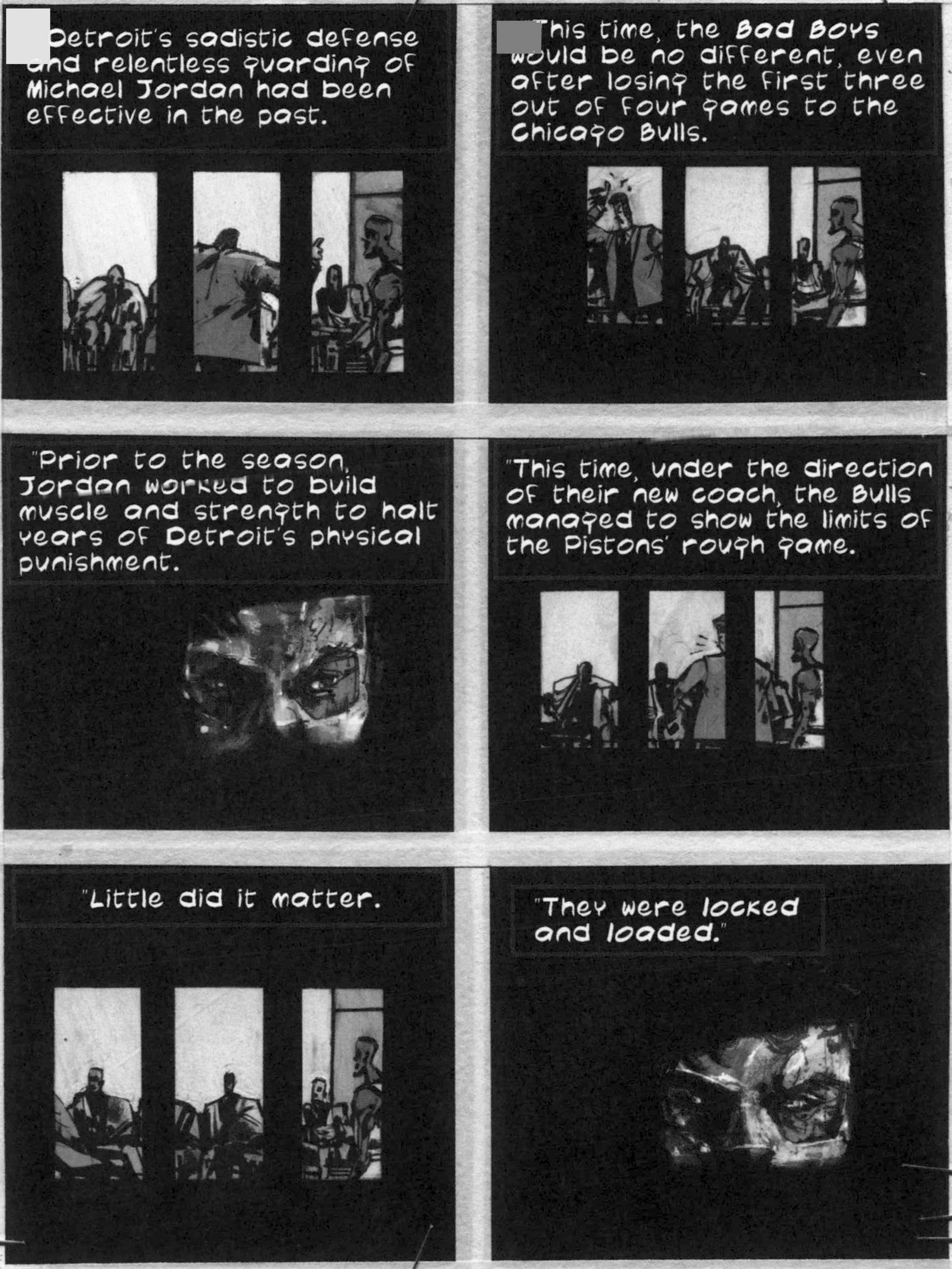
etroit's sadistic defense and relentless guarding of Michael Jordan had been effective in the past.
This time, the Bad Boys would be no different, even after losing the first three out of four games to the Chicago Bulls.
"Prior to the season, Jordan worked to build muscle and strength to halt years of Detroit's physical punishment.
"This time, under the direction of their new coach, the Bulls managed to show the limits of the Pistons' rough game.
"Little did it matter.
"They were locked and loaded."

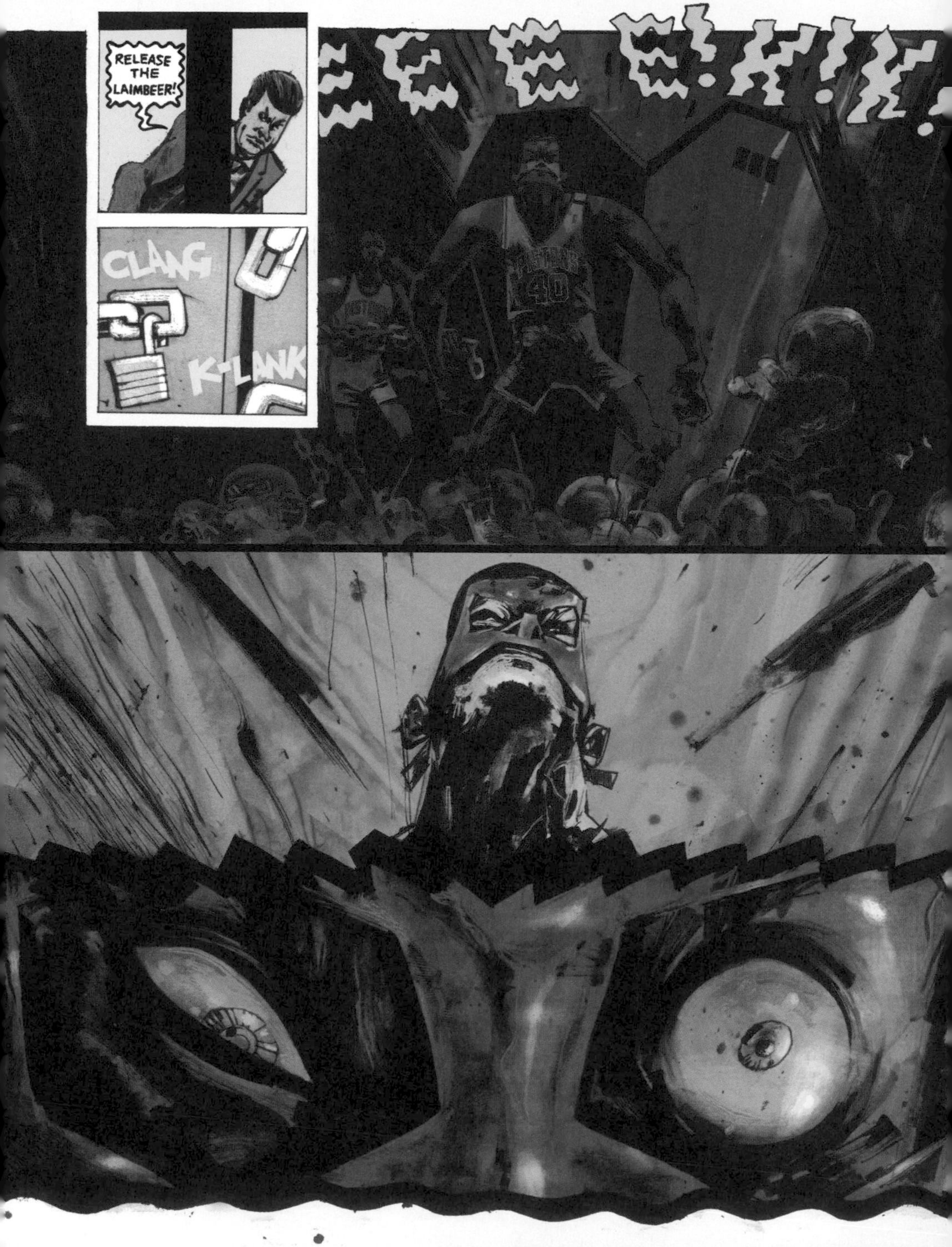
RELEASE THE LAIMBEER!
CLANG
K-LANK
EEEE!K!K!

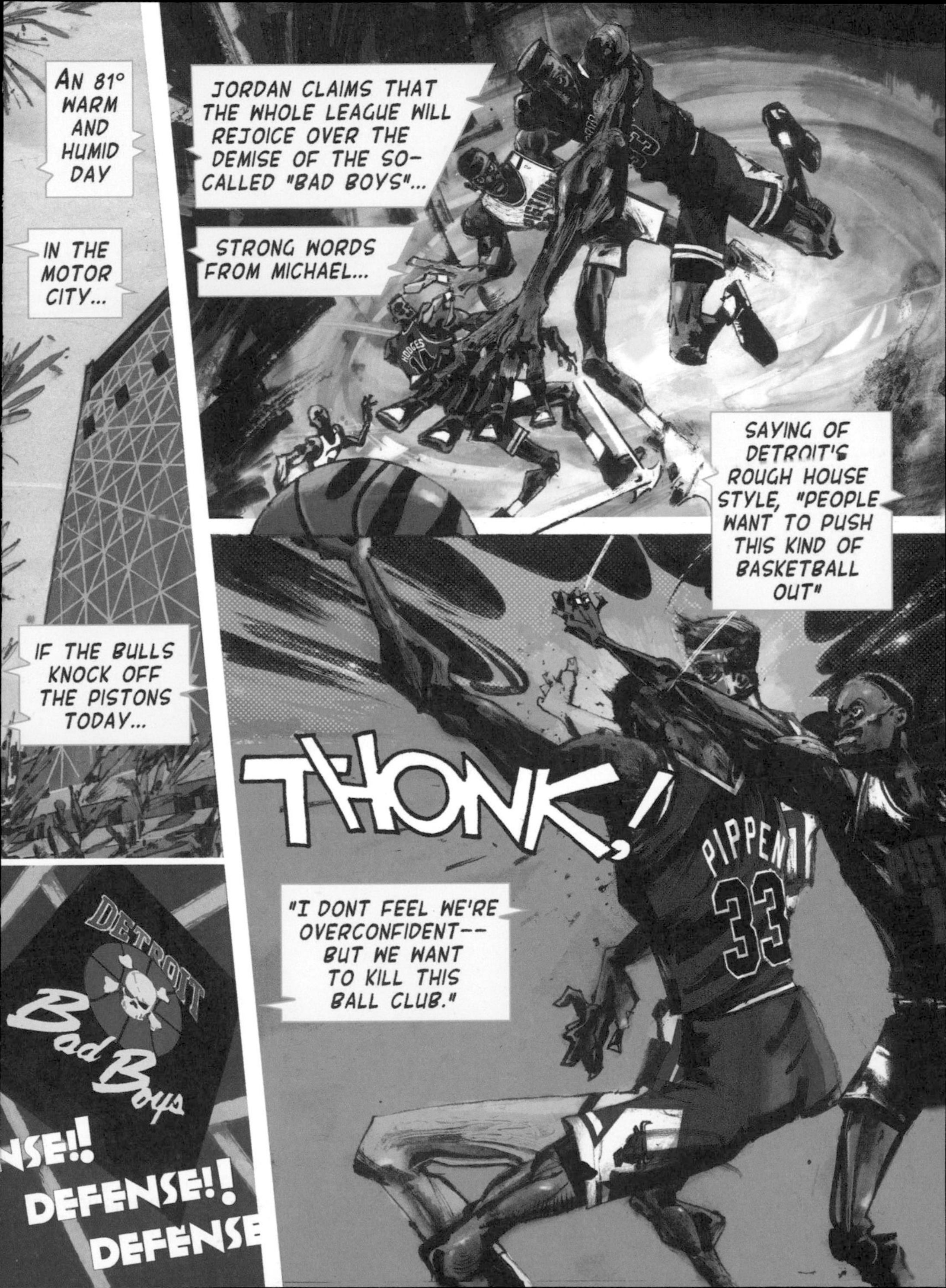
AN 81° WARM AND HUMID DAY
IN THE MOTOR CITY...
JORDAN CLAIMS THAT THE WHOLE LEAGUE WILL REJOICE OVER THE DEMISE OF THE SO-CALLED "BAD BOYS"...
STRONG WORDS FROM MICHAEL...
HODGES
SAYING OF DETROIT'S ROUGH HOUSE STYLE, "PEOPLE WANT TO PUSH THIS KIND OF BASKETBALL OUT"
IF THE BULLS KNOCK OFF THE PISTONS TODAY...
THONK!
PIPPEN
33
"I DONT FEEL WE'RE OVERCONFIDENT-- BUT WE WANT TO KILL THIS BALL CLUB."
DETROIT
Bad Boys
NSE!!
DEFENSE!!
DEFENSE

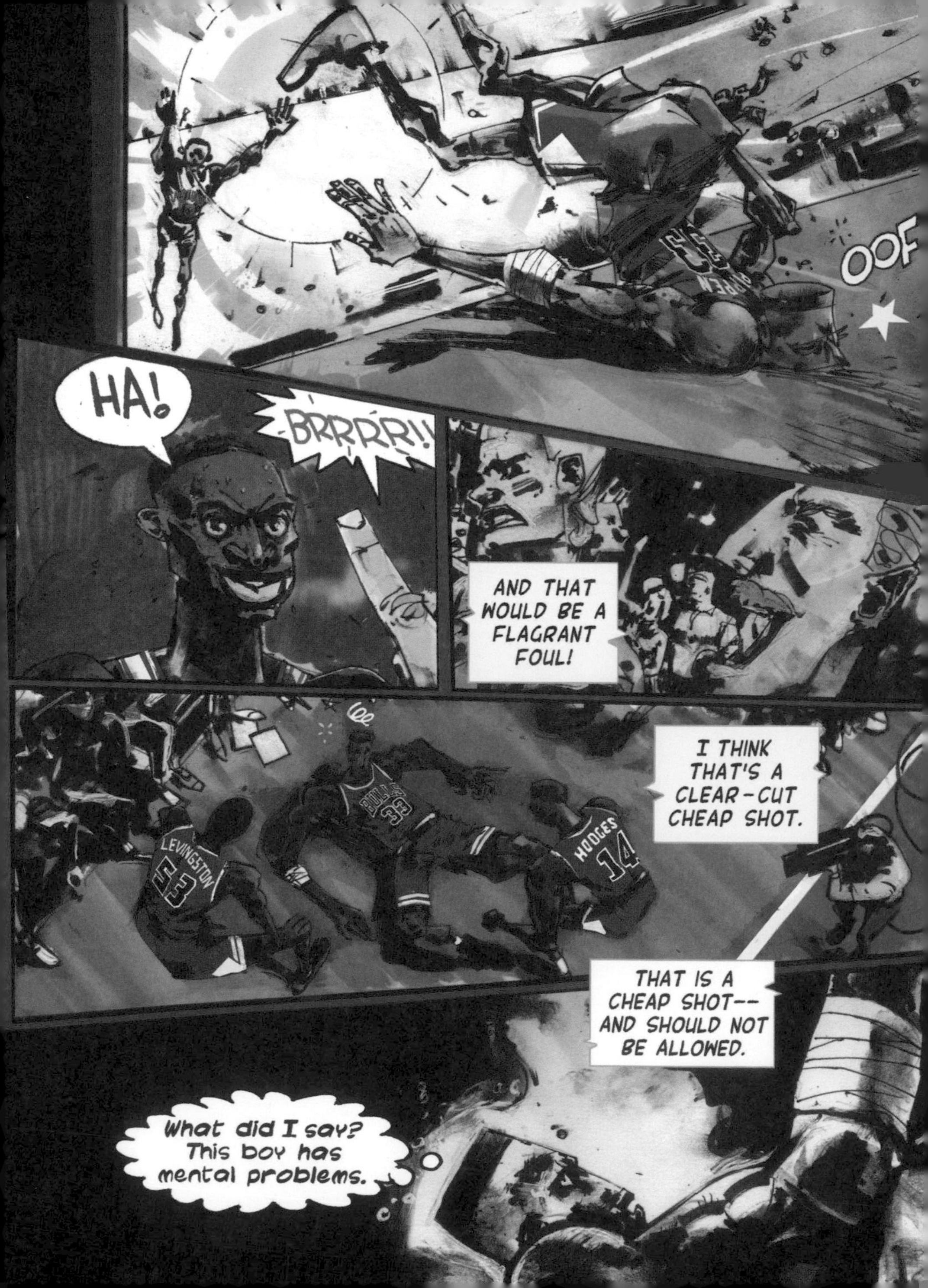
OOF
HA!
BRRRR!!
AND THAT WOULD BE A FLAGRANT FOUL!
LEVINGSTON 53
BULLS 33
HODGES 14
I THINK THAT'S A CLEAR-CUT CHEAP SHOT.
THAT IS A CHEAP SHOT-- AND SHOULD NOT BE ALLOWED.
What did I say? This boy has mental problems.

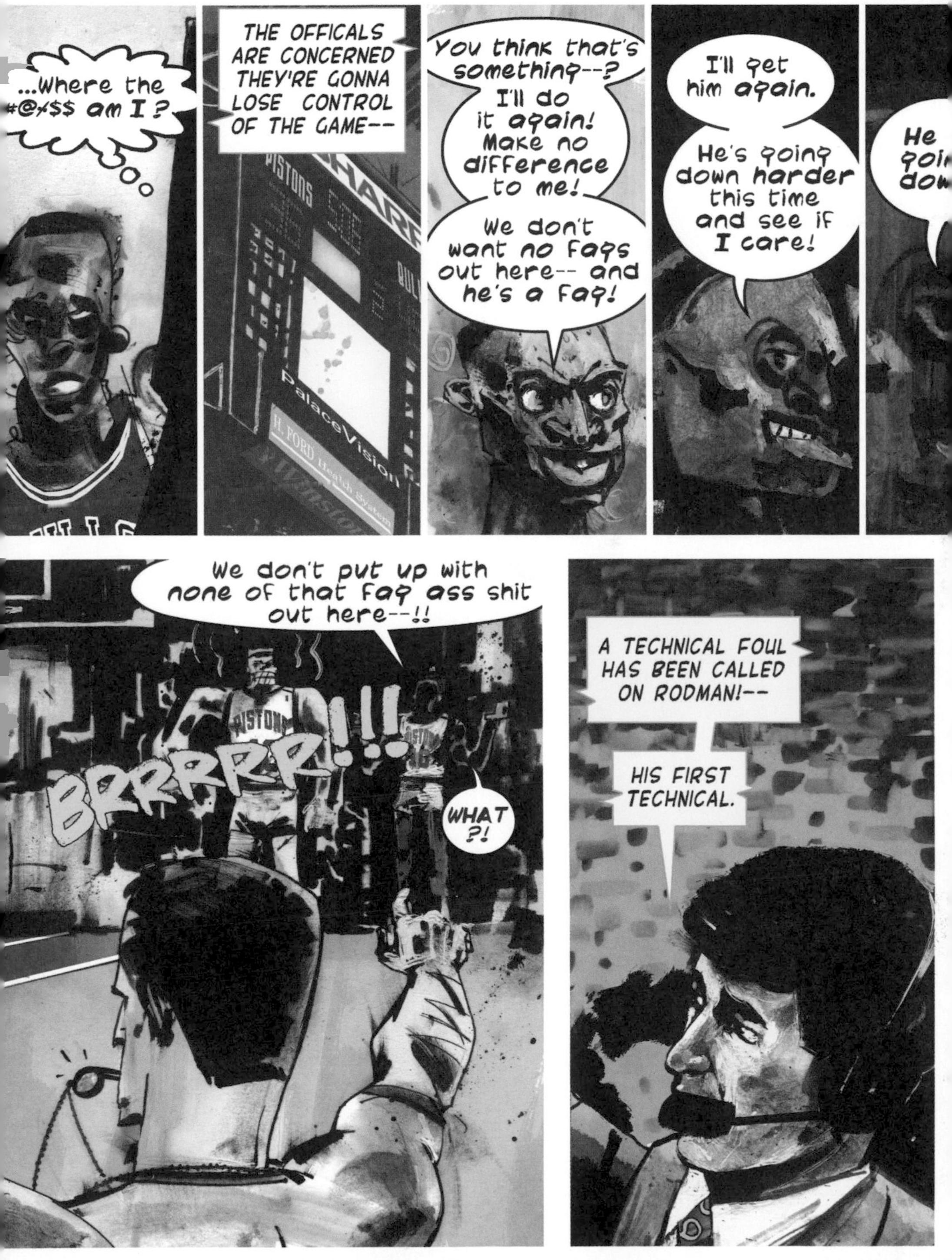
...Where the #@%$$ am I?
THE OFFICALS ARE CONCERNED THEY'RE GONNA LOSE CONTROL OF THE GAME--
PISTONS
PalaceVision
H. FORD Health System
You think that's something--? I'll do it again! Make no difference to me!
We don't want no fags out here-- and he's a fag!
I'll get him again.
He's going down harder this time and see if I care!
He
We don't put up with none of that fag ass shit out here--!!
BRRRRR!!!
WHAT?!
A TECHNICAL FOUL HAS BEEN CALLED ON RODMAN!--
HIS FIRST TECHNICAL.

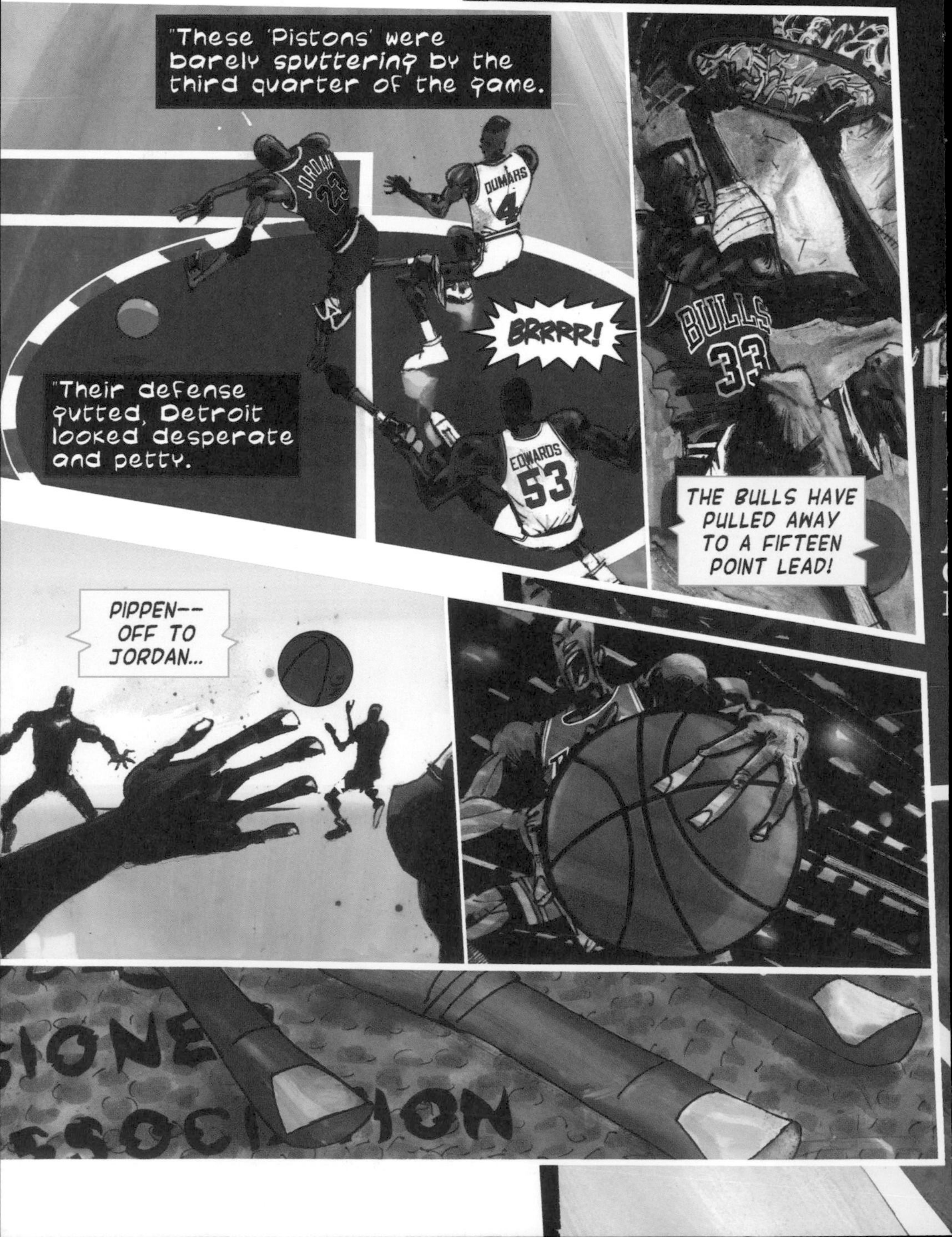
"These 'Pistons' were barely sputtering by the third quarter of the game.
JORDAN 23
DUMARS 4
BRRRR!
"Their defense gutted, Detroit looked desperate and petty.
EDWARDS 53
BULLS 33
THE BULLS HAVE PULLED AWAY TO A FIFTEEN POINT LEAD!
PIPPEN-- OFF TO JORDAN...

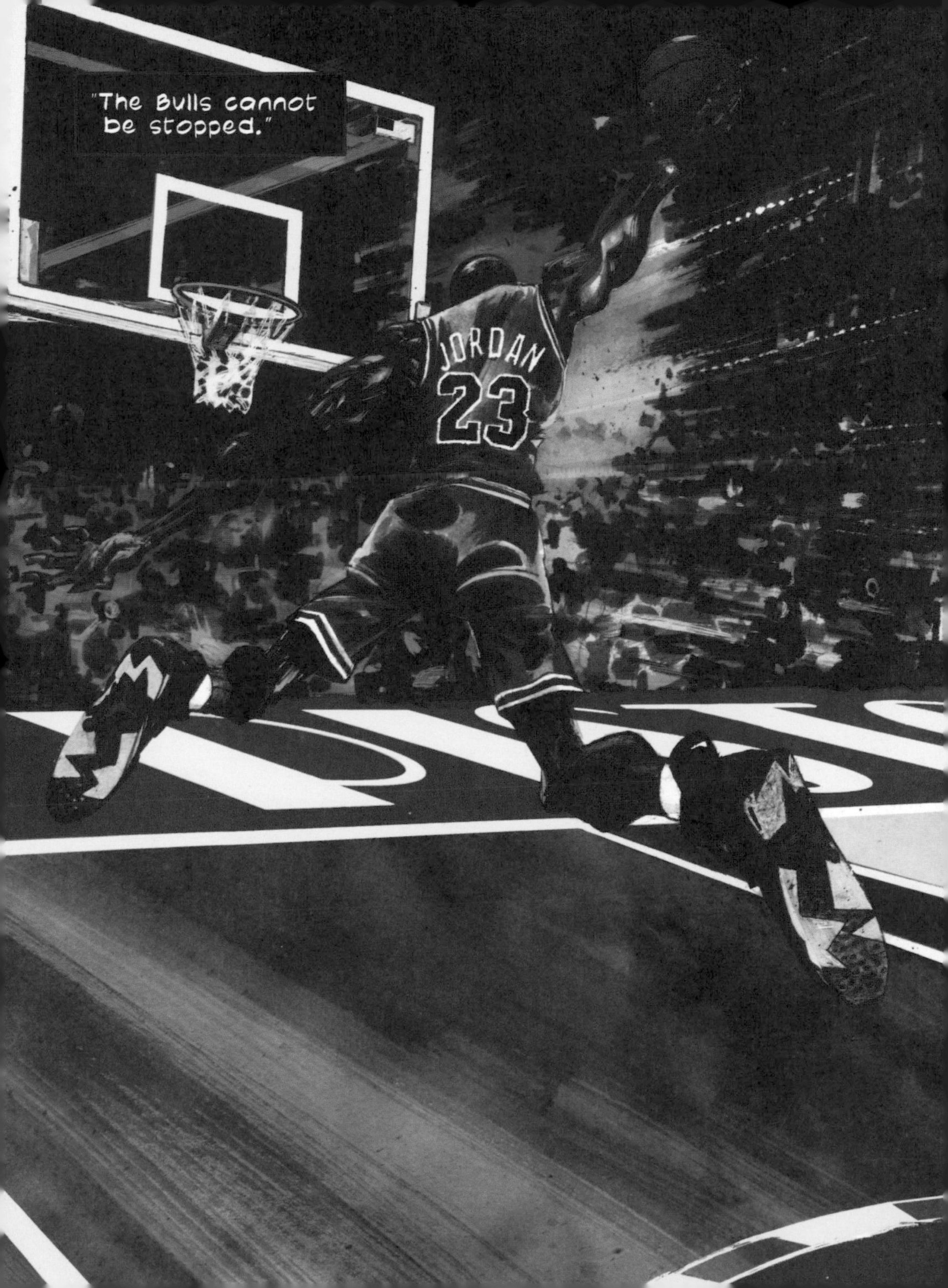
"The Bulls cannot be stopped."
JORDAN
23

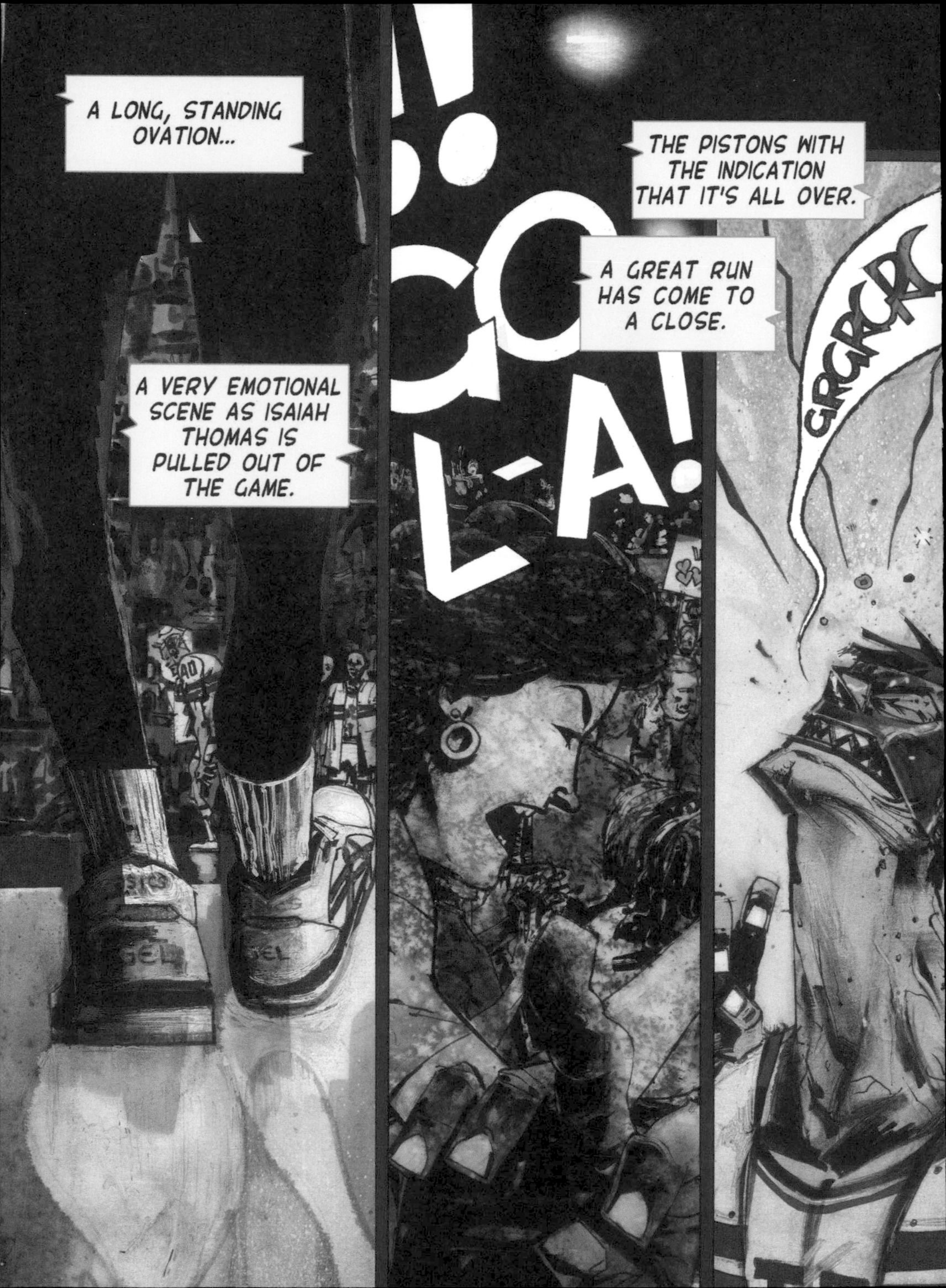
A LONG, STANDING OVATION...
A VERY EMOTIONAL SCENE AS ISAIAH THOMAS IS PULLED OUT OF THE GAME.
GO L-A!
THE PISTONS WITH THE INDICATION THAT IT'S ALL OVER.
A GREAT RUN HAS COME TO A CLOSE.
GRGRGRG

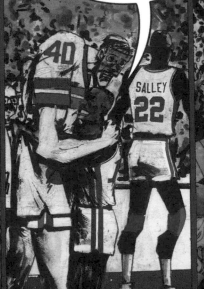

THE CROWD CHANTING, 'GO L-A!'

NOT ACCEPTING THE DEFEAT...

GO L-A!

GO L-A!!

GO-L-A!!

"The Pistons walked away to their locker room... time still remaining on the clock."

Atta boy-- we get'em next time...

SALLEY 22

40

JOHN 3:3

GO-L-A!

whimp

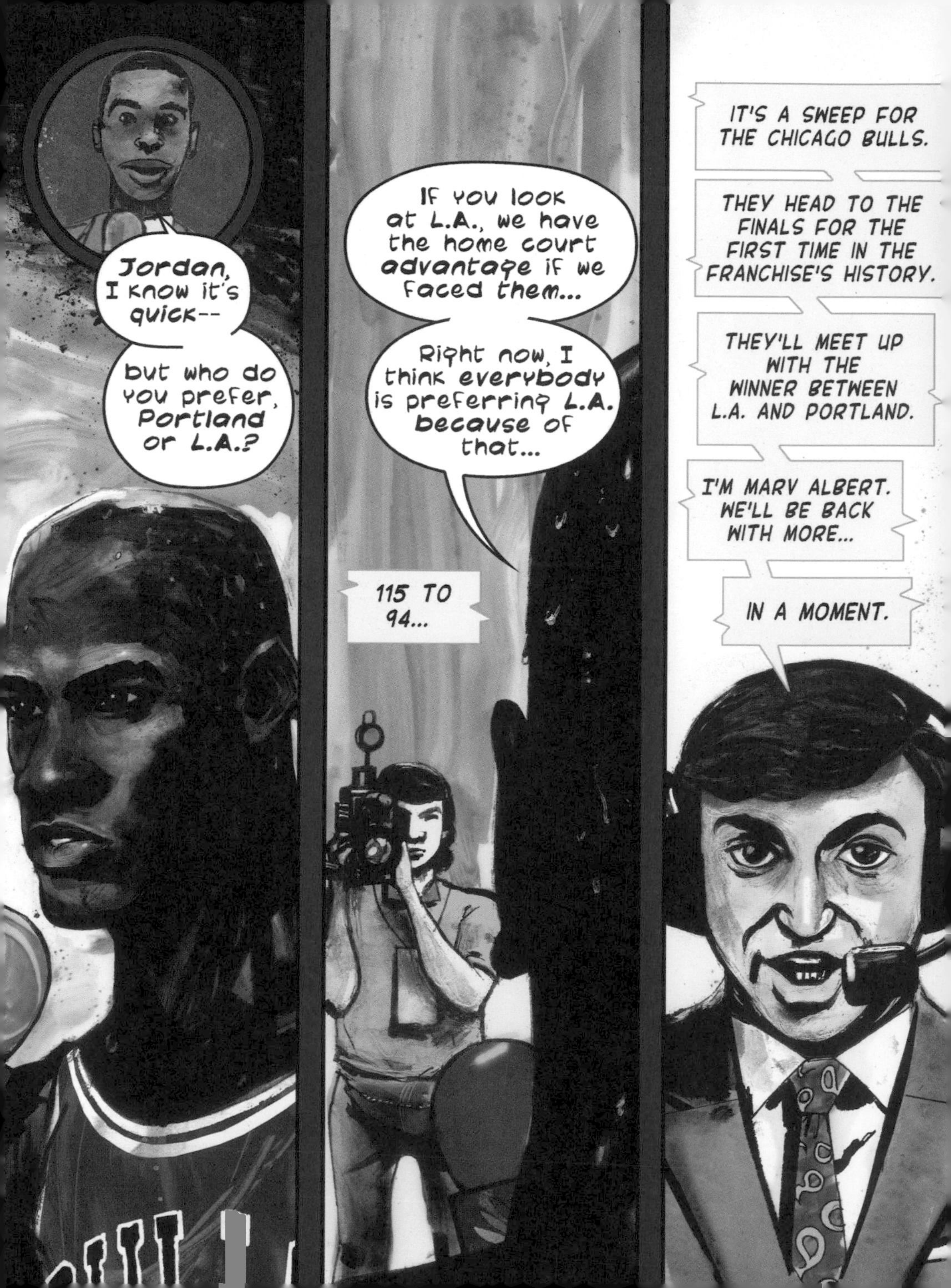
Jordan, I know it's quick--
but who do you prefer, Portland or L.A.?
If you look at L.A., we have the home court advantage if we faced them...
Right now, I think everybody is preferring L.A. because of that...
115 TO 94...
IT'S A SWEEP FOR THE CHICAGO BULLS.
THEY HEAD TO THE FINALS FOR THE FIRST TIME IN THE FRANCHISE'S HISTORY.
THEY'LL MEET UP WITH THE WINNER BETWEEN L.A. AND PORTLAND.
I'M MARV ALBERT. WE'LL BE BACK WITH MORE...
IN A MOMENT.

ONE FINE MORNING IN A CHICAGO SUBURB

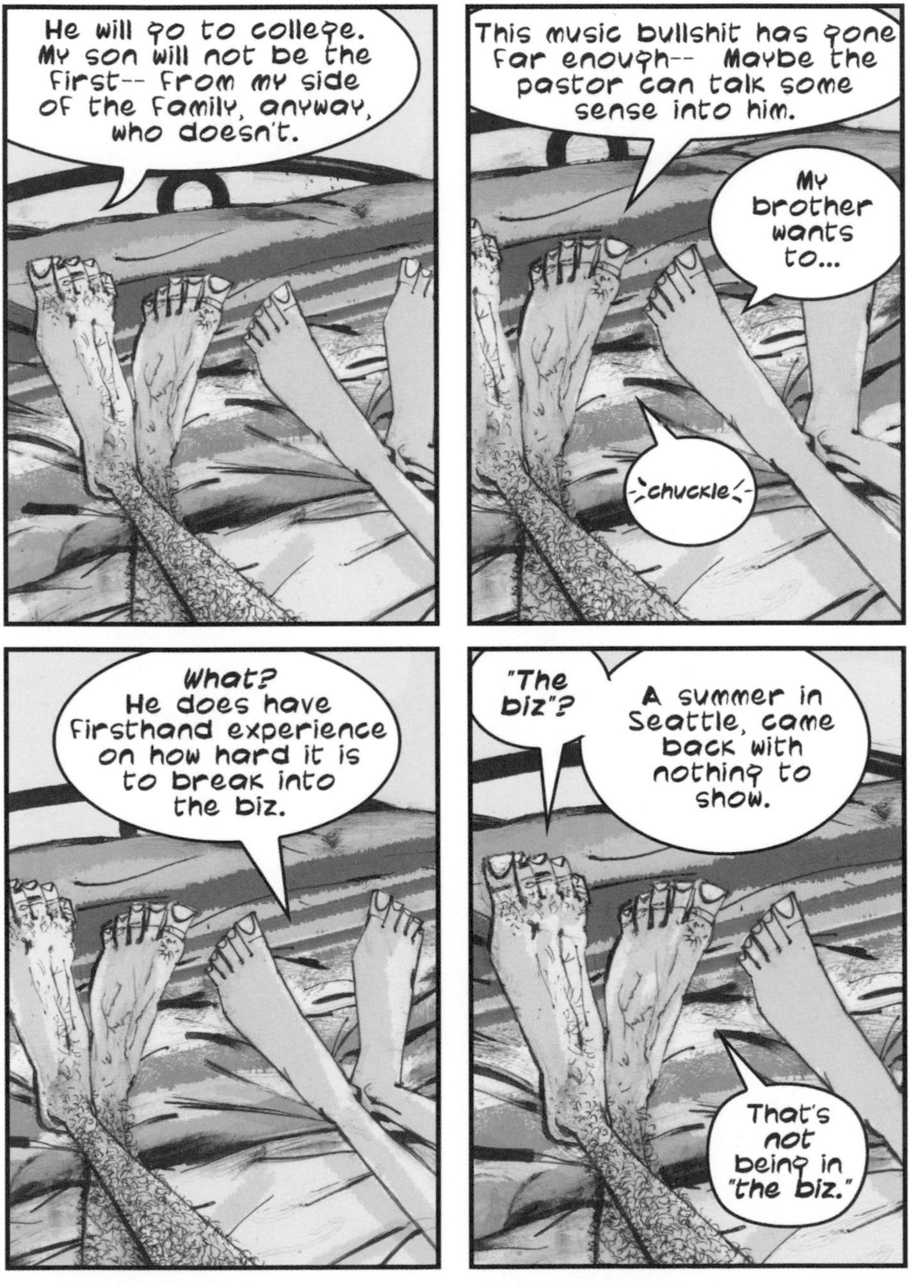

He will go to college. My son will not be the first-- from my side of the family, anyway, who doesn't.
This music bullshit has gone far enough-- Maybe the pastor can talk some sense into him.
My brother wants to...
chuckle
What? He does have firsthand experience on how hard it is to break into the biz.
"The biz"?
A summer in Seattle, came back with nothing to show.
That's *not* being in "the biz."

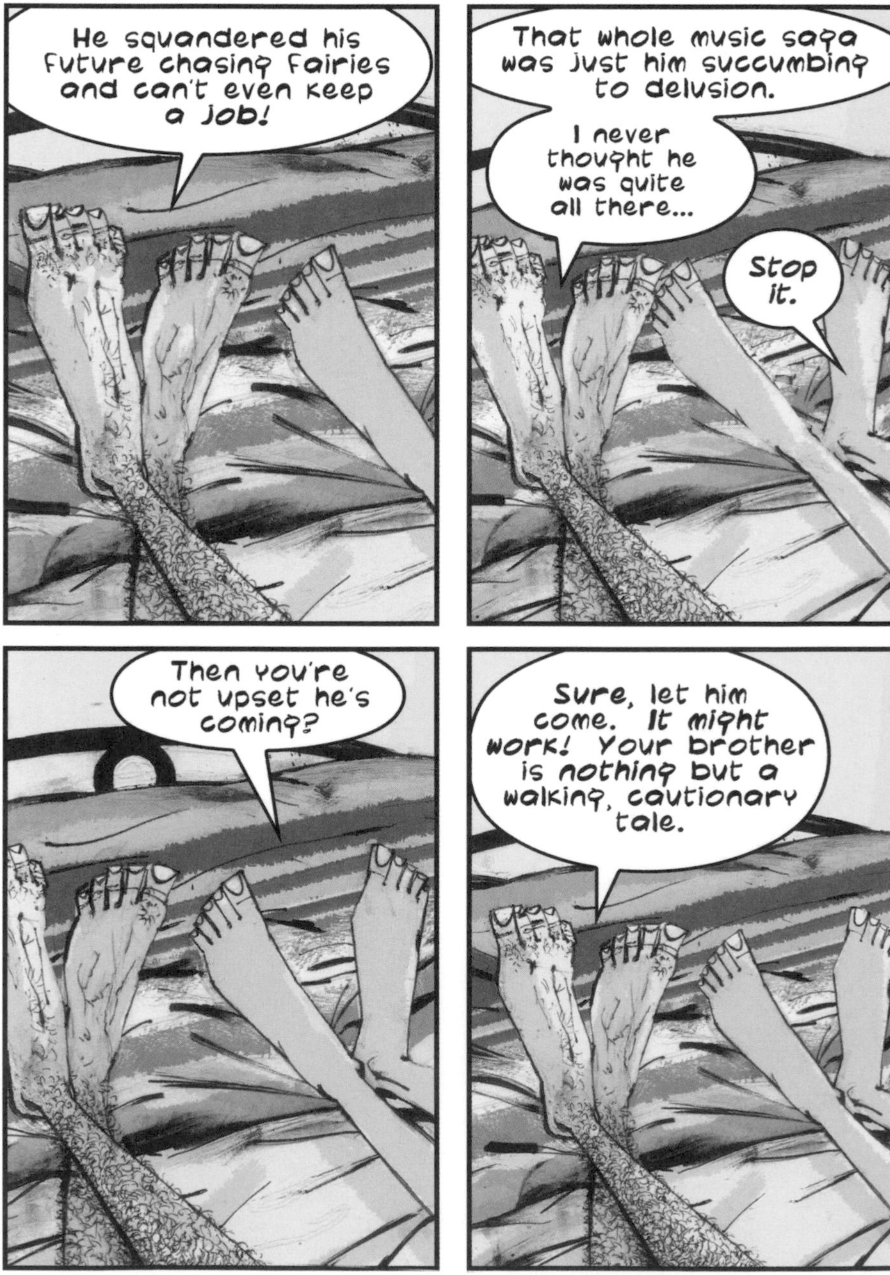
He squandered his future chasing fairies and can't even keep a job!
That whole music saga was just him succumbing to delusion.
I never thought he was quite all there...
Stop it.
Then you're not upset he's coming?
Sure, let him come. *It might work!* Your brother is *nothing* but a walking, cautionary tale.

1:

Wild Horses

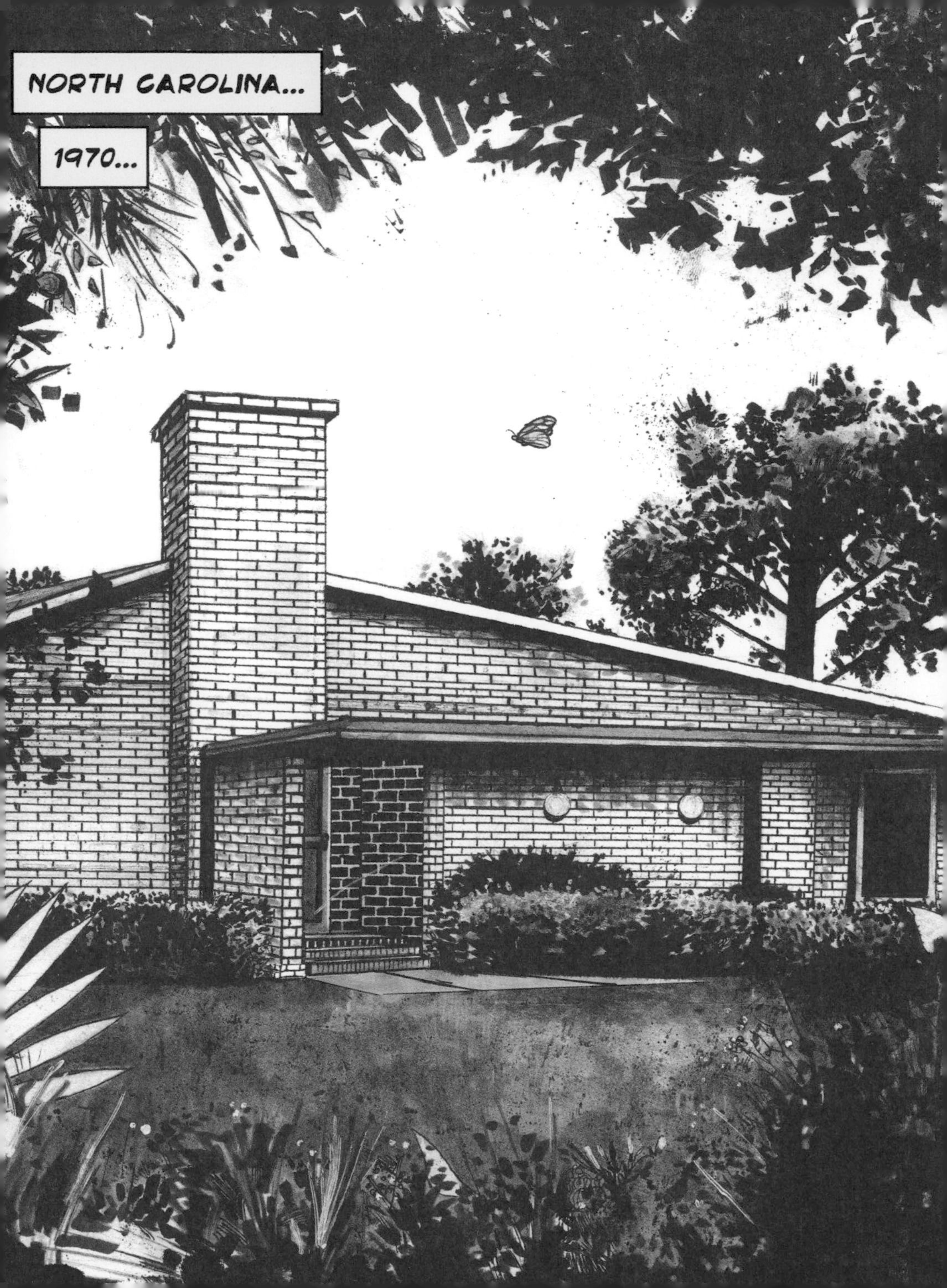
NORTH CAROLINA...
1970...

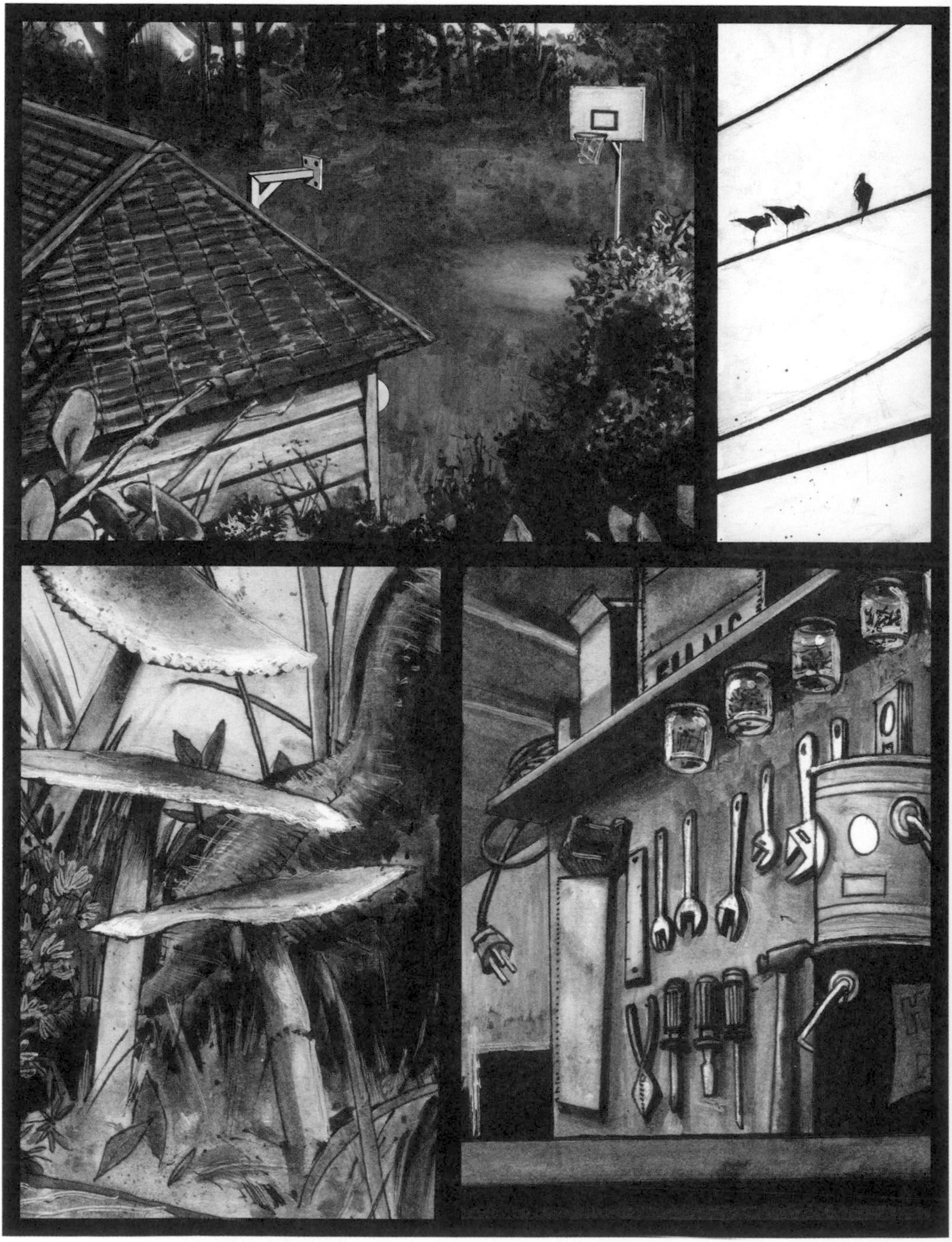

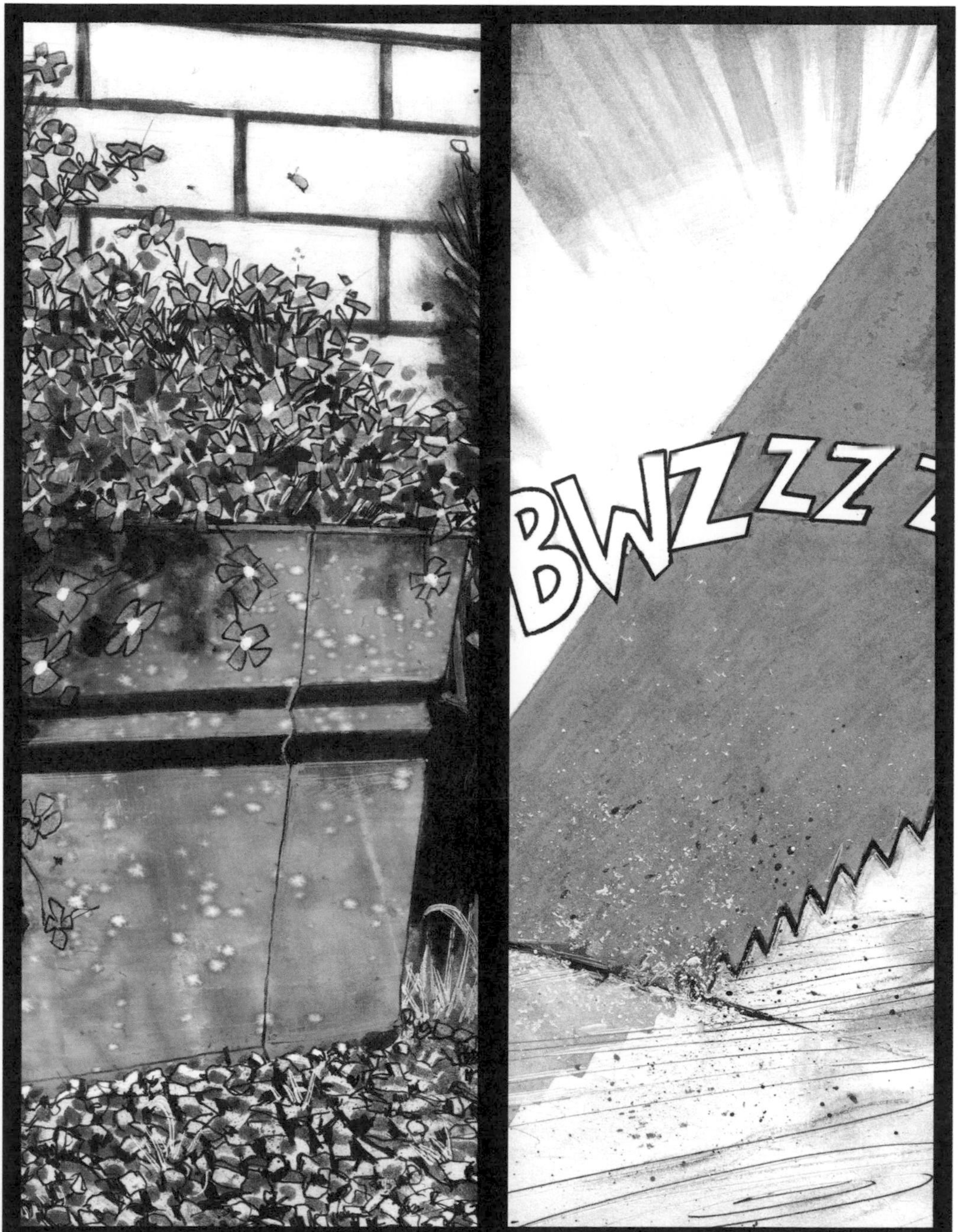
BWZZZ Z

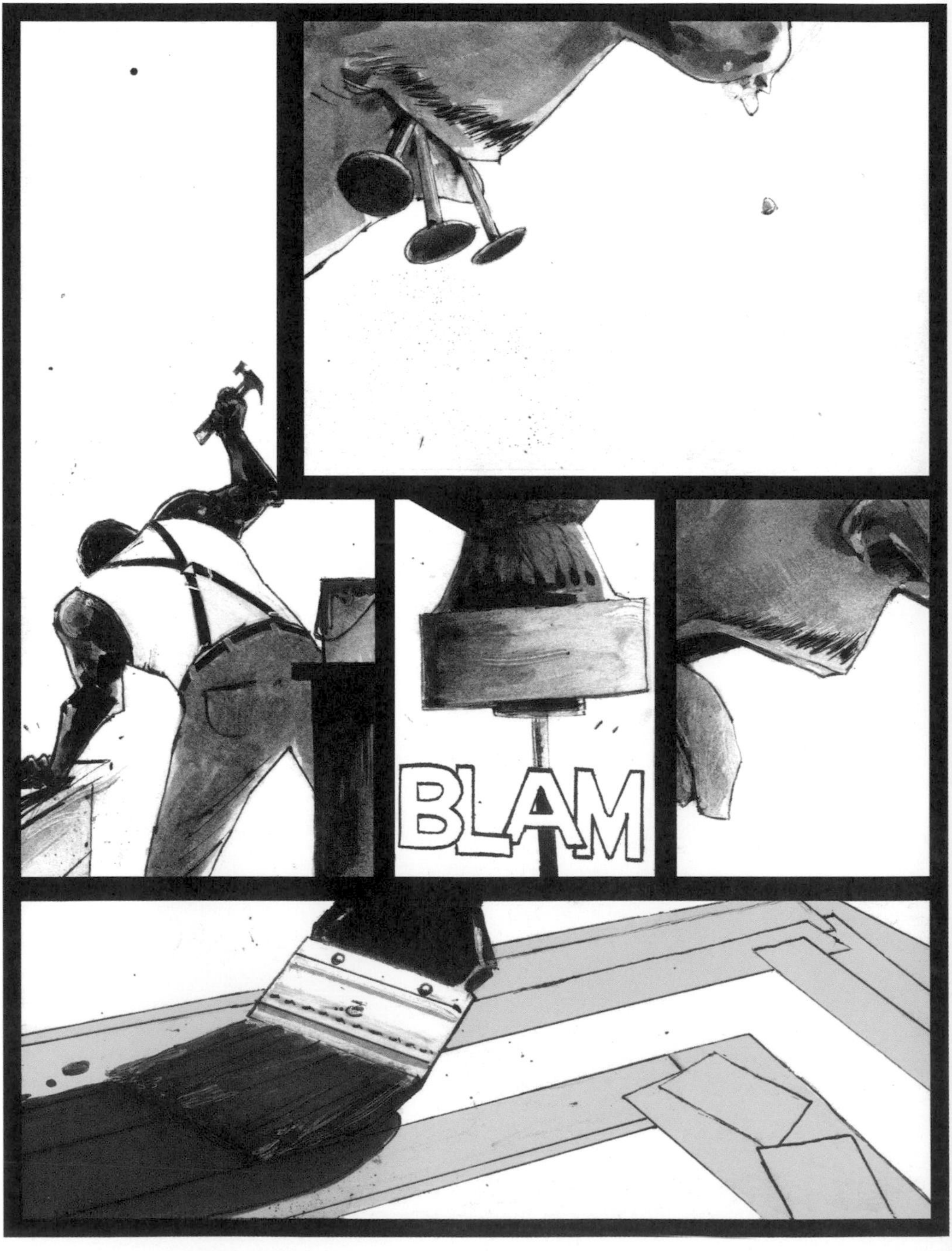
BLAM

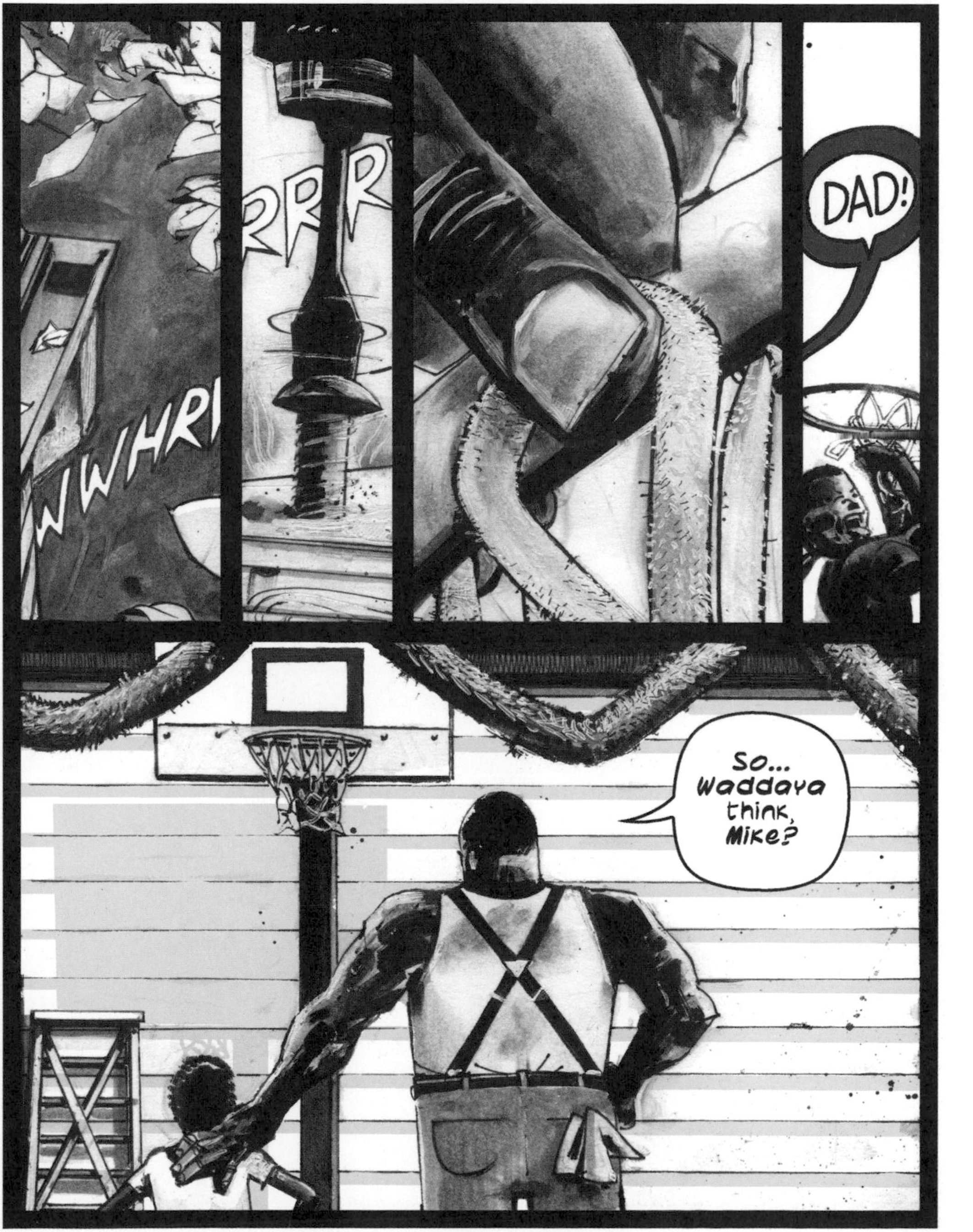
WWHR
RRR
DAD!
So... Waddaya think, Mike?

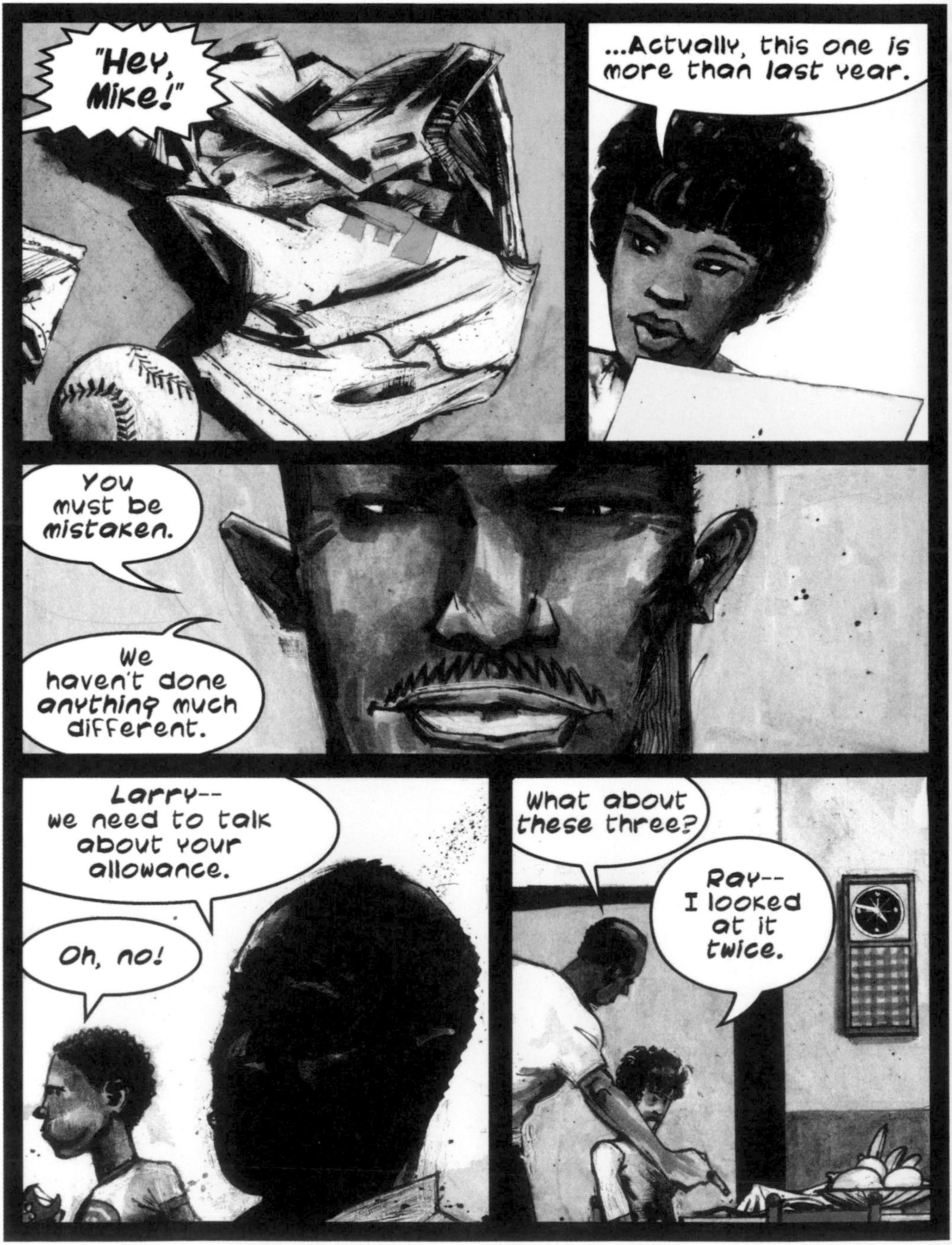
"Hey, Mike!"
...Actually, this one is more than last year.
You must be mistaken.
We haven't done anything much different.
Larry-- we need to talk about your allowance.
Oh, no!
What about these three?
Ray-- I looked at it twice.

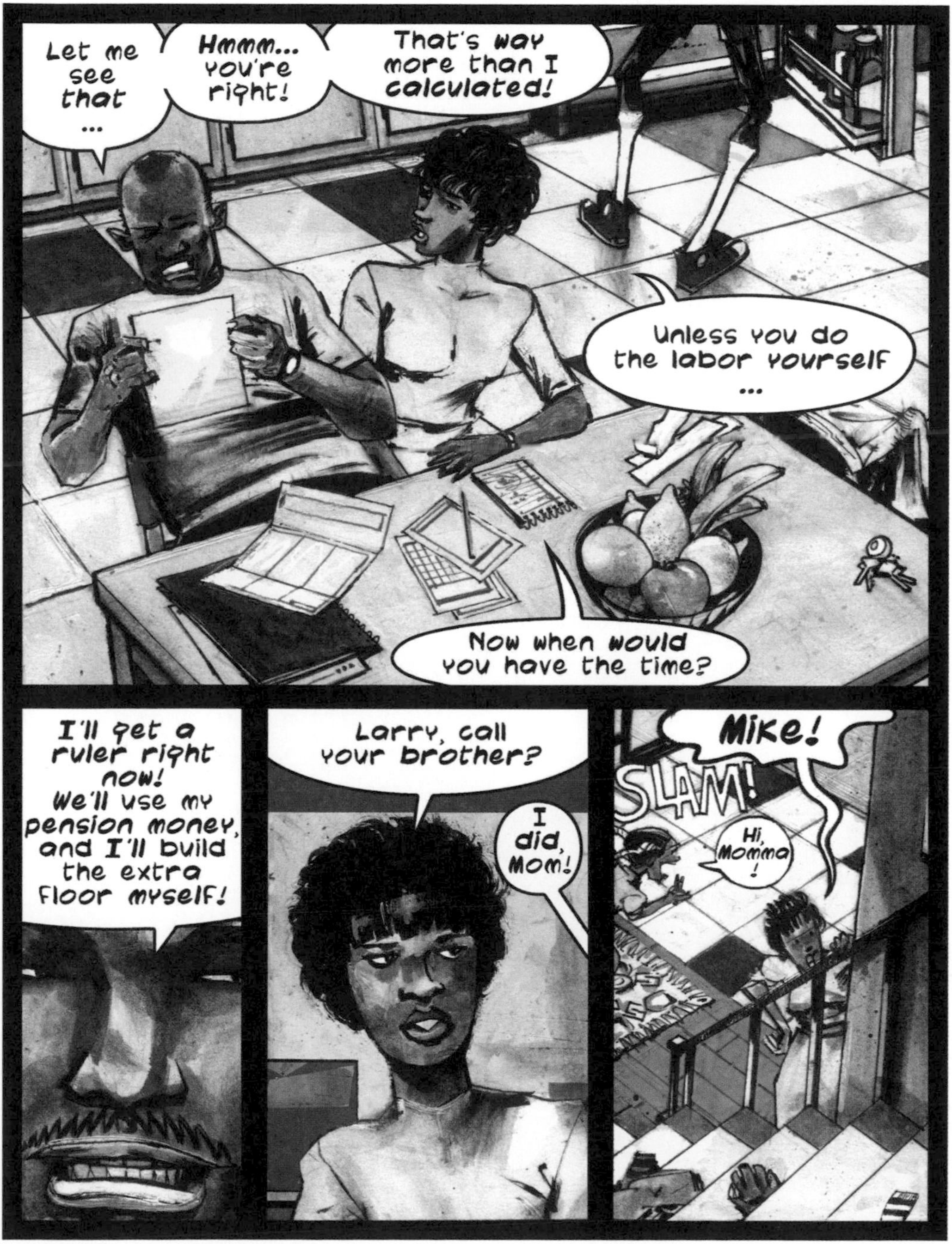

Let me see that ...
Hmmm... you're right!
That's way more than I calculated!
Unless you do the labor yourself ...
Now when would you have the time?
I'll get a ruler right now! We'll use my pension money, and I'll build the extra floor myself!
Larry, call your brother?
I did, Mom!
Mike!
SLAM!
Hi, Momma!

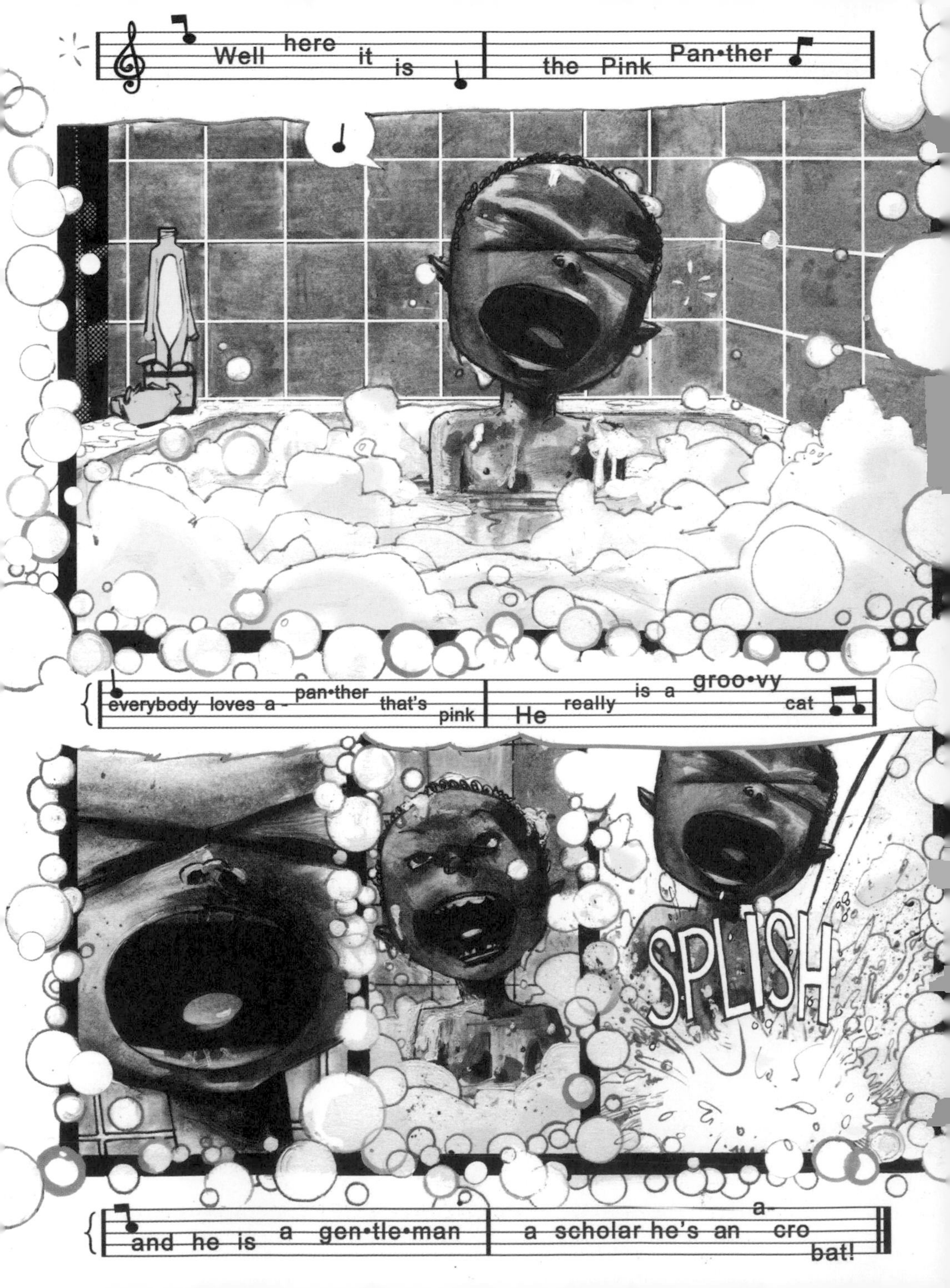
Well here it is
the Pink Pan•ther
everybody loves a pan•ther that's pink
He really is a groo•vy cat
SPLISH
and he is a gen•tle•man
a scholar he's an a-cro bat!

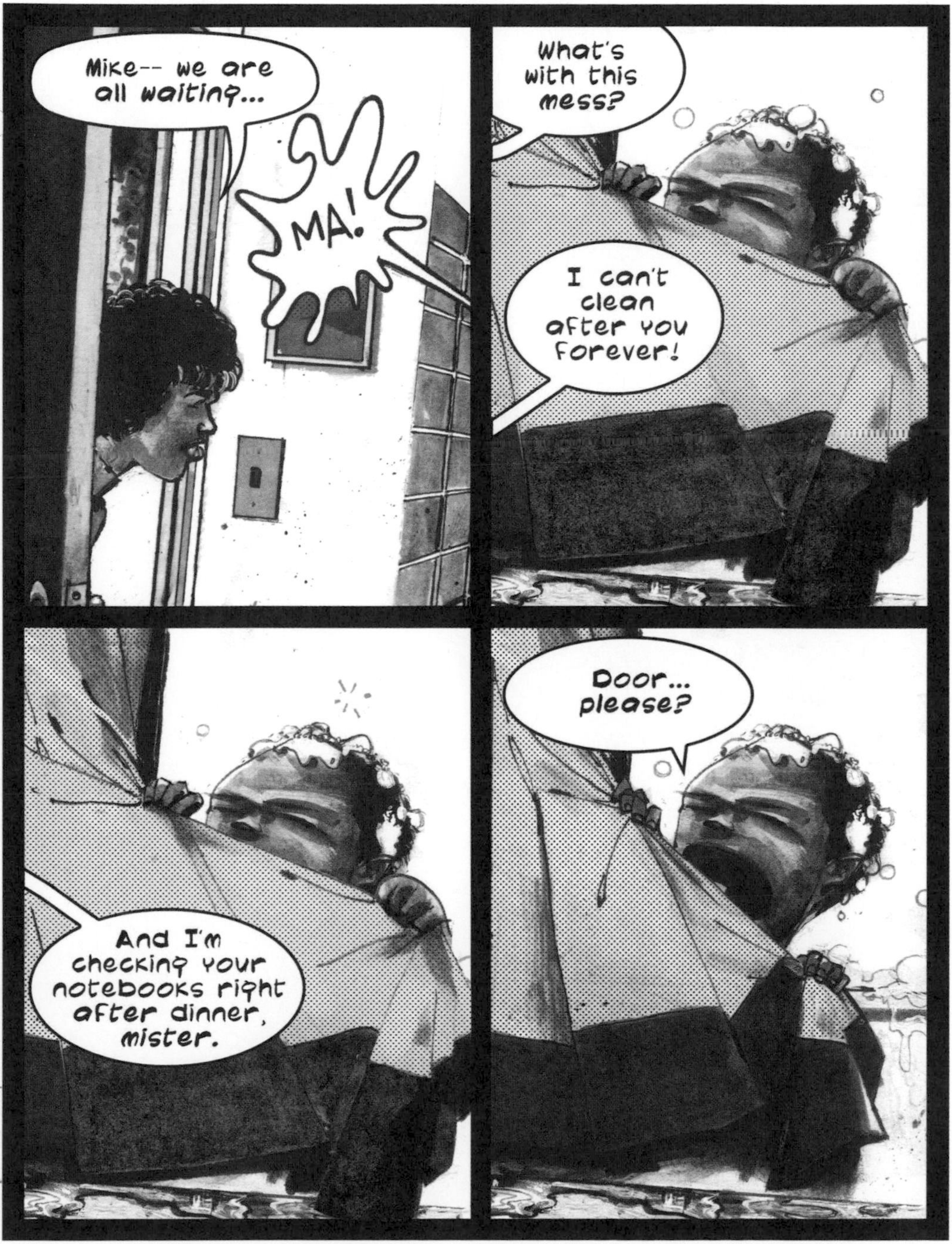
Mike-- we are all waiting...
MA!
What's with this mess?
I can't clean after you forever!
And I'm checking your notebooks right after dinner, mister.
Door... please?

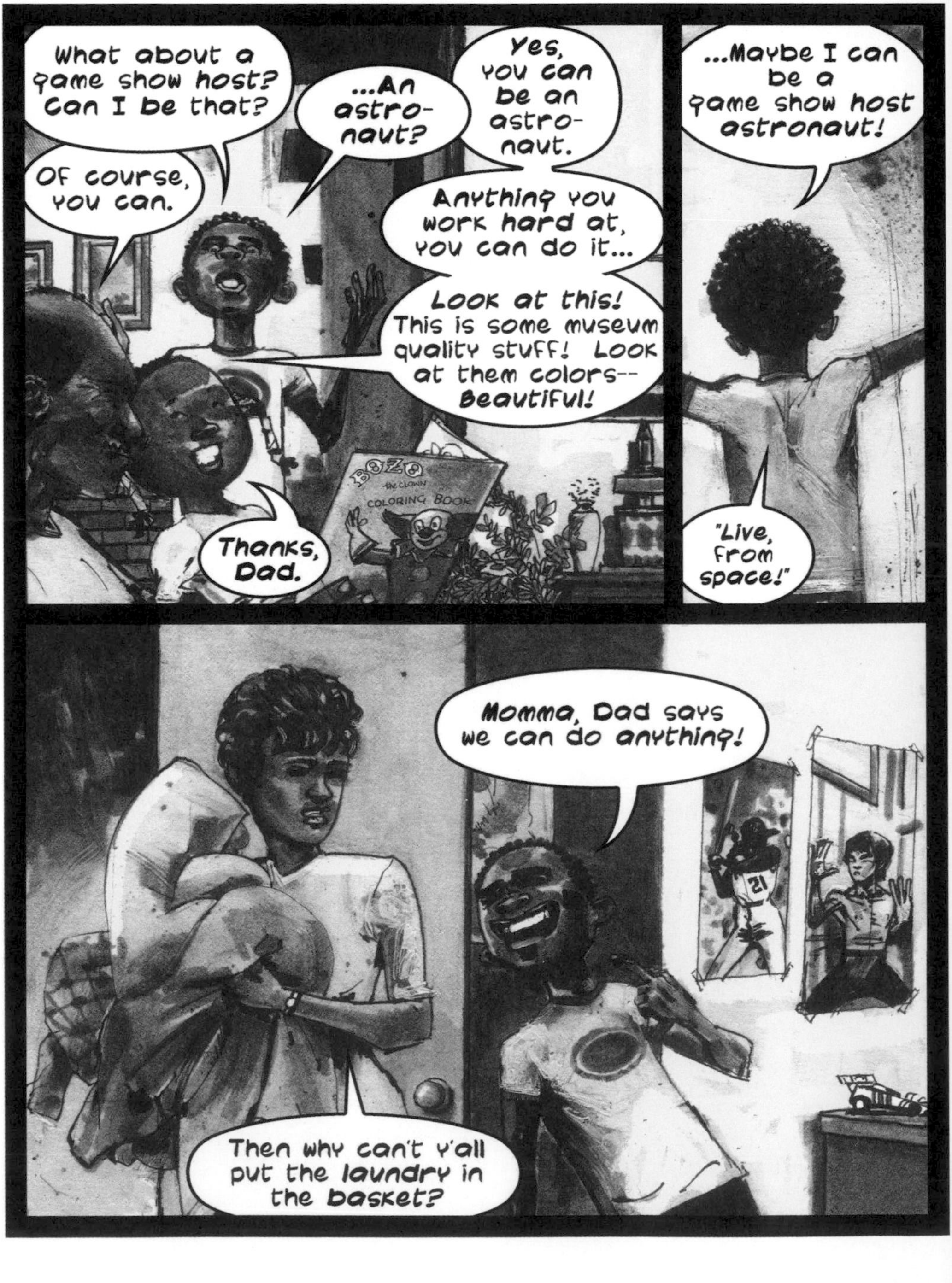
What about a game show host? Can I be that?
Of course, you can.
...An astro-naut?
Yes, you can be an astro-naut.
Anything you work hard at, you can do it...
Look at this! This is some museum quality stuff! Look at them colors-- Beautiful!
BOZO THE CLOWN COLORING BOOK
Thanks, Dad.
...Maybe I can be a game show host astronaut!
"Live, from space!"
Momma, Dad says we can do anything!
21
Then why can't y'all put the laundry in the basket?

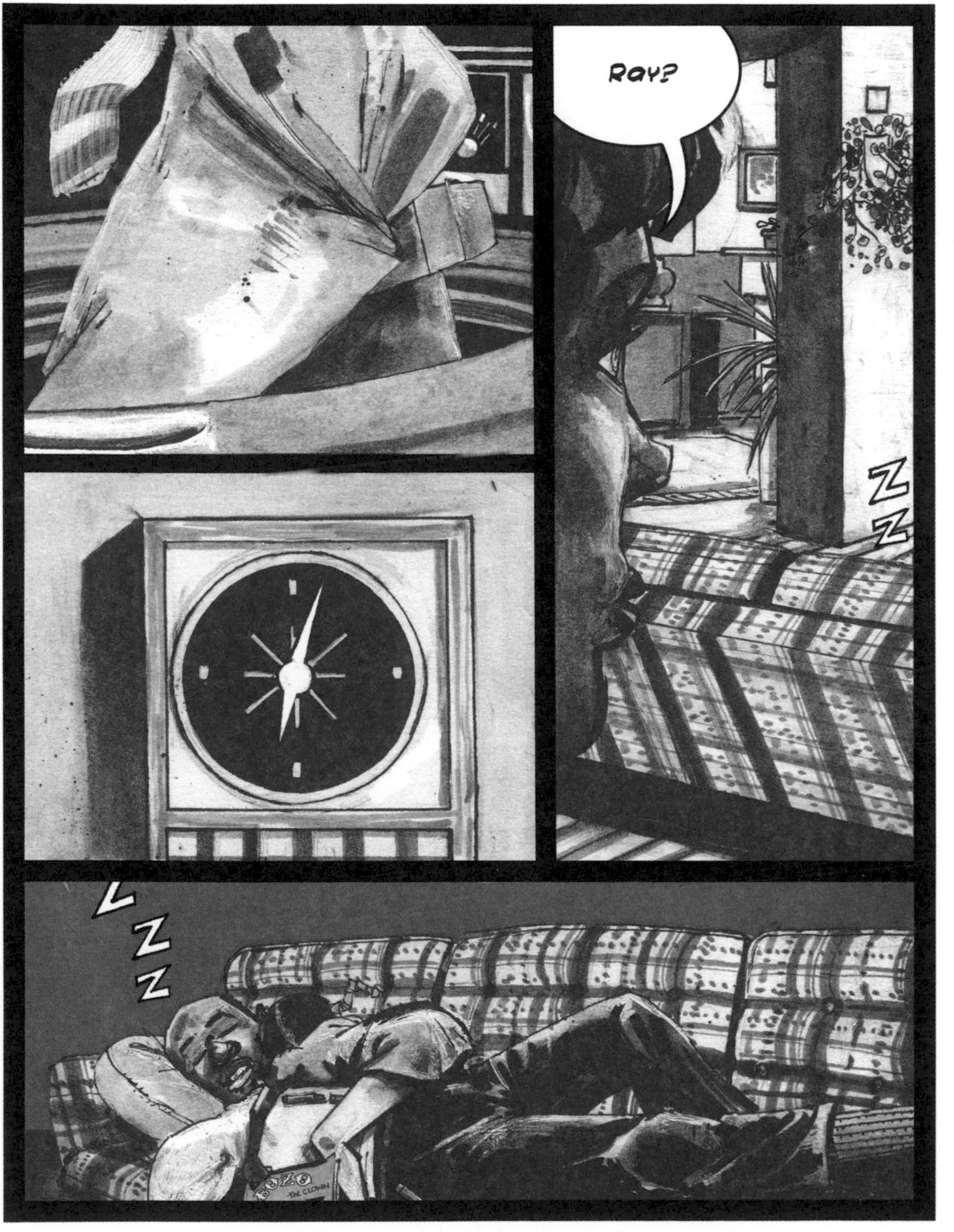

Ray?
Z
Z
Z
Z
Z
BOZO THE CLOWN

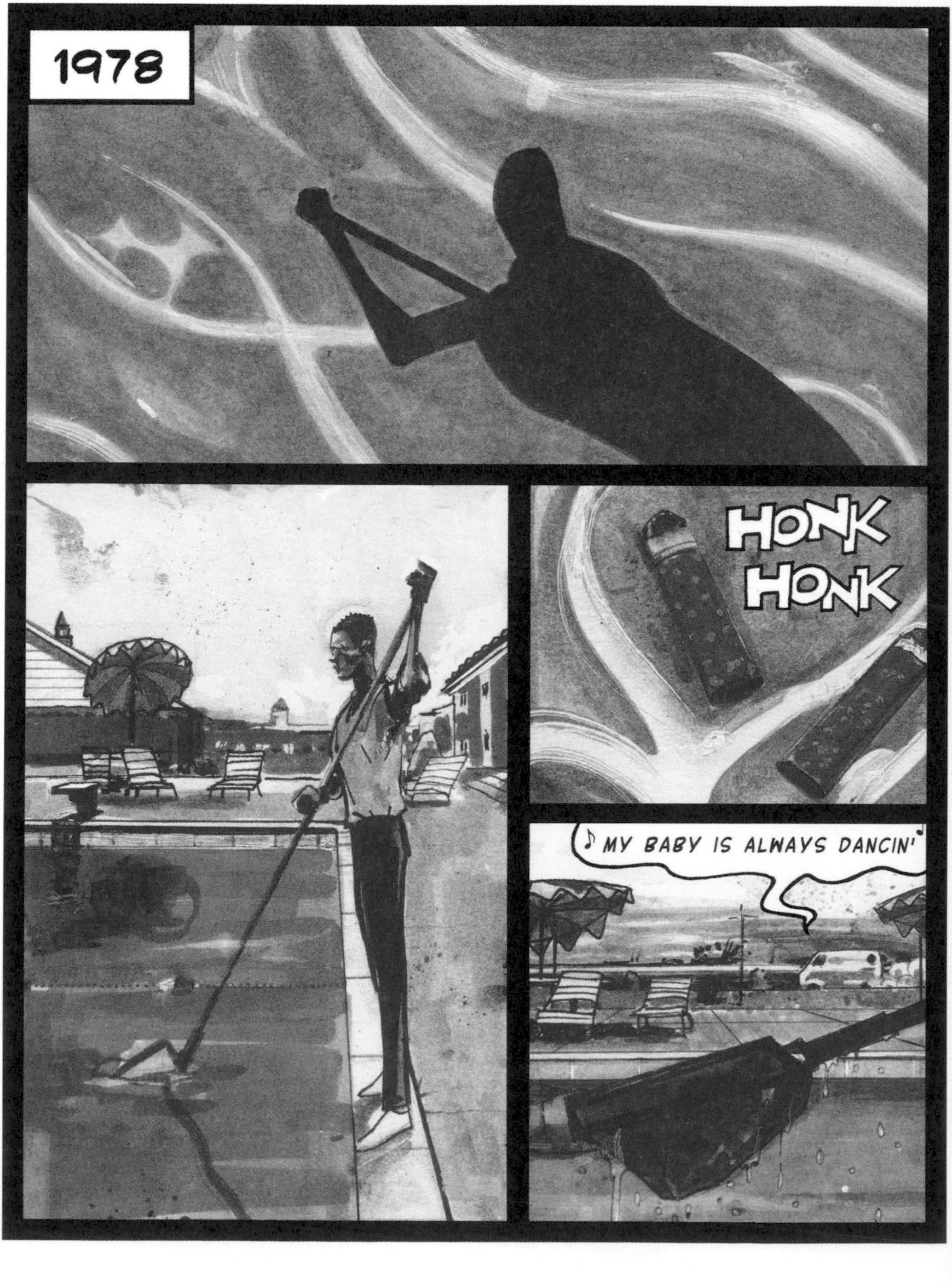
1978
HONK HONK
♪ MY BABY IS ALWAYS DANCIN'

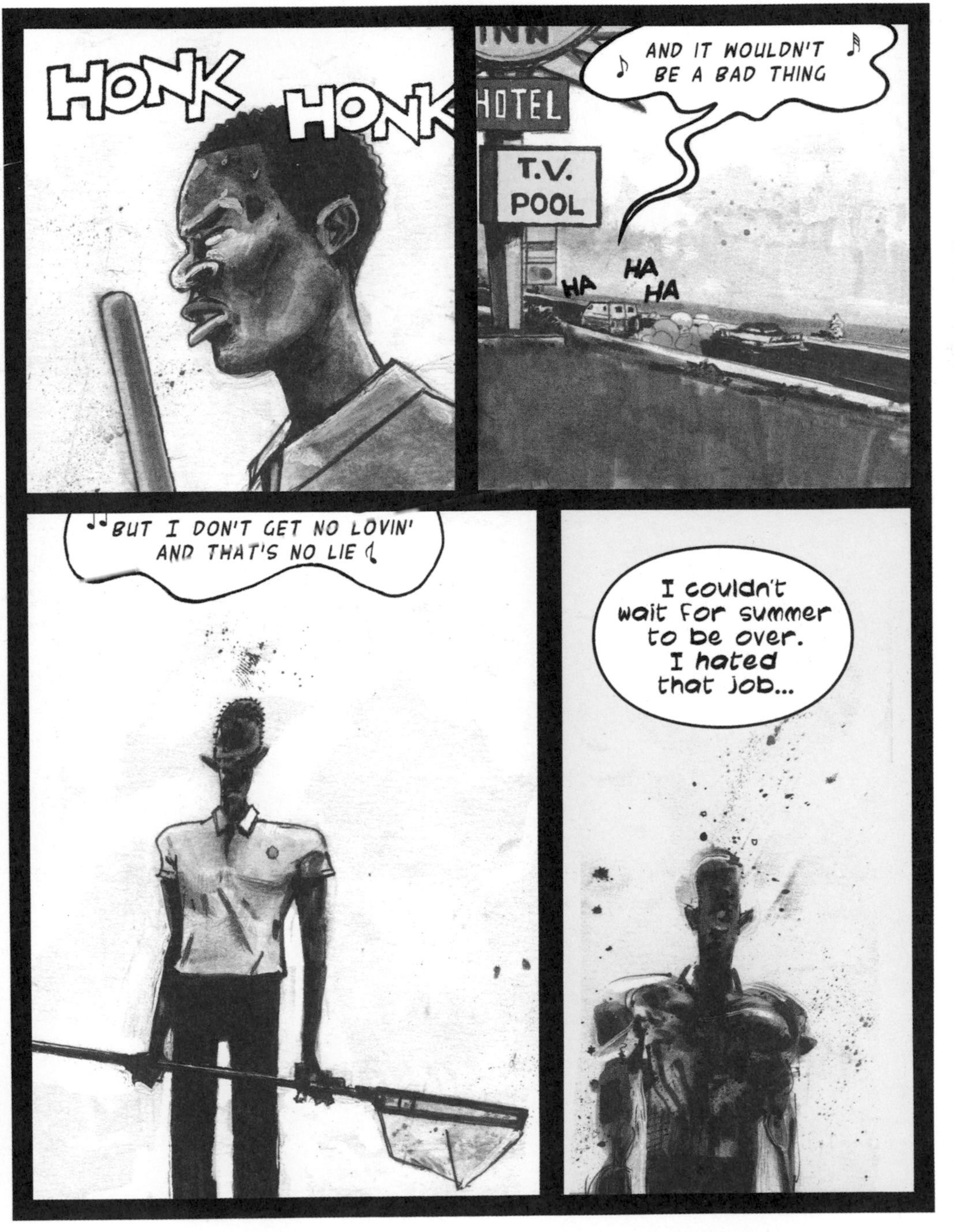
HONK
HONK
INN
HOTEL
T.V. POOL
AND IT WOULDN'T BE A BAD THING
HA
HA HA
BUT I DON'T GET NO LOVIN' AND THAT'S NO LIE
I couldn't wait for summer to be over. I hated that job...

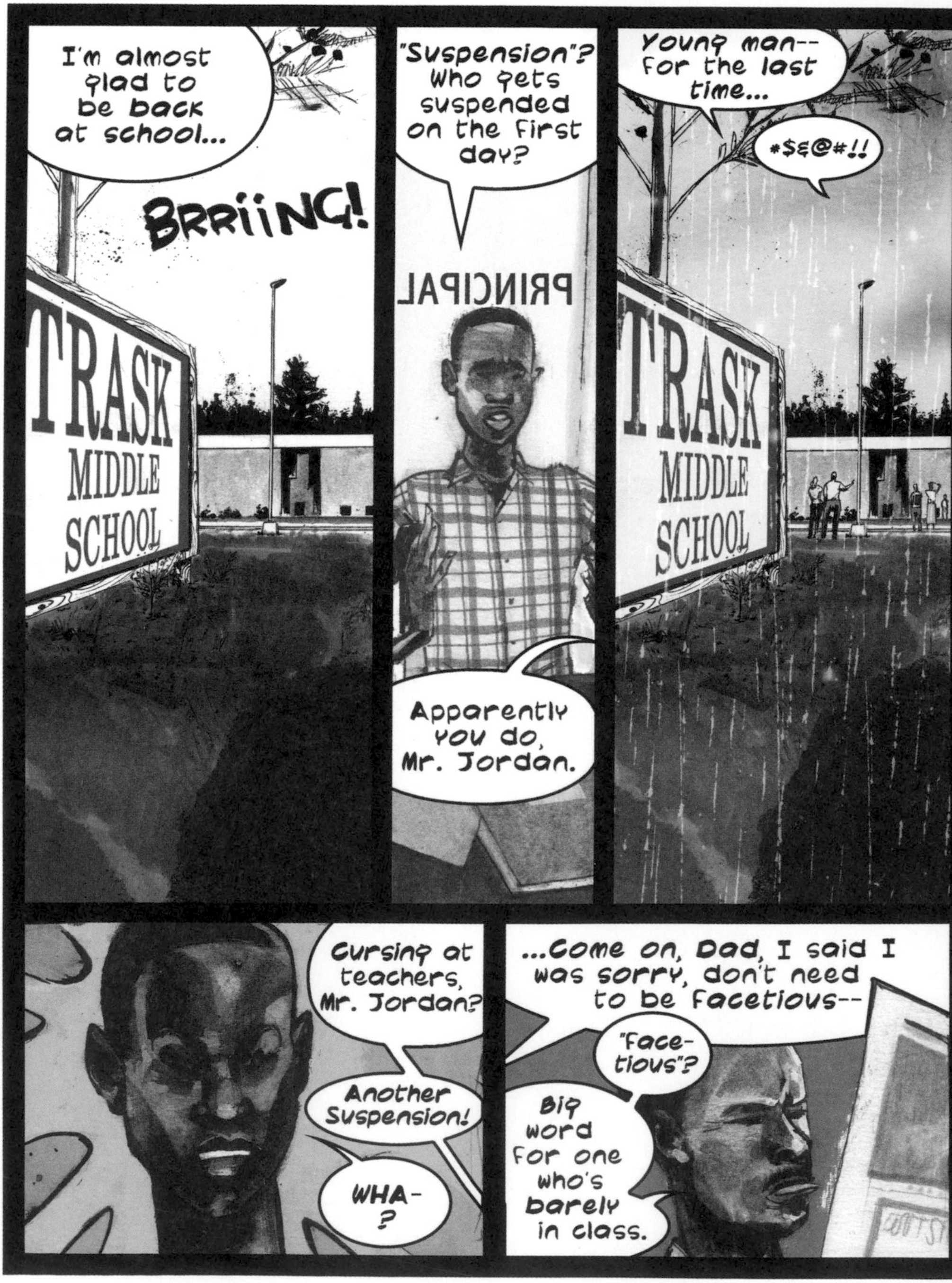
I'm almost glad to be back at school...
BRRiiNG!
TRASK MIDDLE SCHOOL
"Suspension"? Who gets suspended on the first day?
PRINCIPAL
Apparently you do, Mr. Jordan.
Young man-- for the last time...
#$&@#!!
TRASK MIDDLE SCHOOL
Cursing at teachers, Mr. Jordan?
Another Suspension!
WHA-?
...Come on, Dad, I said I was sorry, don't need to be facetious--
"Face-tious"?
Big word for one who's barely in class.

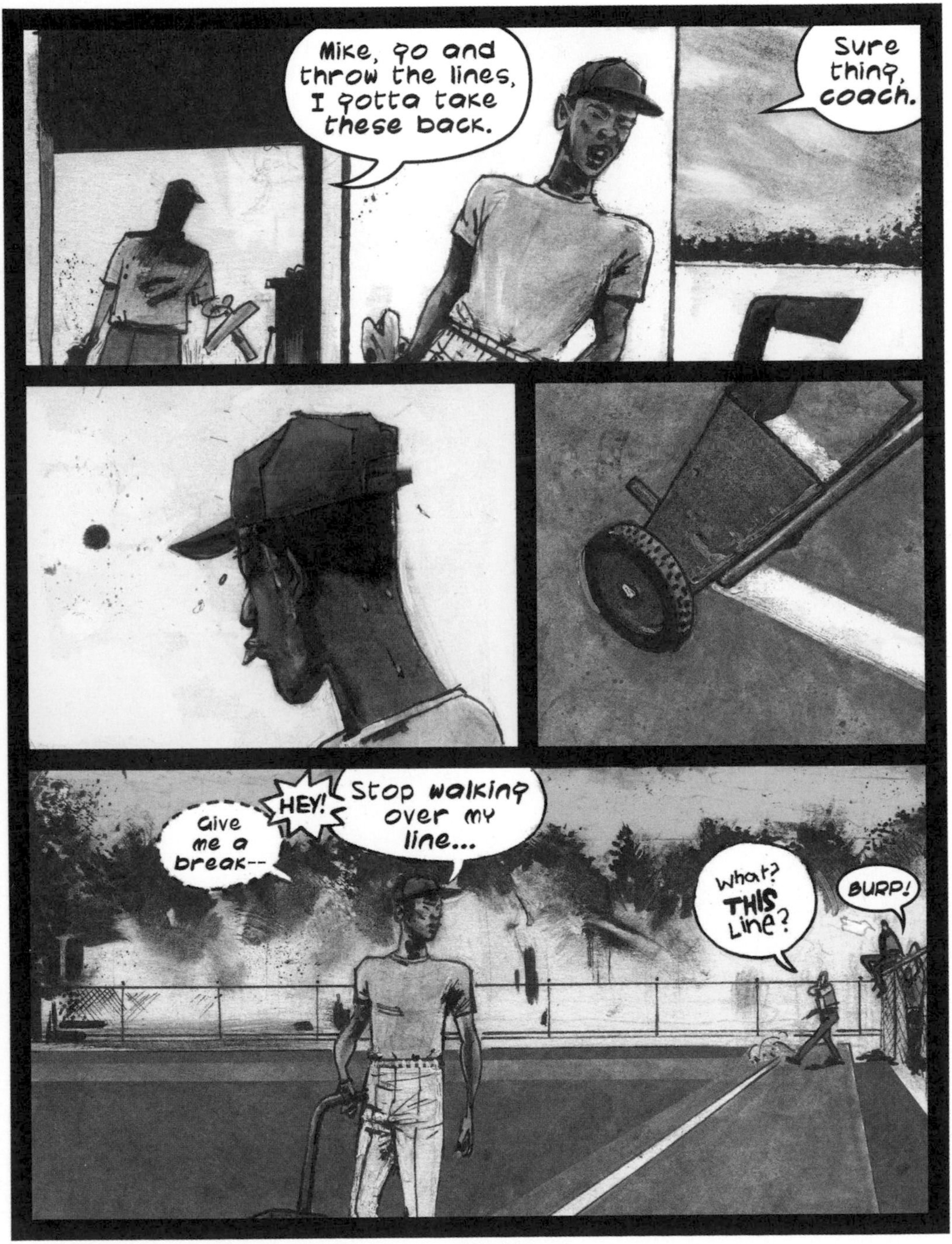
Mike, go and throw the lines, I gotta take these back.
Sure thing, coach.
Give me a break--
HEY!
Stop walking over my line...
What? THIS Line?
BURP!

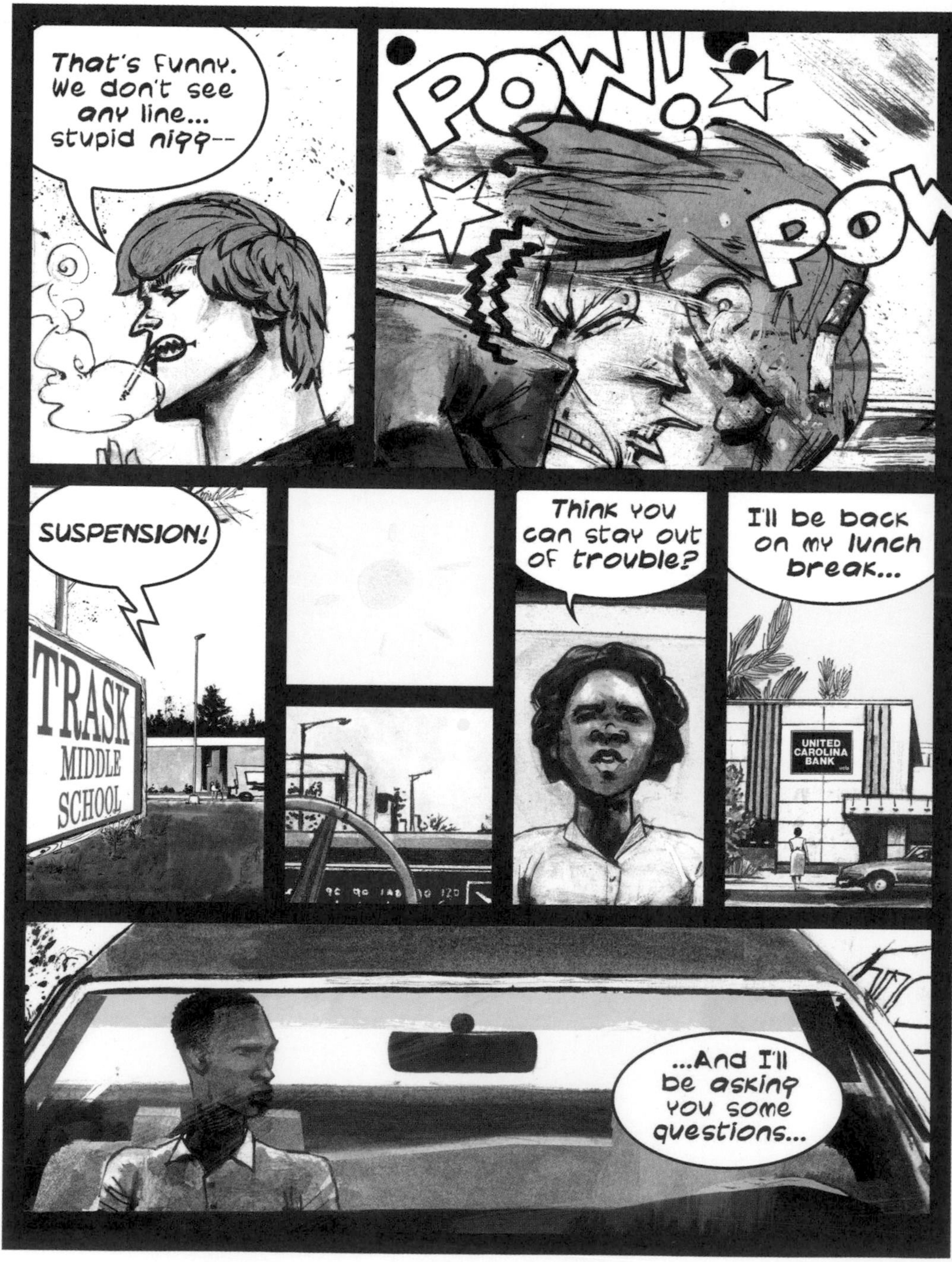
That's funny. We don't see any line... stupid nigg--
POW!
POW
SUSPENSION!
TRASK MIDDLE SCHOOL
Think you can stay out of trouble?
I'll be back on my lunch break...
UNITED CAROLINA BANK
...And I'll be asking you some questions...

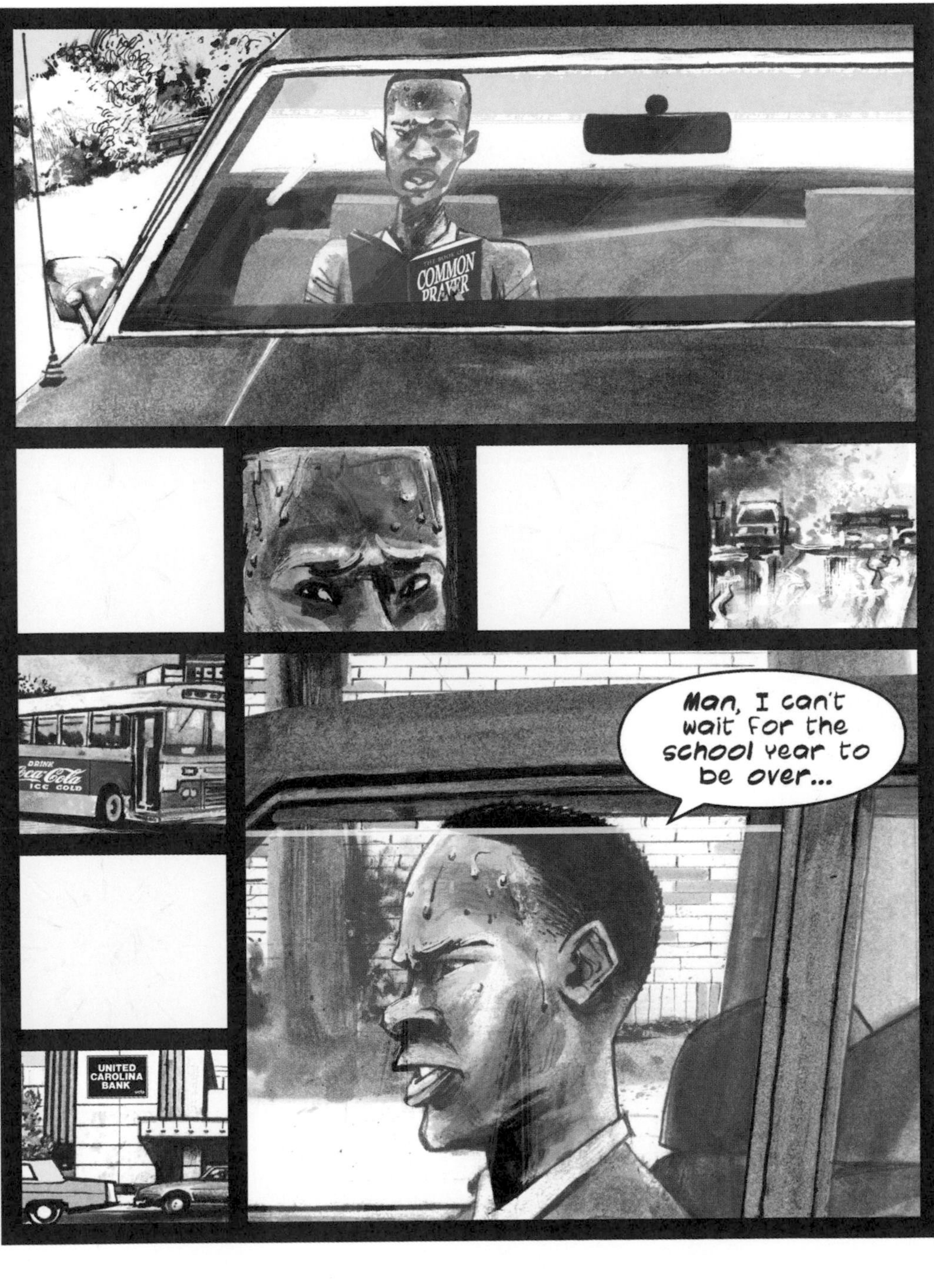
THE BOOK OF COMMON PRAYER
DRINK Coca-Cola ICE COLD
UNITED CAROLINA BANK
Man, I can't wait for the school year to be over...

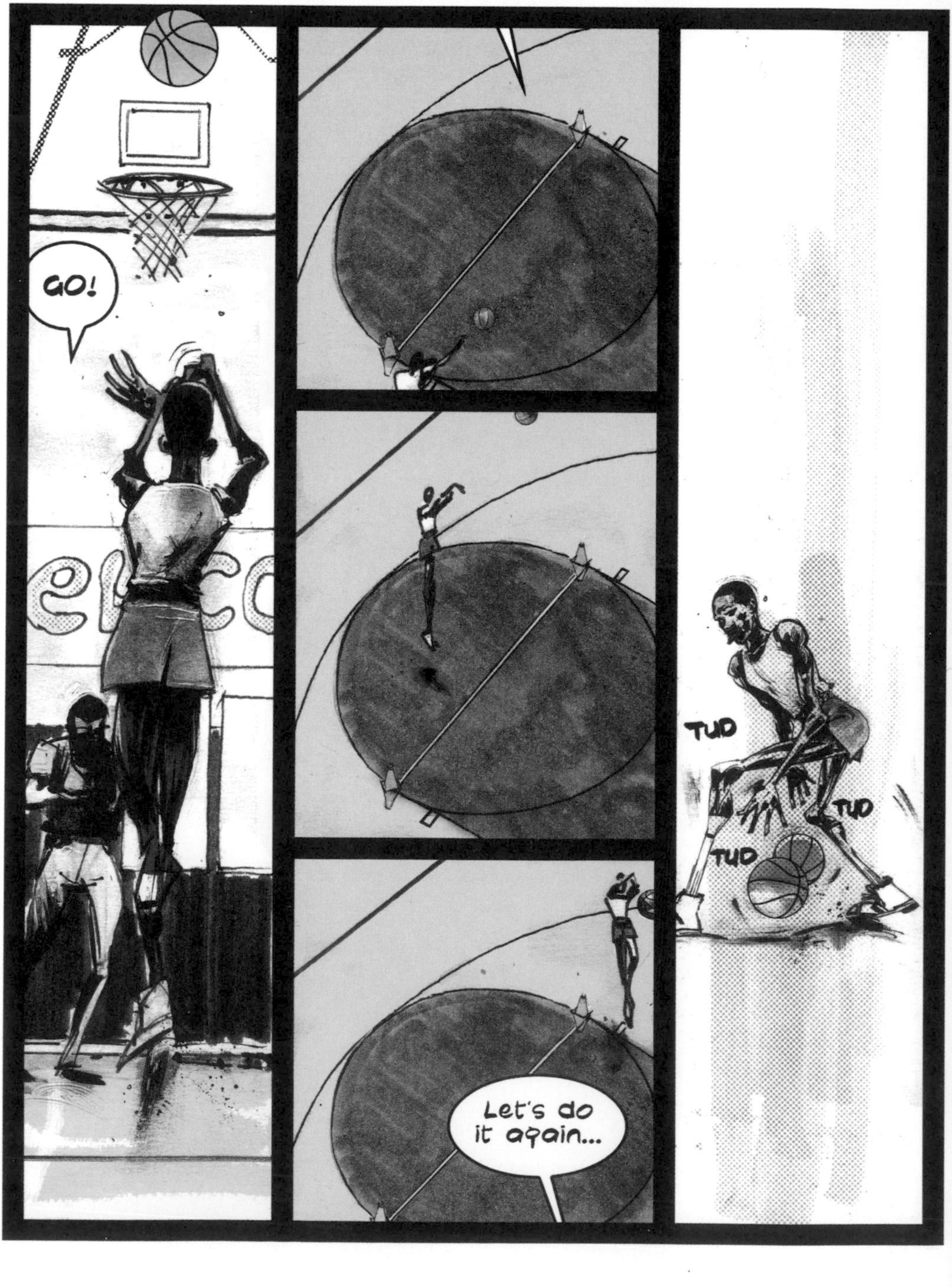
GO!
Let's do it again...
TUD
TUD
TUD

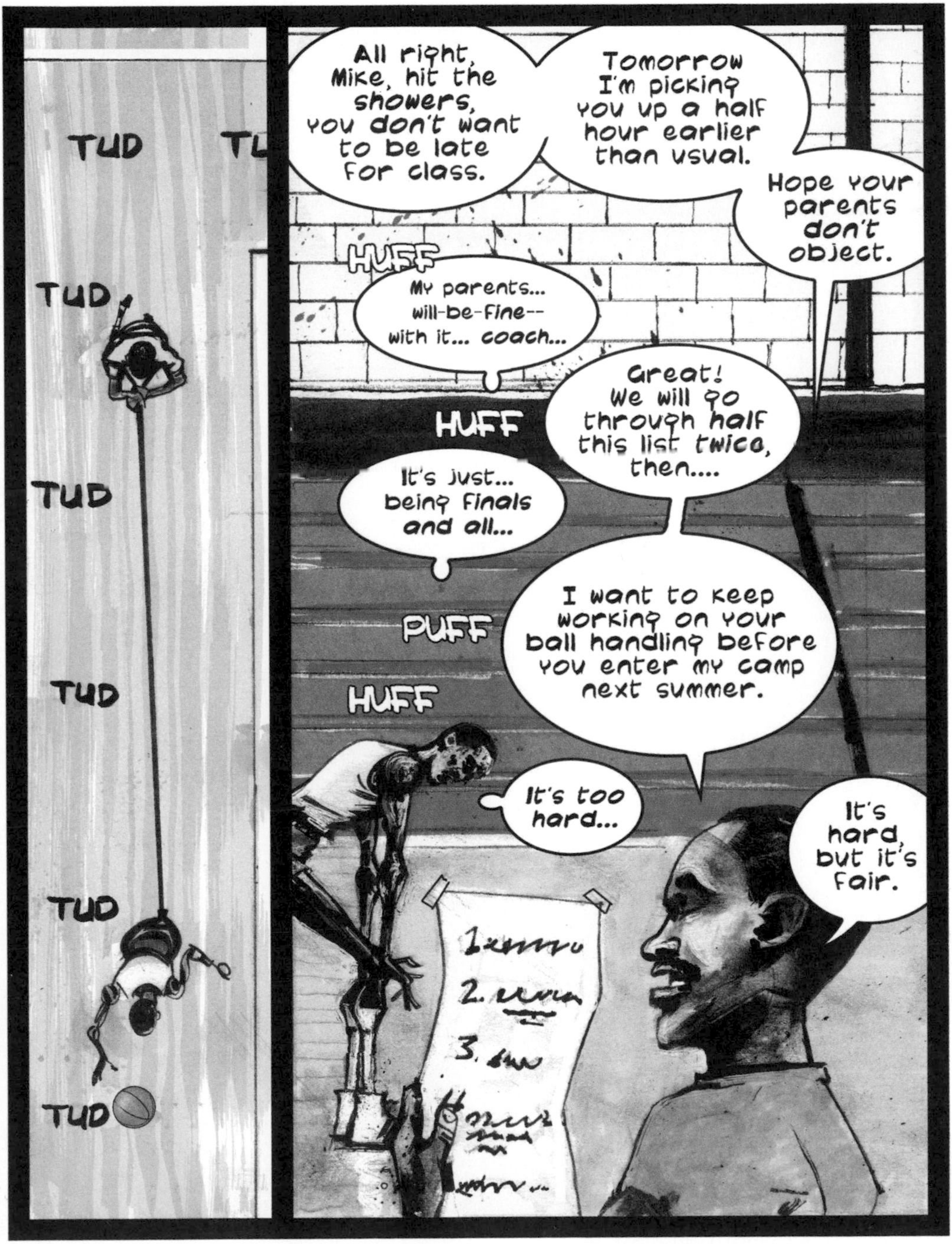
TUD
TUD
TUD
TUD
TUD
TUD
All right, Mike, hit the showers, you don't want to be late for class.
Tomorrow I'm picking you up a half hour earlier than usual.
Hope your parents don't object.
HUFF
My parents... will-be-fine-- with it... coach...
HUFF
Great! We will go through half this list twice, then....
It's just... being finals and all...
PUFF
I want to keep working on your ball handling before you enter my camp next summer.
HUFF
It's too hard...
It's hard, but it's fair.

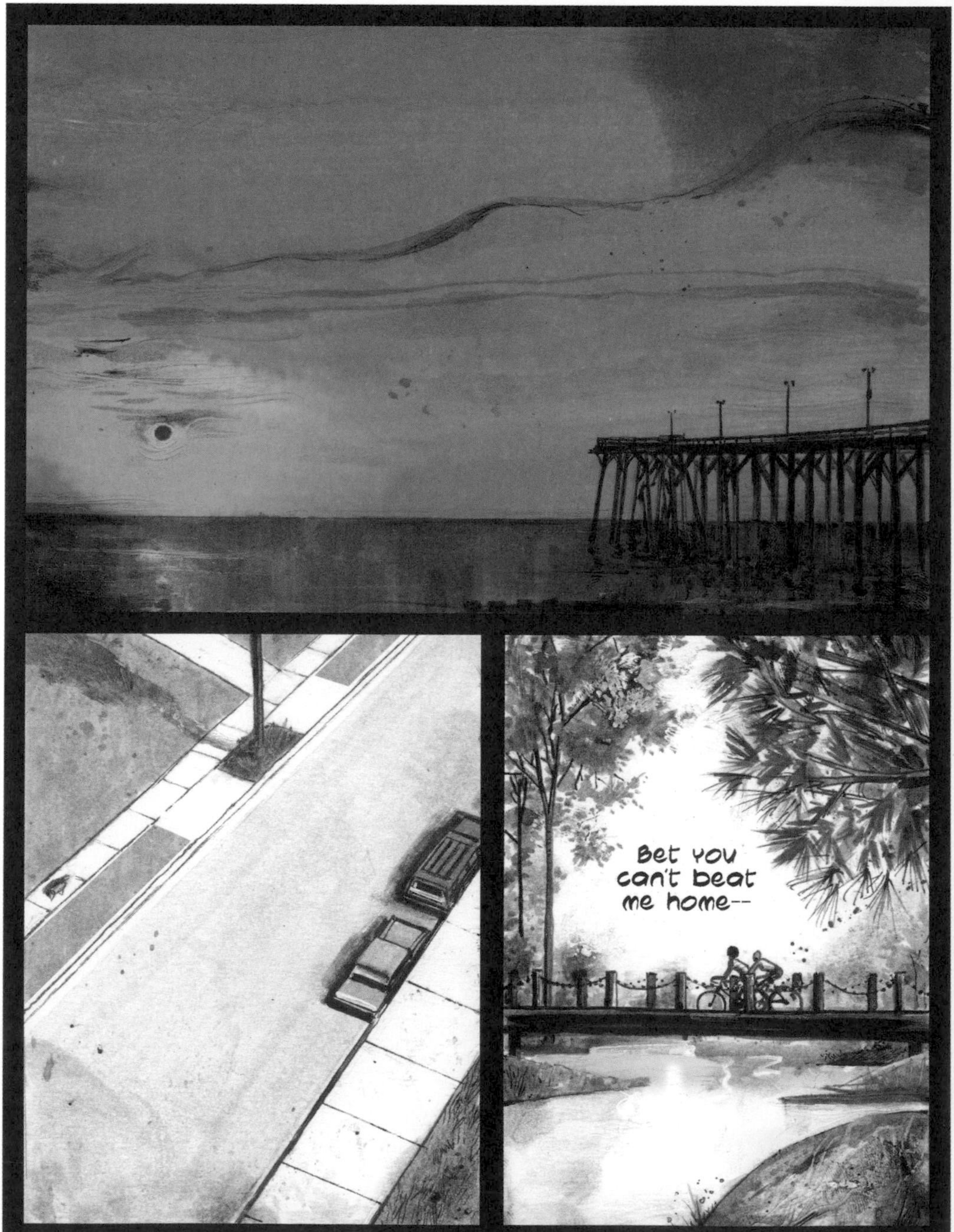
Bet you can't beat me home--

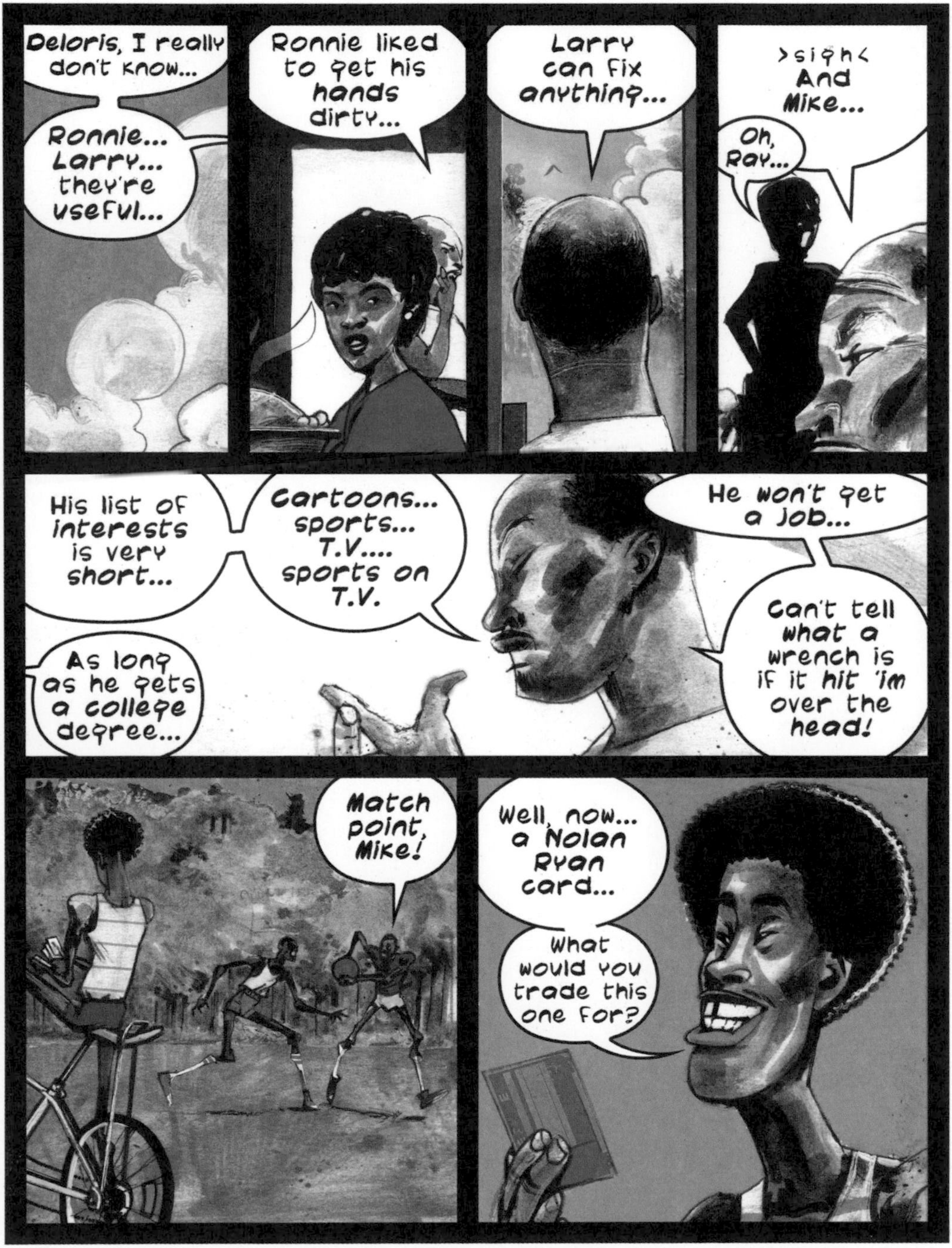
Deloris, I really don't know...
Ronnie... Larry... they're useful...
Ronnie liked to get his hands dirty...
Larry can fix anything...
>sigh< And Mike...
Oh, Ray...
His list of interests is very short...
Cartoons... sports... T.V.... sports on T.V.
He won't get a job...
Can't tell what a wrench is if it hit 'im over the head!
As long as he gets a college degree...
Match point, Mike!
Well, now... a Nolan Ryan card...
What would you trade this one for?

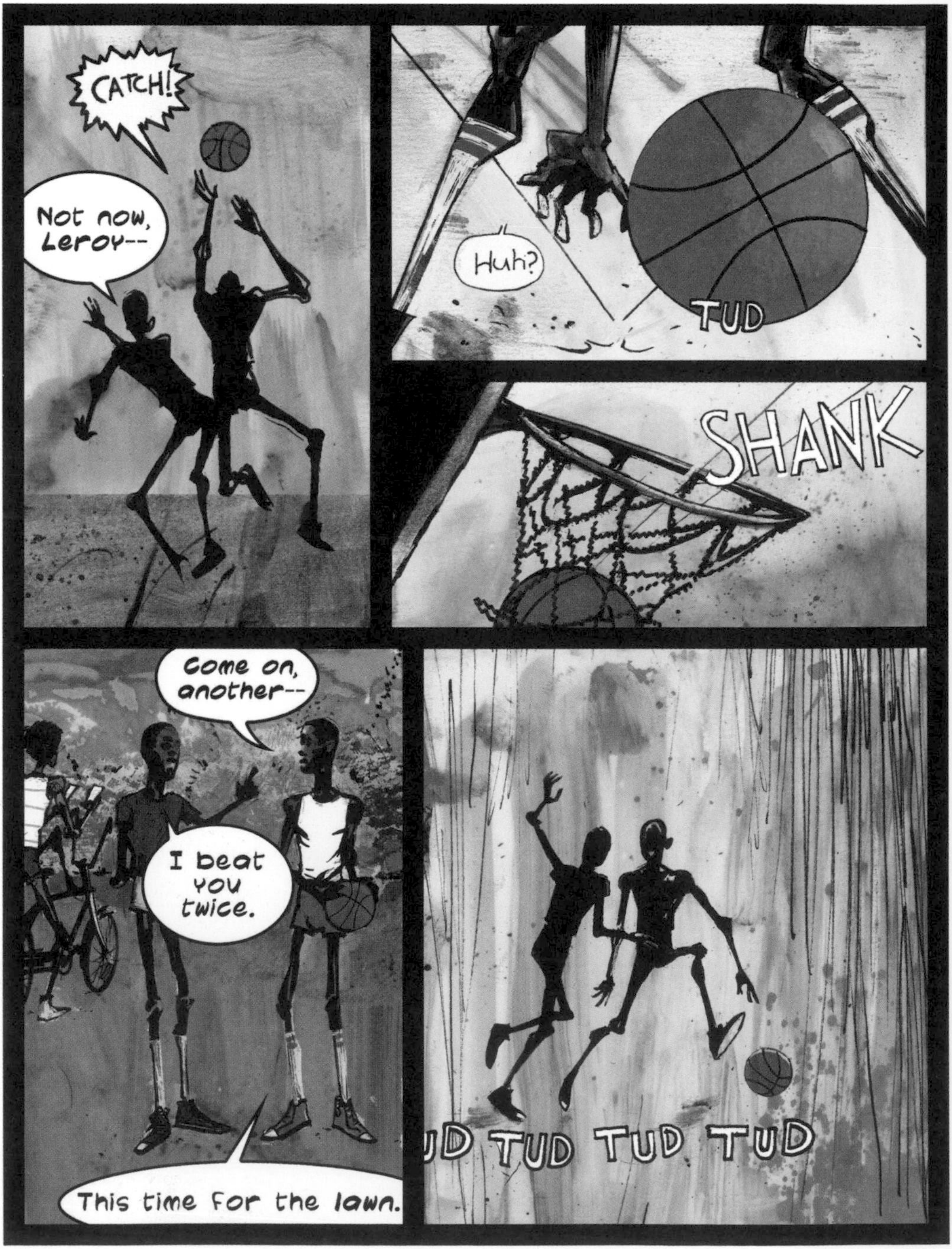
CATCH!
Not now, Leroy--
Huh?
TUD
SHANK
Come on, another--
I beat you twice.
This time for the lawn.
UD TUD TUD TUD

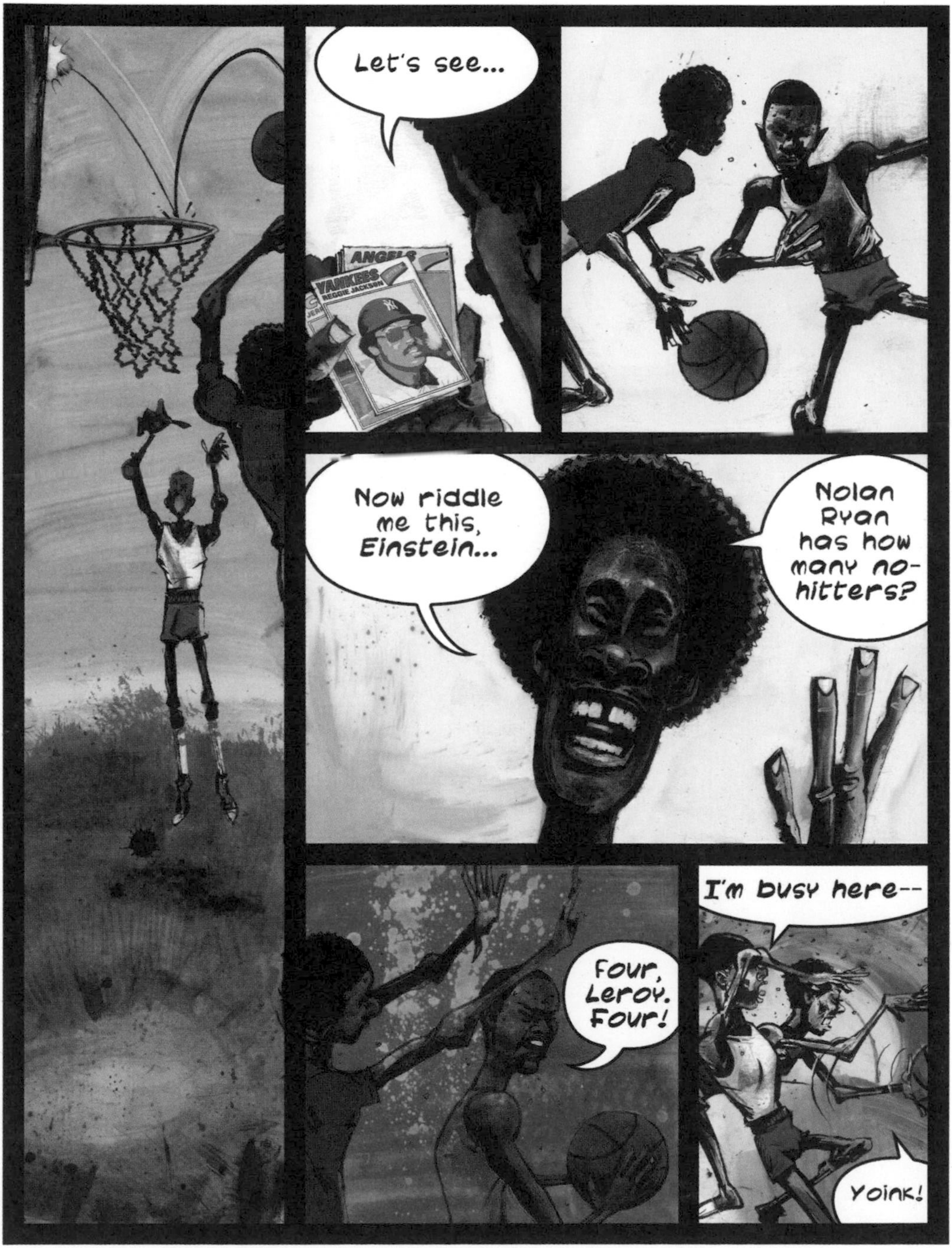
Let's see...
YANKEES
REGGIE JACKSON
ANGELS
Now riddle me this, Einstein...
Nolan Ryan has how many no-hitters?
Four, Leroy. Four!
I'm busy here--
Yoink!

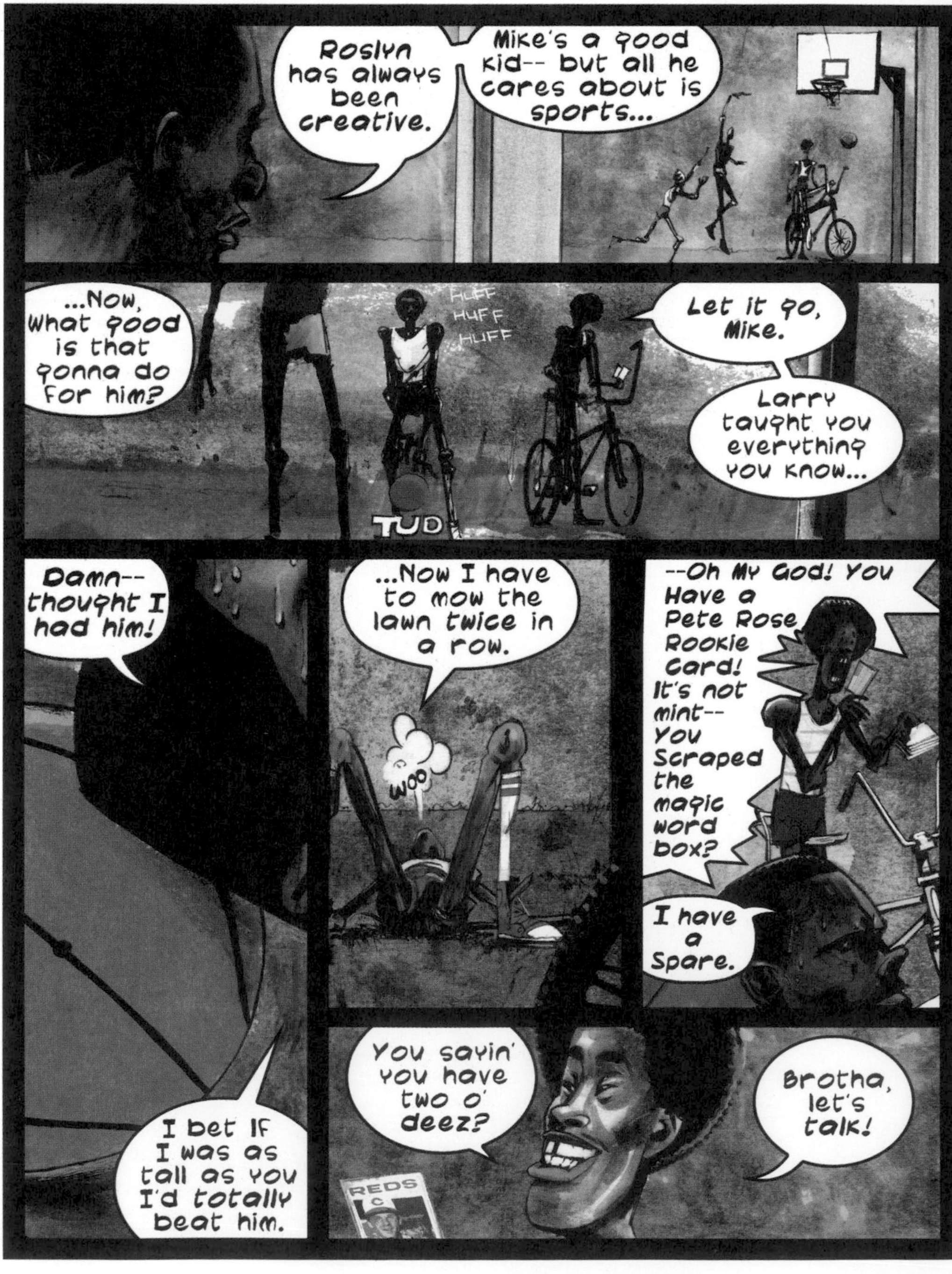
Roslyn has always been creative.
Mike's a good kid-- but all he cares about is sports...
...Now, what good is that gonna do for him?
HUFF HUFF HUFF
Let it go, Mike.
Larry taught you everything you know...
TUD
Damn-- thought I had him!
...Now I have to mow the lawn twice in a row.
WOO
--Oh My God! You Have a Pete Rose Rookie Card! It's not mint-- You Scraped the magic word box?
I have a Spare.
I bet If I was as tall as you I'd totally beat him.
You sayin' you have two o' deez?
Brotha, let's talk!
REDS

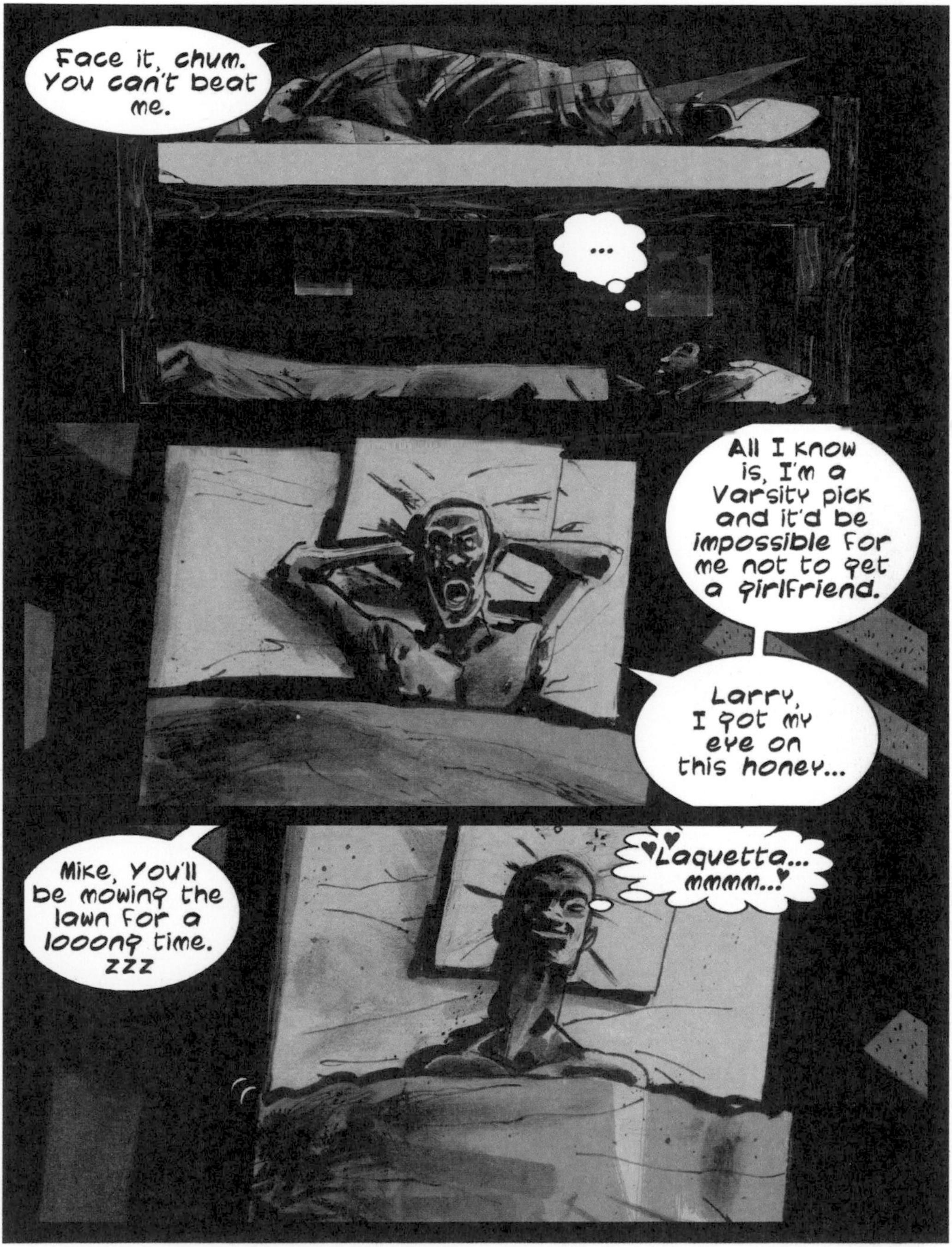
Face it, chum. You can't beat me.
...
All I know is, I'm a Varsity pick and it'd be impossible for me not to get a girlfriend.
Larry, I got my eye on this honey...
Mike, you'll be mowing the lawn for a looong time. ZZZ
Laquetta... mmmm...

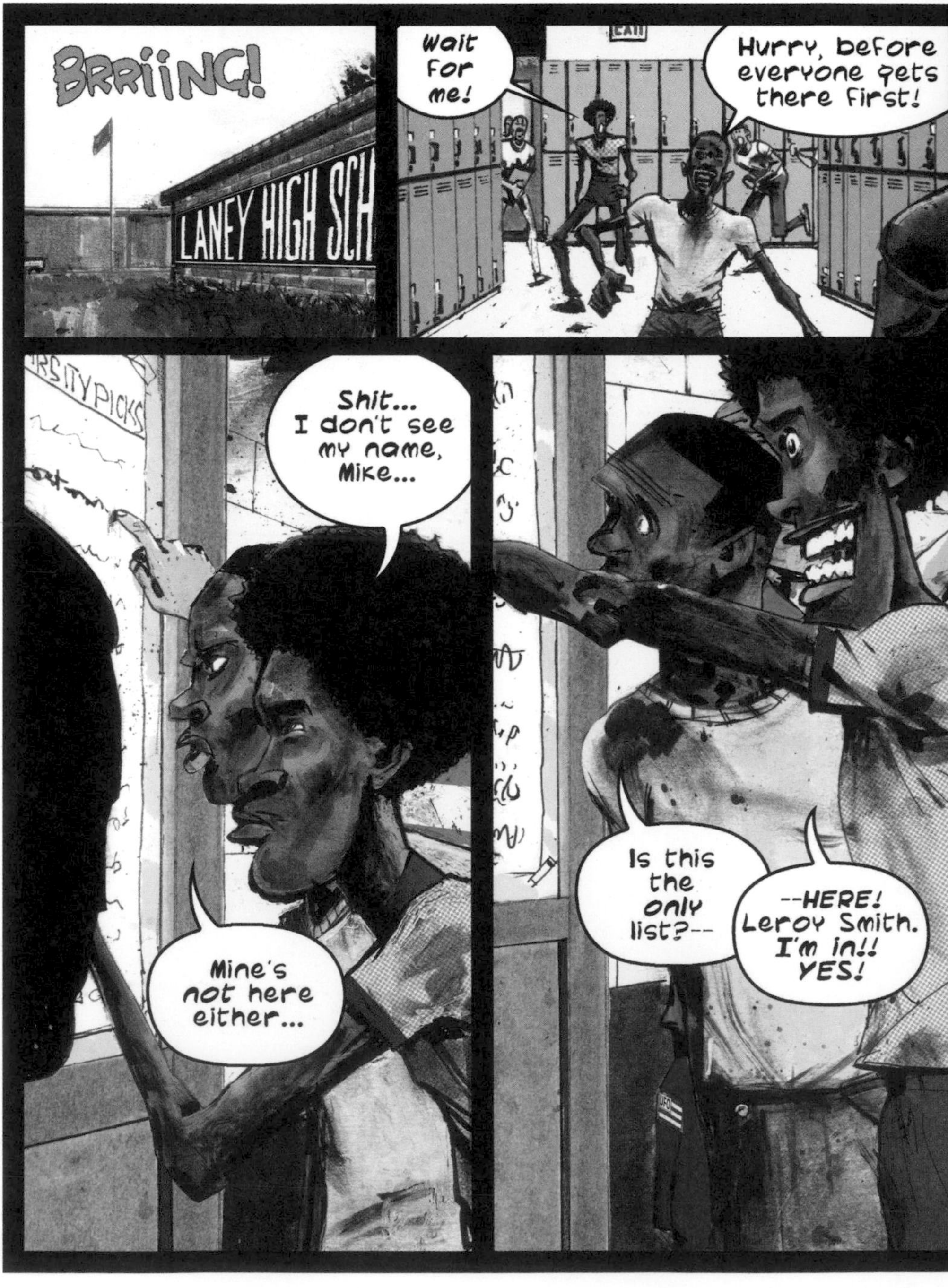
BRRIING!
LANEY HIGH SCH
Wait for me!
Hurry, before everyone gets there first!
RSITY PICKS
Shit... I don't see my name, Mike...
Mine's not here either...
Is this the only list?--
--HERE! Leroy Smith. I'm in!! YES!

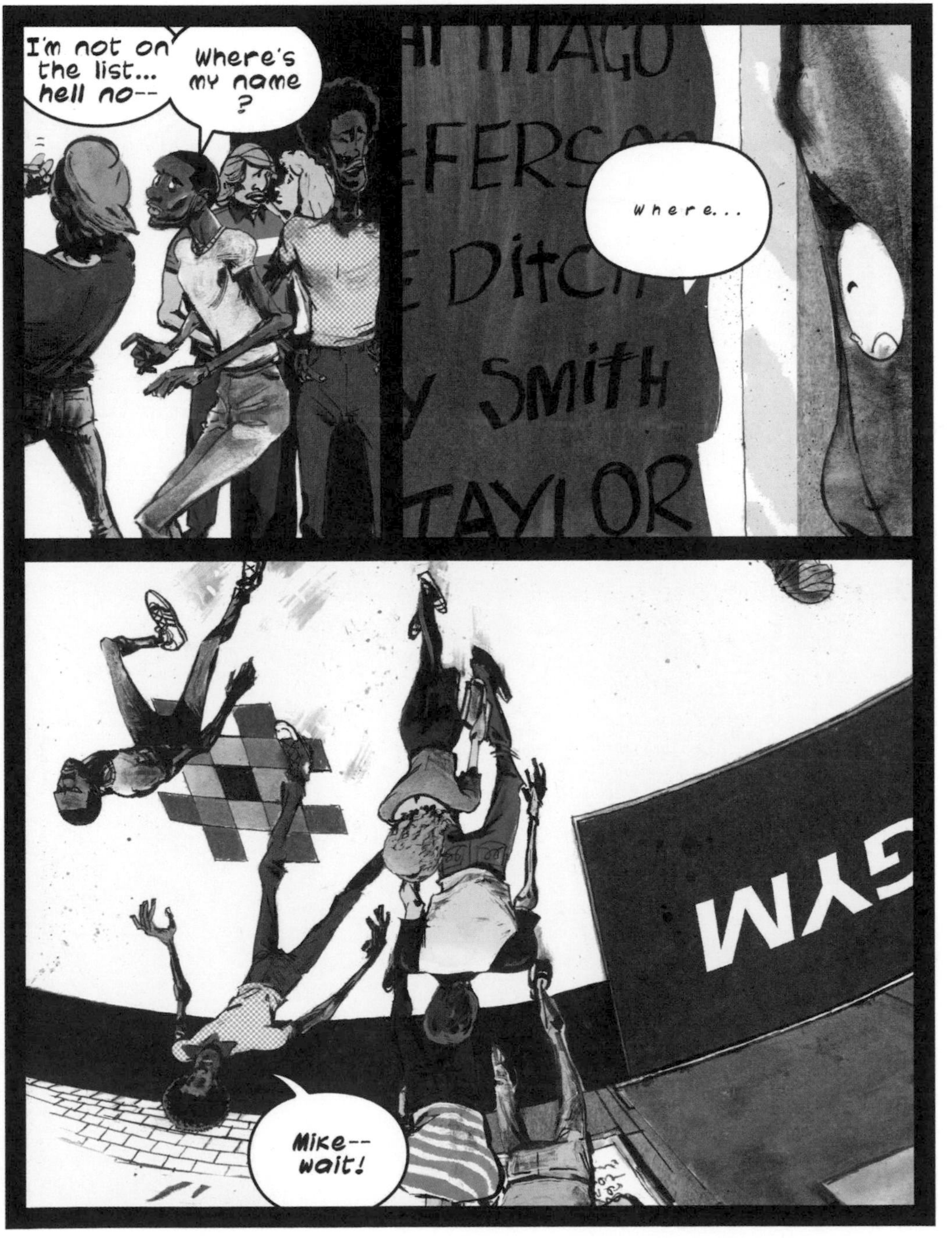
I'm not on the list... hell no--
Where's my name?
Where...
Mike-- wait!

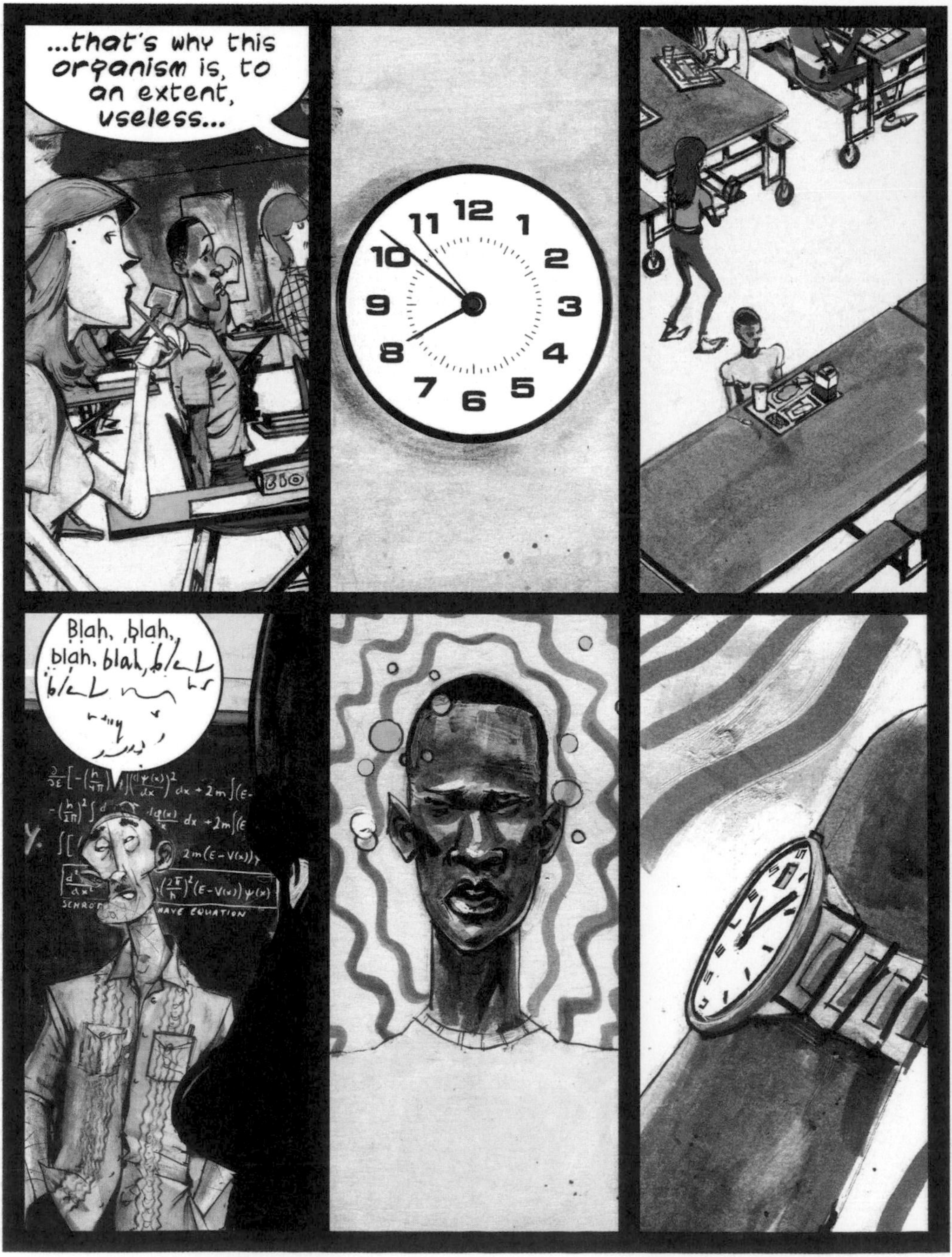
...that's why this organism is, to an extent, useless...
Blah, blah, blah, blah,
WAVE EQUATION

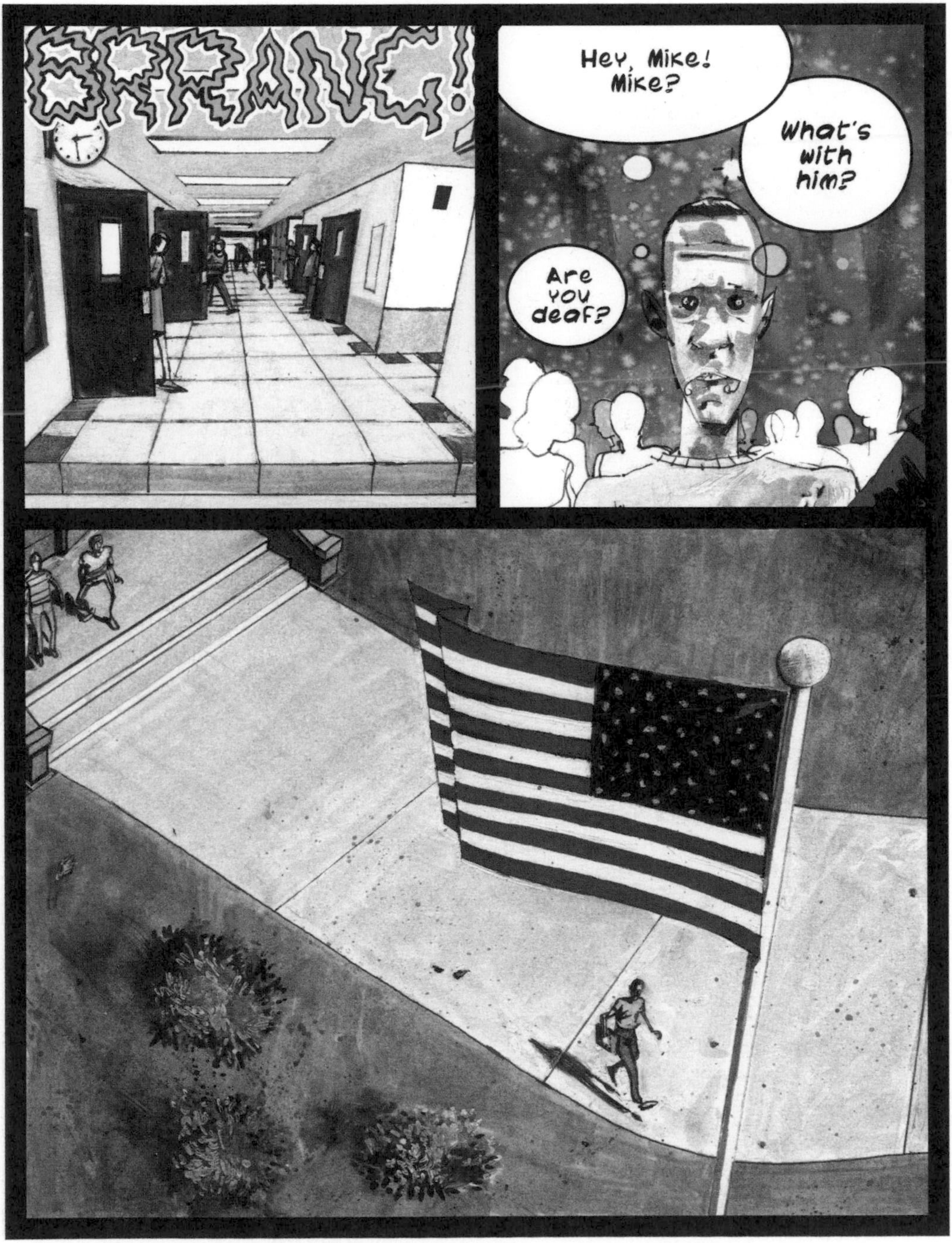
BRRANG!
Hey, Mike! Mike?
What's with him?
Are you deaf?

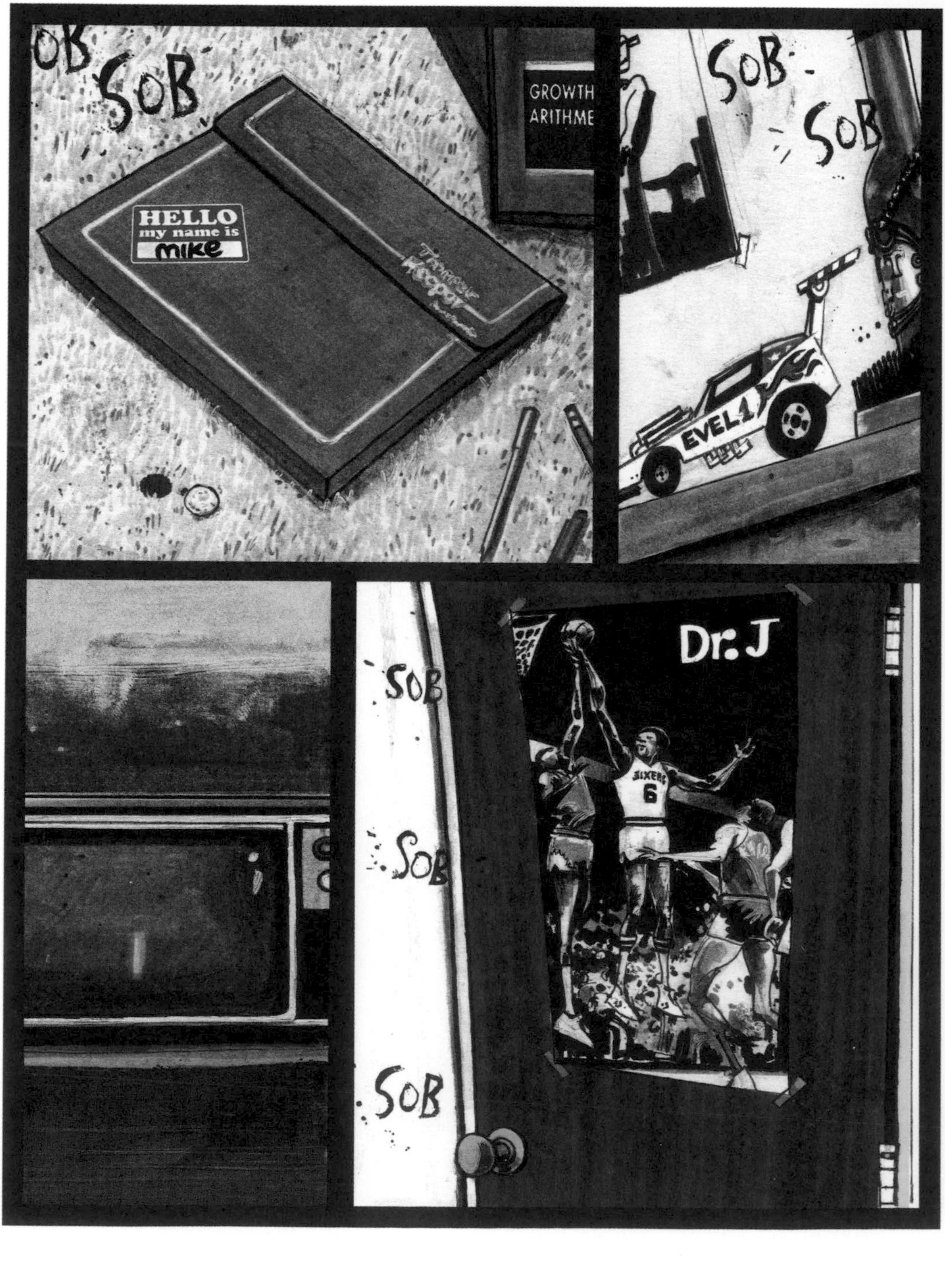

OB
SOB
GROWTH
ARITHME
HELLO
my name is
mike
SOB
SOB
EVEL 1
SOB
SOB
SOB
Dr. J
SIXERS
6

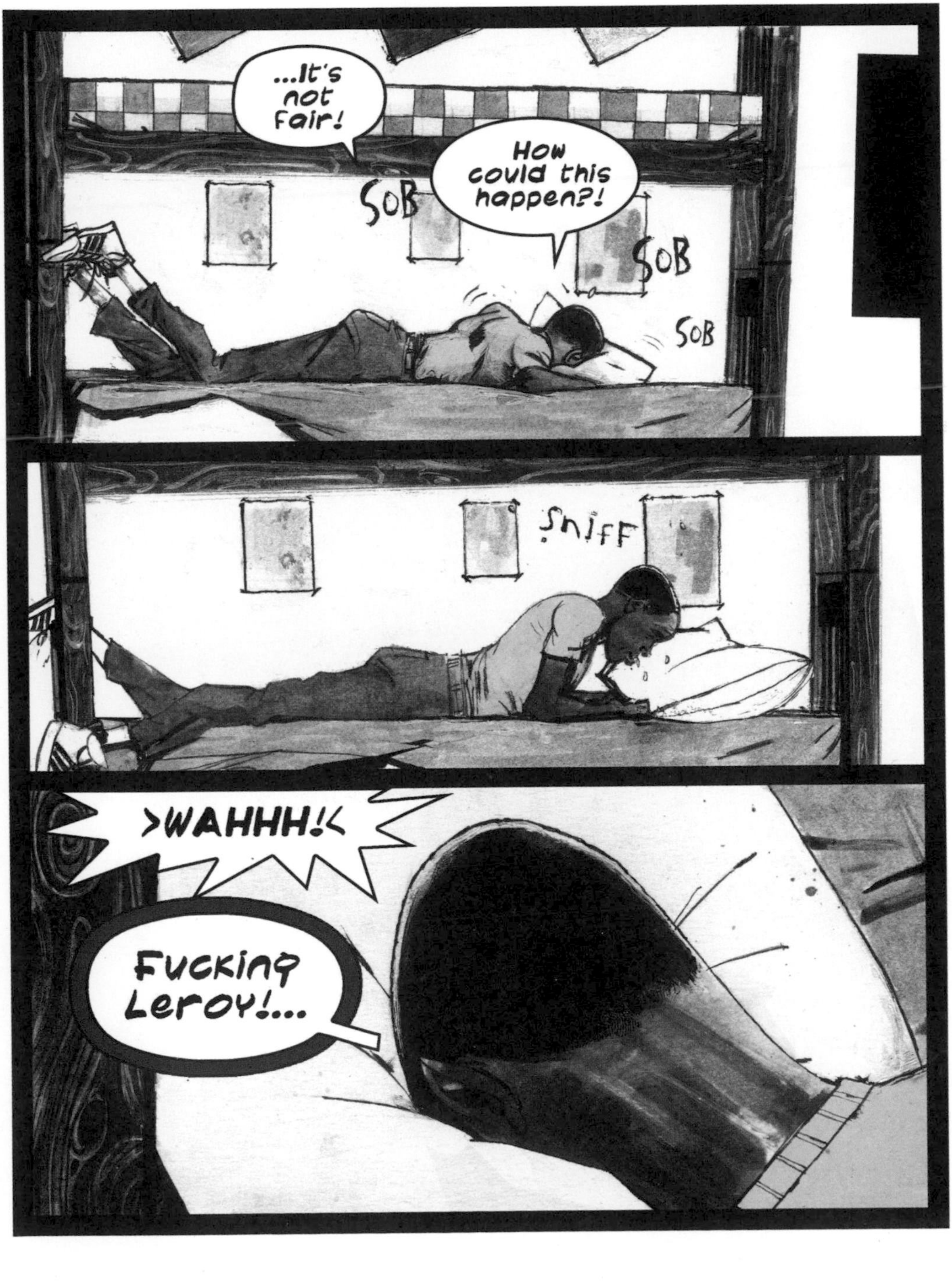
...It's not fair!
How could this happen?!
SOB
SOB
SOB
Sniff
>WAHHH!<
Fucking Leroy!...

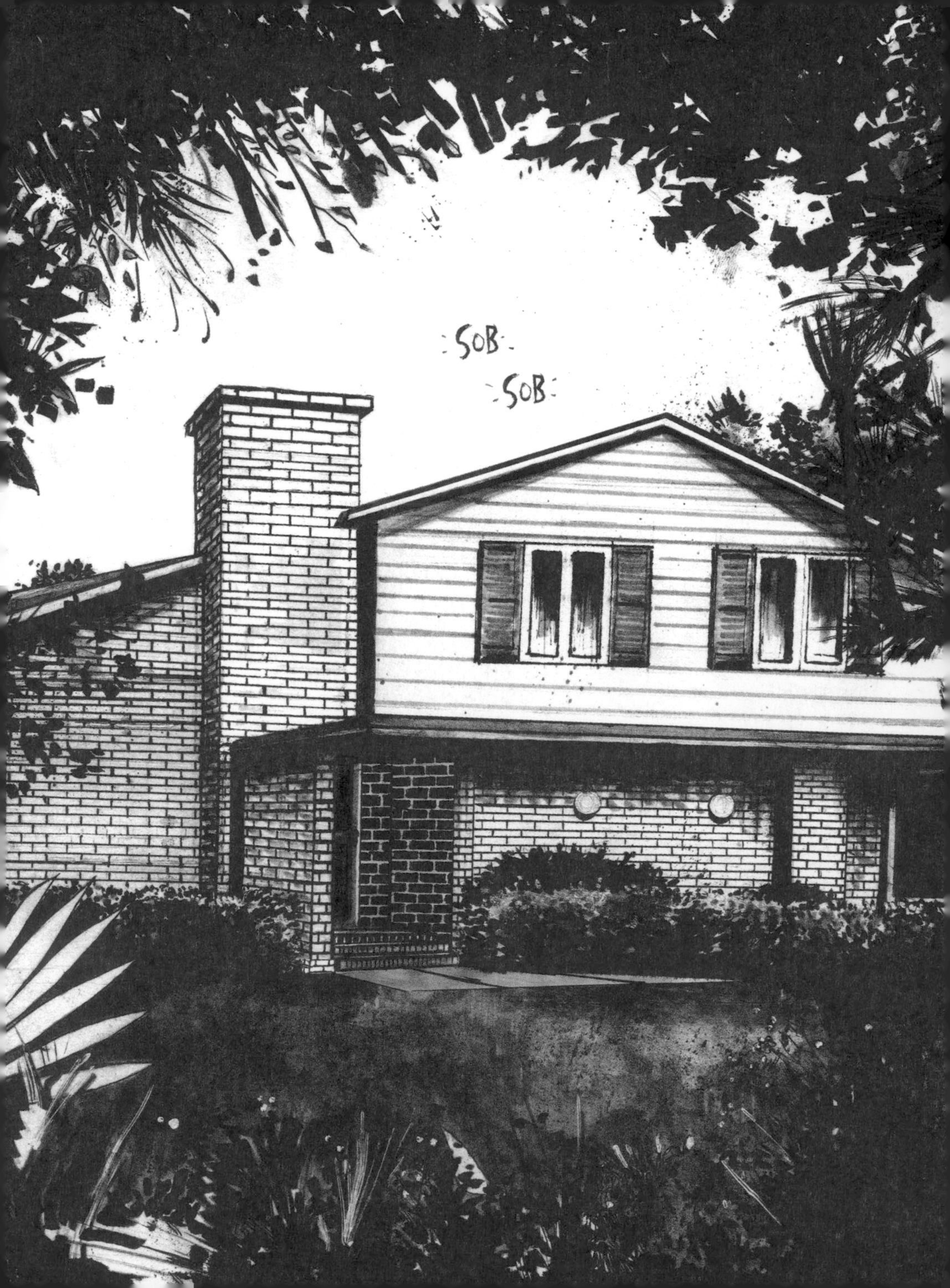
SOB
SOB

ONE FINE NOON IN A CHICAGO SUBURB

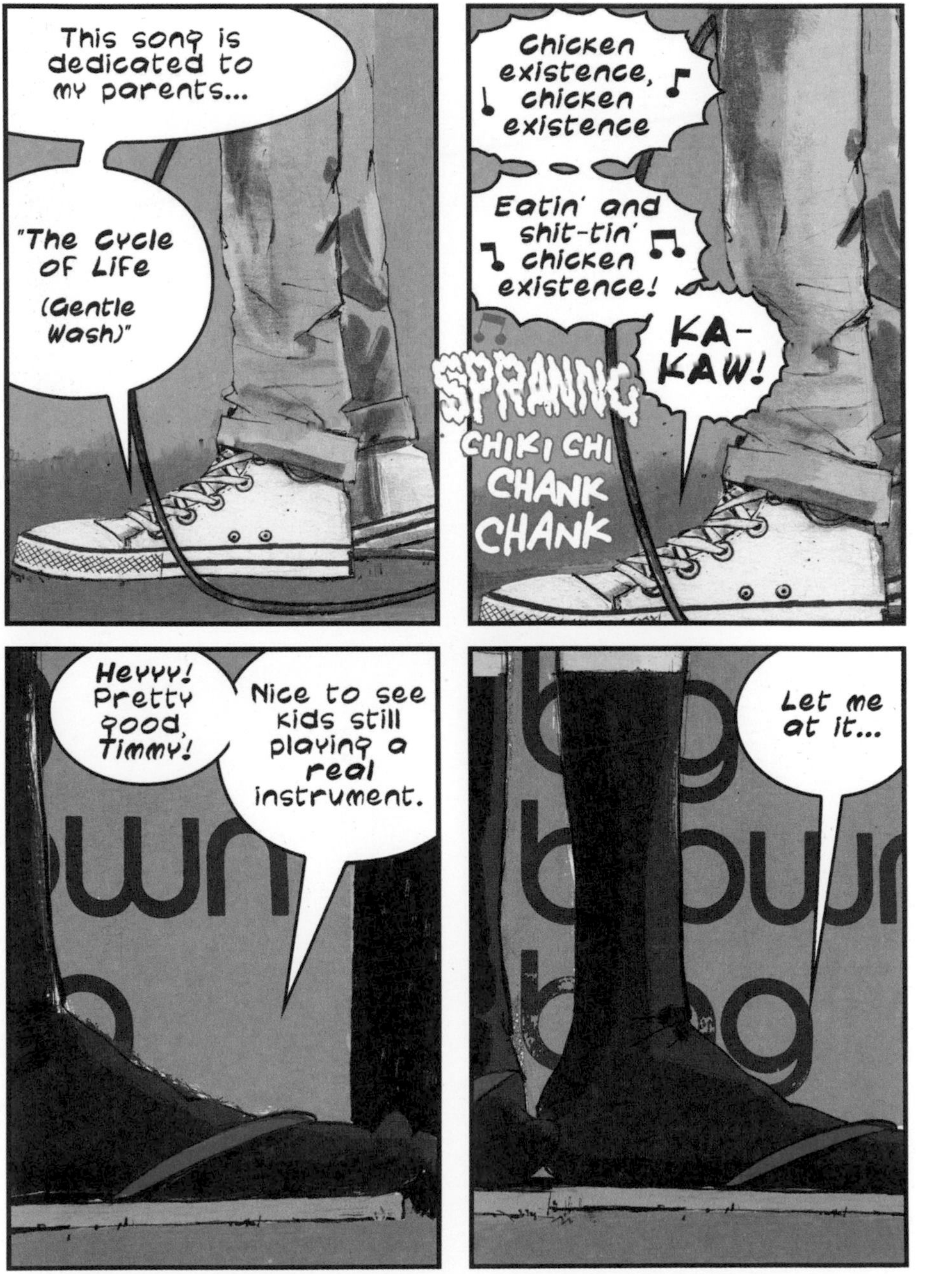

This song is dedicated to my parents...
"The Cycle of Life (Gentle Wash)"
Chicken existence, chicken existence
Eatin' and shit-tin' chicken existence!
SPRANNG
CHIKI CHI CHANK CHANK
KA-KAW!
Heyyy! Pretty good, Timmy!
Nice to see kids still playing a *real* instrument.
Let me at it...

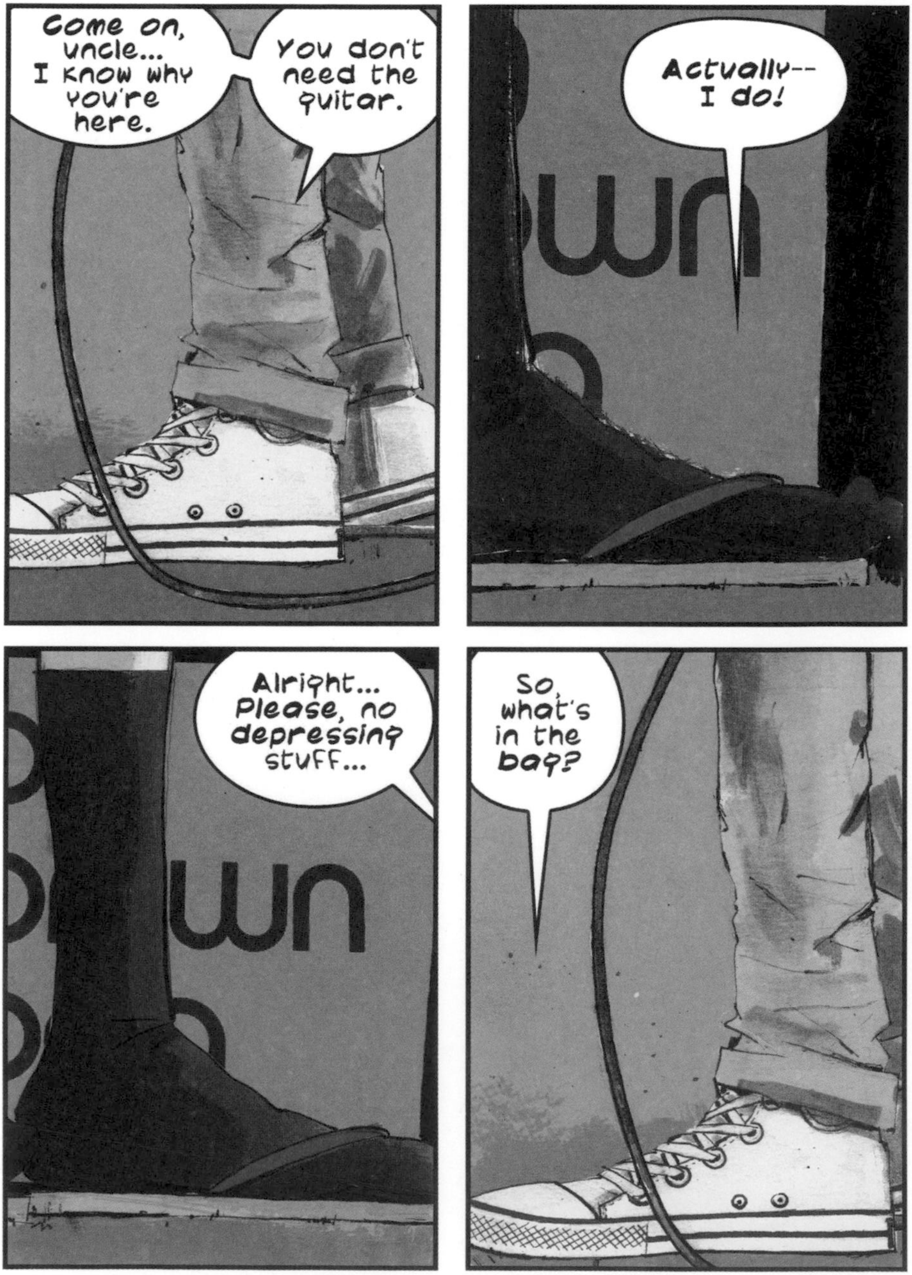

Come on, uncle... I know why you're here.
You don't need the guitar.
Actually-- I do!
Alright... Please, no depressing stuff...
So, what's in the bag?

2:
Gonna Make You Sweat

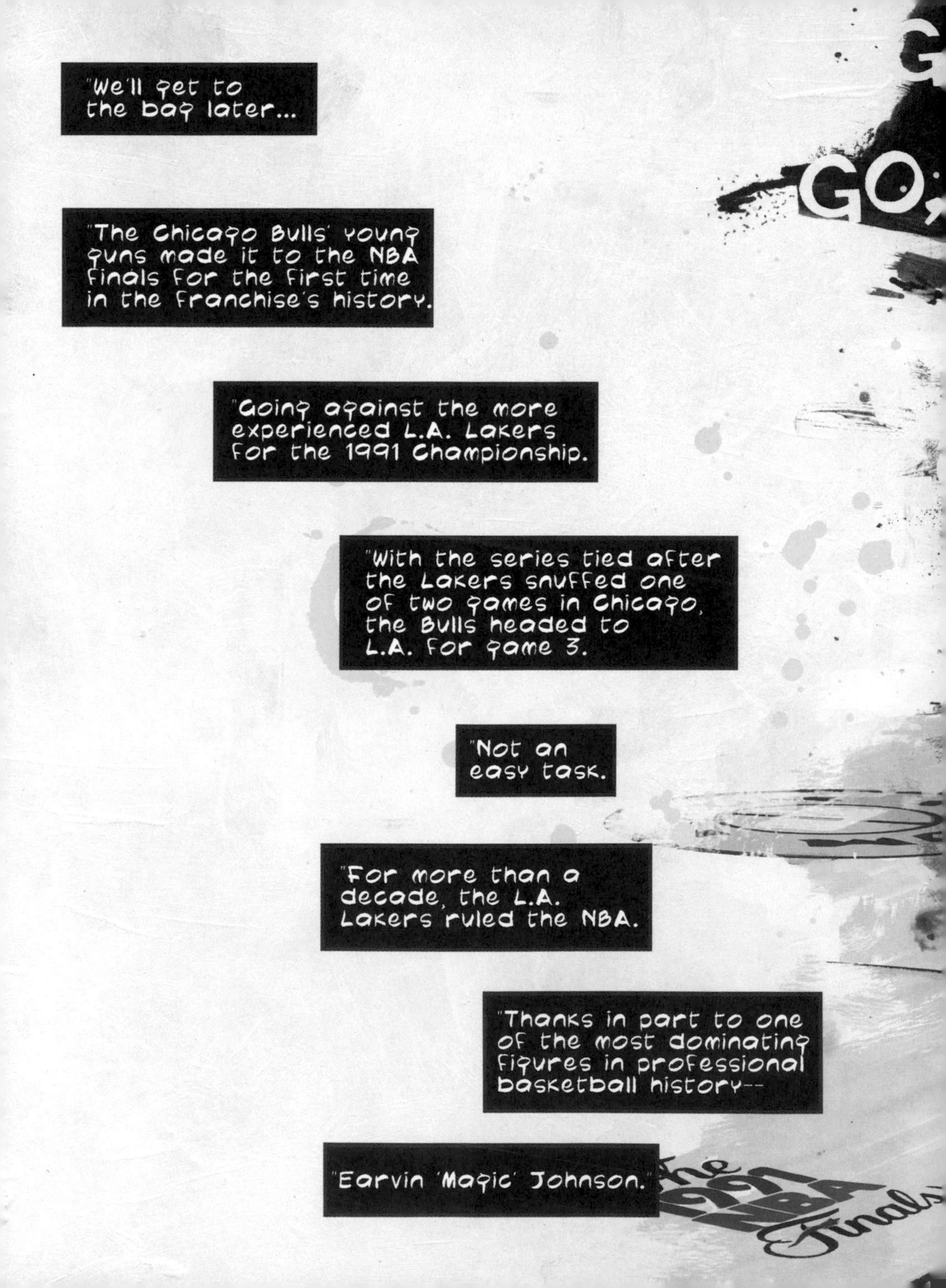
"We'll get to the bag later...
"The Chicago Bulls' young guns made it to the NBA finals for the first time in the franchise's history.
"Going against the more experienced L.A. Lakers for the 1991 Championship.
"With the series tied after the Lakers snuffed one of two games in Chicago, the Bulls headed to L.A. for game 3.
"Not an easy task.
"For more than a decade, the L.A. Lakers ruled the NBA.
"Thanks in part to one of the most dominating figures in professional basketball history--
"Earvin 'Magic' Johnson."

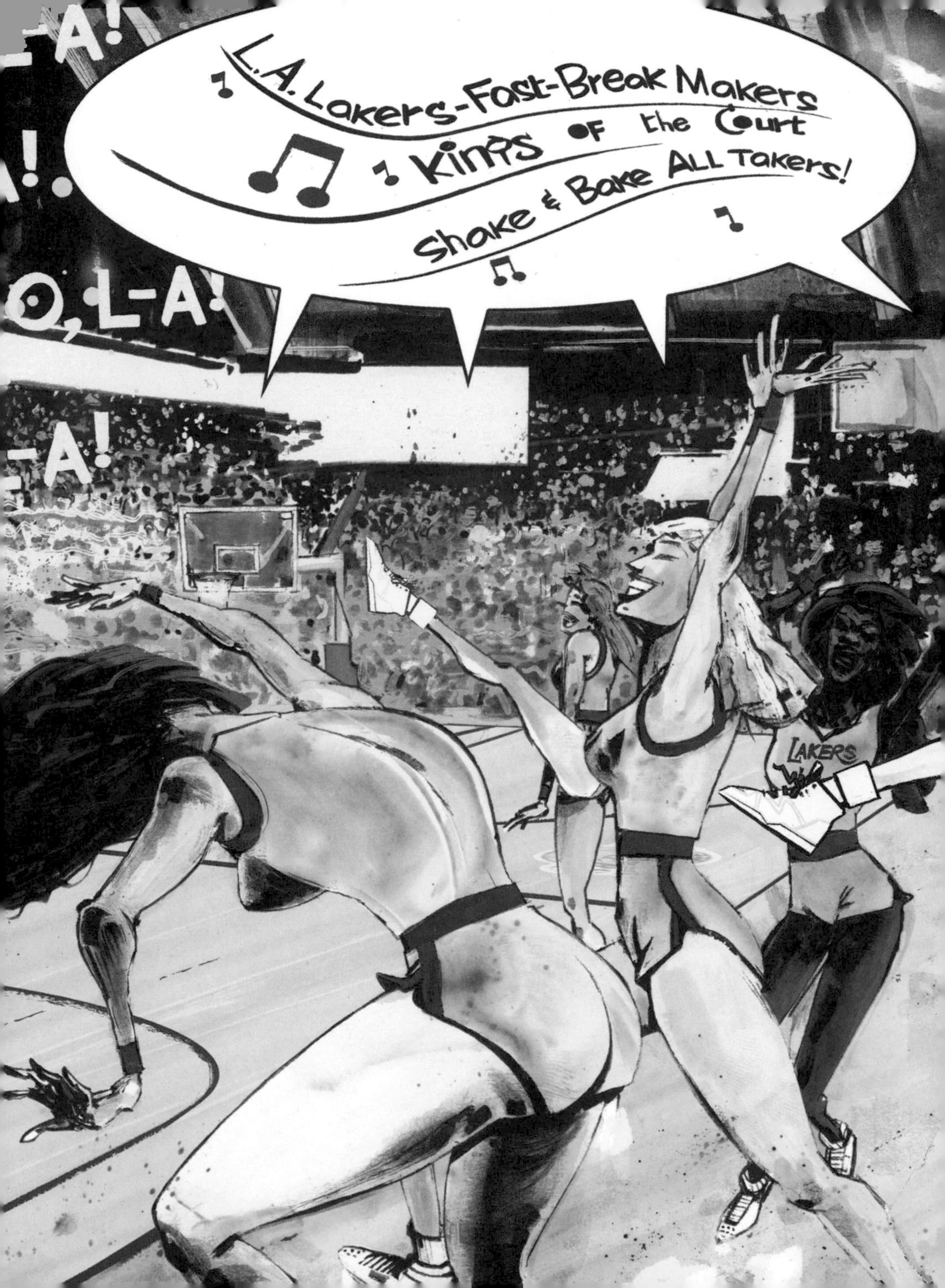

L.A. Lakers-Fast-Break Makers
Kings of the Court
Shake & Bake ALL Takers!
O, L-A!
LAKERS

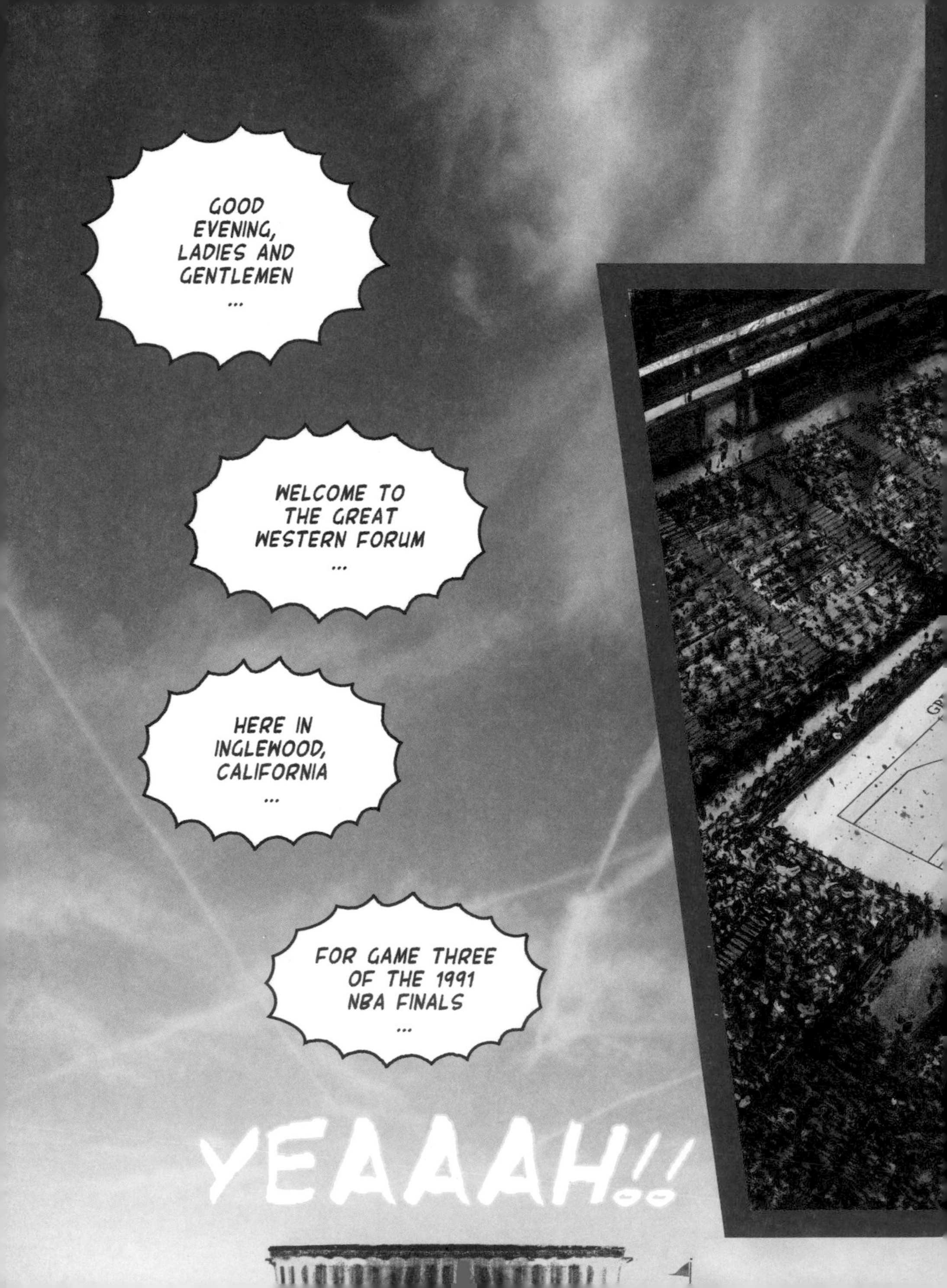
GOOD EVENING, LADIES AND GENTLEMEN ...
WELCOME TO THE GREAT WESTERN FORUM ...
HERE IN INGLEWOOD, CALIFORNIA ...
FOR GAME THREE OF THE 1991 NBA FINALS ...
YEAAAH!!

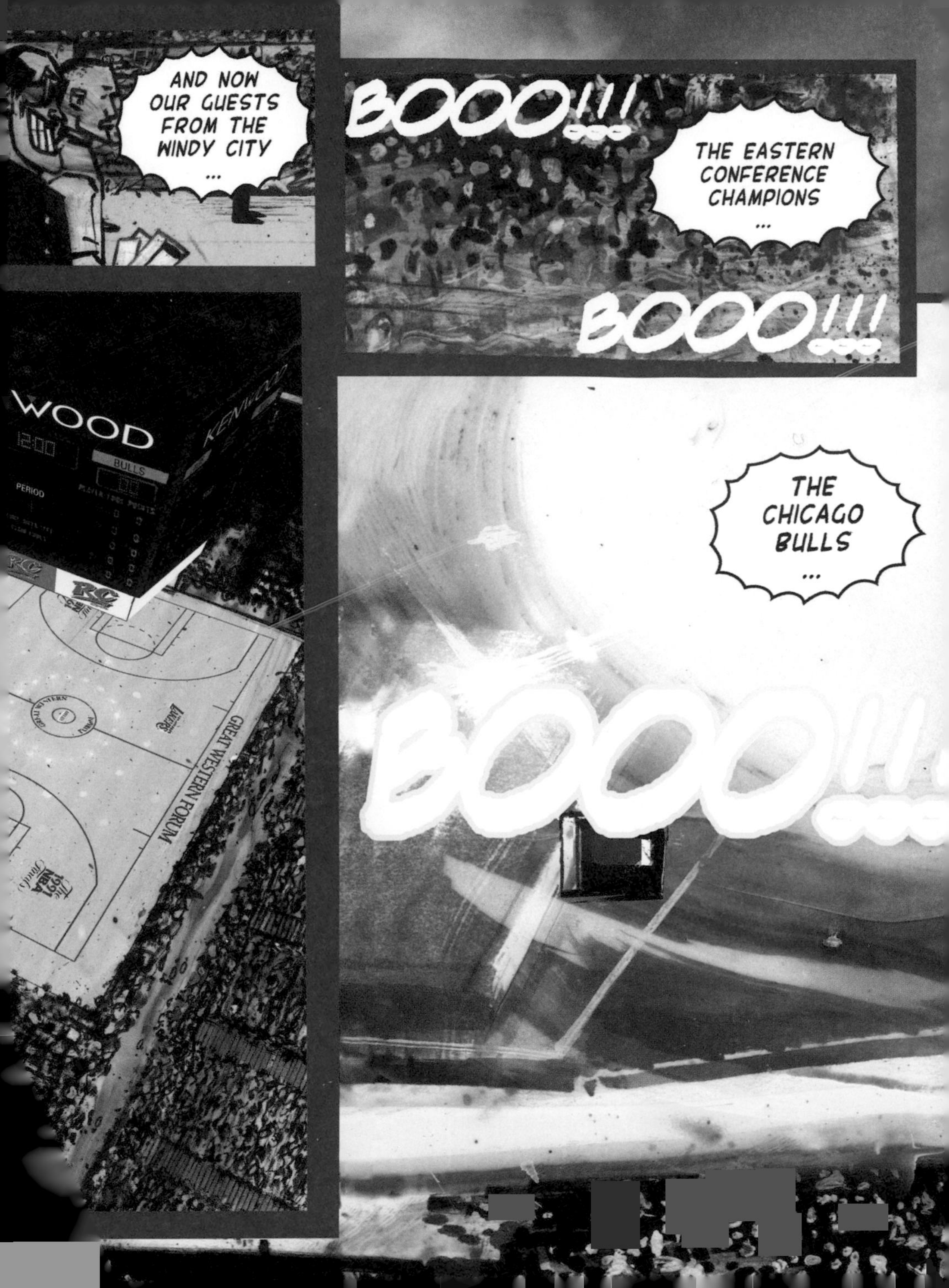
AND NOW OUR GUESTS FROM THE WINDY CITY ...
BOOO!!!...
THE EASTERN CONFERENCE CHAMPIONS ...
BOOO!!!...
WOOD
KENWOOD
BULLS
PERIOD
GREAT WESTERN FORUM
THE CHICAGO BULLS ...
BOOO!!!...

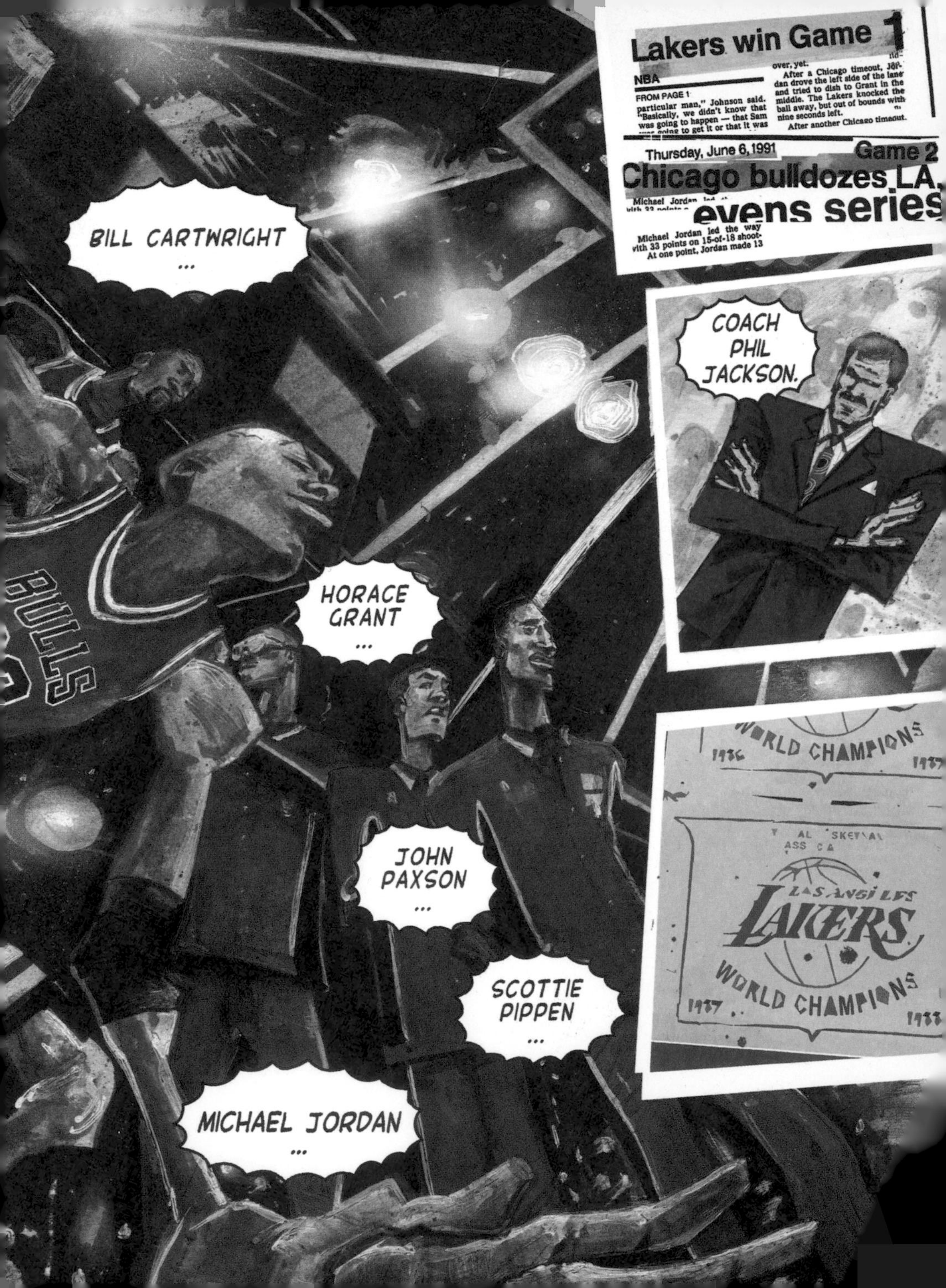
Lakers win Game 1
NBA
FROM PAGE 1
particular man," Johnson said. "Basically, we didn't know that was going to happen — that Sam
over, yet.
After a Chicago timeout, Jordan drove the left side of the lane and tried to dish to Grant in the middle. The Lakers knocked the ball away, but out of bounds with nine seconds left.
After another Chicago timeout.
Thursday, June 6, 1991
Game 2
Chicago bulldozes LA, evens series
Michael Jordan led the way with 33 points on 15-of-18 shooting. At one point, Jordan made 13
BILL CARTWRIGHT ...
HORACE GRANT ...
JOHN PAXSON ...
SCOTTIE PIPPEN ...
MICHAEL JORDAN ...
COACH PHIL JACKSON.
WORLD CHAMPIONS
LAKERS
WORLD CHAMPIONS

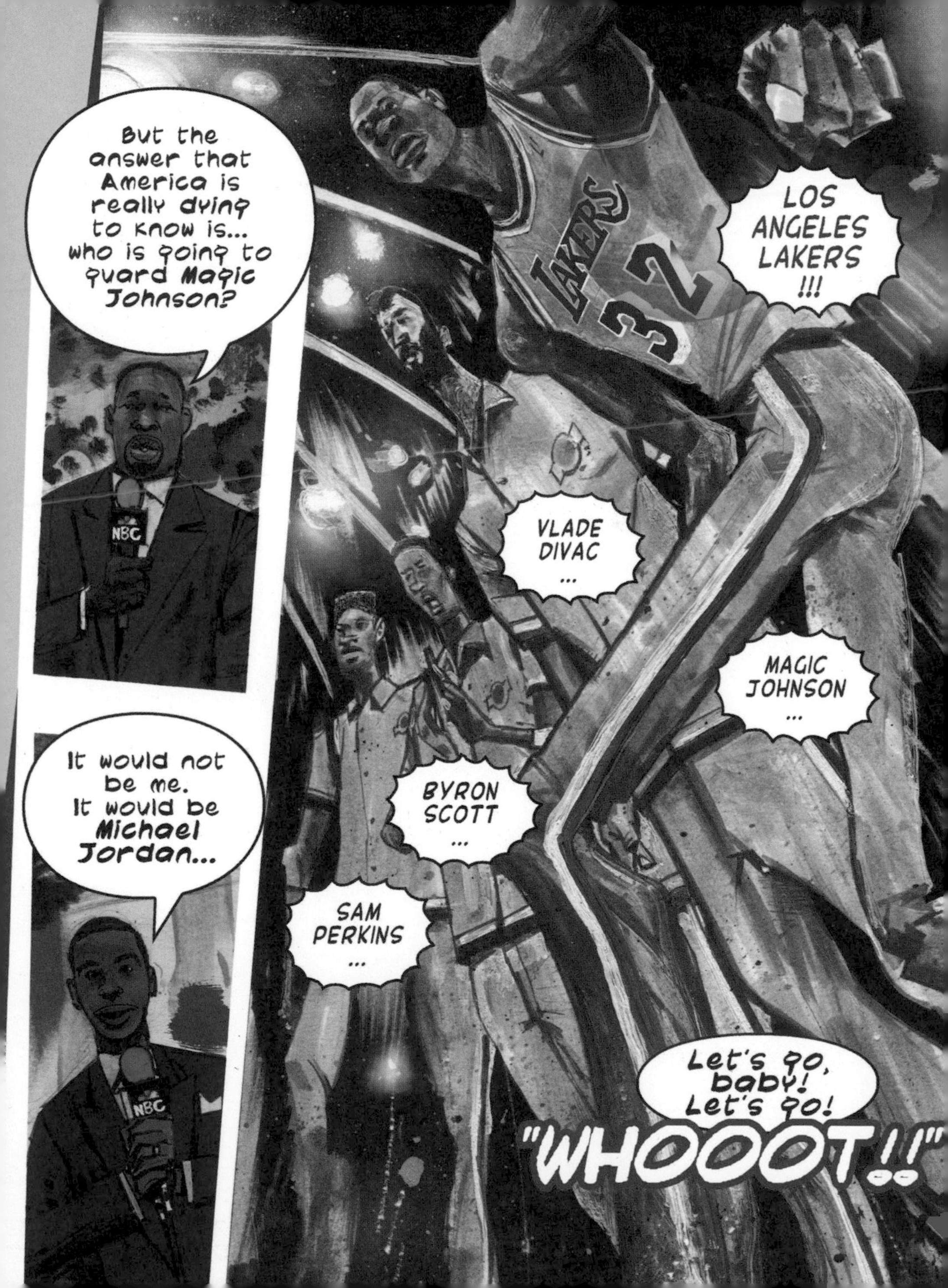
But the answer that America is really dying to know is... who is going to guard Magic Johnson?
It would not be me. It would be Michael Jordan...
LOS ANGELES LAKERS !!!
VLADE DIVAC ...
MAGIC JOHNSON ...
BYRON SCOTT ...
SAM PERKINS ...
Let's go, baby! Let's go!
"WHOOOT!!"

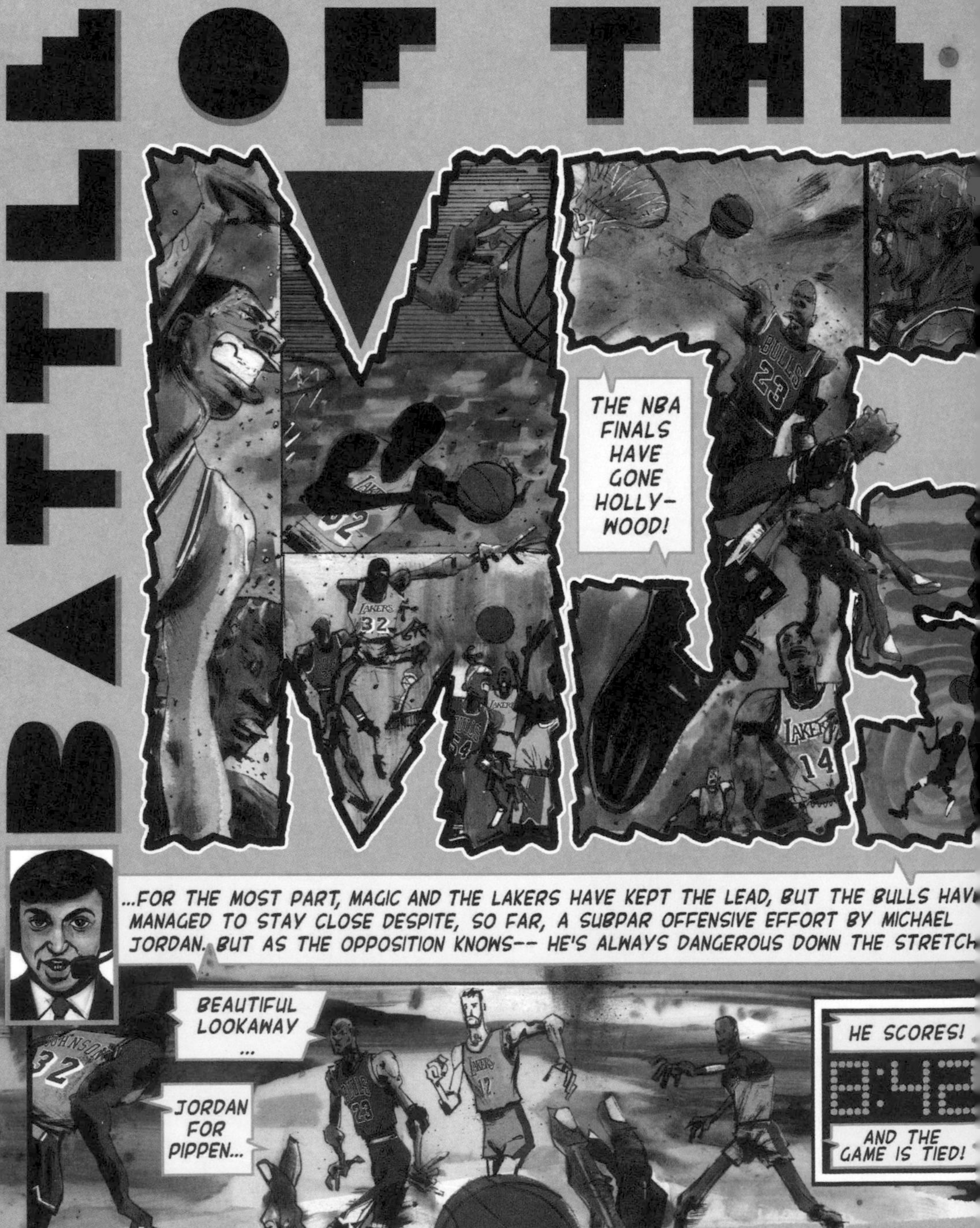
BATTLE OF THE
THE NBA FINALS HAVE GONE HOLLY-WOOD!
...FOR THE MOST PART, MAGIC AND THE LAKERS HAVE KEPT THE LEAD, BUT THE BULLS HAV
MANAGED TO STAY CLOSE DESPITE, SO FAR, A SUBPAR OFFENSIVE EFFORT BY MICHAEL
JORDAN. BUT AS THE OPPOSITION KNOWS-- HE'S ALWAYS DANGEROUS DOWN THE STRETCH
BEAUTIFUL LOOKAWAY ...
JORDAN FOR PIPPEN...
HE SCORES!
AND THE GAME IS TIED!

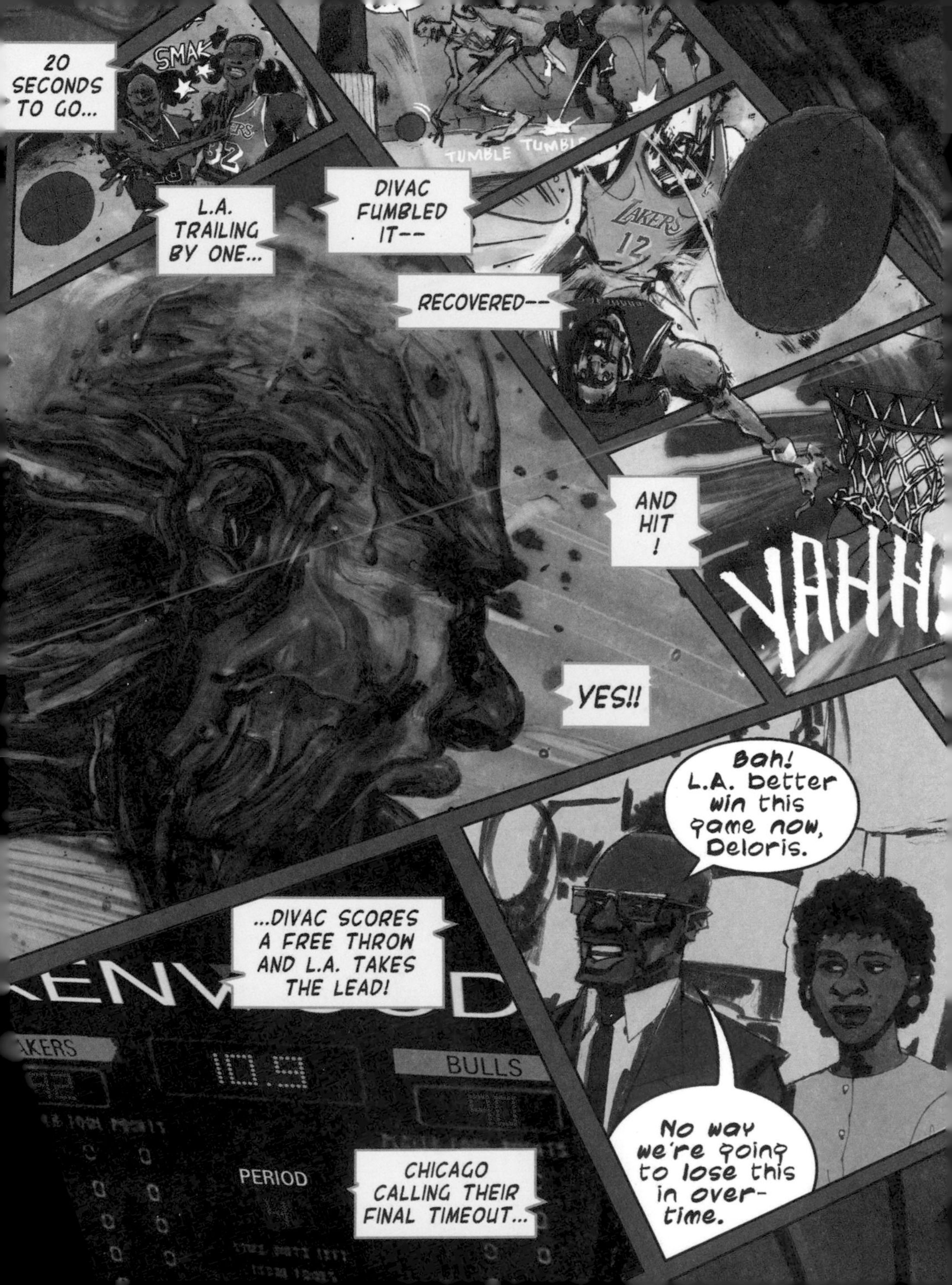
20 SECONDS TO GO...
SMAK
TUMBLE TUMBLE
L.A. TRAILING BY ONE...
DIVAC FUMBLED IT--
RECOVERED--
AND HIT !
YAHH
YES!!
Bah! L.A. better win this game now, Deloris.
...DIVAC SCORES A FREE THROW AND L.A. TAKES THE LEAD!
CHICAGO CALLING THEIR FINAL TIMEOUT...
No way we're going to lose this in over-time.
KENWOOD
LAKERS
10.9
BULLS
PERIOD

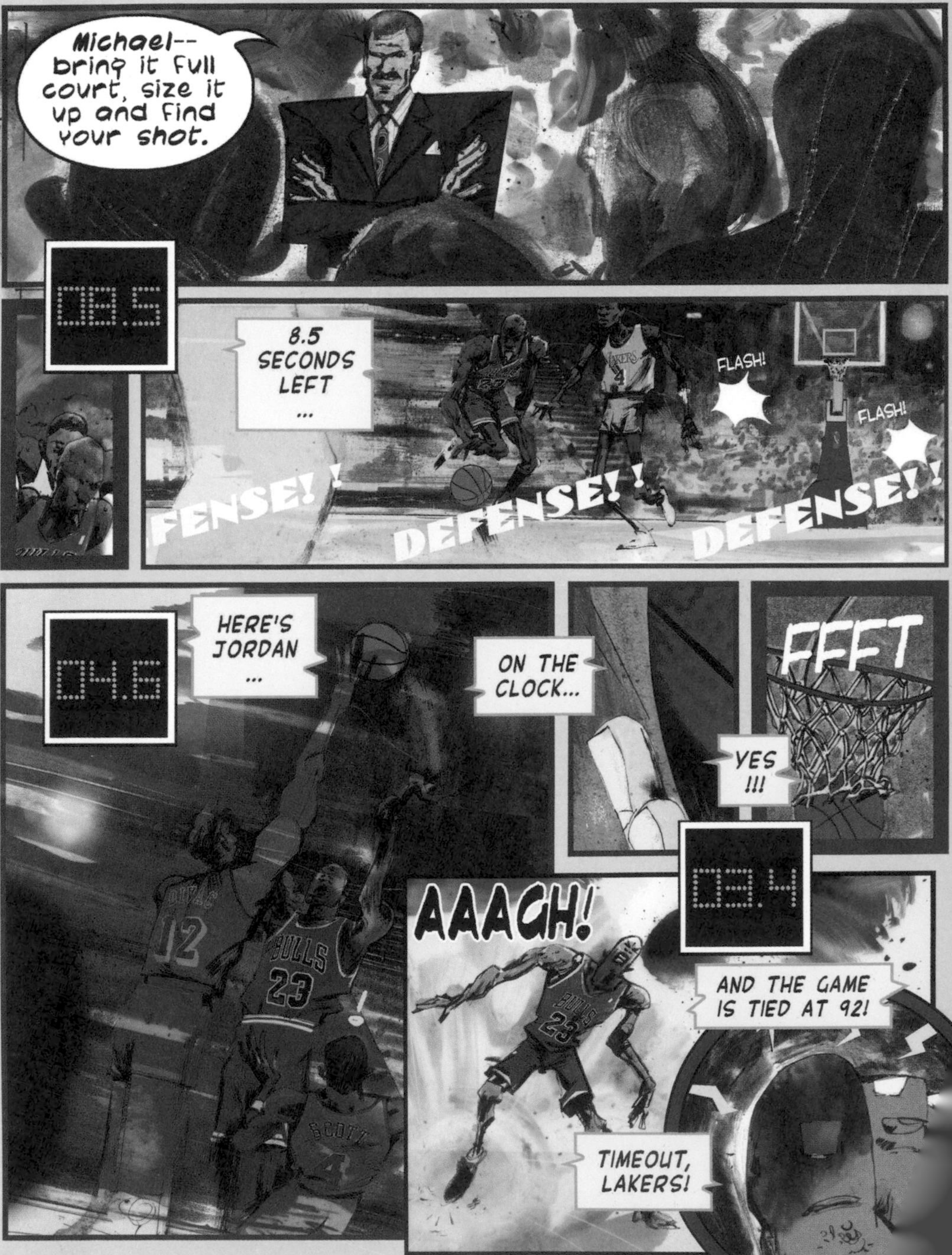
Michael--
bring it full court, size it up and find your shot.
08.5
8.5 SECONDS LEFT ...
FLASH!
FLASH!
FENSE!!
DEFENSE!!
DEFENSE!!
04.6
HERE'S JORDAN ...
ON THE CLOCK...
FFFT
YES !!!
03.4
AAAGH!
AND THE GAME IS TIED AT 92!
TIMEOUT, LAKERS!

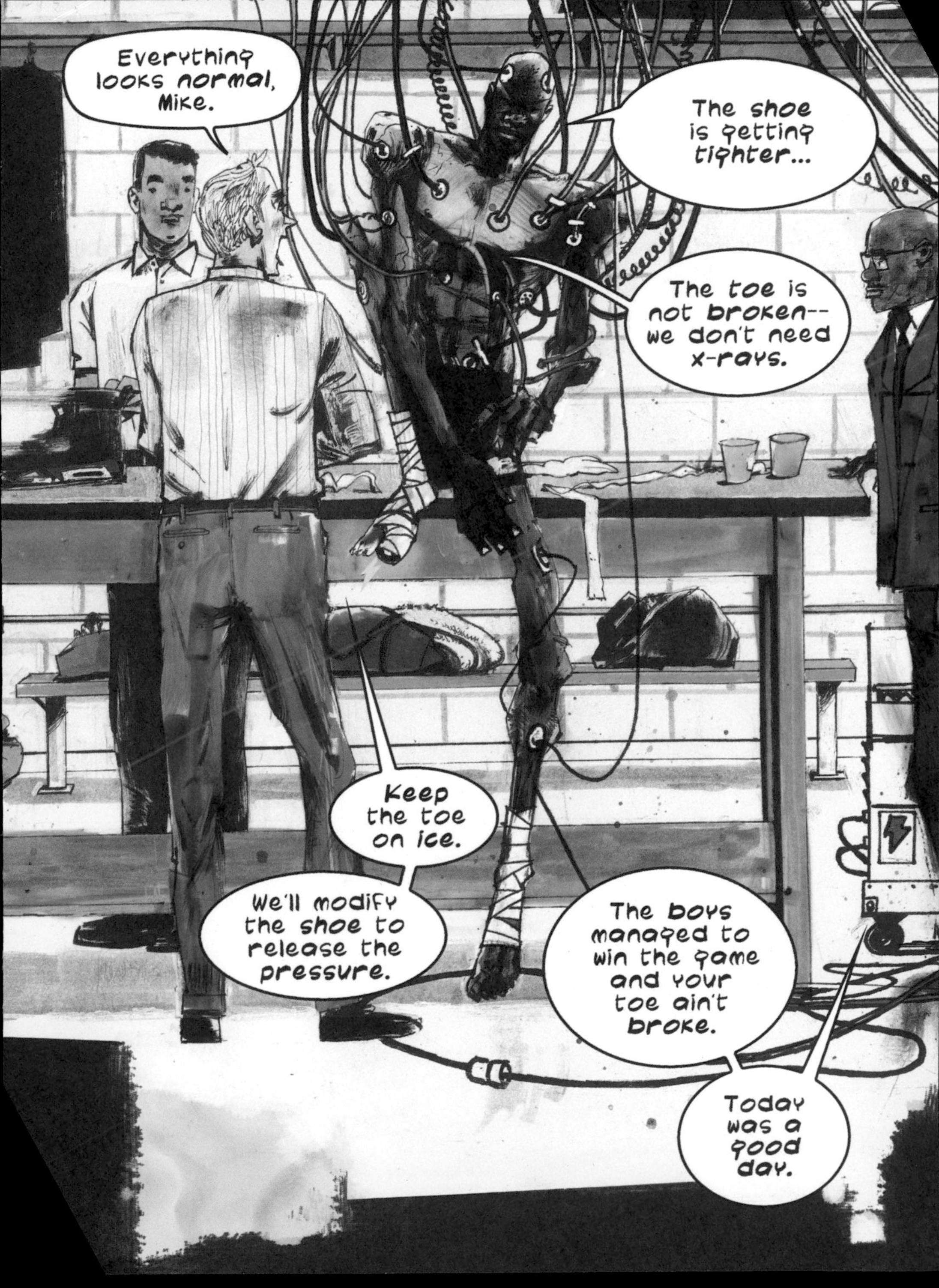
Everything looks normal, Mike.
The shoe is getting tighter...
The toe is not broken-- we don't need x-rays.
Keep the toe on ice.
We'll modify the shoe to release the pressure.
The boys managed to win the game and your toe ain't broke.
Today was a good day.

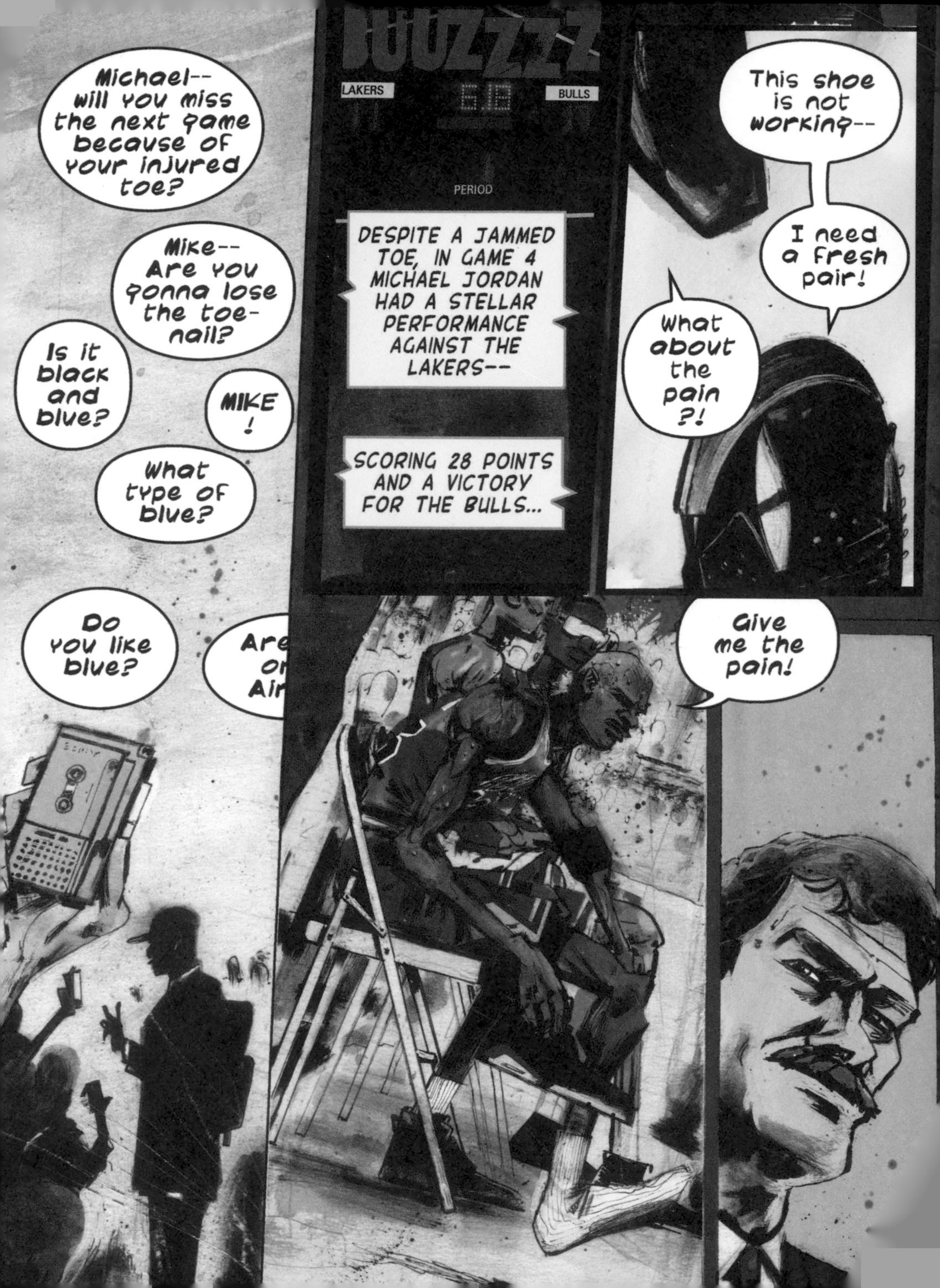
Michael-- will you miss the next game because of your injured toe?
Mike-- Are you gonna lose the toe-nail?
Is it black and blue?
MIKE!
What type of blue?
BUUZZZZ
LAKERS
BULLS
PERIOD
DESPITE A JAMMED TOE, IN GAME 4 MICHAEL JORDAN HAD A STELLAR PERFORMANCE AGAINST THE LAKERS--
SCORING 28 POINTS AND A VICTORY FOR THE BULLS...
This shoe is not working--
I need a fresh pair!
What about the pain?!
Do you like blue?
Are
Give me the pain!

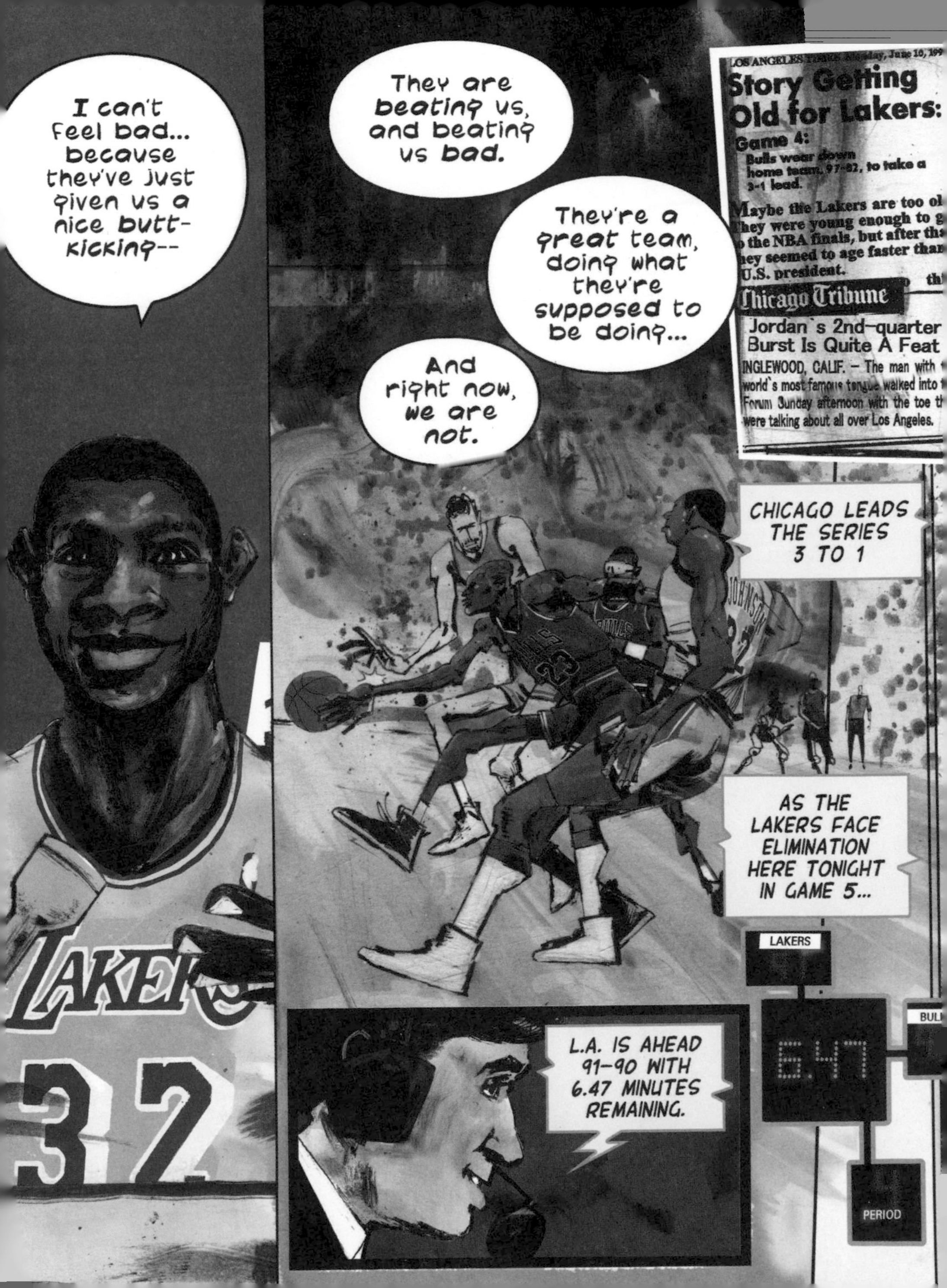
I can't feel bad... because they've just given us a nice butt-kicking--
They are beating us, and beating us bad.
They're a great team, doing what they're supposed to be doing...
And right now, we are not.
LOS ANGELES TIMES Monday, June 10, 199
Story Getting Old for Lakers:
Game 4:
Bulls wear down home team, 97-82, to take a 3-1 lead.
Maybe the Lakers are too ol
They were young enough to g
the NBA finals, but after th
hey seemed to age faster than
U.S. president.
Chicago Tribune
Jordan's 2nd-quarter Burst Is Quite A Feat
INGLEWOOD, CALIF. – The man with
world's most famous tongue walked into
Forum Sunday afternoon with the toe th
were talking about all over Los Angeles.
CHICAGO LEADS THE SERIES 3 TO 1
AS THE LAKERS FACE ELIMINATION HERE TONIGHT IN GAME 5...
LAKERS
L.A. IS AHEAD 91–90 WITH 6.47 MINUTES REMAINING.
6.47
PERIOD

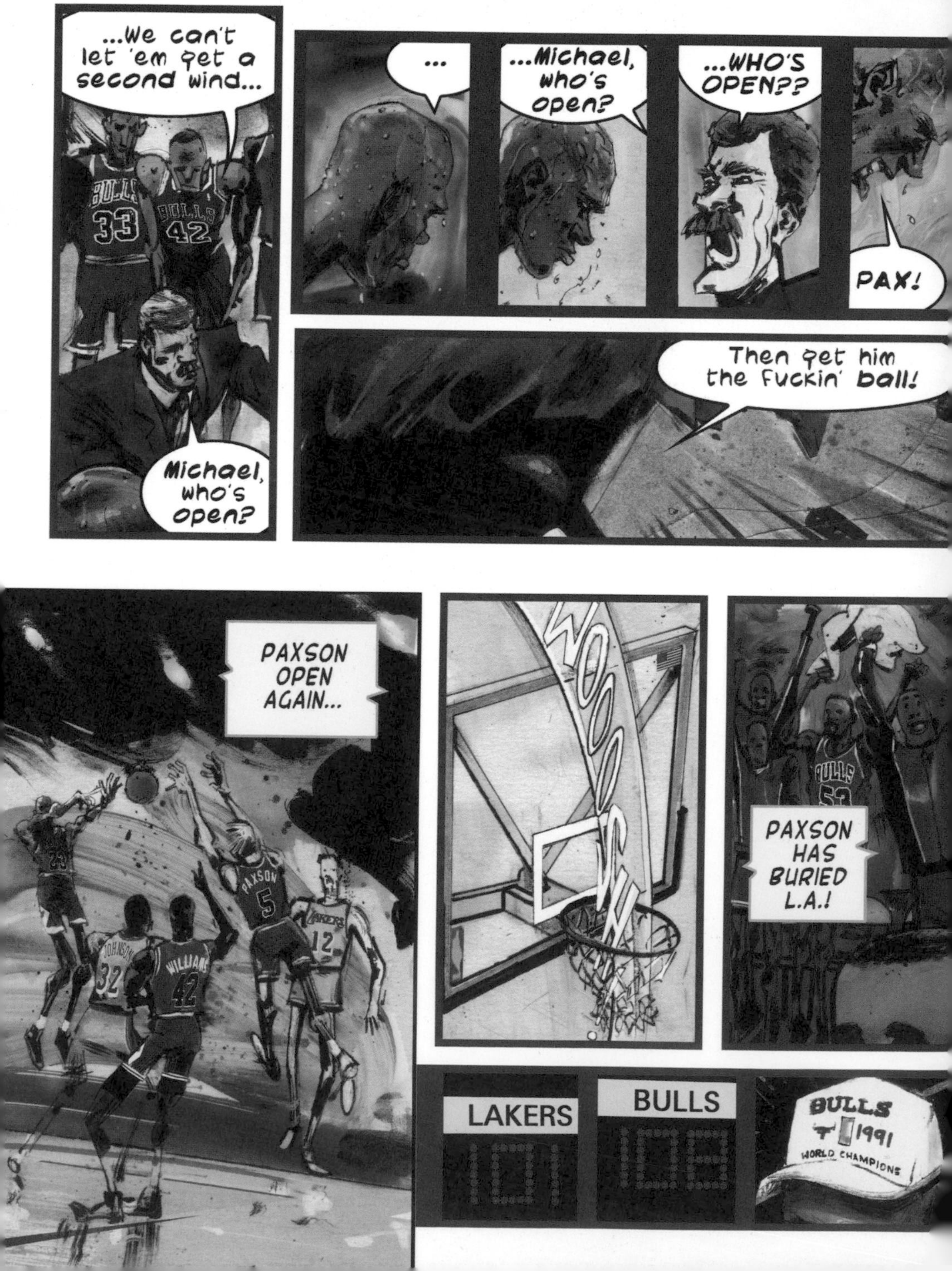
...We can't let 'em get a second wind...
Michael, who's open?
...
...Michael, who's open?
...WHO'S OPEN??
PAX!
Then get him the fuckin' ball!
PAXSON OPEN AGAIN...
WOOOOSSHH
PAXSON HAS BURIED L.A.!
LAKERS
BULLS
BULLS 1991 WORLD CHAMPIONS

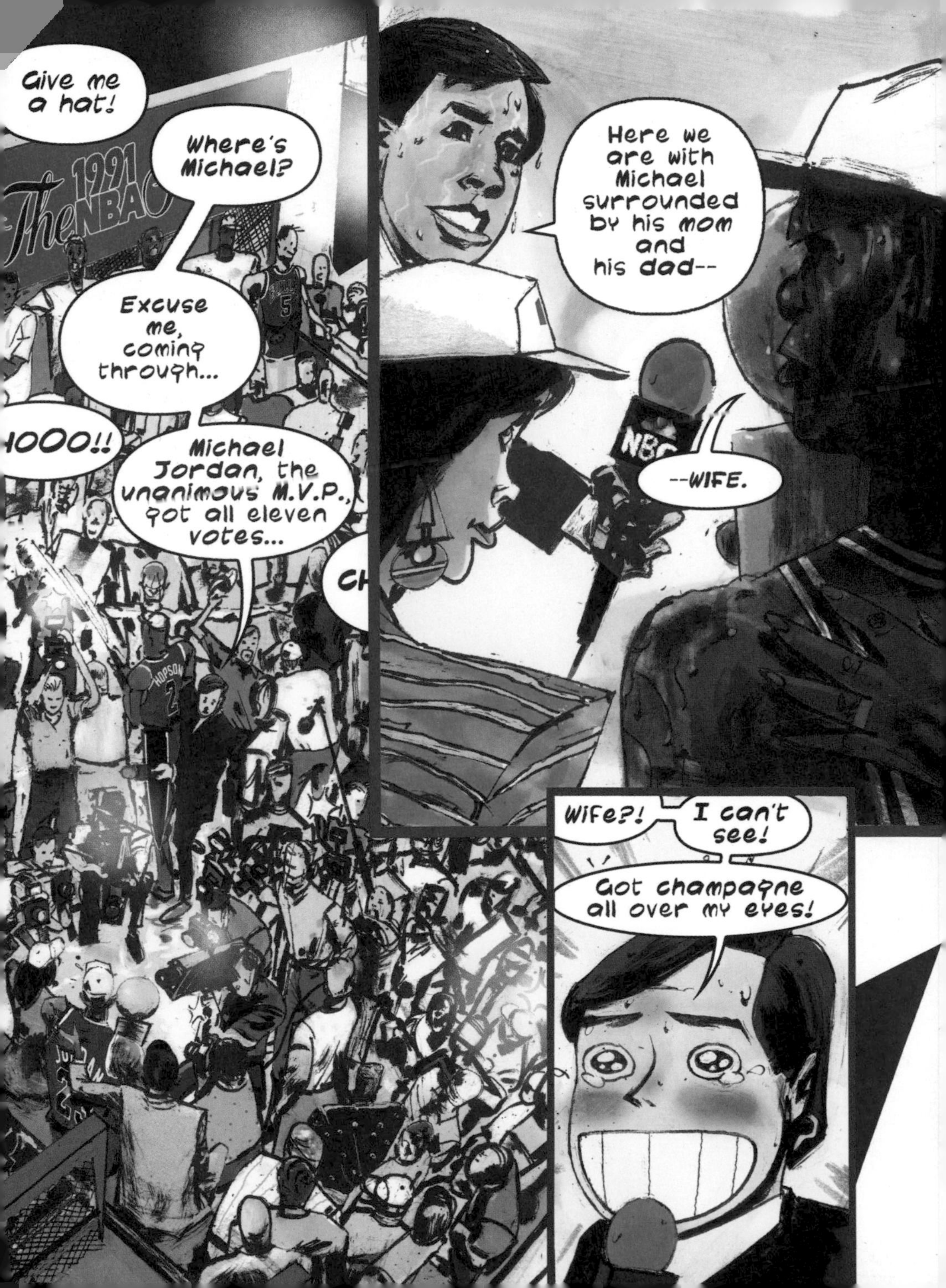
Give me a hat!
Where's Michael?
Excuse me, coming through...
OOOO!!
Michael Jordan, the unanimous M.V.P., got all eleven votes...
CH
Here we are with Michael surrounded by his mom and his dad--
--WIFE.
Wife?!
I can't see!
Got champagne all over my eyes!

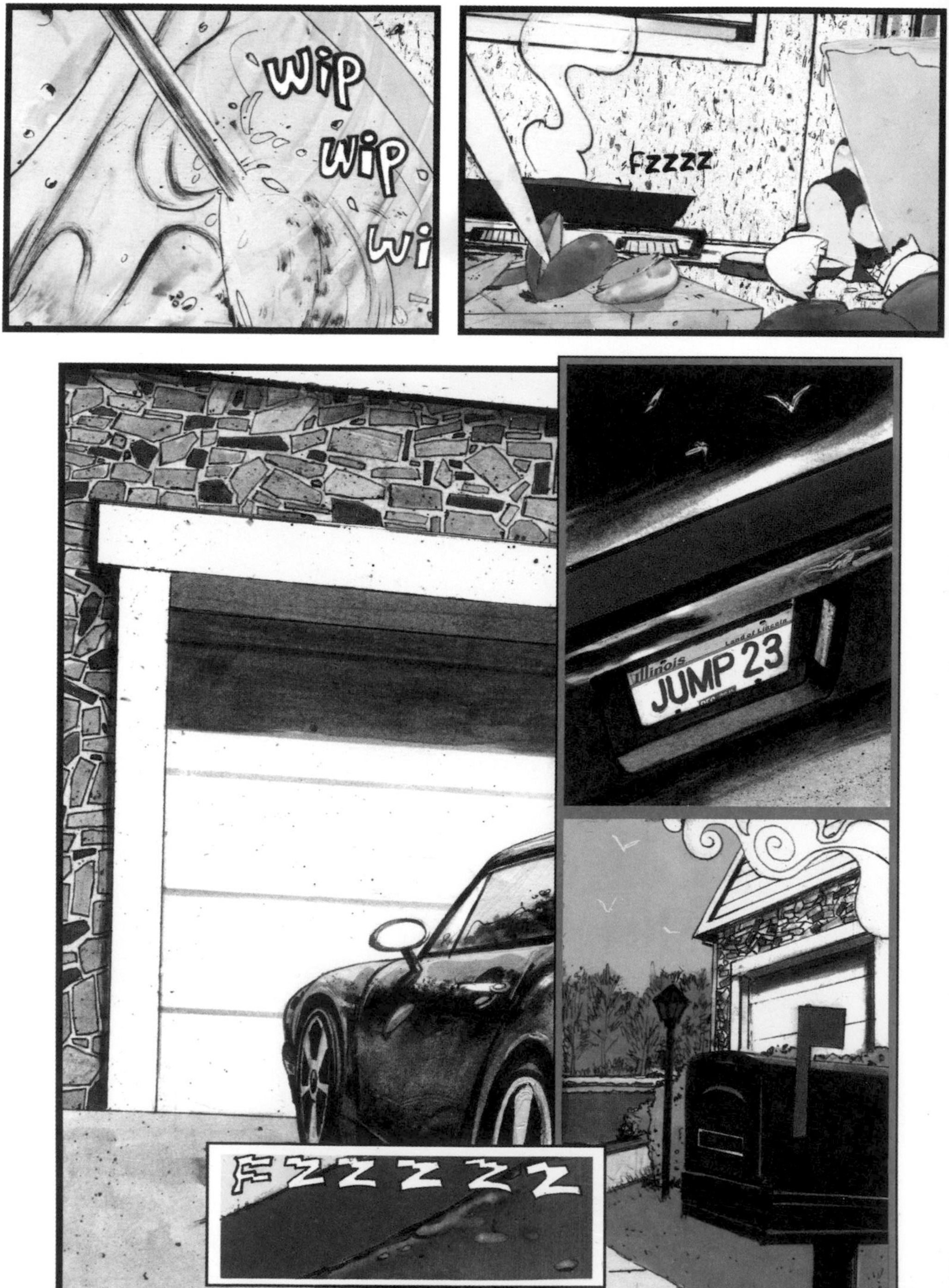
wip
wip
wi
Fzzzz
FZZZZZZ
Illinois
Land of Lincoln
JUMP 23

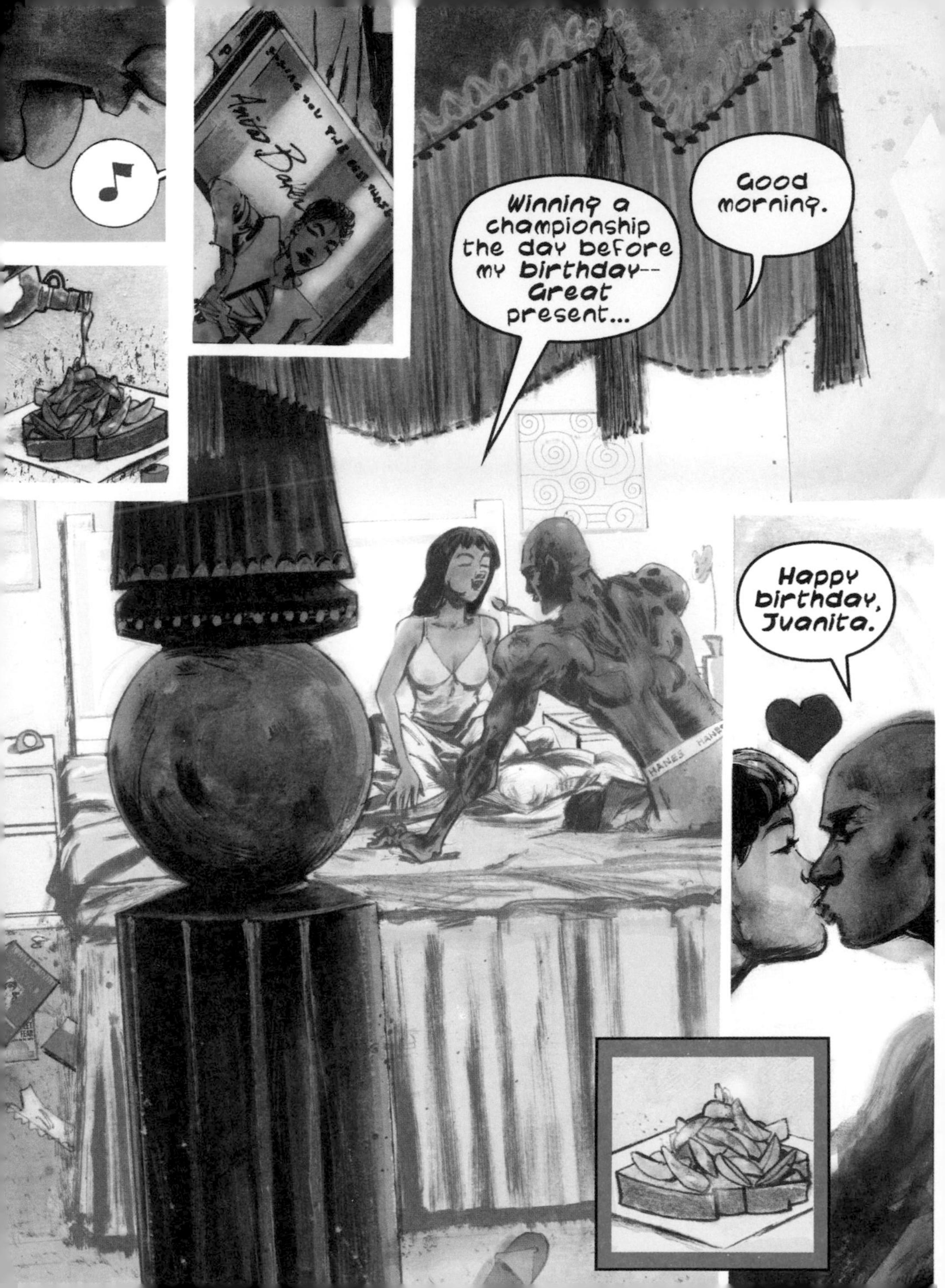
Winning a championship the day before my birthday-- Great present...
Good morning.
HANES
Happy birthday, Juanita.

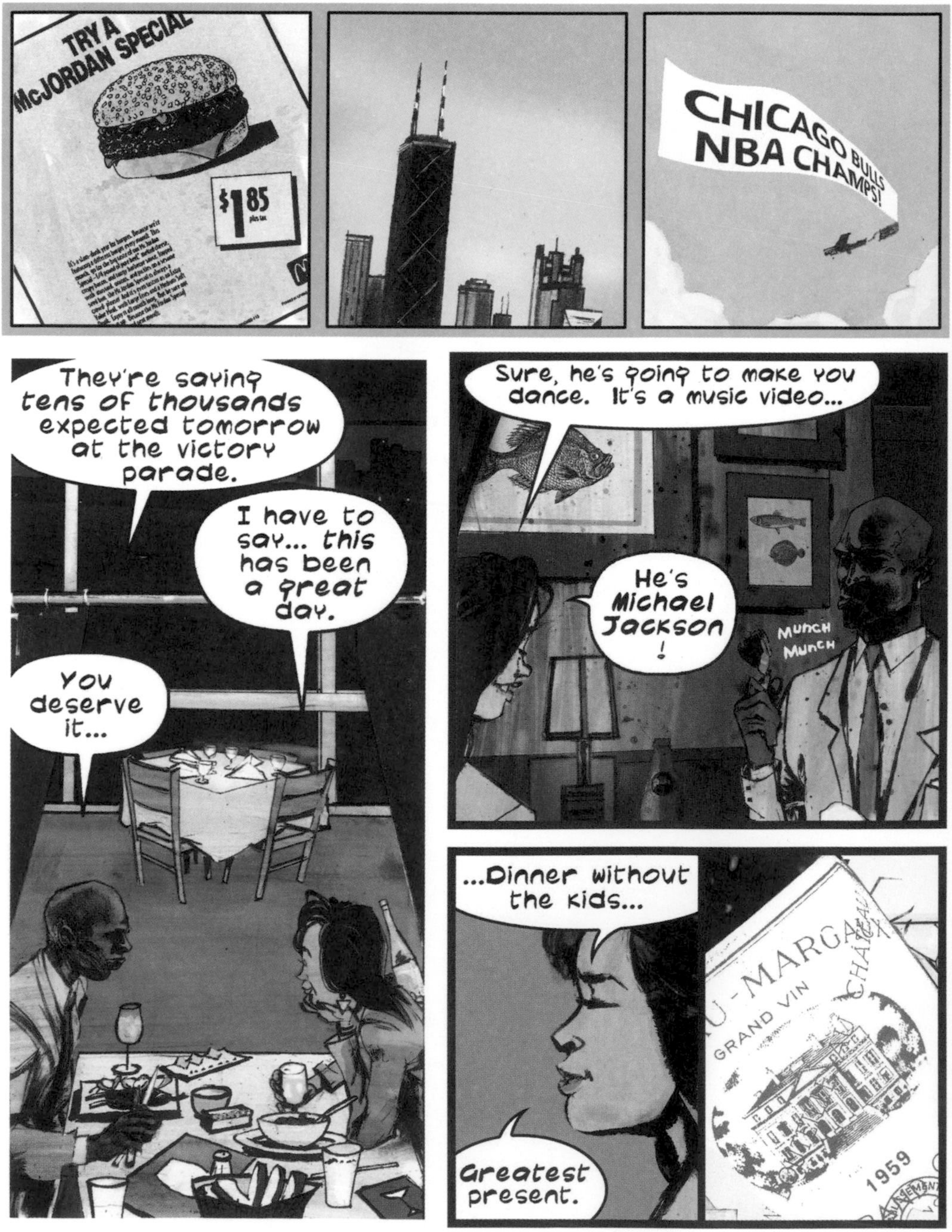

TRY A McJORDAN SPECIAL
$1.85
CHICAGO BULLS NBA CHAMPS!
They're saying tens of thousands expected tomorrow at the victory parade.
I have to say... this has been a great day.
You deserve it...
Sure, he's going to make you dance. It's a music video...
He's Michael Jackson!
MUNCH MUNCH
...Dinner without the kids...
Greatest present.
U-MARGA
GRAND VIN
CHATEAU
1959

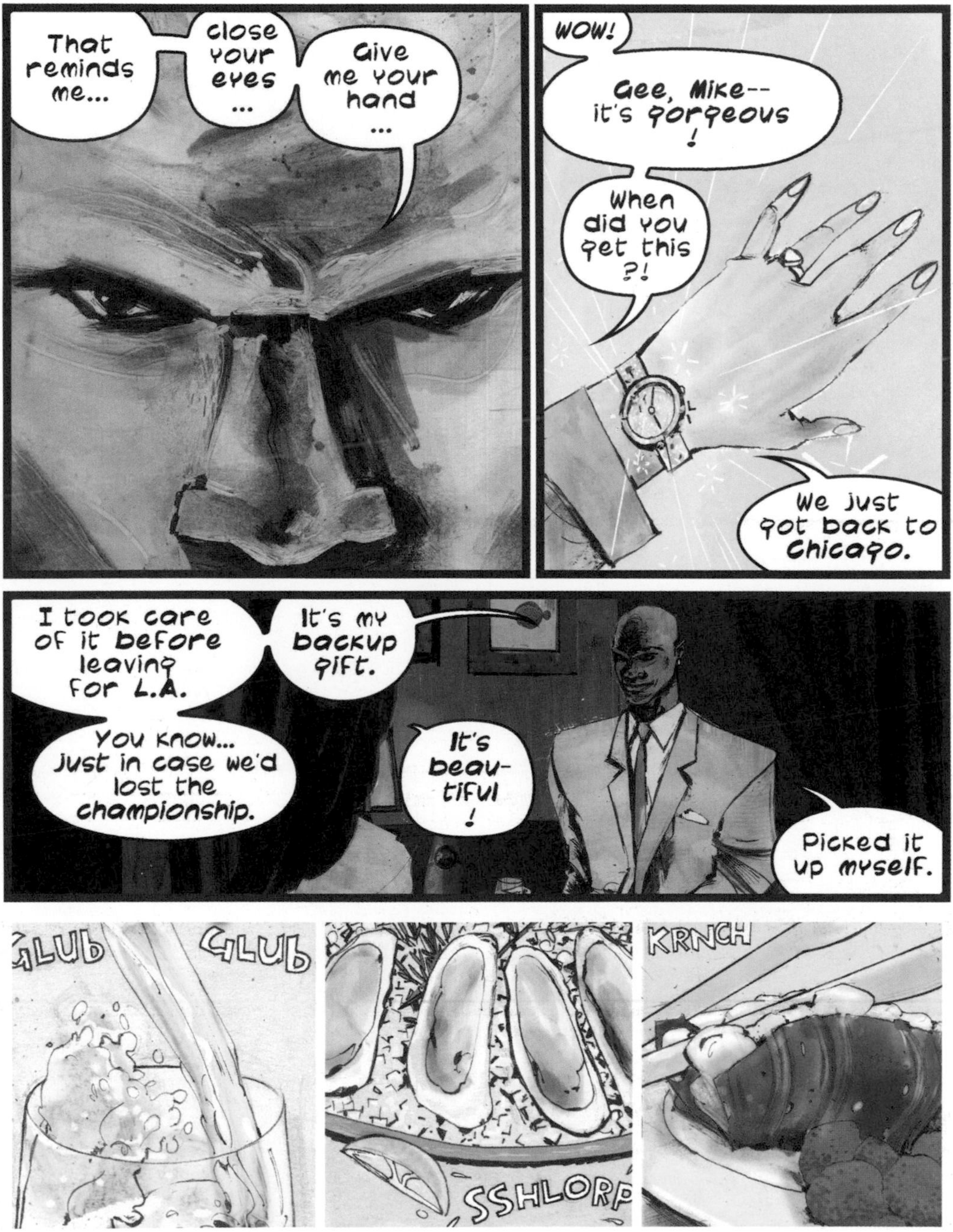

That reminds me...
close your eyes ...
Give me your hand ...
WOW!
Gee, Mike-- it's gorgeous!
When did you get this ?!
We just got back to Chicago.
I took care of it before leaving for L.A.
It's my backup gift.
You know... just in case we'd lost the championship.
It's beau-tiful!
Picked it up myself.
GLUB GLUB
SSHLORP
KRNCH

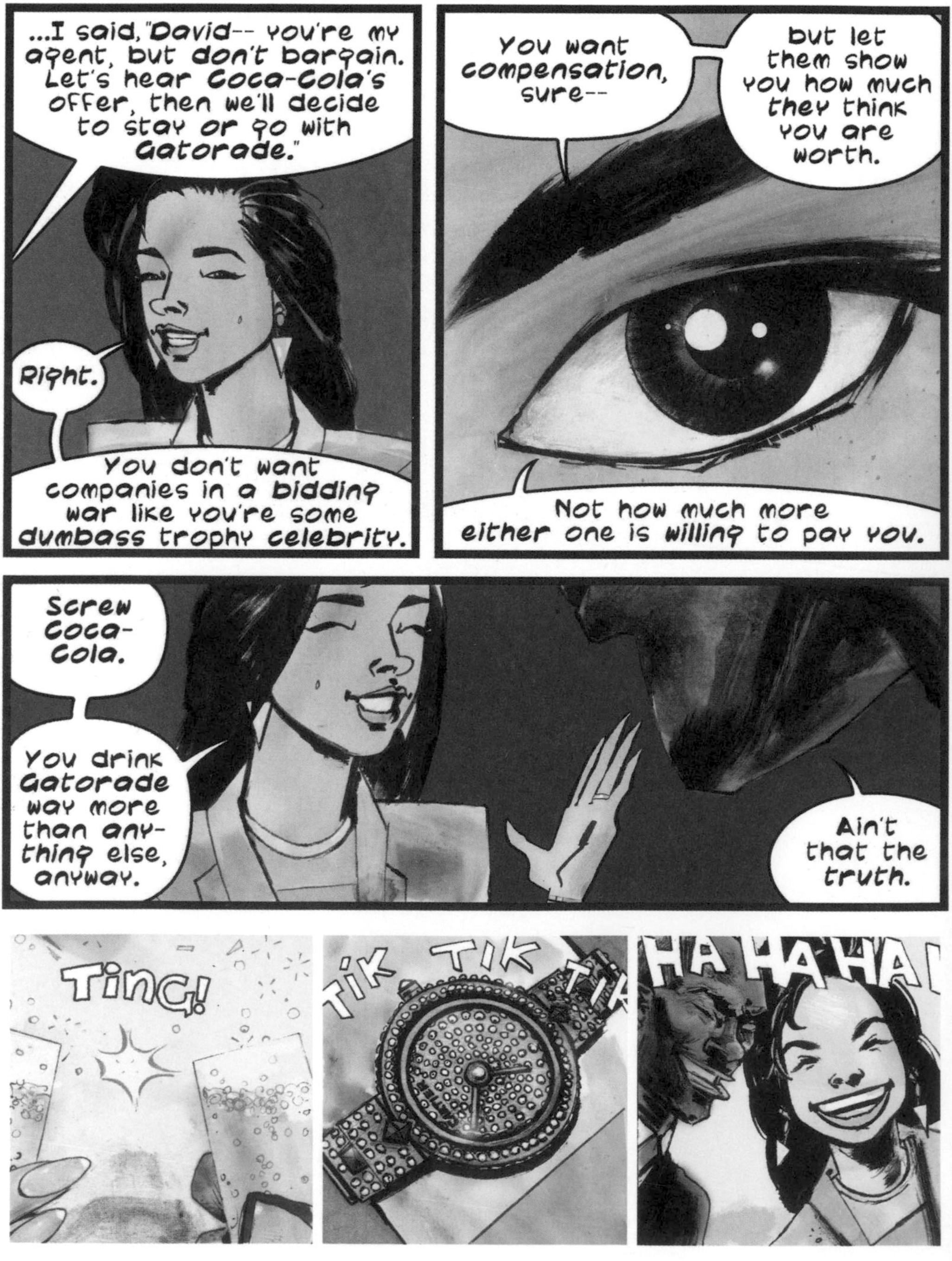
...I said, "David-- you're my agent, but don't bargain. Let's hear Coca-Cola's offer, then we'll decide to stay or go with Gatorade."
Right.
You don't want companies in a bidding war like you're some dumbass trophy celebrity.
You want compensation, sure--
but let them show you how much they think you are worth.
Not how much more either one is willing to pay you.
Screw Coca-Cola.
You drink Gatorade way more than anything else, anyway.
Ain't that the truth.
TING!
TIK TIK TIK
HA HA HA!

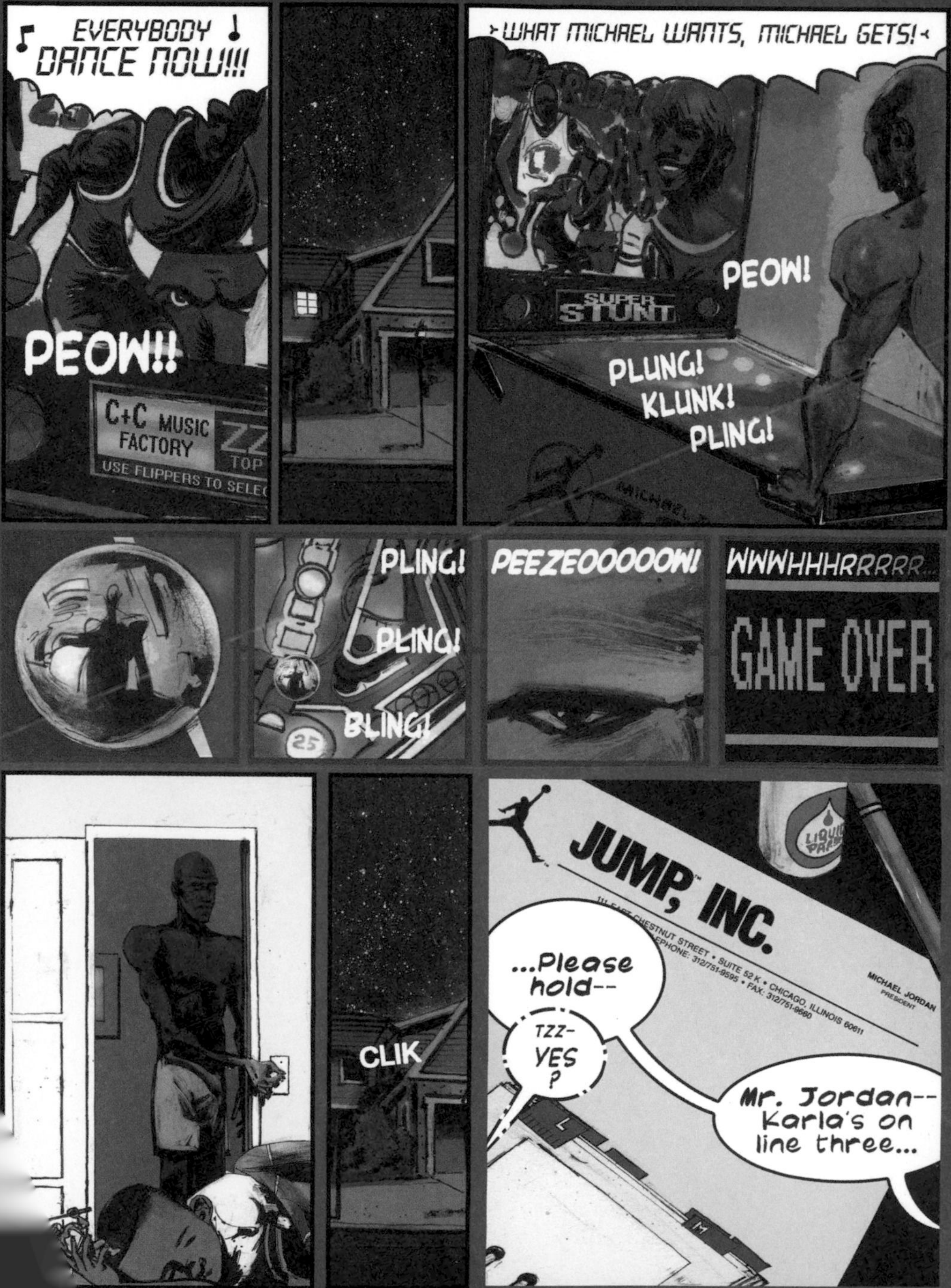

EVERYBODY DANCE NOW!!!
PEOW!!
C+C MUSIC FACTORY
ZZ TOP
USE FLIPPERS TO SELEC
WHAT MICHAEL WANTS, MICHAEL GETS!
SUPER STUNT
PEOW!
PLUNG! KLUNK! PLING!
PLING!
BLING!
BLING!
25
PEEZEOOOOOW!
WWWHHHRRRRR...
GAME OVER
CLIK
JUMP, INC.
CHESTNUT STREET • SUITE 52 K • CHICAGO, ILLINOIS 60611
312/751-9595 • FAX: 312/751-9660
MICHAEL JORDAN
PRESIDENT
...Please hold--
TZZ-YES?
Mr. Jordan--Karla's on line three...

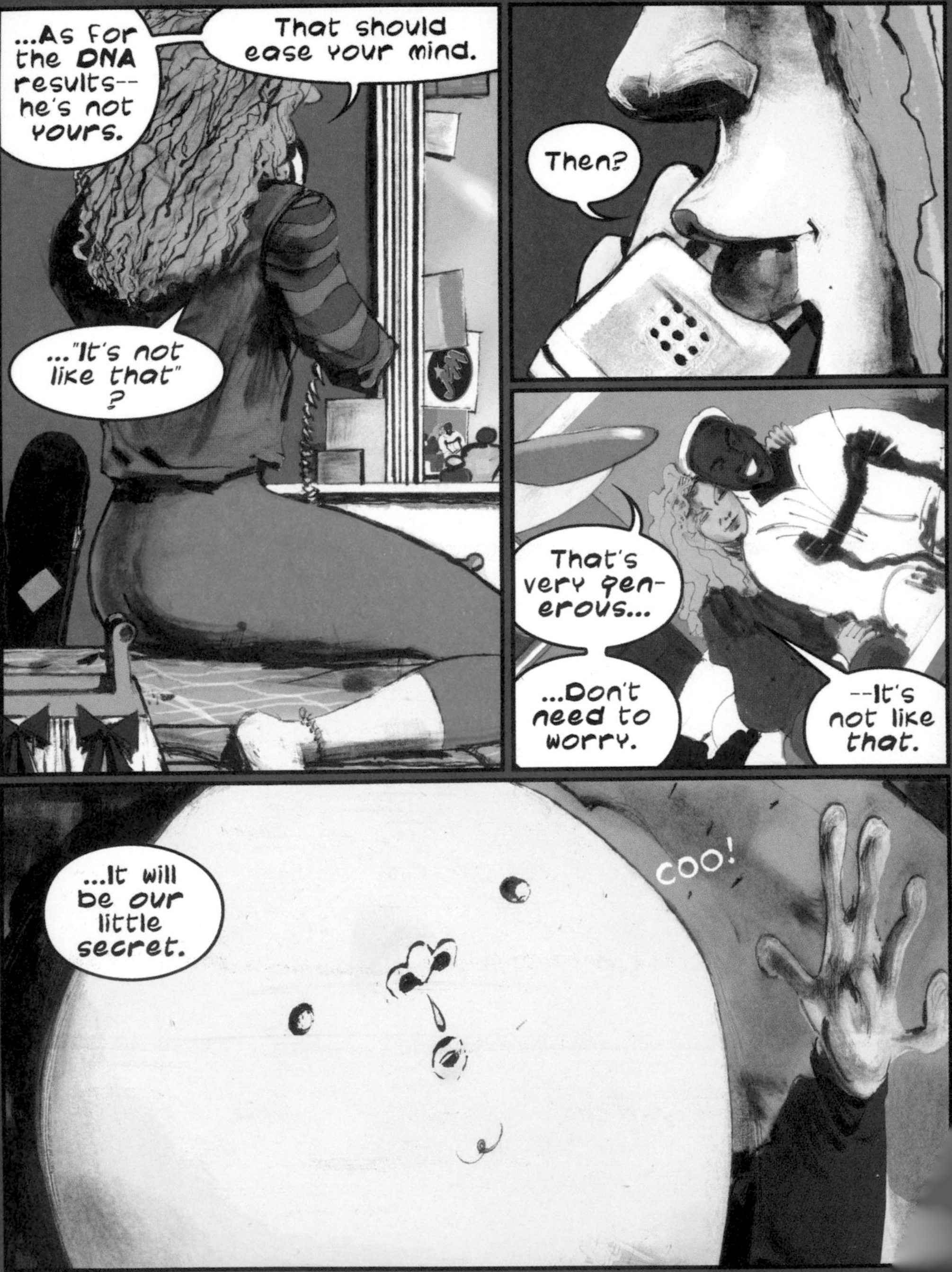
...As for the DNA results--he's not yours.
That should ease your mind.
Then?
..."It's not like that"?
That's very gen-erous...
...Don't need to worry.
--It's not like that.
...It will be our little secret.
COO!

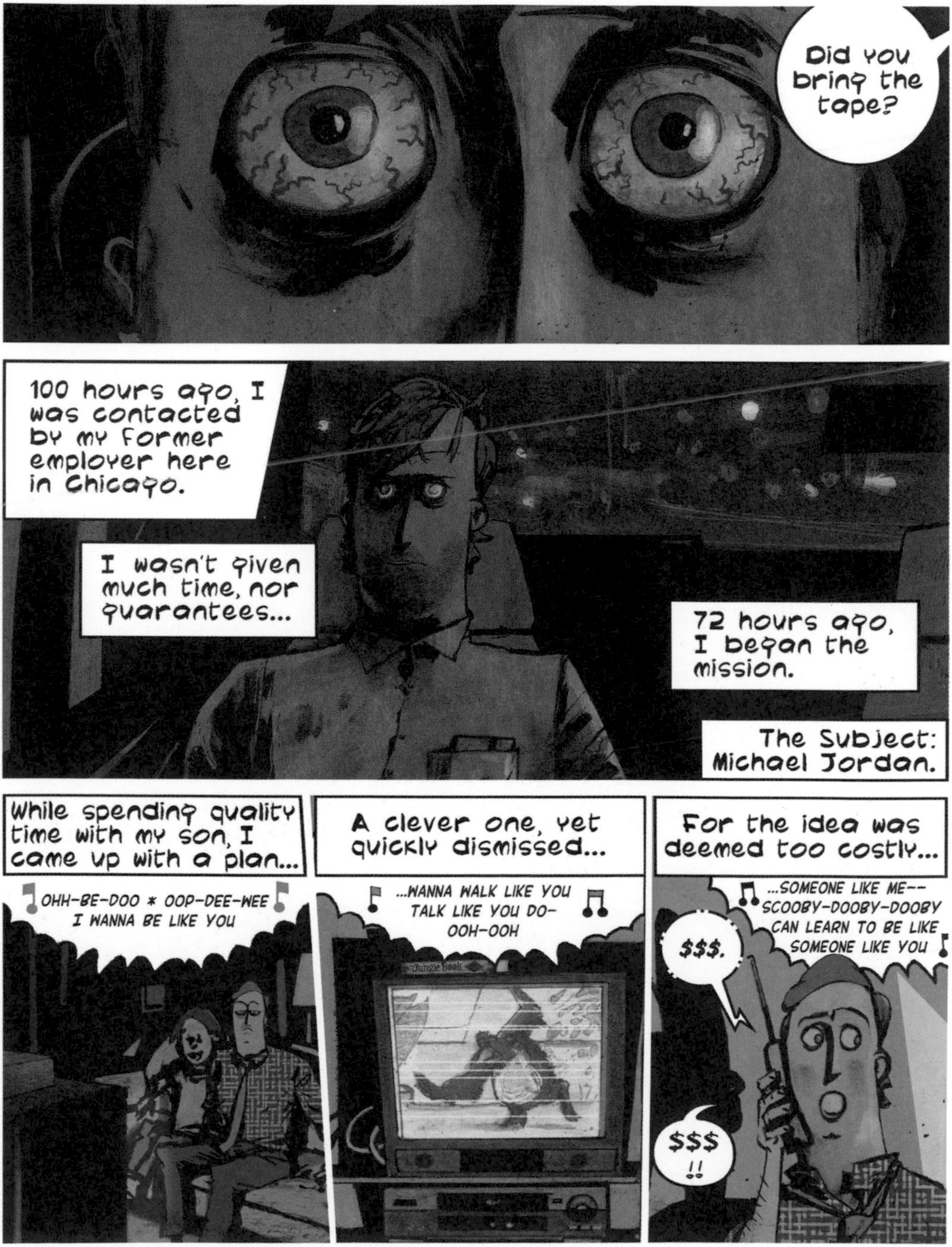
Did you bring the tape?
100 hours ago, I was contacted by my former employer here in Chicago.
I wasn't given much time, nor guarantees...
72 hours ago, I began the mission.
The Subject: Michael Jordan.
While spending quality time with my son, I came up with a plan...
OHH-BE-DOO * OOP-DEE-WEE
I WANNA BE LIKE YOU
A clever one, yet quickly dismissed...
...WANNA WALK LIKE YOU
TALK LIKE YOU DO-
OOH-OOH
Jungle Book
For the idea was deemed too costly...
...SOMEONE LIKE ME--
SCOOBY-DOOBY-DOOBY
CAN LEARN TO BE LIKE
SOMEONE LIKE YOU
$$$.
$$$
!!

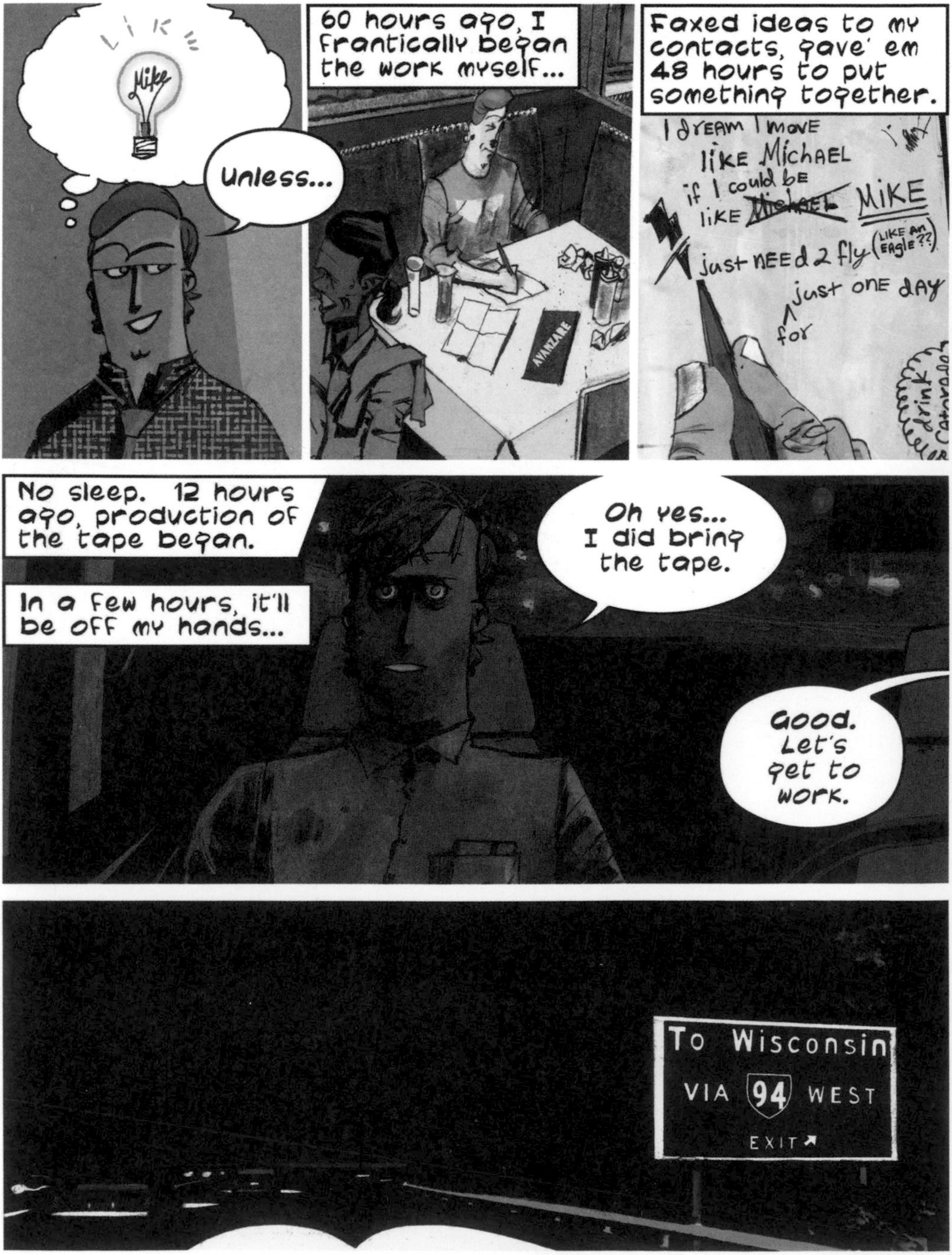
LIKE
Mike
Unless...
60 hours ago, I frantically began the work myself...
AVANZARE
Faxed ideas to my contacts, gave' em 48 hours to put something together.
I dream I move like Michael
if I could be like Michael MIKE
just need 2 fly (LIKE AN EAGLE??)
for just one day
drink
No sleep. 12 hours ago, production of the tape began.
In a few hours, it'll be off my hands...
Oh yes... I did bring the tape.
Good. Let's get to work.
To Wisconsin
VIA 94 WEST
EXIT

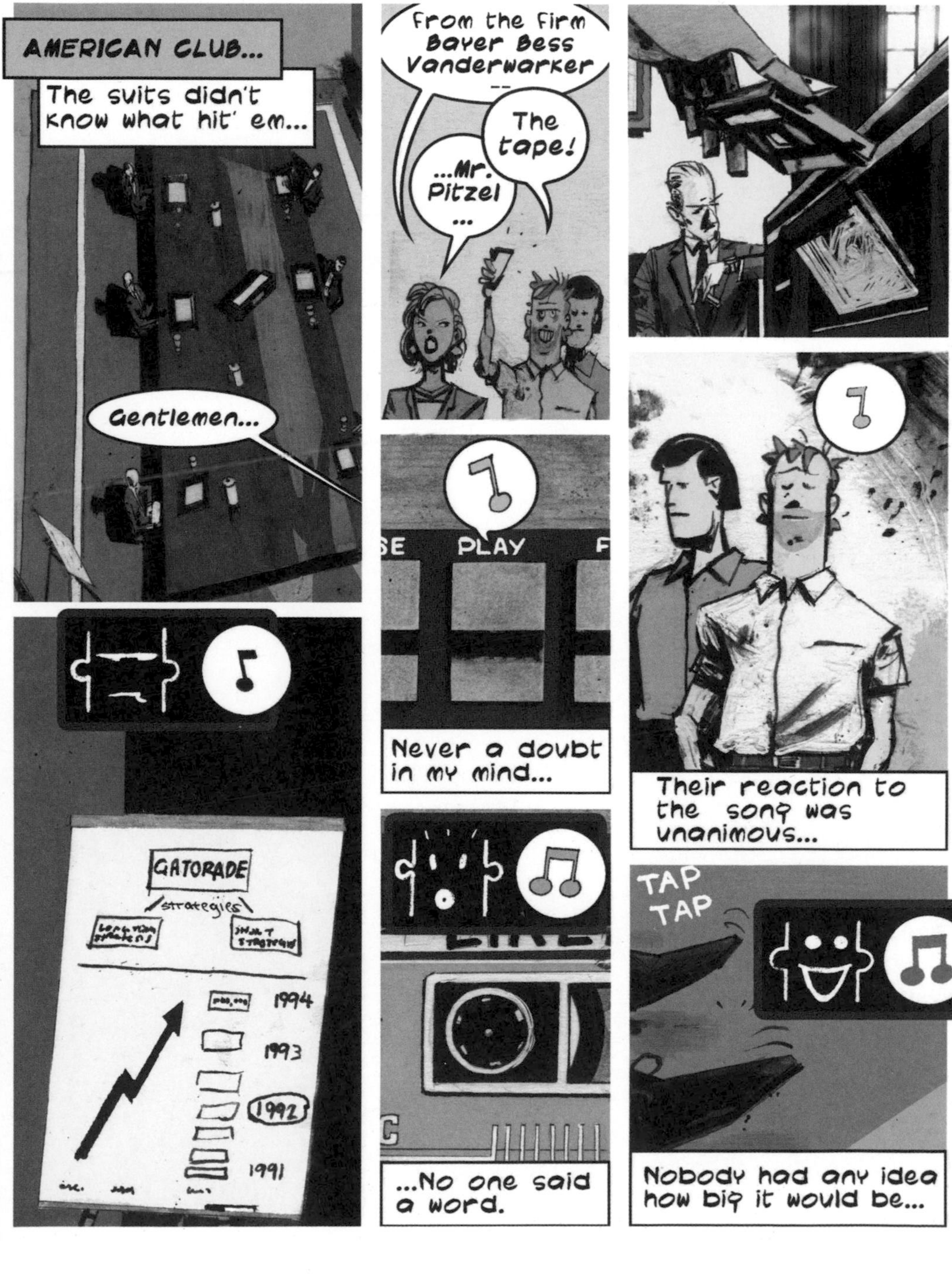
AMERICAN CLUB...
The suits didn't know what hit' em...
Gentlemen...
GATORADE
strategies
1994
1993
1992
1991
From the firm Bayer Bess Vanderwarker --
...Mr. Pitzel ...
The tape!
PLAY
Never a doubt in my mind...
...No one said a word.
Their reaction to the song was unanimous...
TAP TAP
Nobody had any idea how big it would be...

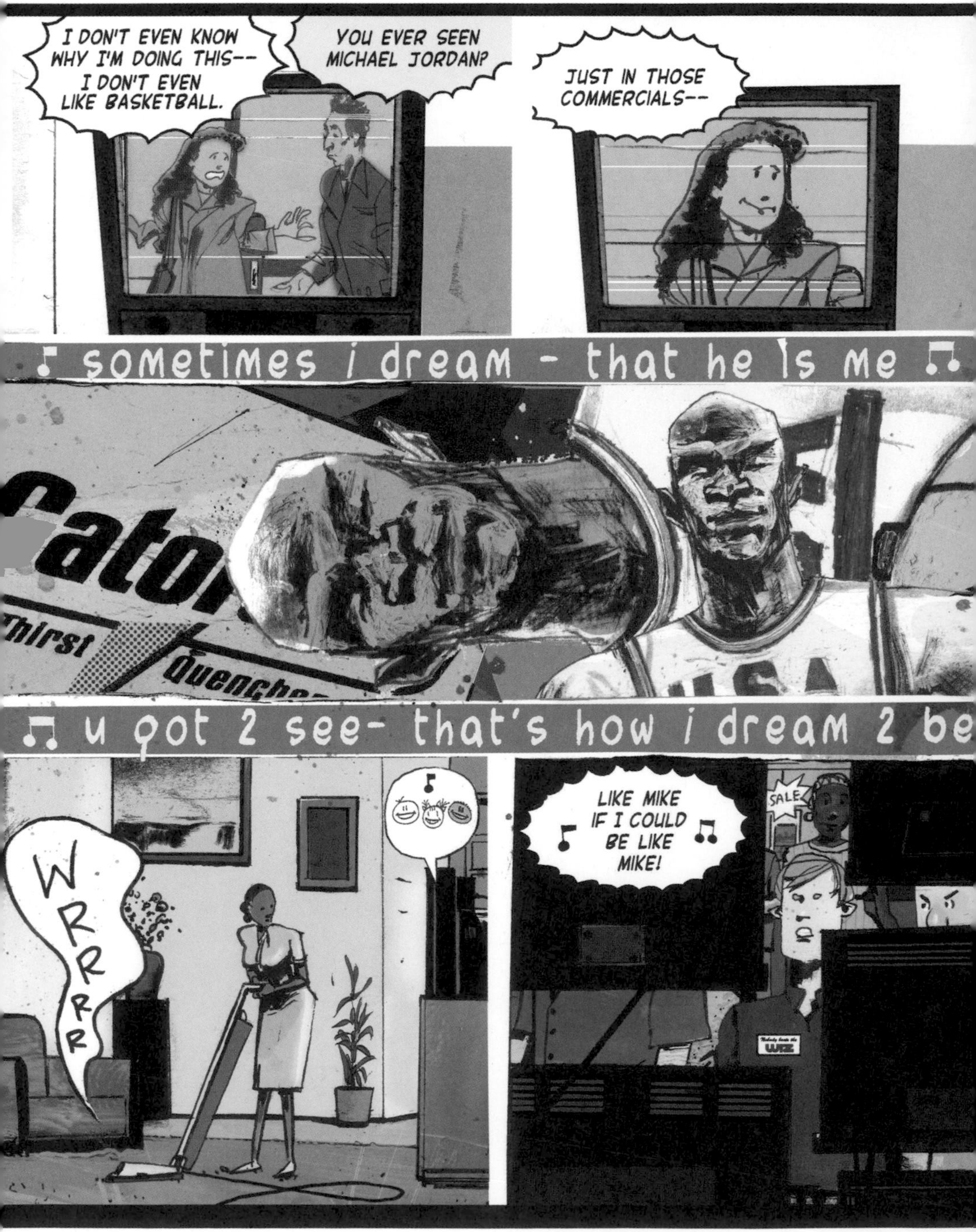
I DON'T EVEN KNOW WHY I'M DOING THIS-- I DON'T EVEN LIKE BASKETBALL.
YOU EVER SEEN MICHAEL JORDAN?
JUST IN THOSE COMMERCIALS--
sometimes i dream - that he is me
u got 2 see- that's how i dream 2 be
WRRRRR
SALE
LIKE MIKE IF I COULD BE LIKE MIKE!

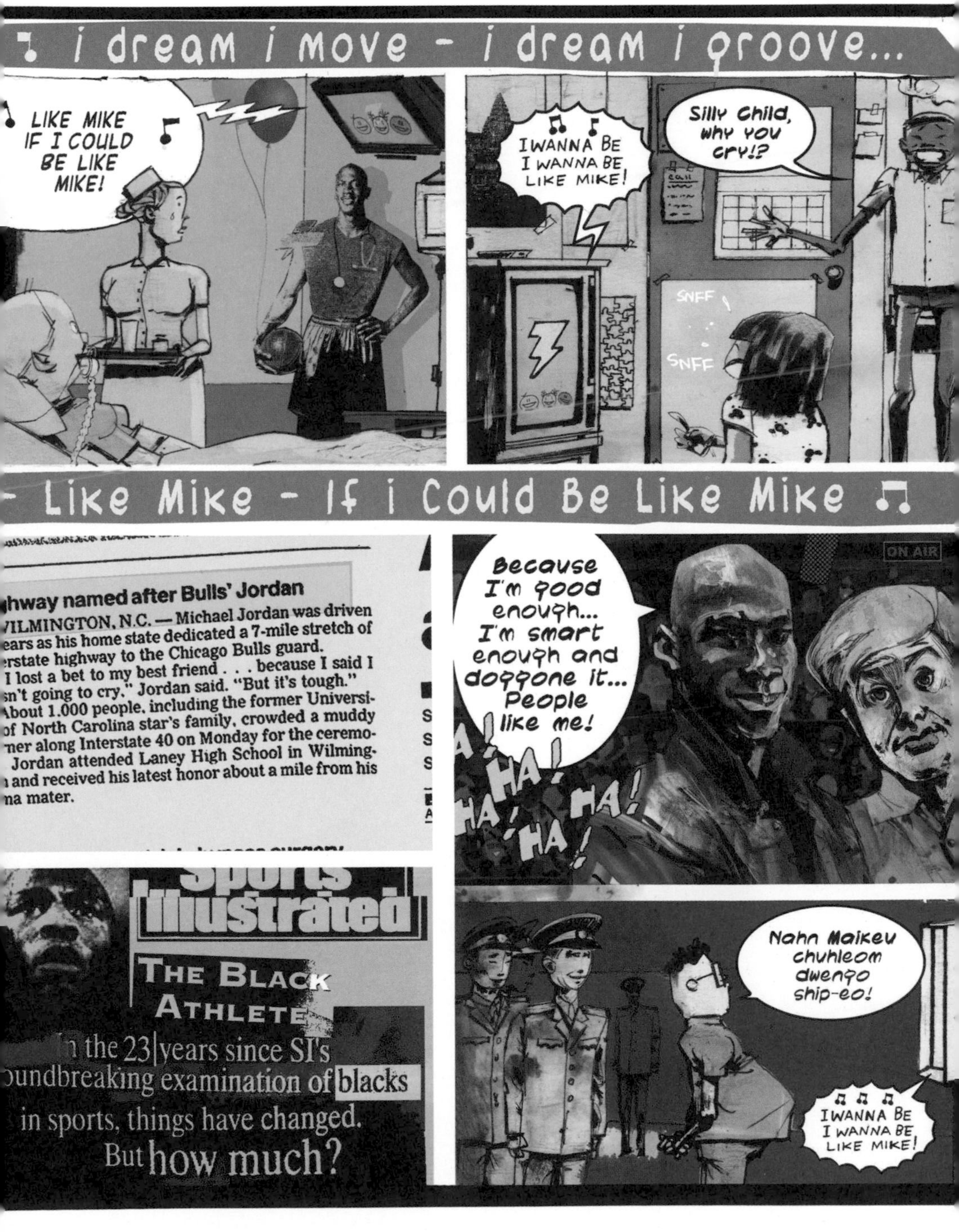
i dream i move - i dream i groove...
LIKE MIKE IF I COULD BE LIKE MIKE!
I WANNA BE I WANNA BE LIKE MIKE!
Silly Child, why you cry!?
SNFF
SNFF
- Like Mike - If i Could Be Like Mike
ghway named after Bulls' Jordan
VILMINGTON, N.C. — Michael Jordan was driven
ears as his home state dedicated a 7-mile stretch of
erstate highway to the Chicago Bulls guard.
I lost a bet to my best friend . . . because I said I
sn't going to cry," Jordan said. "But it's tough."
About 1,000 people, including the former Universi-
of North Carolina star's family, crowded a muddy
ner along Interstate 40 on Monday for the ceremo-
Jordan attended Laney High School in Wilming-
n and received his latest honor about a mile from his
na mater.
ON AIR
Because I'm good enough... I'm smart enough and doggone it... People like me!
HA! HA! HA! HA! HA!
Sports Illustrated
THE BLACK ATHLETE
In the 23 years since SI's
oundbreaking examination of blacks
in sports, things have changed.
But how much?
Nahn Maikeu chuhleom dwengo ship-eo!
I WANNA BE I WANNA BE LIKE MIKE!

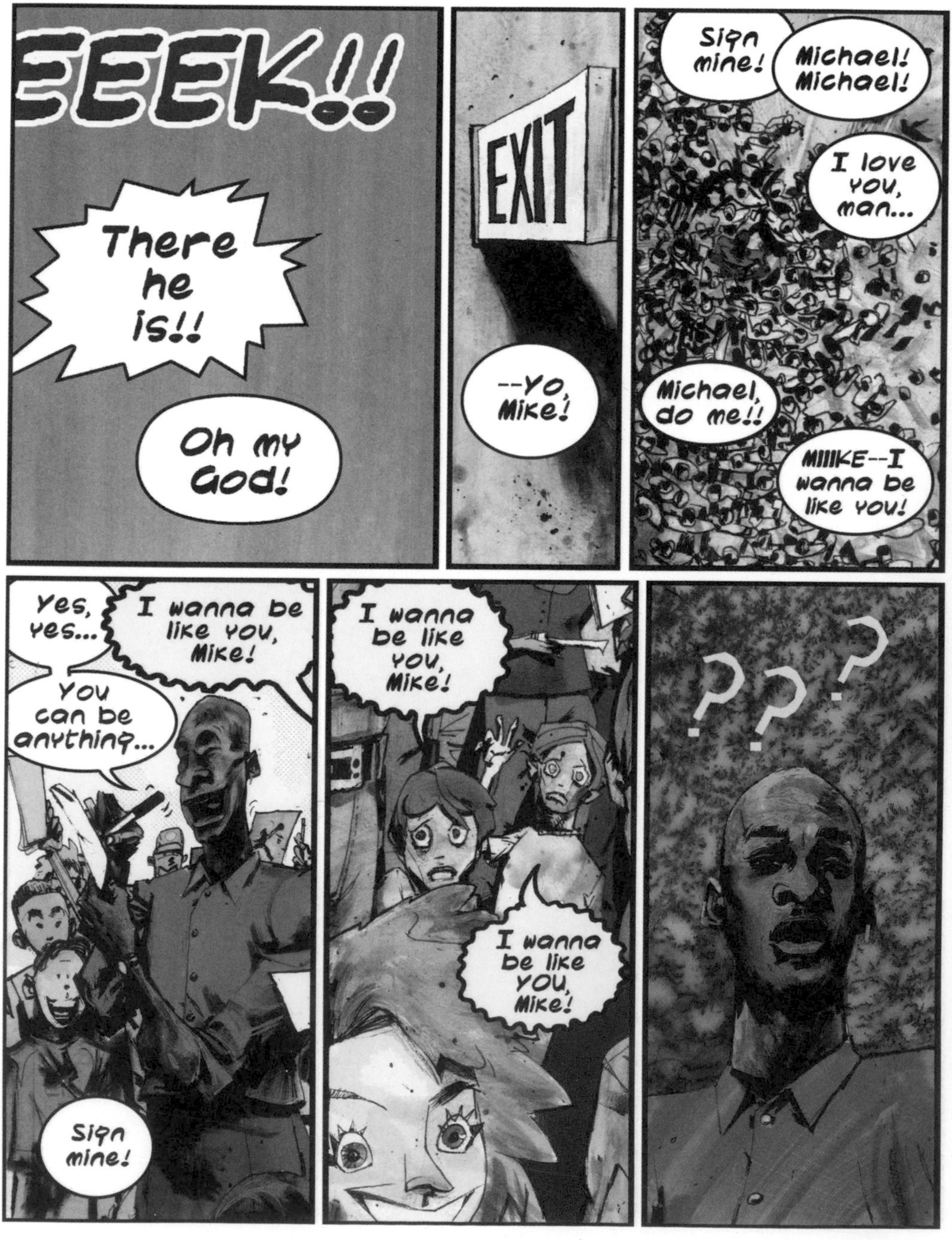
EEEK!!
There he is!!
Oh my God!
EXIT
--Yo, Mike!
Sign mine!
Michael! Michael!
I love you, man...
Michael, do me!!
MIIIKE--I wanna be like you!
Yes, yes...
I wanna be like you, Mike!
You can be anything...
Sign mine!
I wanna be like you, Mike!
I wanna be like you, Mike!
???

I Wanna Be Like Mike

STILL A FINE NOON IN A CHICAGO SUBURB

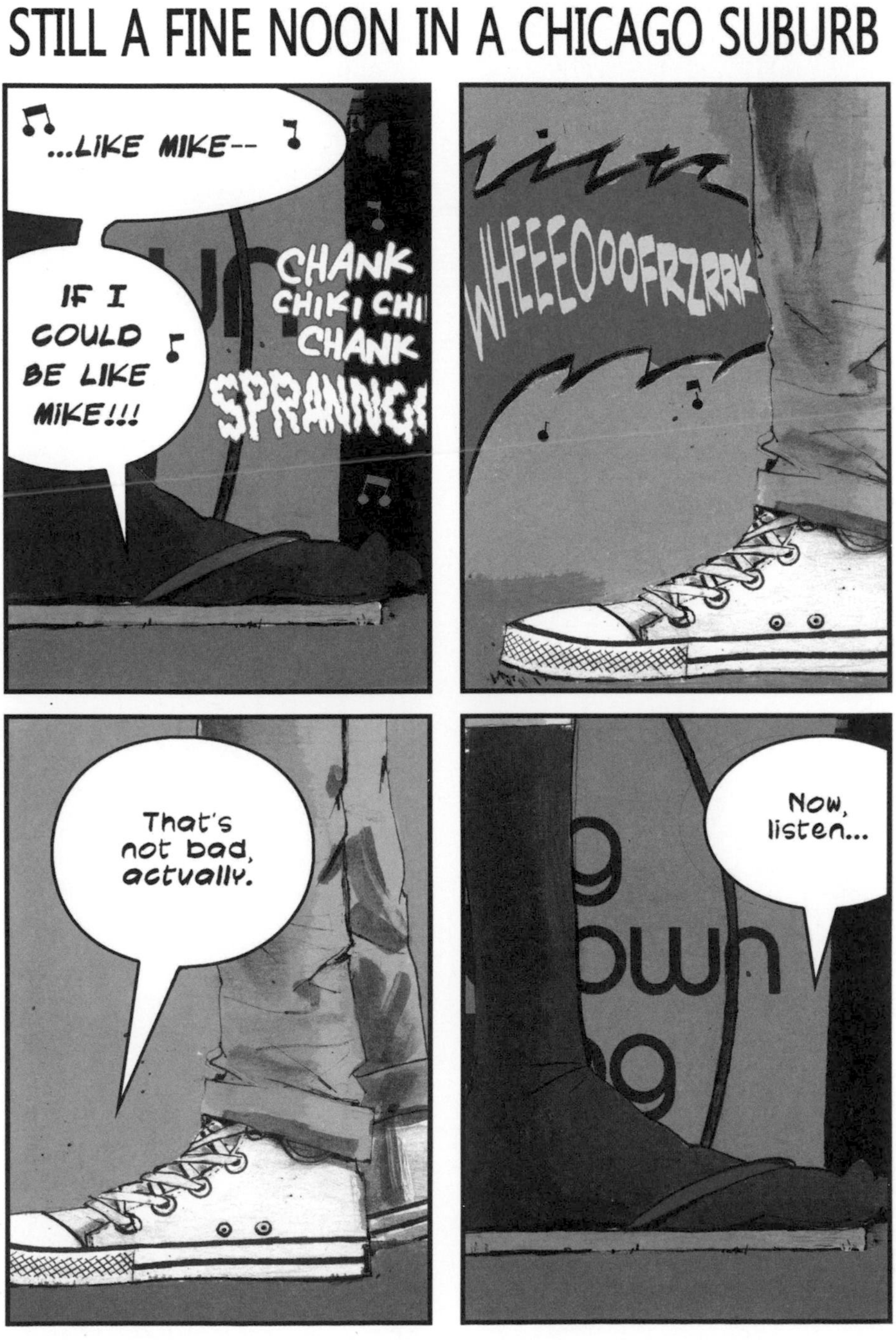
...LIKE MIKE--
IF I COULD BE LIKE MIKE!!!
CHANK
CHIKI CHI
CHANK
SPRANNG
WHEEEOOOFRZRRK
That's not bad, actually.
Now, listen...

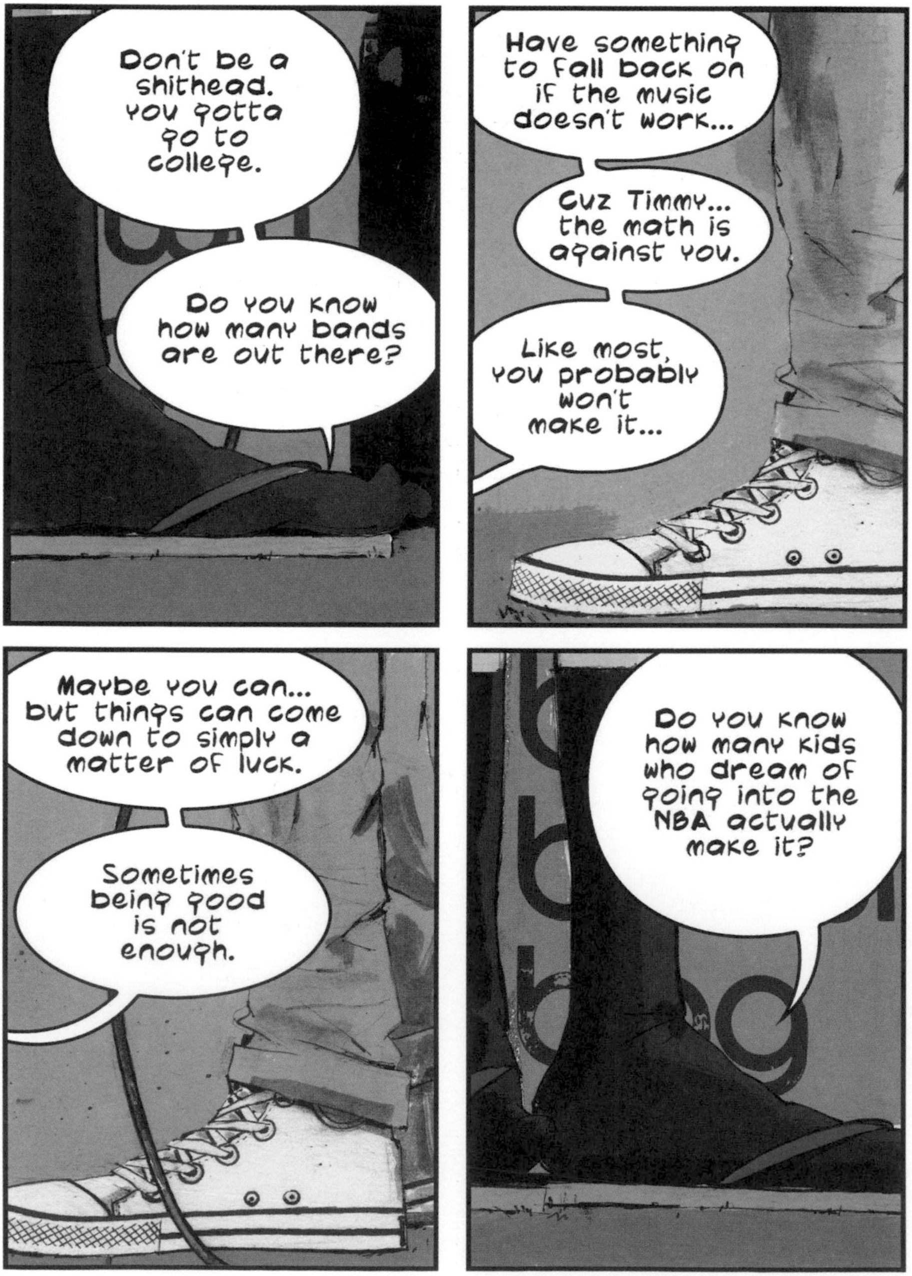
Don't be a shithead. You gotta go to college.
Do you know how many bands are out there?
Have something to fall back on if the music doesn't work...
Cuz Timmy... the math is against you.
Like most, you probably won't make it...
Maybe you can... but things can come down to simply a matter of luck.
Sometimes being good is not enough.
Do you know how many kids who dream of going into the NBA actually make it?

3:
In 3's

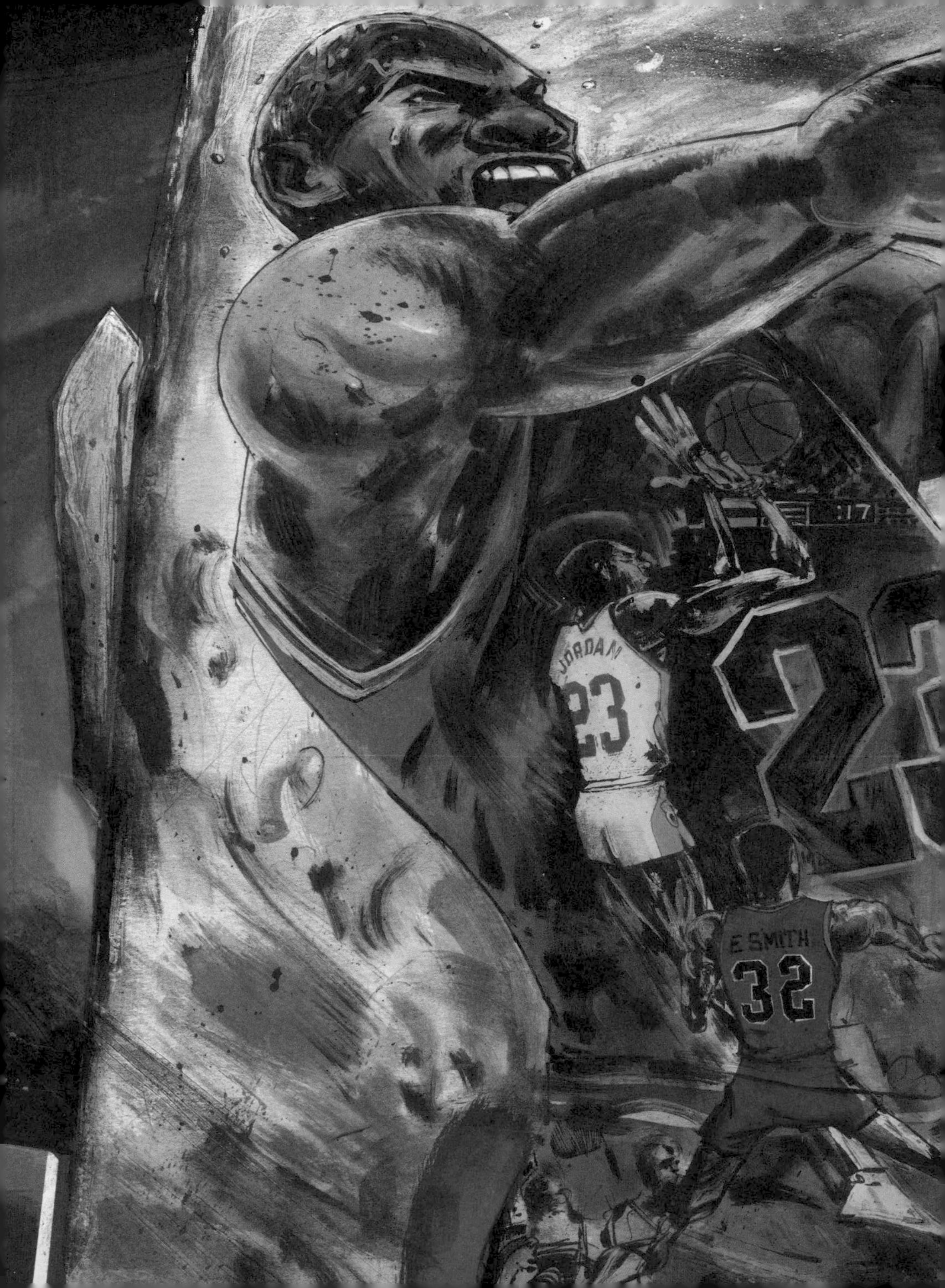
:17
JORDAN
23
E SMITH
32

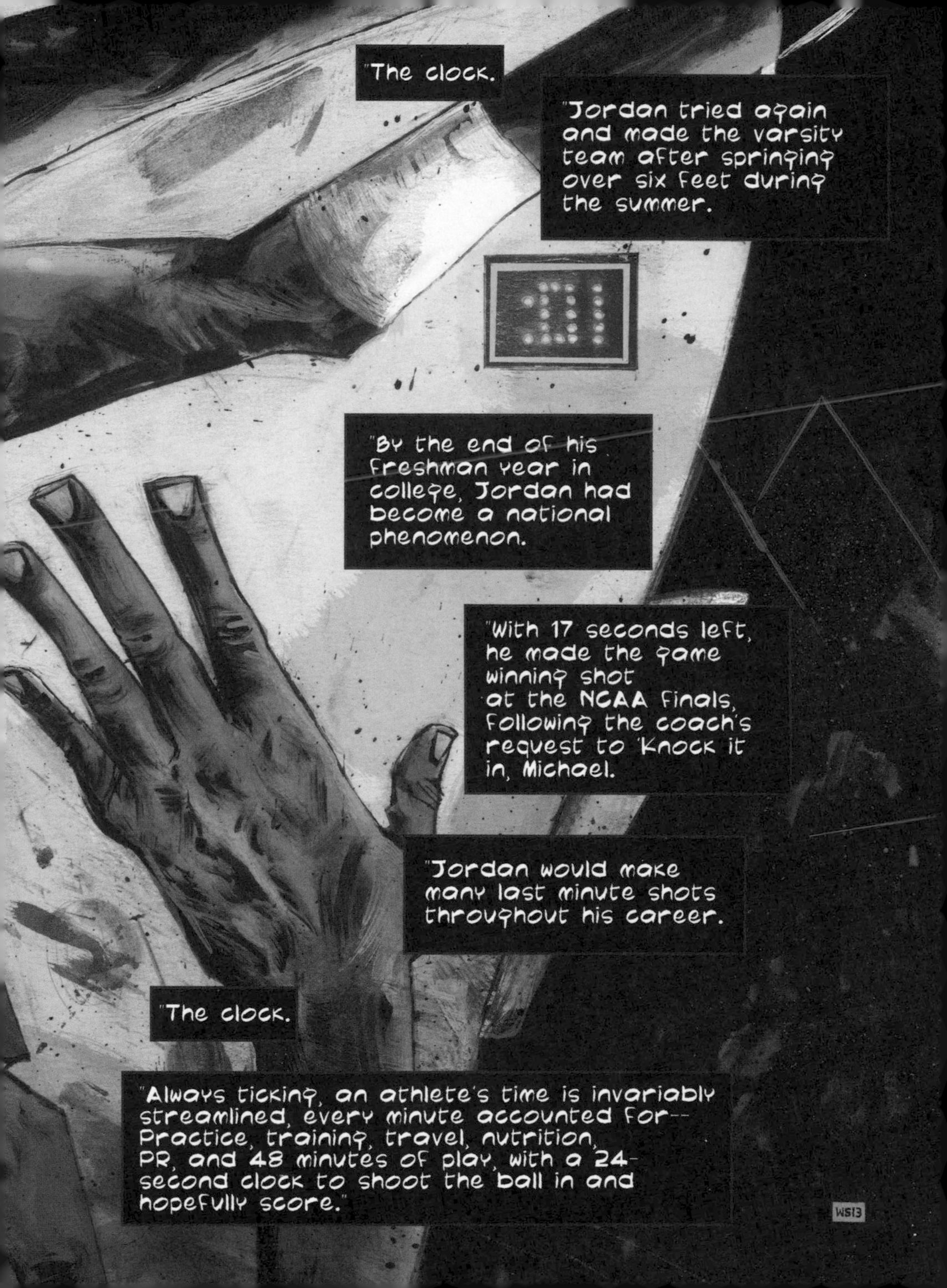
"The clock.
"Jordan tried again and made the varsity team after springing over six feet during the summer.
"By the end of his freshman year in college, Jordan had become a national phenomenon.
"With 17 seconds left, he made the game winning shot at the NCAA finals, following the coach's request to 'Knock it in, Michael.
"Jordan would make many last minute shots throughout his career.
"The clock.
"Always ticking, an athlete's time is invariably streamlined, every minute accounted for-- Practice, training, travel, nutrition, PR, and 48 minutes of play, with a 24-second clock to shoot the ball in and hopefully score."
WS13

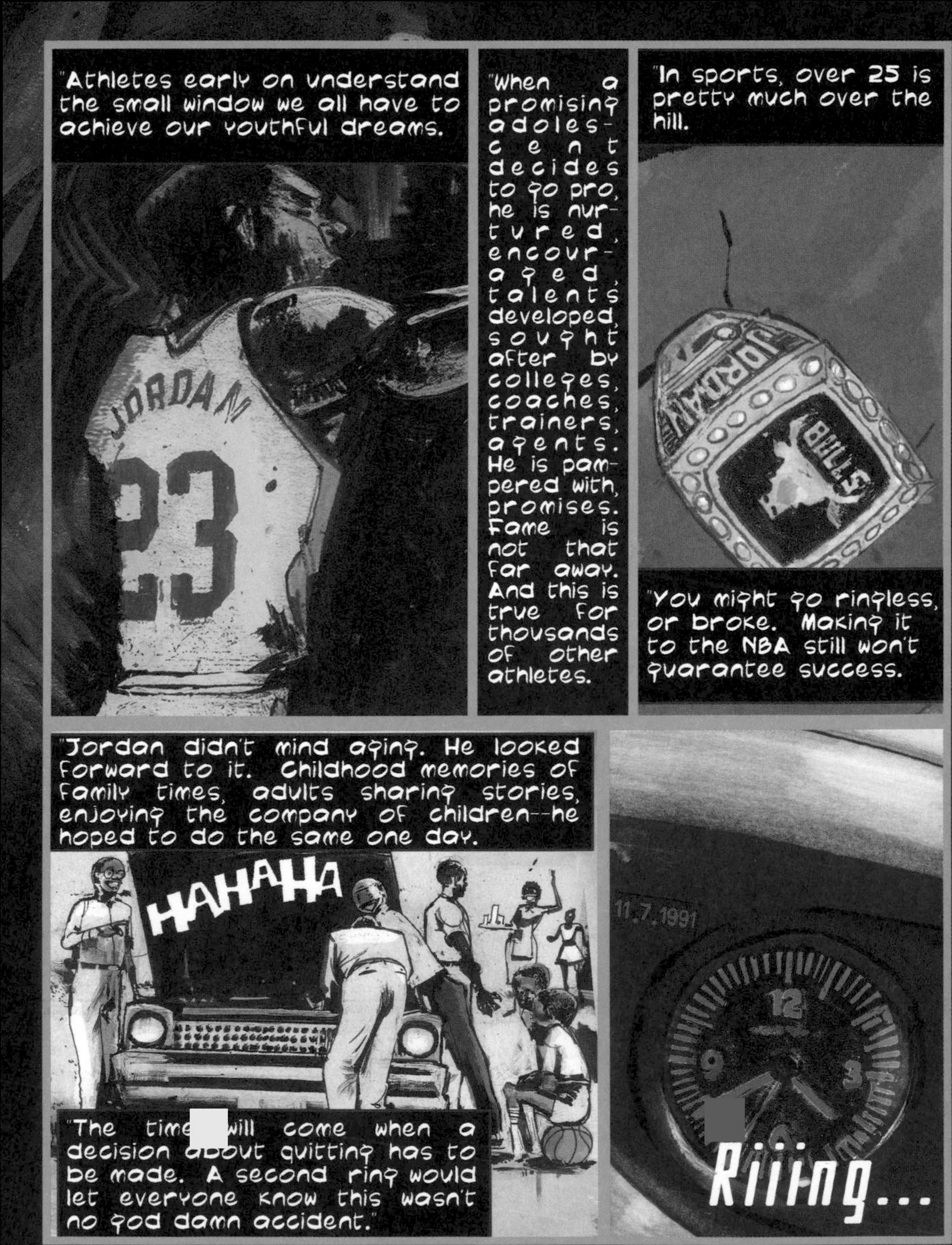
"Athletes early on understand the small window we all have to achieve our youthful dreams.
JORDAN
23
"When a promising adolescent decides to go pro, he is nurtured, encouraged, talents developed, sought after by colleges, coaches, trainers, agents. He is pampered with promises. Fame is not that far away. And this is true for thousands of other athletes.
"In sports, over 25 is pretty much over the hill.
JORDAN
BULLS
"You might go ringless, or broke. Making it to the NBA still won't guarantee success.
"Jordan didn't mind aging. He looked forward to it. Childhood memories of family times, adults sharing stories, enjoying the company of children--he hoped to do the same one day.
HAHAHA
"The time will come when a decision about quitting has to be made. A second ring would let everyone know this wasn't no god damn accident."
11.7.1991
12
9
3
Riiing...

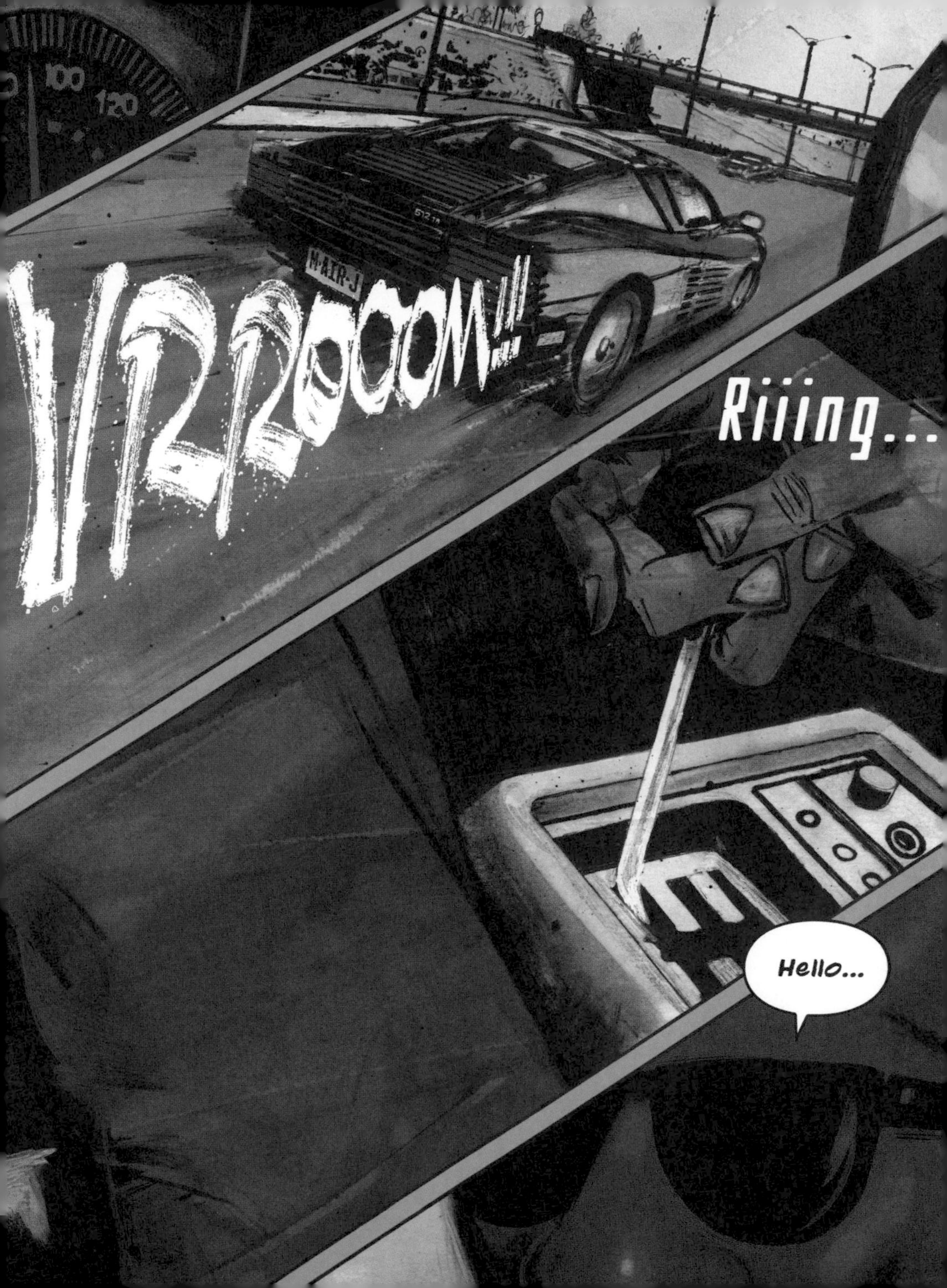

100
120
M-AIR-J
VRROOOM!!!
Riiing...
Hello...

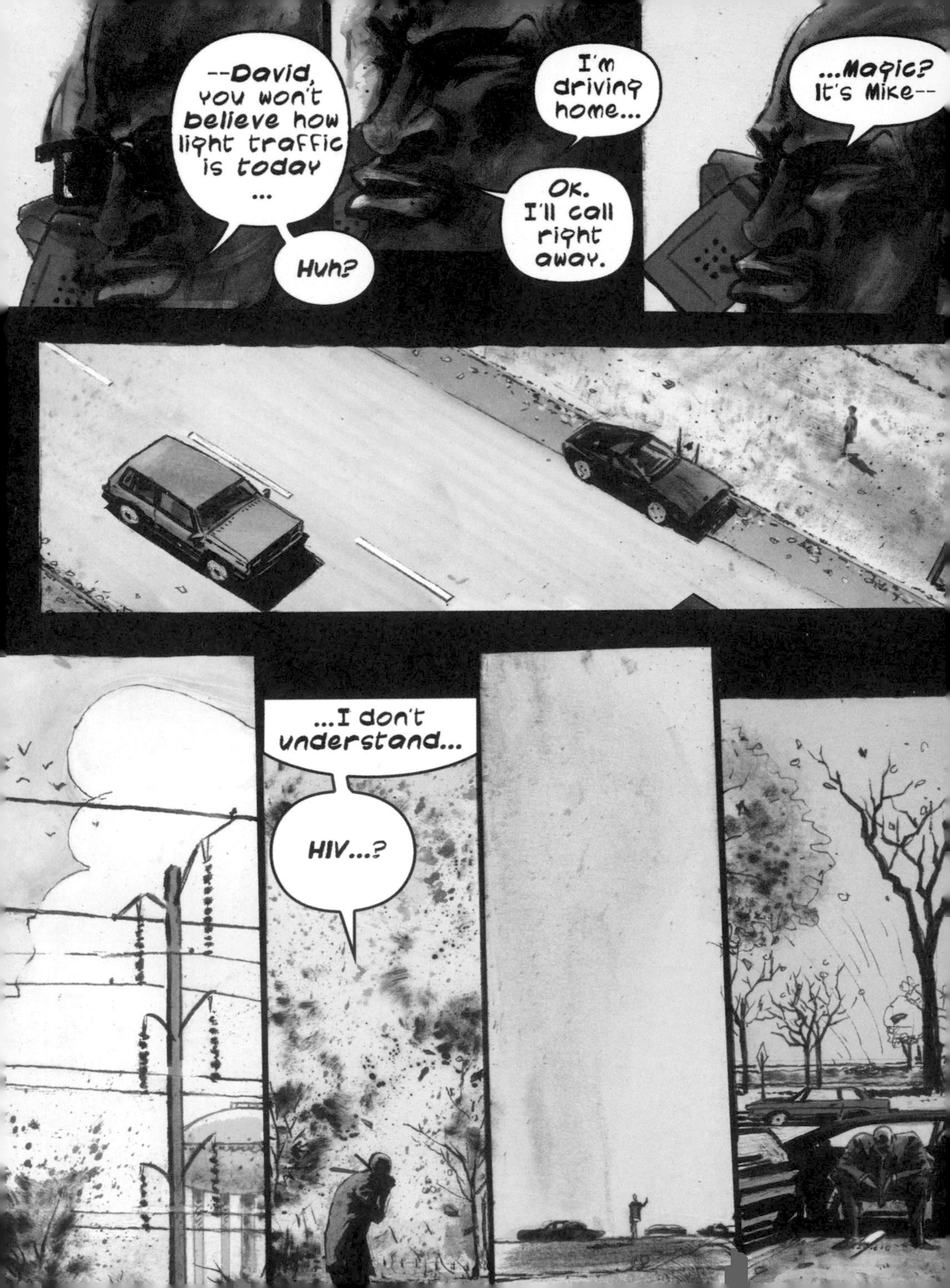
--David, you won't believe how light traffic is today ...
Huh?
I'm driving home...
Ok. I'll call right away.
...Magic? It's Mike--
...I don't understand...
HIV...?

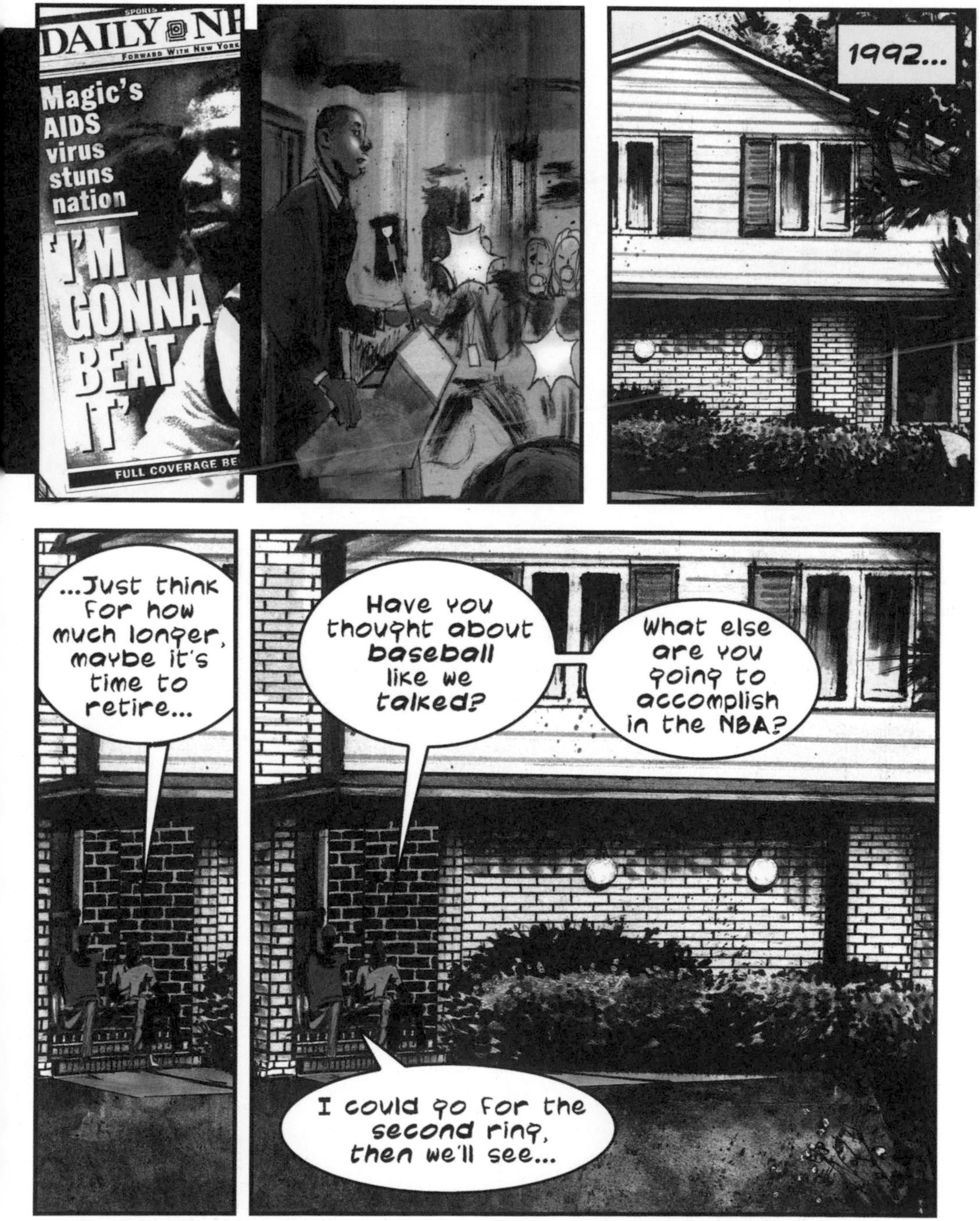
DAILY NE
FORWARD WITH NEW YORK
Magic's AIDS virus stuns nation
'I'M GONNA BEAT IT'
FULL COVERAGE BE
1992...
...Just think for how much longer, maybe it's time to retire...
Have you thought about baseball like we talked?
What else are you going to accomplish in the NBA?
I could go for the second ring, then we'll see...

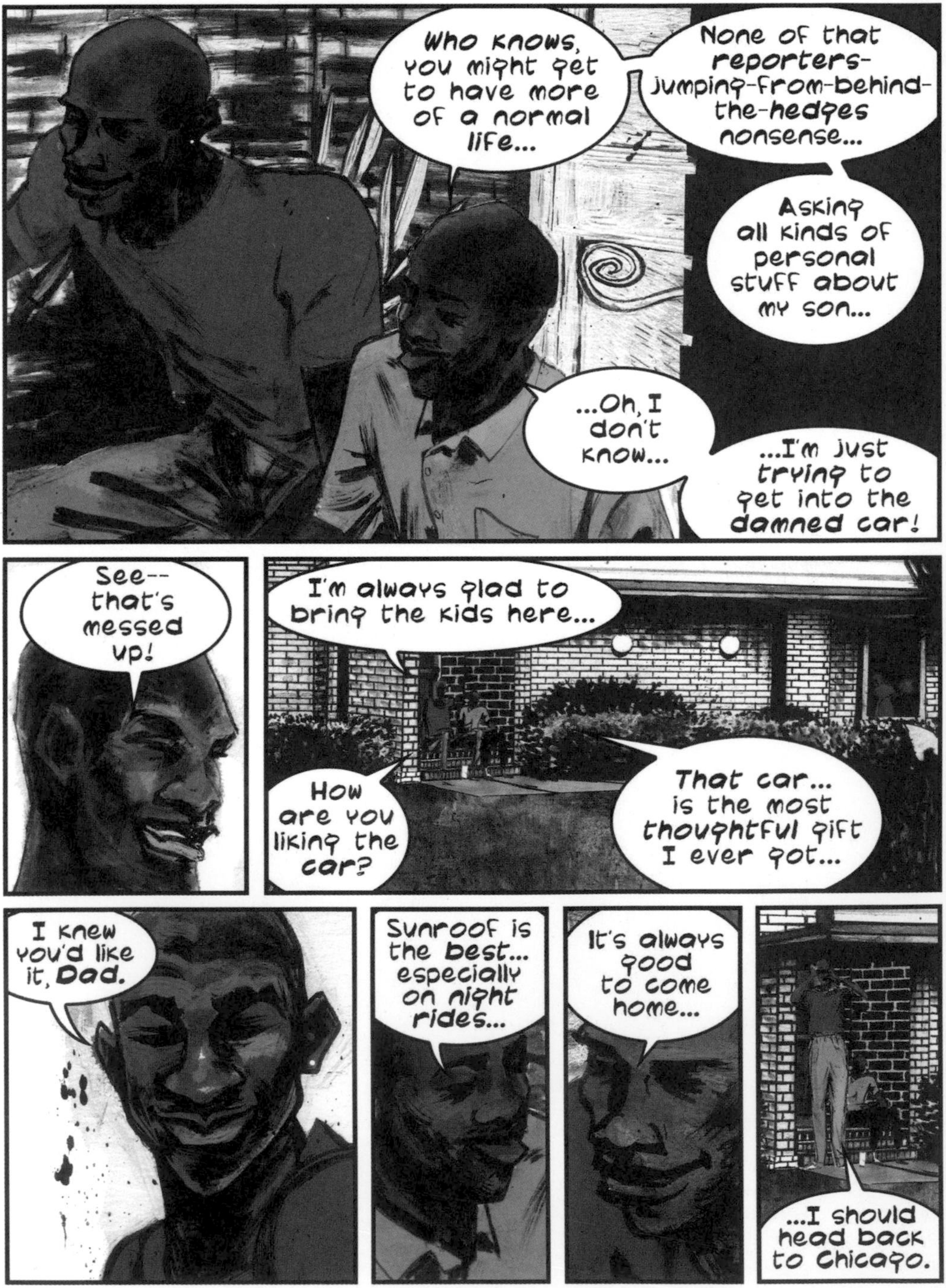
Who knows, you might get to have more of a normal life...
None of that reporters-jumping-from-behind-the-hedges nonsense...
Asking all kinds of personal stuff about my son...
...Oh, I don't know...
...I'm just trying to get into the damned car!
See--that's messed up!
I'm always glad to bring the kids here...
How are you liking the car?
That car... is the most thoughtful gift I ever got...
I knew you'd like it, Dad.
Sunroof is the best... especially on night rides...
It's always good to come home...
...I should head back to Chicago.

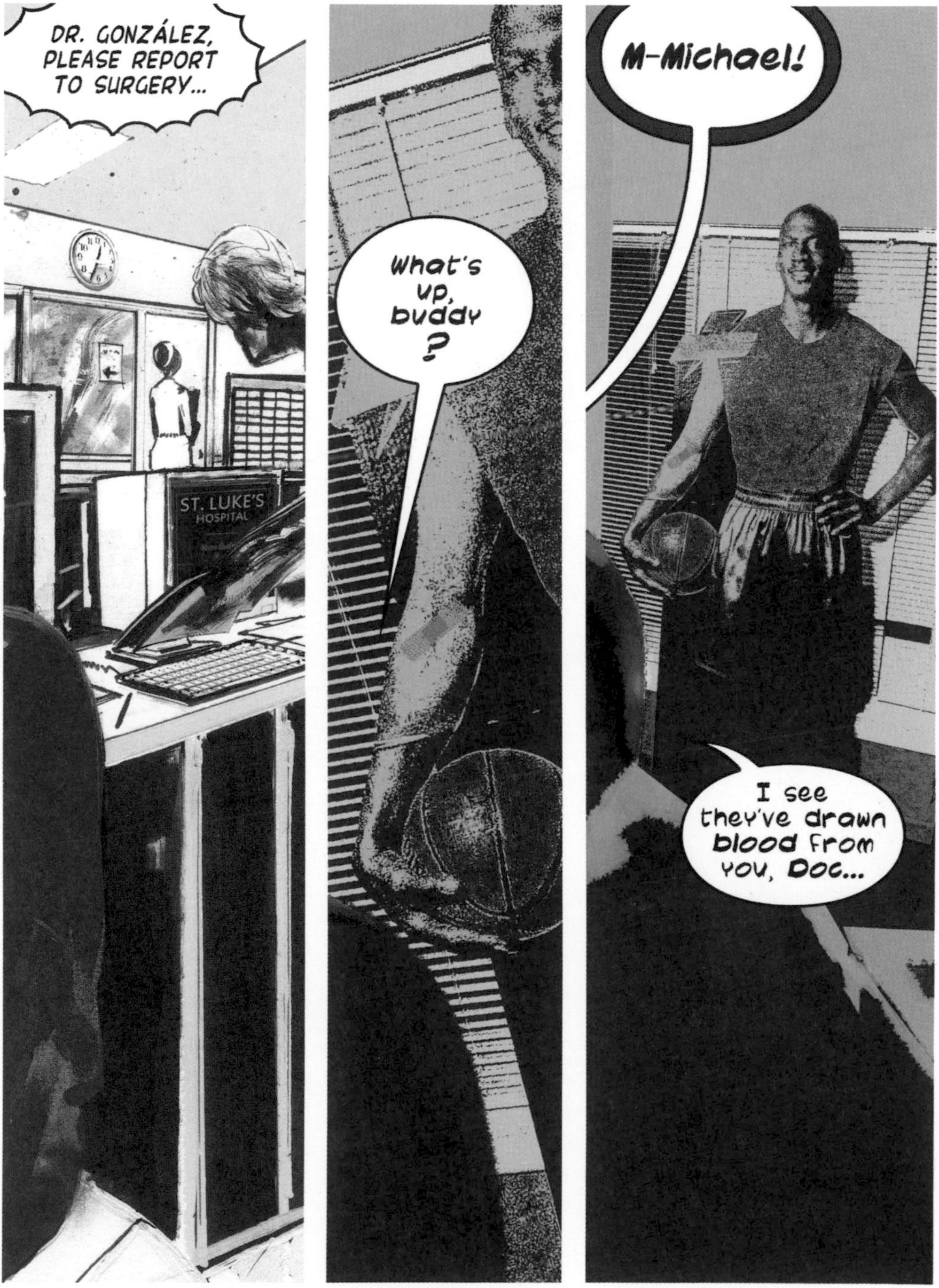
DR. GONZÁLEZ, PLEASE REPORT TO SURGERY...
ST. LUKE'S HOSPITAL
What's up, buddy?
M-Michael!
I see they've drawn blood from you, Doc...

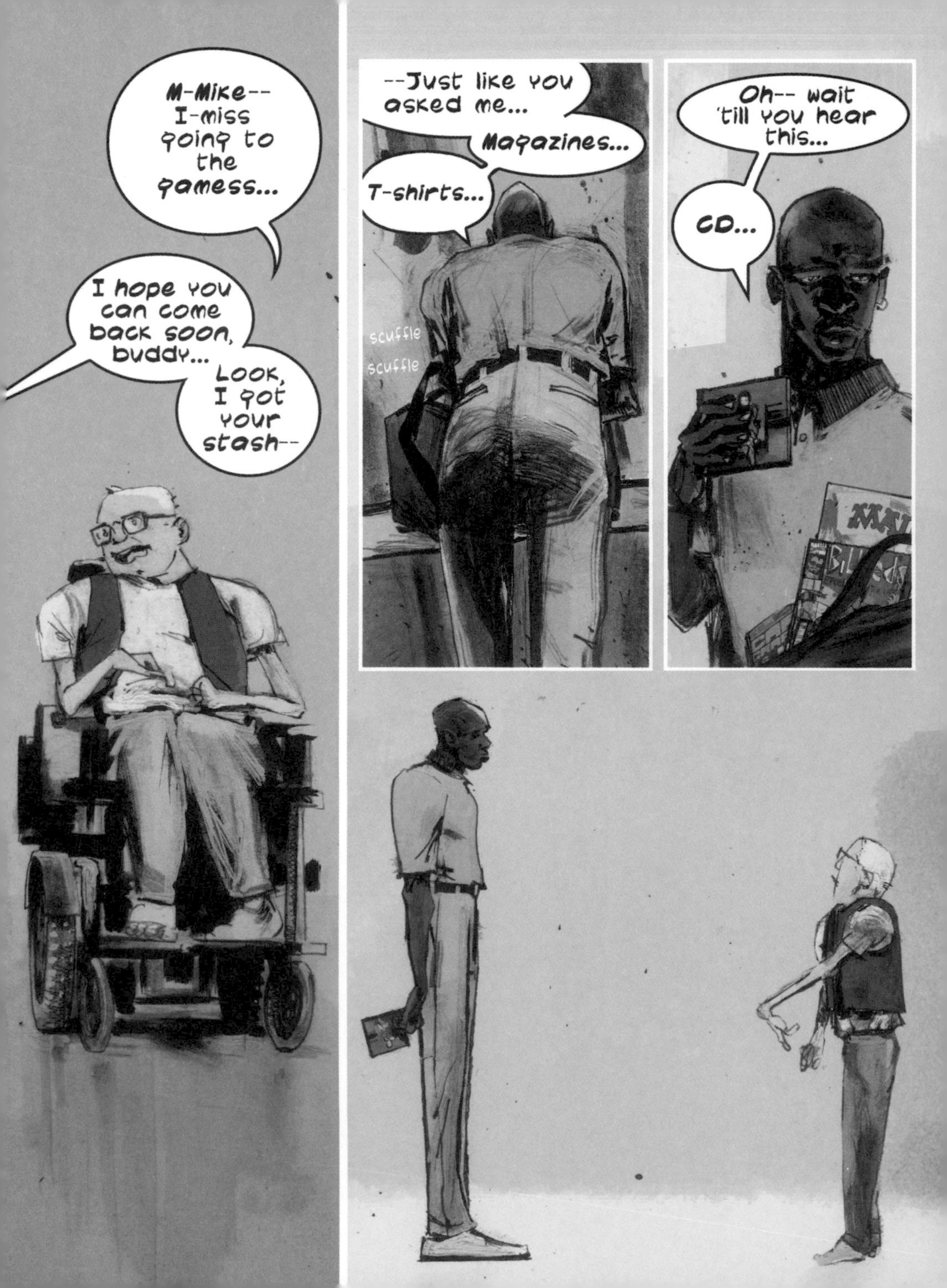
M-Mike-- I-miss going to the gamess...
I hope you can come back soon, buddy...
Look, I got your stash--
--Just like you asked me...
Magazines...
T-shirts...
scuffle
scuffle
Oh-- wait 'till you hear this...
CD...

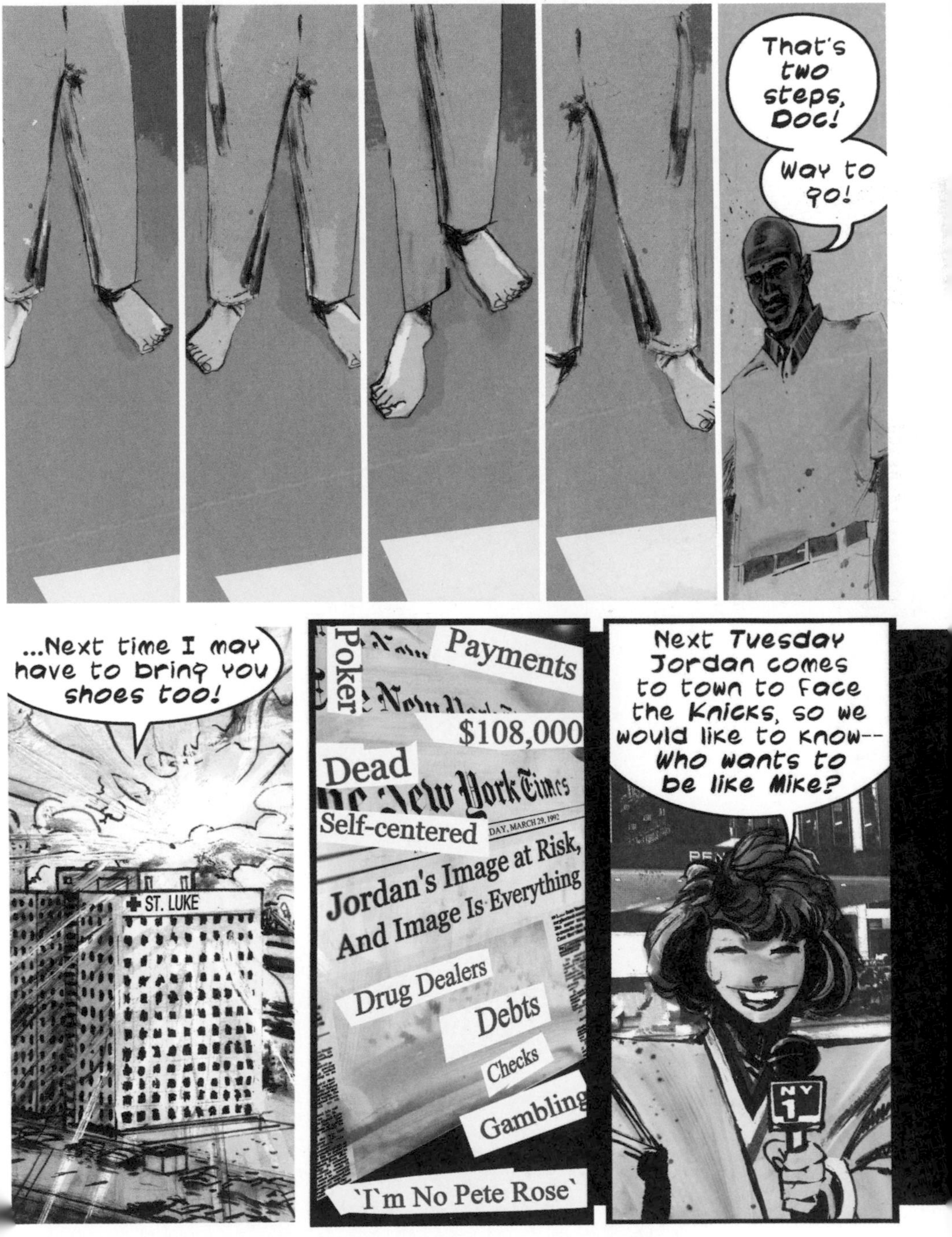
That's two steps, Doc!
Way to go!
...Next time I may have to bring you shoes too!
ST. LUKE
Poker
Payments
$108,000
Dead
The New York Times
Self-centered
DAY, MARCH 29, 1992
Jordan's Image at Risk, And Image Is Everything
Drug Dealers
Debts
Checks
Gambling
`I`m No Pete Rose`
Next Tuesday Jordan comes to town to face the Knicks, so we would like to know-- Who wants to be like Mike?
NY 1

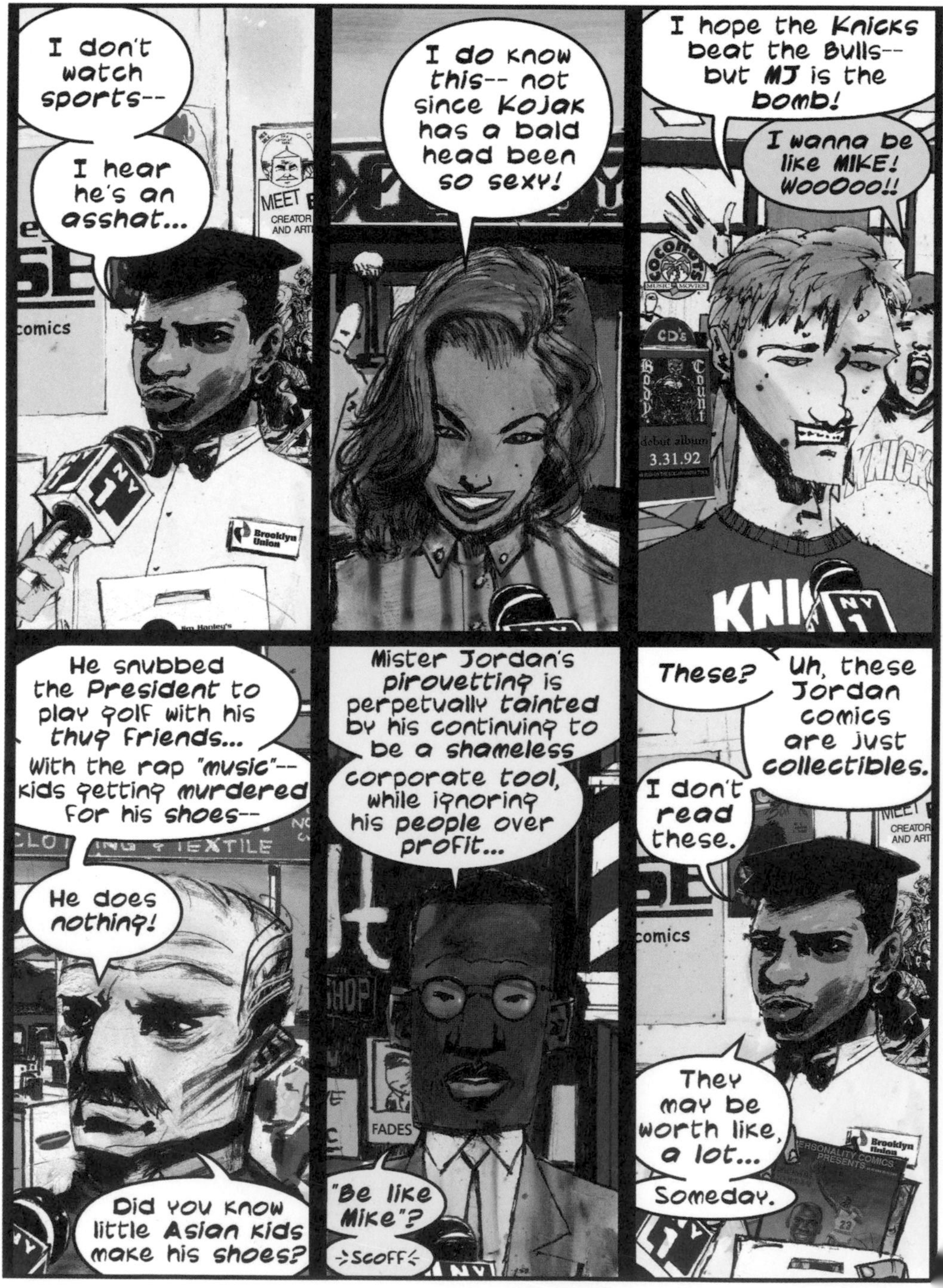
I don't watch sports--
I hear he's an asshat...
MEET
CREATOR AND ART
comics
Brooklyn Union
I do know this-- not since Kojak has a bald head been so sexy!
I hope the Knicks beat the Bulls-- but MJ is the bomb!
I wanna be like MIKE! WooOoo!!
COCONUTS MUSIC MOVIES
CD's
Body Count
debut album 3.31.92
KNICKS
He snubbed the President to play golf with his thug friends...
With the rap "music"-- kids getting murdered for his shoes--
He does nothing!
Did you know little Asian kids make his shoes?
Mister Jordan's pirouetting is perpetually tainted by his continuing to be a shameless
corporate tool, while ignoring his people over profit...
FADES
"Be like Mike"?
SCOFF
These?
Uh, these Jordan comics are just collectibles.
I don't read these.
comics
They may be worth like, a lot...
Someday.
PERSONALITY COMICS PRESENTS
Brooklyn Union

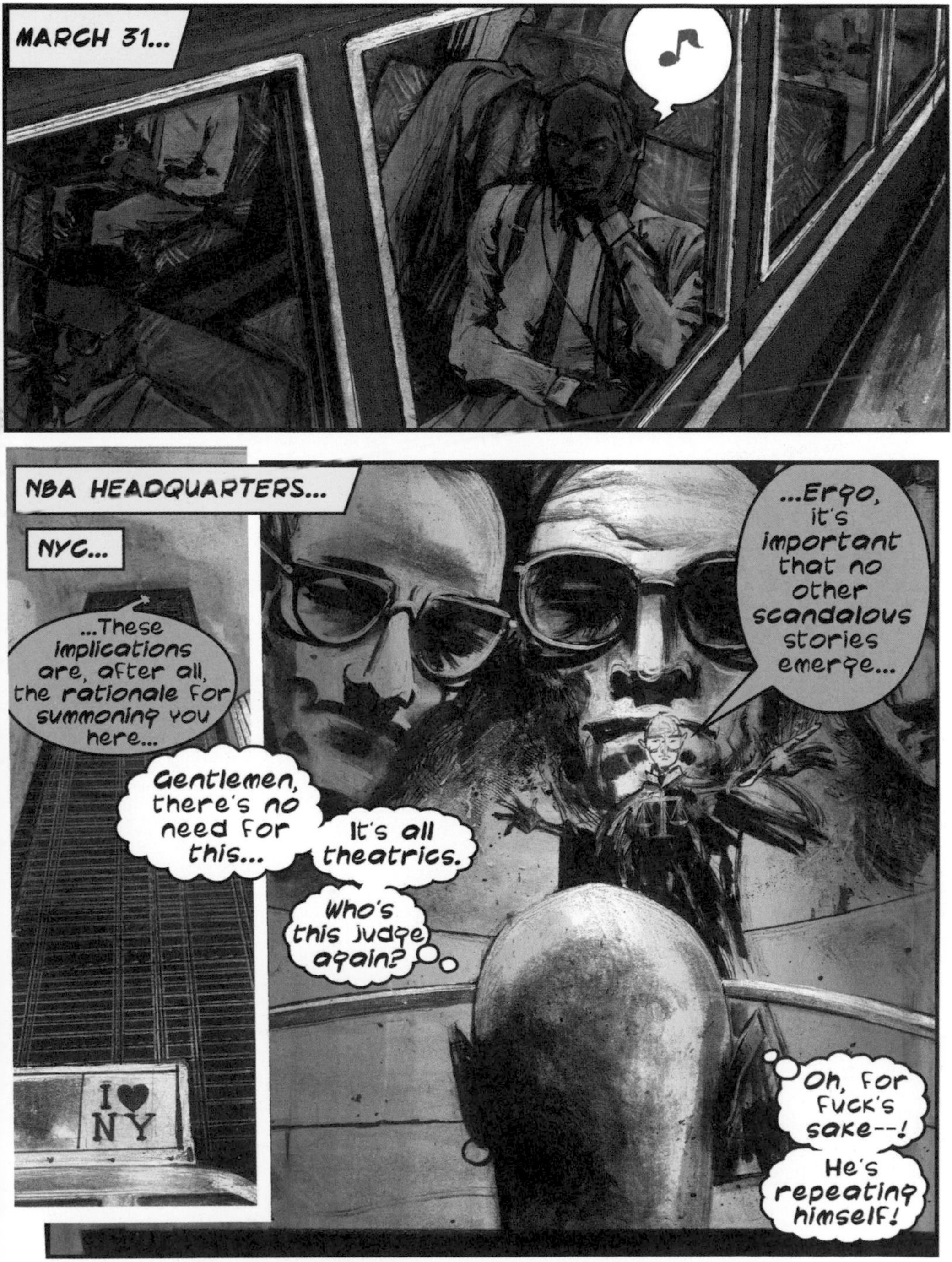
MARCH 31...
NBA HEADQUARTERS...
NYC...
...These implications are, after all, the rationale for summoning you here...
Gentlemen, there's no need for this...
It's all theatrics.
Who's this judge again?
...Ergo, it's important that no other scandalous stories emerge...
Oh, for fuck's sake--!
He's repeating himself!
I NY

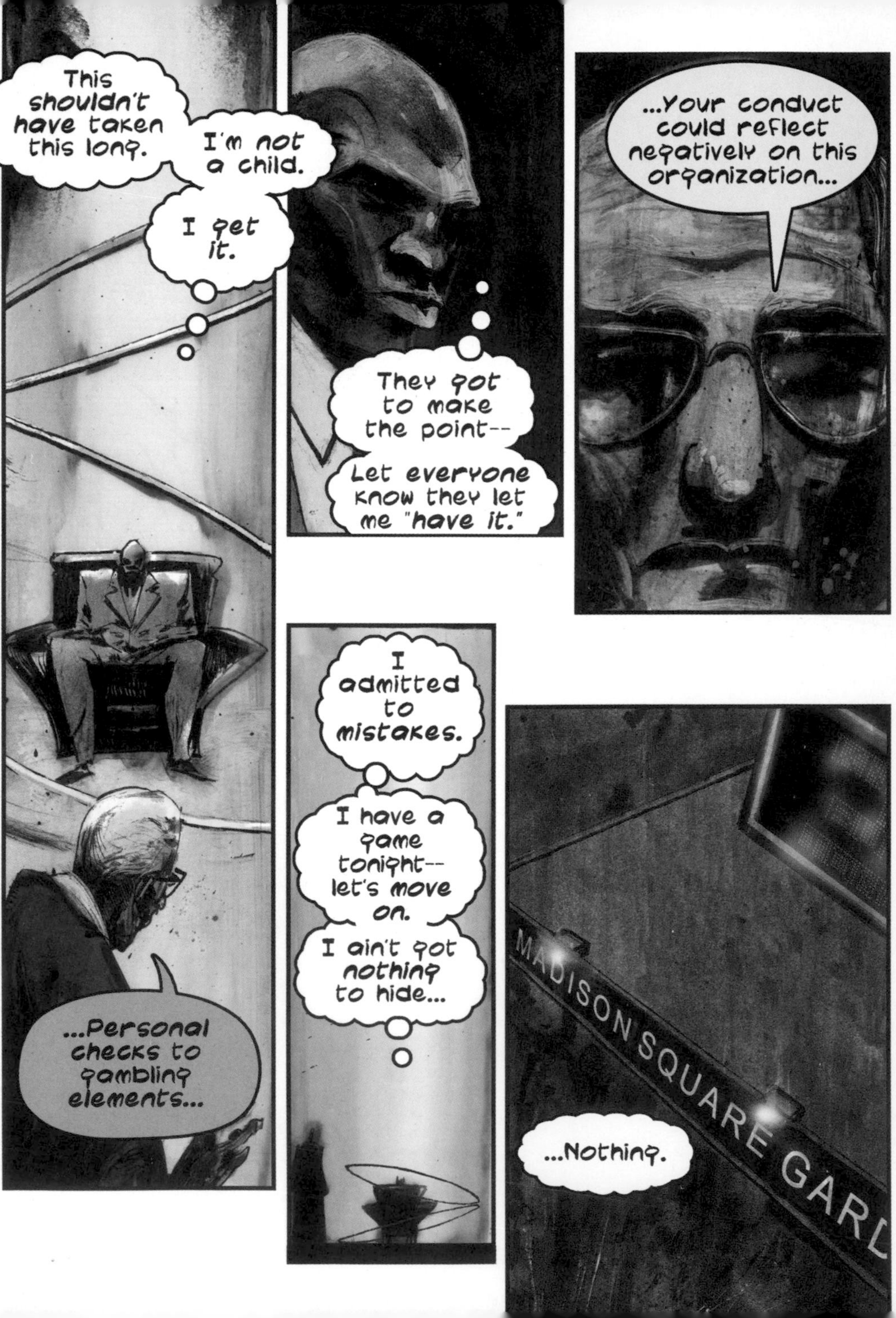
This shouldn't have taken this long.
I'm not a child.
I get it.
They got to make the point--
Let everyone know they let me "have it."
...Your conduct could reflect negatively on this organization...
...Personal checks to gambling elements...
I admitted to mistakes.
I have a game tonight-- let's move on.
I ain't got nothing to hide...
MADISON SQUARE GARD
...Nothing.

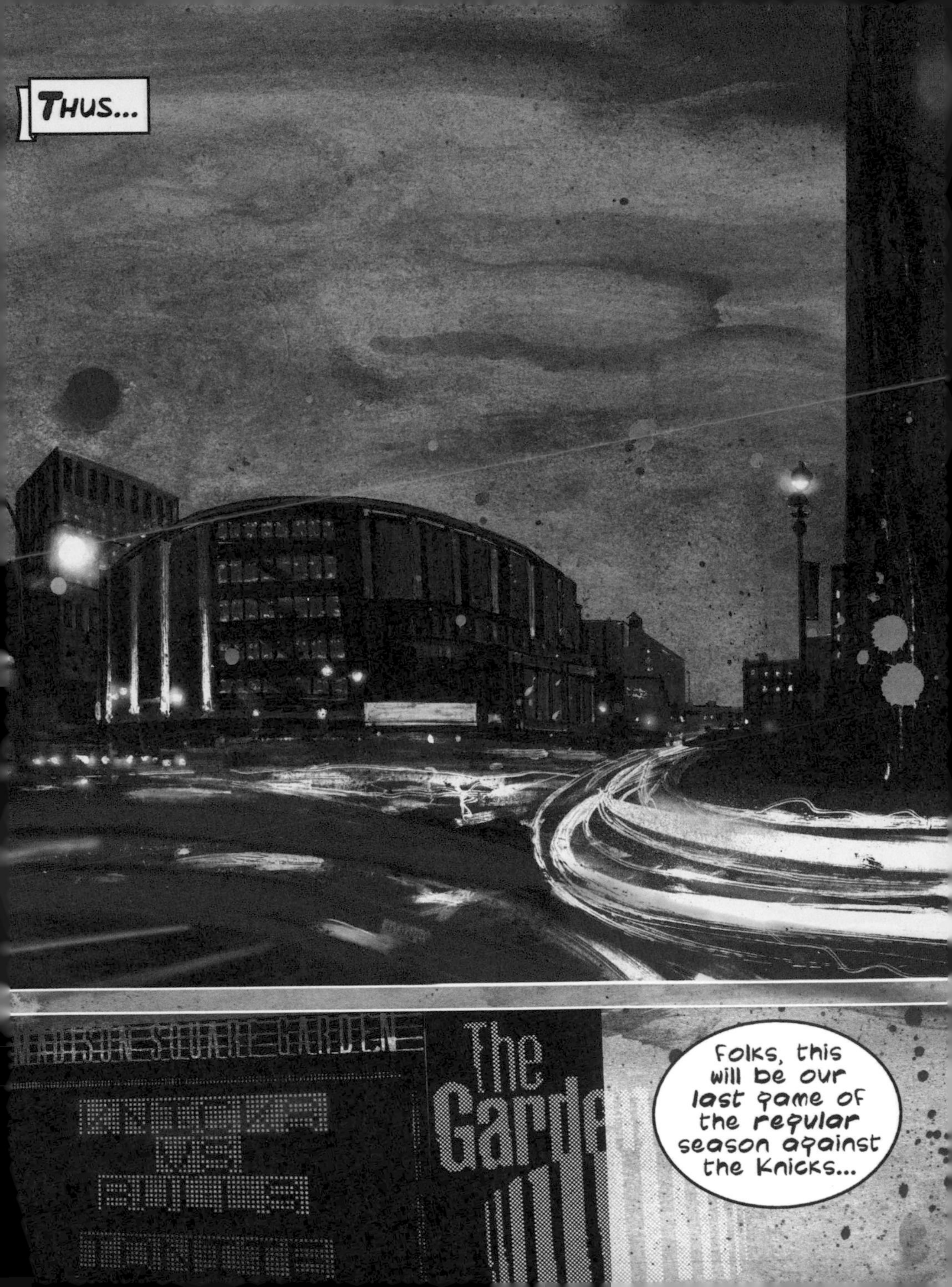
Thus...
Folks, this will be our last game of the regular season against the Knicks...

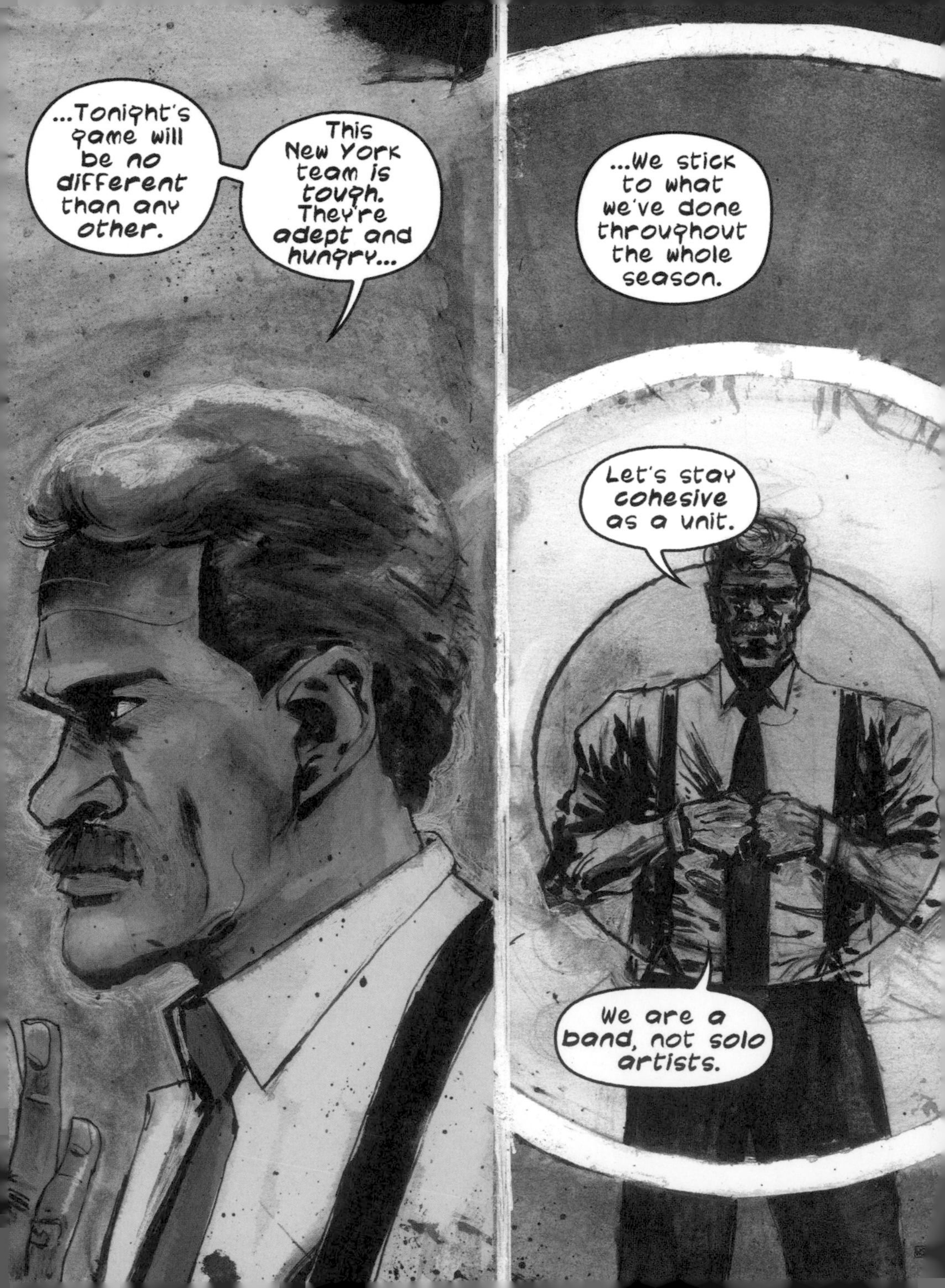
...Tonight's game will be no different than any other.
This New York team is tough. They're adept and hungry...
...We stick to what we've done throughout the whole season.
Let's stay cohesive as a unit.
We are a band, not solo artists.

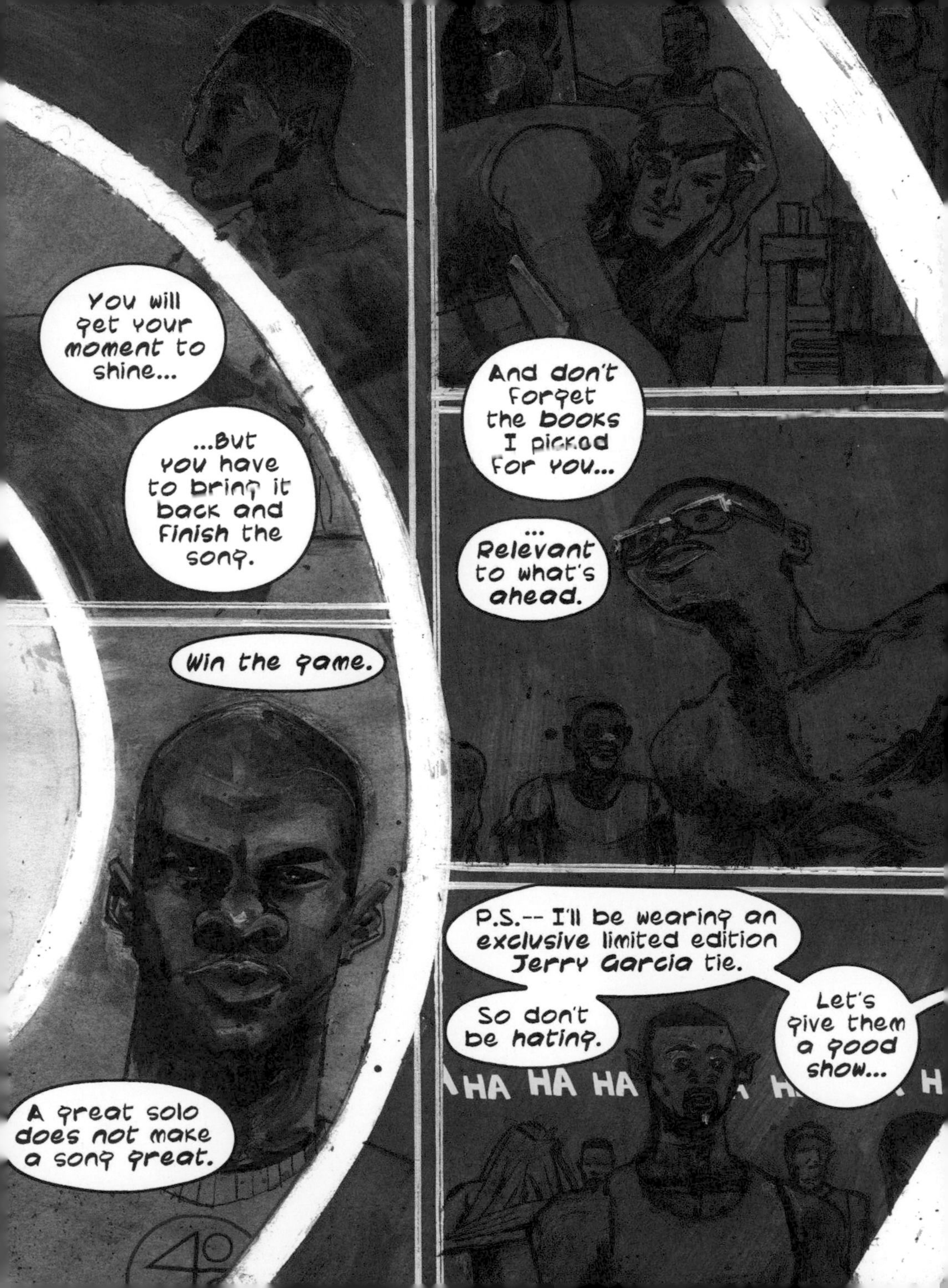
You will get your moment to shine...
...But you have to bring it back and finish the song.
Win the game.
A great solo does not make a song great.
And don't forget the books I picked for you...
...Relevant to what's ahead.
P.S.-- I'll be wearing an exclusive limited edition Jerry Garcia tie.
So don't be hating.
Let's give them a good show...
HA HA HA

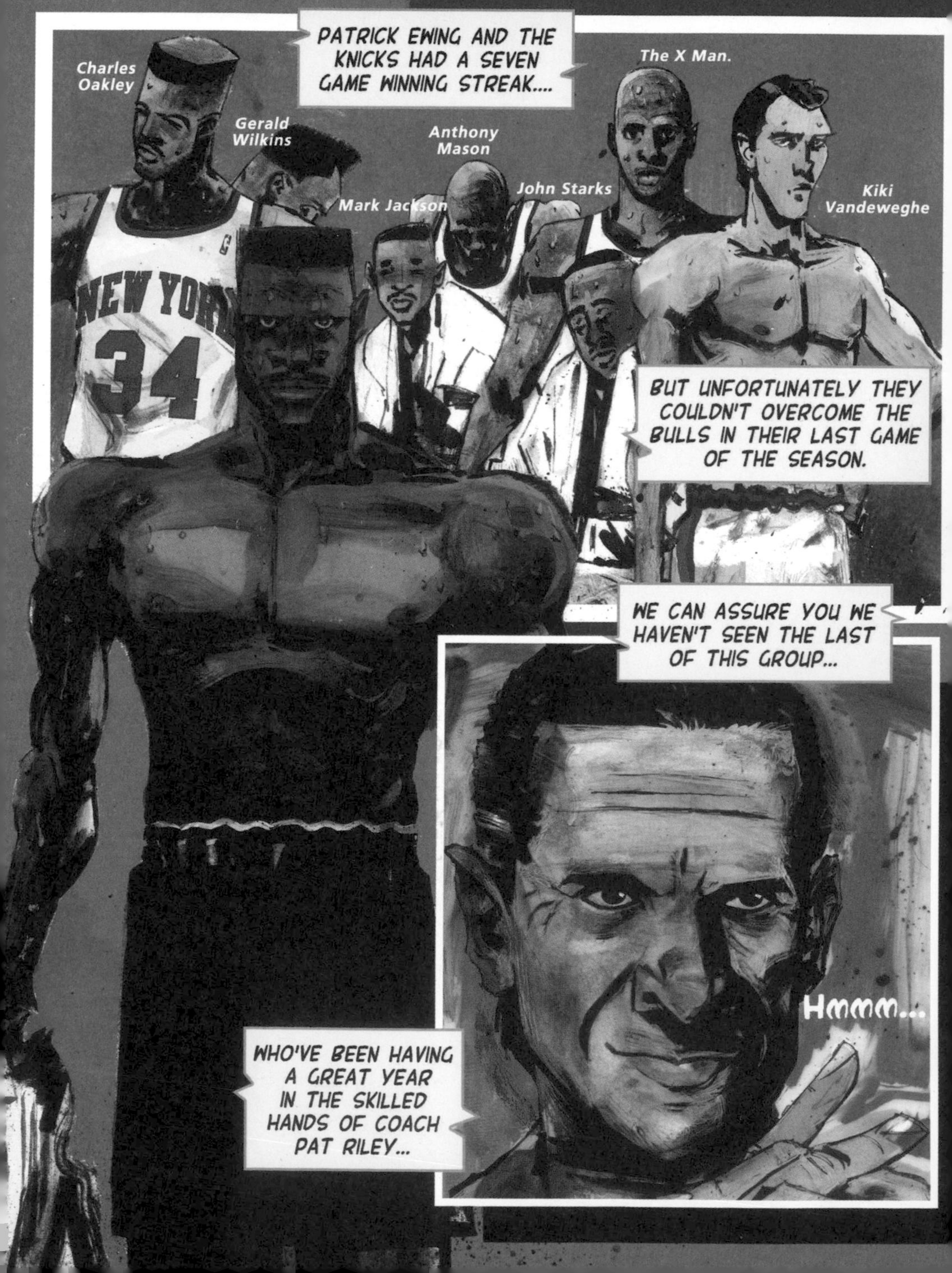

PATRICK EWING AND THE KNICKS HAD A SEVEN GAME WINNING STREAK....
Charles Oakley
Gerald Wilkins
Anthony Mason
Mark Jackson
John Starks
The X Man.
Kiki Vandeweghe
BUT UNFORTUNATELY THEY COULDN'T OVERCOME THE BULLS IN THEIR LAST GAME OF THE SEASON.
WE CAN ASSURE YOU WE HAVEN'T SEEN THE LAST OF THIS GROUP...
WHO'VE BEEN HAVING A GREAT YEAR IN THE SKILLED HANDS OF COACH PAT RILEY...
Hmmm...

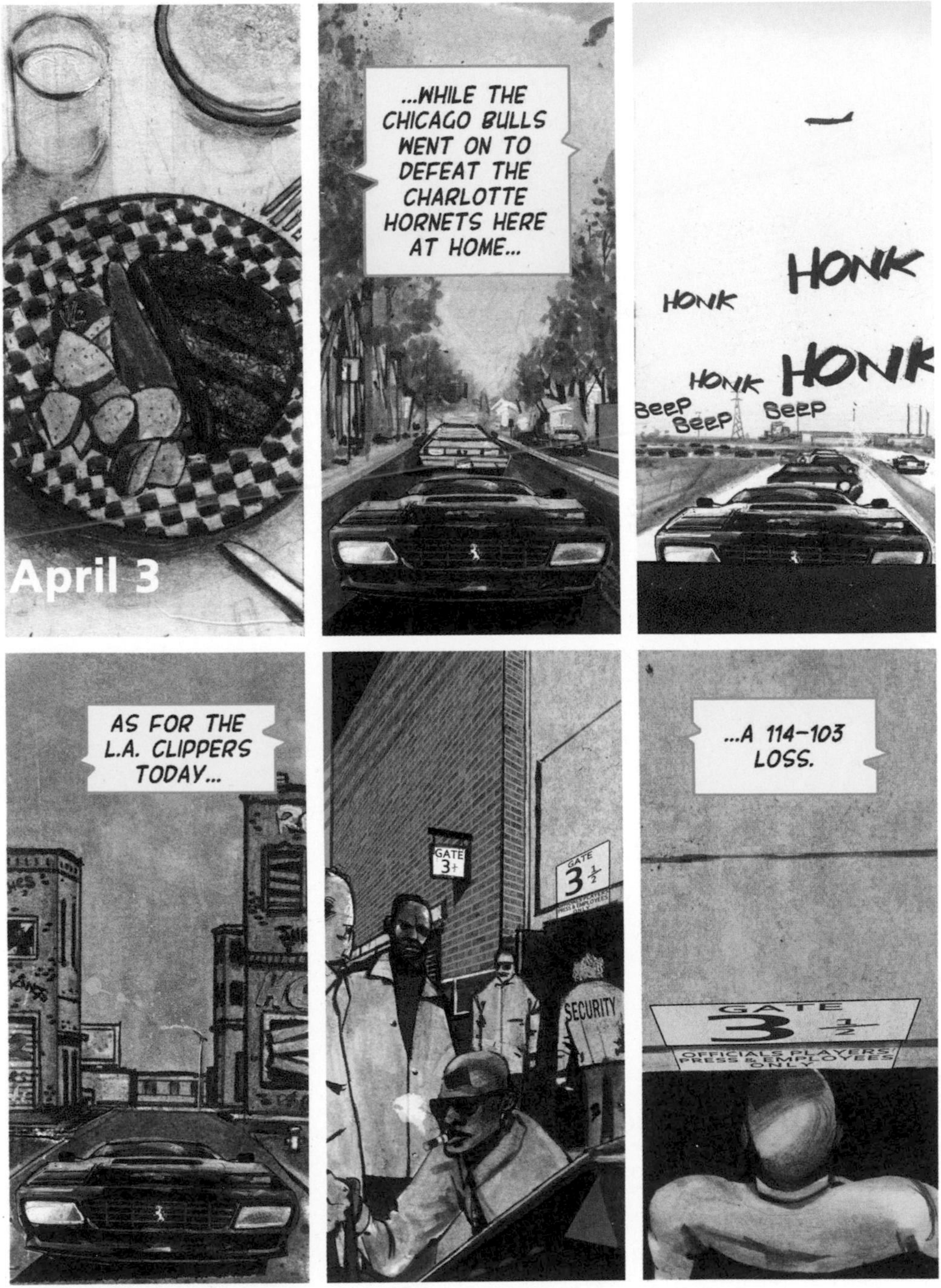

April 3
...WHILE THE CHICAGO BULLS WENT ON TO DEFEAT THE CHARLOTTE HORNETS HERE AT HOME...
HONK
HONK
HONK
HONK
Beep
Beep
Beep
AS FOR THE L.A. CLIPPERS TODAY...
SECURITY
...A 114-103 LOSS.
GATE 3 1/2
OFFICIALS PLAYERS PRESS & EMPLOYEES ONLY

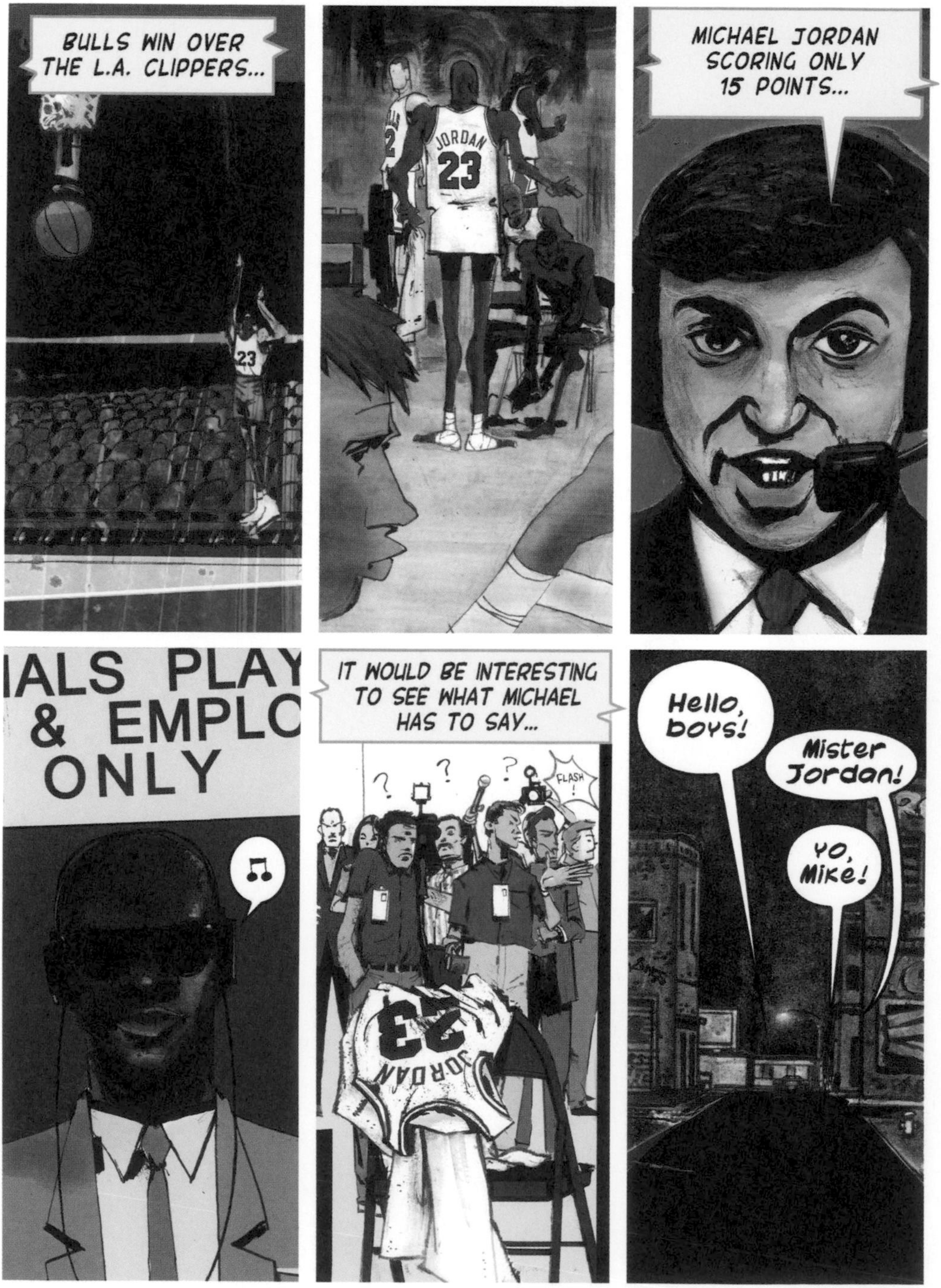
BULLS WIN OVER THE L.A. CLIPPERS...
JORDAN 23
MICHAEL JORDAN SCORING ONLY 15 POINTS...
IALS PLAY
& EMPLO
ONLY
IT WOULD BE INTERESTING TO SEE WHAT MICHAEL HAS TO SAY...
FLASH !
JORDAN 23
Hello, boys!
Mister Jordan!
YO, Mike!

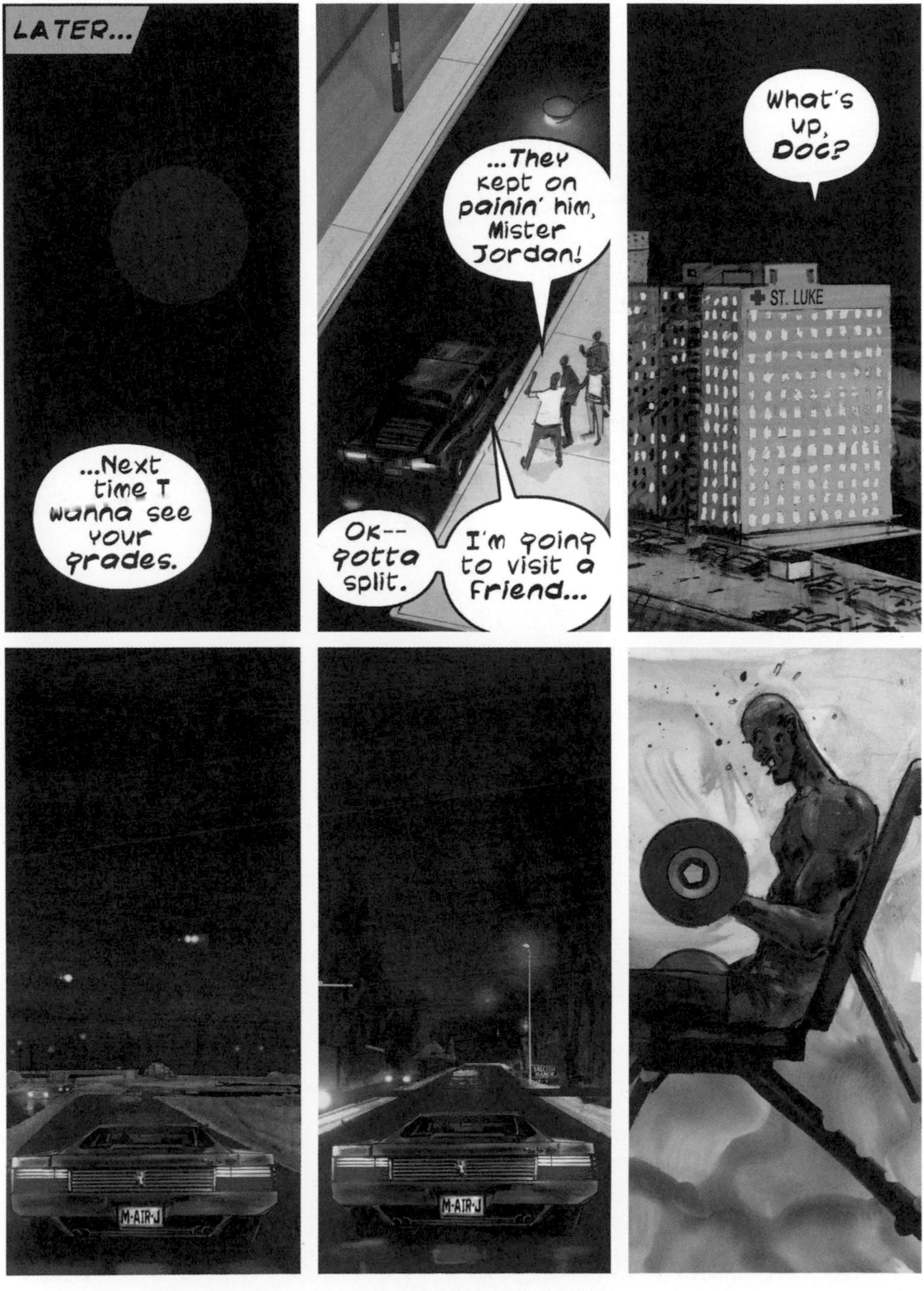
LATER...
...Next time I wanna see your grades.
...They kept on painin' him, Mister Jordan!
Ok-- gotta split.
I'm going to visit a friend...
What's up, Doc?
ST. LUKE
M-AIR-J
M-AIR-J

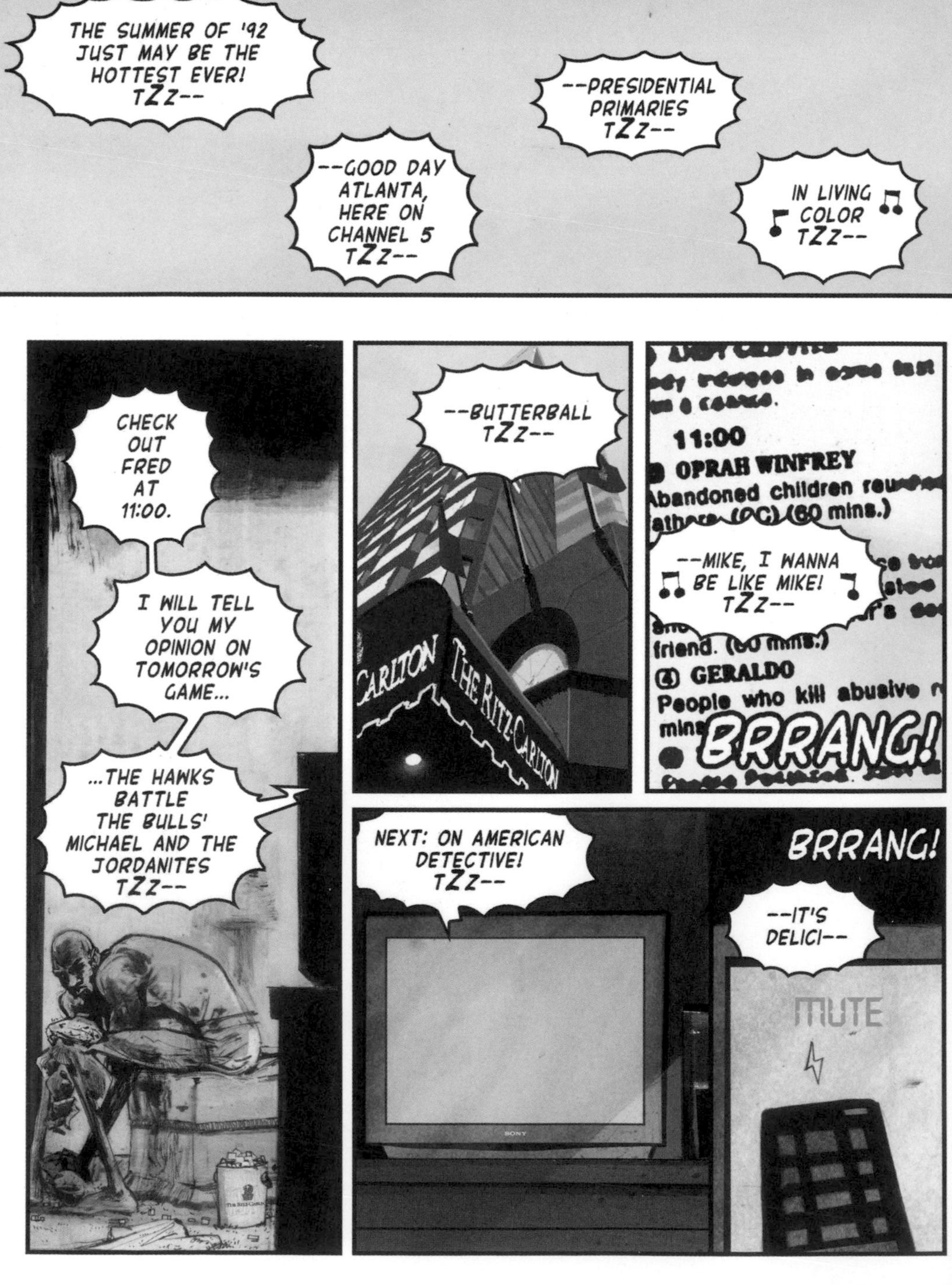
THE SUMMER OF '92 JUST MAY BE THE HOTTEST EVER! TZZ--
--GOOD DAY ATLANTA, HERE ON CHANNEL 5 TZZ--
--PRESIDENTIAL PRIMARIES TZZ--
IN LIVING COLOR TZZ--
CHECK OUT FRED AT 11:00.
I WILL TELL YOU MY OPINION ON TOMORROW'S GAME...
...THE HAWKS BATTLE THE BULLS' MICHAEL AND THE JORDANITES TZZ--
--BUTTERBALL TZZ--
THE RITZ-CARLTON
11:00
OPRAH WINFREY
friend.
GERALDO
People who kill abusive
--MIKE, I WANNA BE LIKE MIKE! TZZ--
BRRANG!
NEXT: ON AMERICAN DETECTIVE! TZZ--
BRRANG!
--IT'S DELICI--
MUTE
SONY

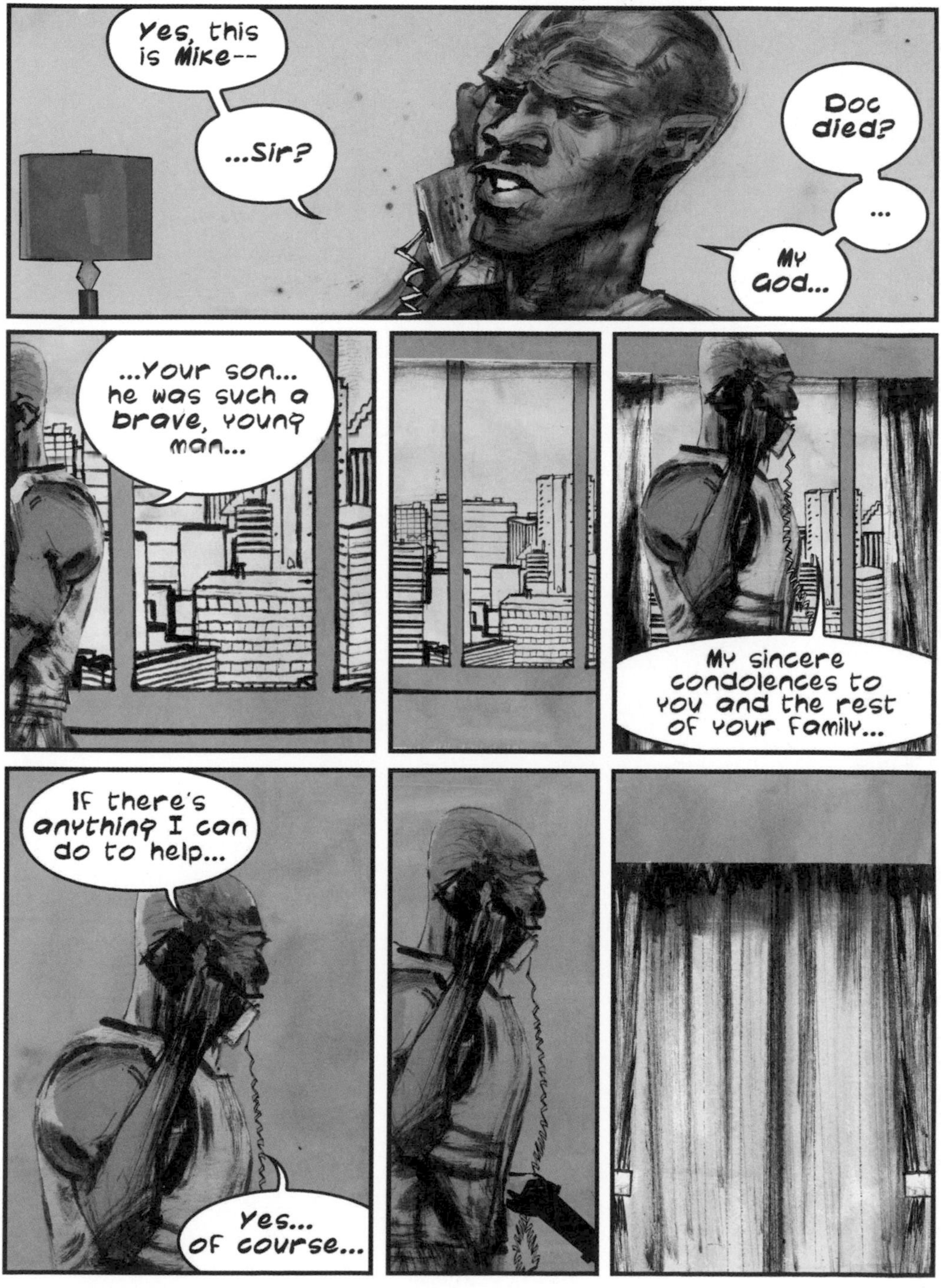
Yes, this is Mike--
...Sir?
Doc died?
...
My God...
...Your son... he was such a brave, young man...
My sincere condolences to you and the rest of your family...
If there's anything I can do to help...
Yes... of course...

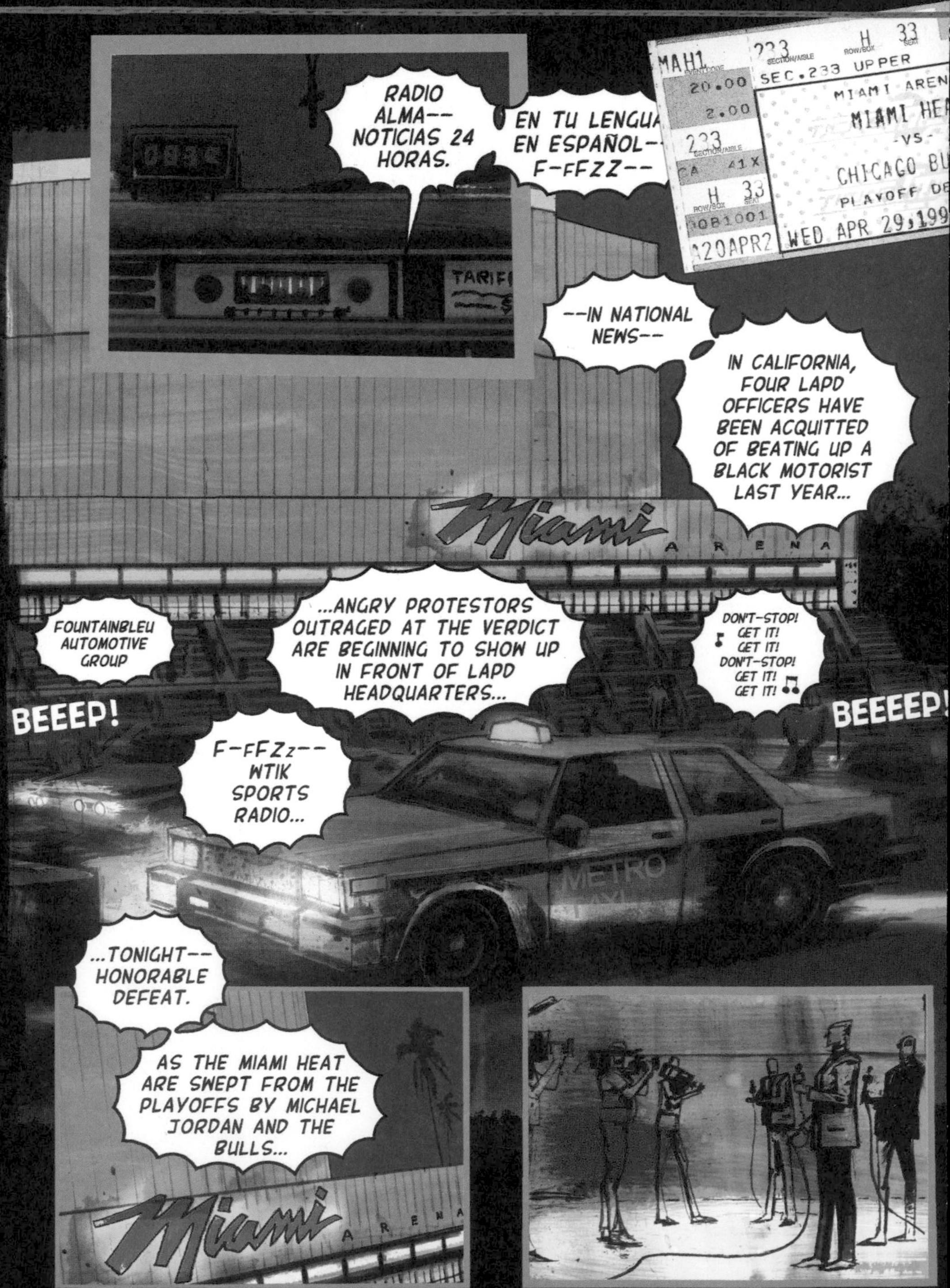
RADIO ALMA-- NOTICIAS 24 HORAS.
EN TU LENGUA EN ESPAÑOL-- F-FFZZ--
MAH1 233 H 33
SEC.233 UPPER
MIAMI AREN
MIAMI HEA
-VS-
CHICAGO BU
PLAYOFF DE
WED APR 29,199
--IN NATIONAL NEWS--
IN CALIFORNIA, FOUR LAPD OFFICERS HAVE BEEN ACQUITTED OF BEATING UP A BLACK MOTORIST LAST YEAR...
Miami ARENA
FOUNTAINBLEU AUTOMOTIVE GROUP
...ANGRY PROTESTORS OUTRAGED AT THE VERDICT ARE BEGINNING TO SHOW UP IN FRONT OF LAPD HEADQUARTERS...
DON'T-STOP! GET IT! GET IT! DON'T-STOP! GET IT! GET IT!
BEEEP!
BEEEEP!
F-FFZz-- WTIK SPORTS RADIO...
METRO
...TONIGHT-- HONORABLE DEFEAT.
AS THE MIAMI HEAT ARE SWEPT FROM THE PLAYOFFS BY MICHAEL JORDAN AND THE BULLS...
Miami ARENA

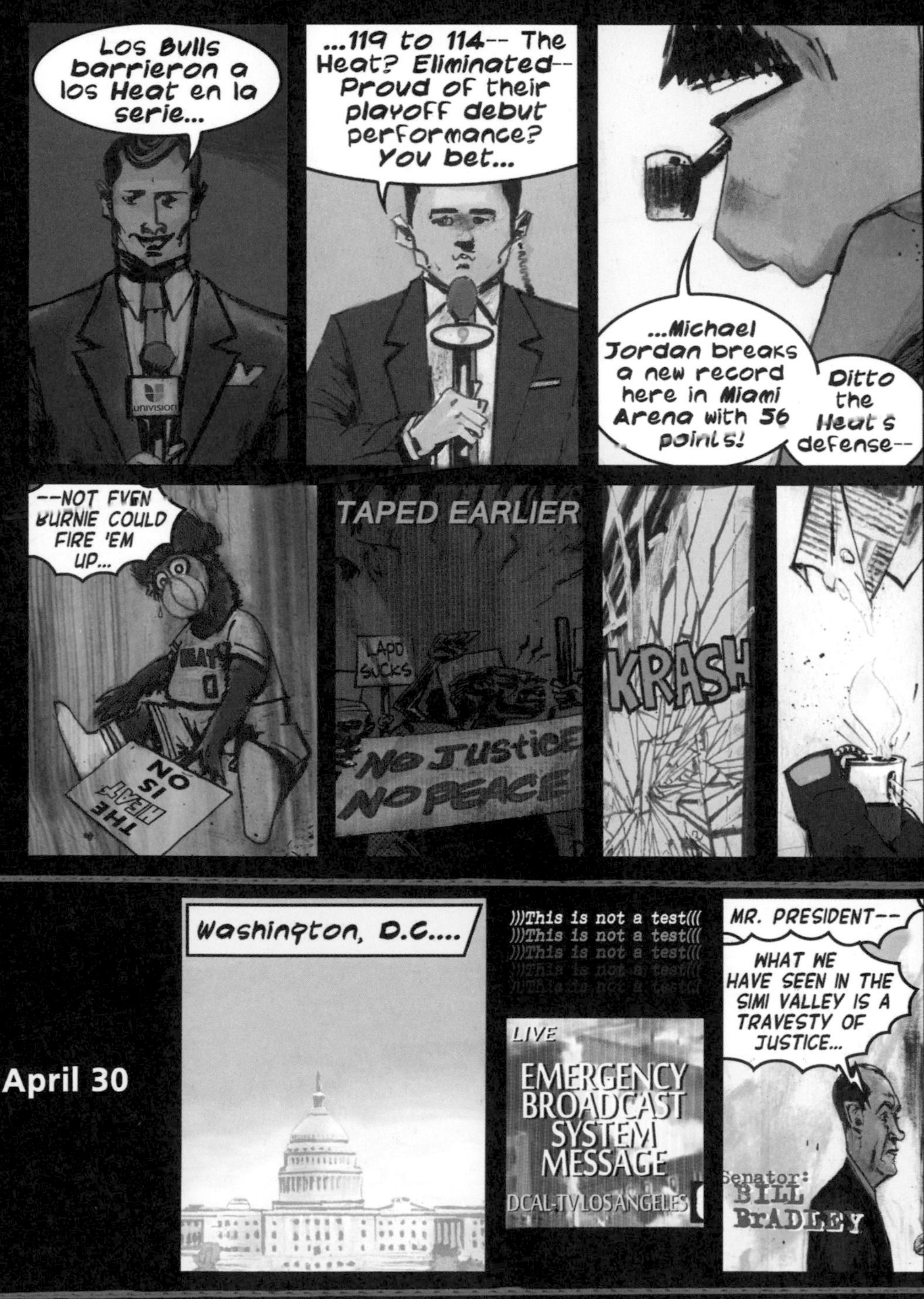
Los Bulls barrieron a los Heat en la serie...
univision
...119 to 114-- The Heat? Eliminated-- Proud of their playoff debut performance? You bet...
...Michael Jordan breaks a new record here in Miami Arena with 56 points!
Ditto the Heat's defense--
--NOT EVEN BURNIE COULD FIRE 'EM UP...
THE HEAT IS ON
TAPED EARLIER
LAPD SUCKS
NO JUSTICE NO PEACE
KRASH
April 30
Washington, D.C....
)))This is not a test(((
)))This is not a test(((
)))This is not a test(((
LIVE
EMERGENCY BROADCAST SYSTEM MESSAGE
DCAL-TV LOS ANGELES
MR. PRESIDENT--
WHAT WE HAVE SEEN IN THE SIMI VALLEY IS A TRAVESTY OF JUSTICE...
Senator: BILL BRADLEY

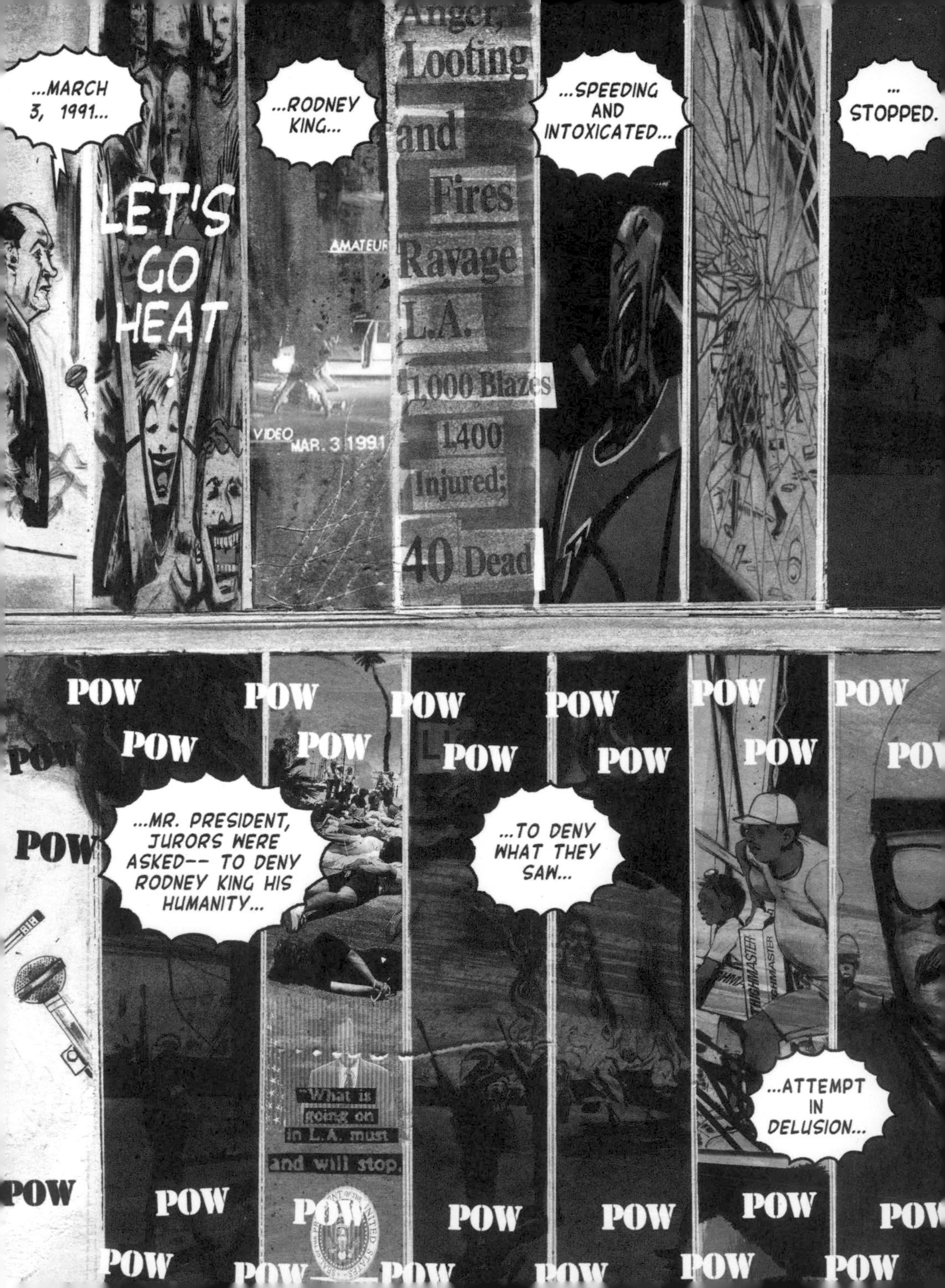
...MARCH 3, 1991...
LET'S GO HEAT!
...RODNEY KING...
AMATEUR
VIDEO MAR. 3 1991
Anger, Looting and Fires Ravage L.A.
1,000 Blazes
1,400 Injured;
40 Dead
...SPEEDING AND INTOXICATED...
... STOPPED.
POW
...MR. PRESIDENT, JURORS WERE ASKED-- TO DENY RODNEY KING HIS HUMANITY...
...TO DENY WHAT THEY SAW...
"What is going on in L.A. must and will stop."
...ATTEMPT IN DELUSION...

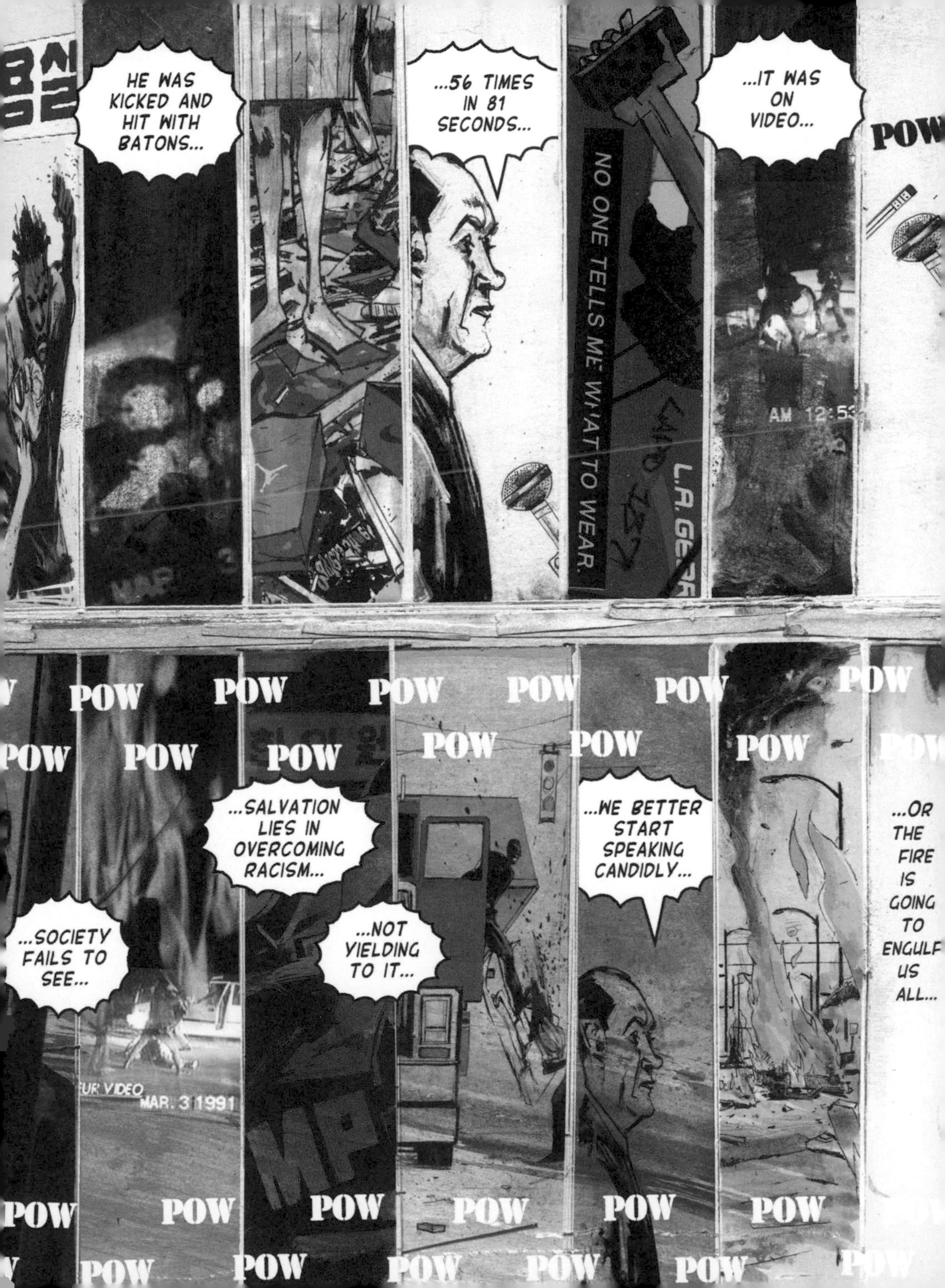
HE WAS KICKED AND HIT WITH BATONS...
...56 TIMES IN 81 SECONDS...
NO ONE TELLS ME WHAT TO WEAR.
L.A. GEAR
...IT WAS ON VIDEO...
POW
AM 12:53
POW
POW
POW
POW
POW
POW
POW
POW
POW
POW
POW
POW
POW
...SALVATION LIES IN OVERCOMING RACISM...
...WE BETTER START SPEAKING CANDIDLY...
...OR THE FIRE IS GOING TO ENGULF US ALL...
...SOCIETY FAILS TO SEE...
...NOT YIELDING TO IT...
MAR. 3 1991
POW
POW
POW
POW
POW
POW
POW
POW
POW
POW
POW
POW
POW

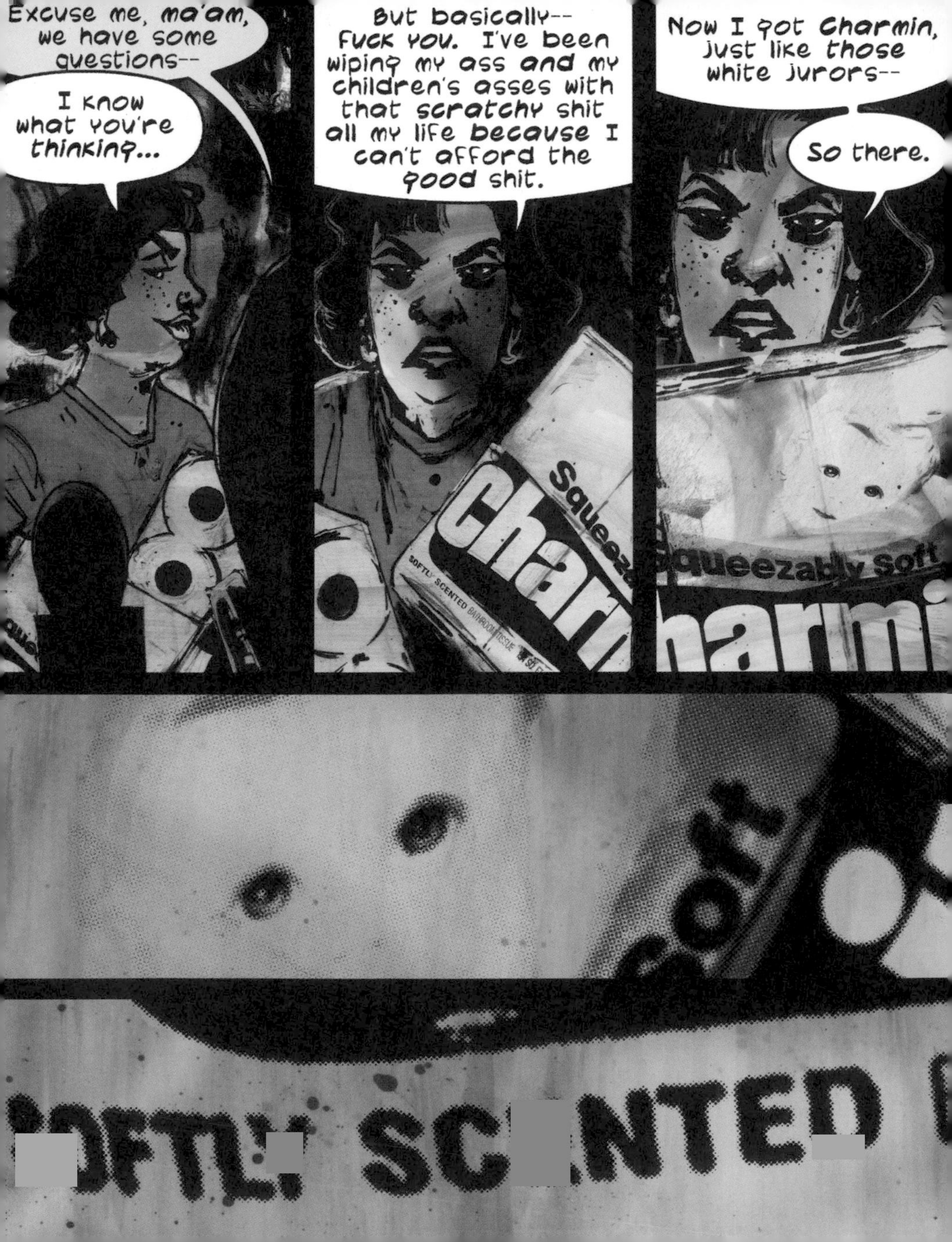
Excuse me, ma'am, we have some questions--
I know what you're thinking...
But basically-- Fuck you. I've been wiping my ass and my children's asses with that scratchy shit all my life because I can't afford the good shit.
Now I got Charmin, just like those white jurors--
So there.
Squeezably soft
soft

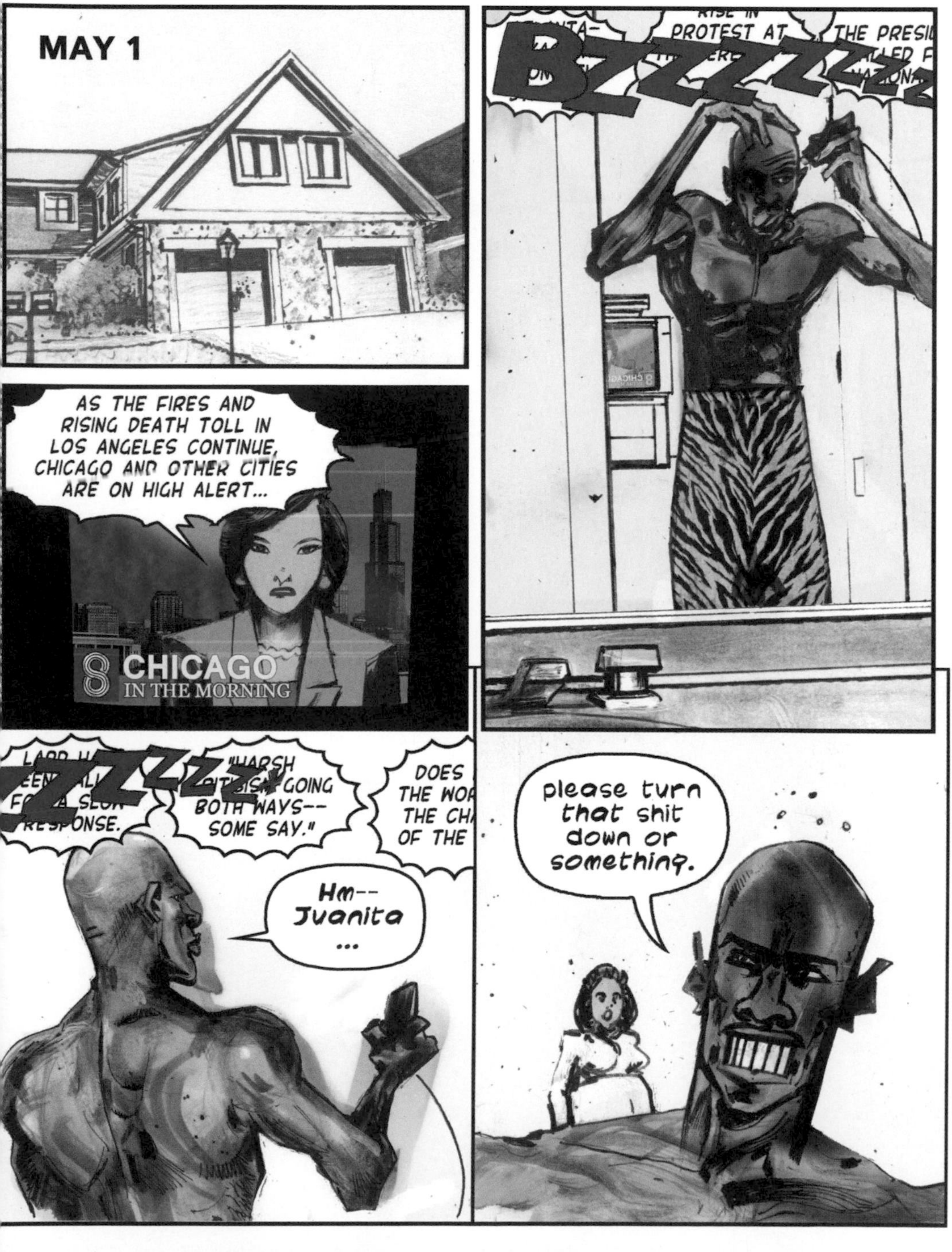
MAY 1
AS THE FIRES AND RISING DEATH TOLL IN LOS ANGELES CONTINUE, CHICAGO AND OTHER CITIES ARE ON HIGH ALERT...
CHICAGO
IN THE MORNING
PROTEST AT
THE PRESI
BZZZZZzzz
RESPONSE.
BOTH WAYS--
SOME SAY."
DOES
THE WOR
THE CH
OF THE
Hm--
Juanita
...
please turn that shit down or something.

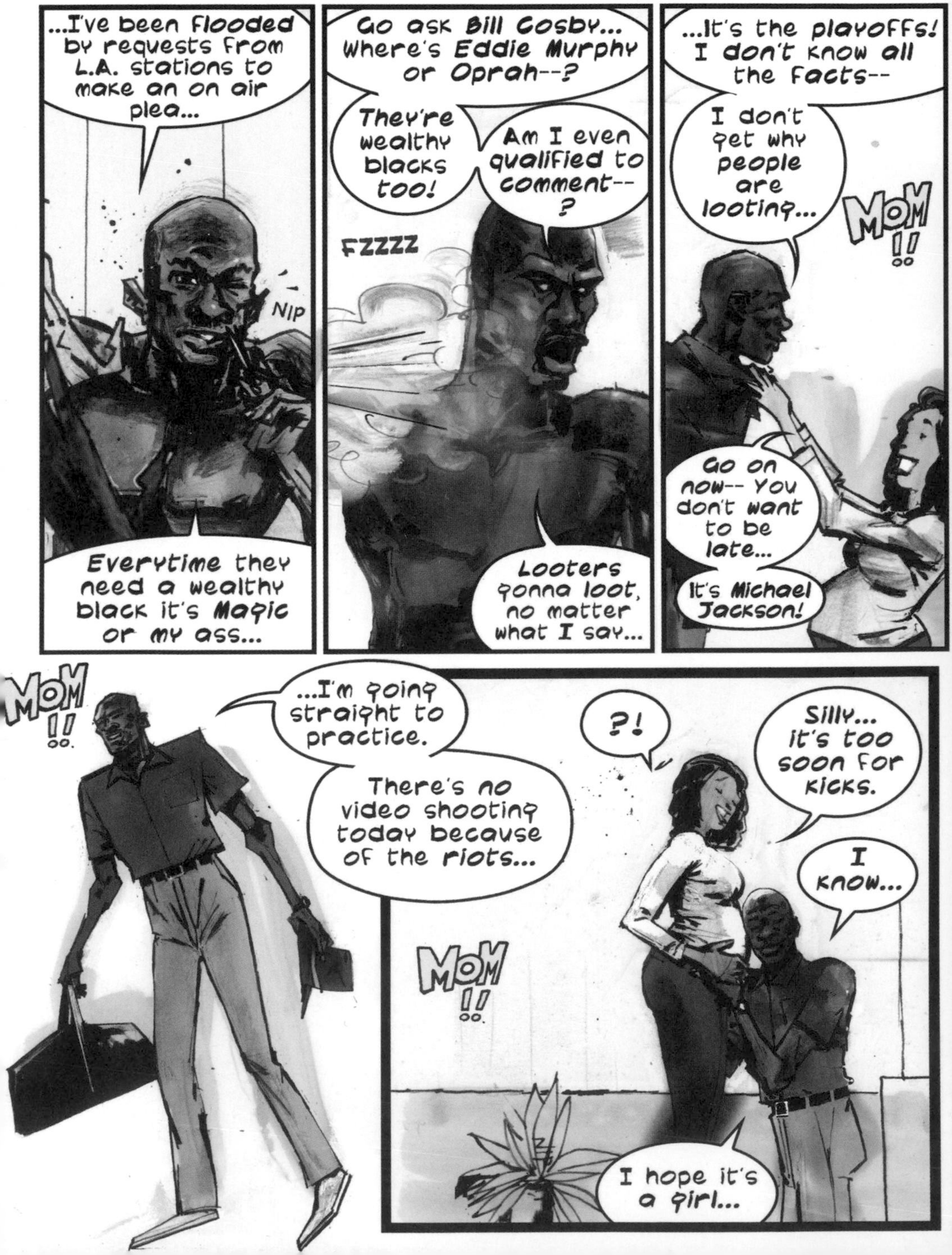
...I've been flooded by requests from L.A. stations to make an on air plea...
NIP
Everytime they need a wealthy black it's Magic or my ass...
Go ask Bill Cosby... Where's Eddie Murphy or Oprah--?
They're wealthy blacks too!
Am I even qualified to comment--?
FZZZZ
Looters gonna loot, no matter what I say...
...It's the playoffs! I don't know all the facts--
I don't get why people are looting...
MOM!!
Go on now-- You don't want to be late...
It's Michael Jackson!
MOM!!
...I'm going straight to practice.
There's no video shooting today because of the riots...
?!
Silly... it's too soon for kicks.
I know...
MOM!!
I hope it's a girl...

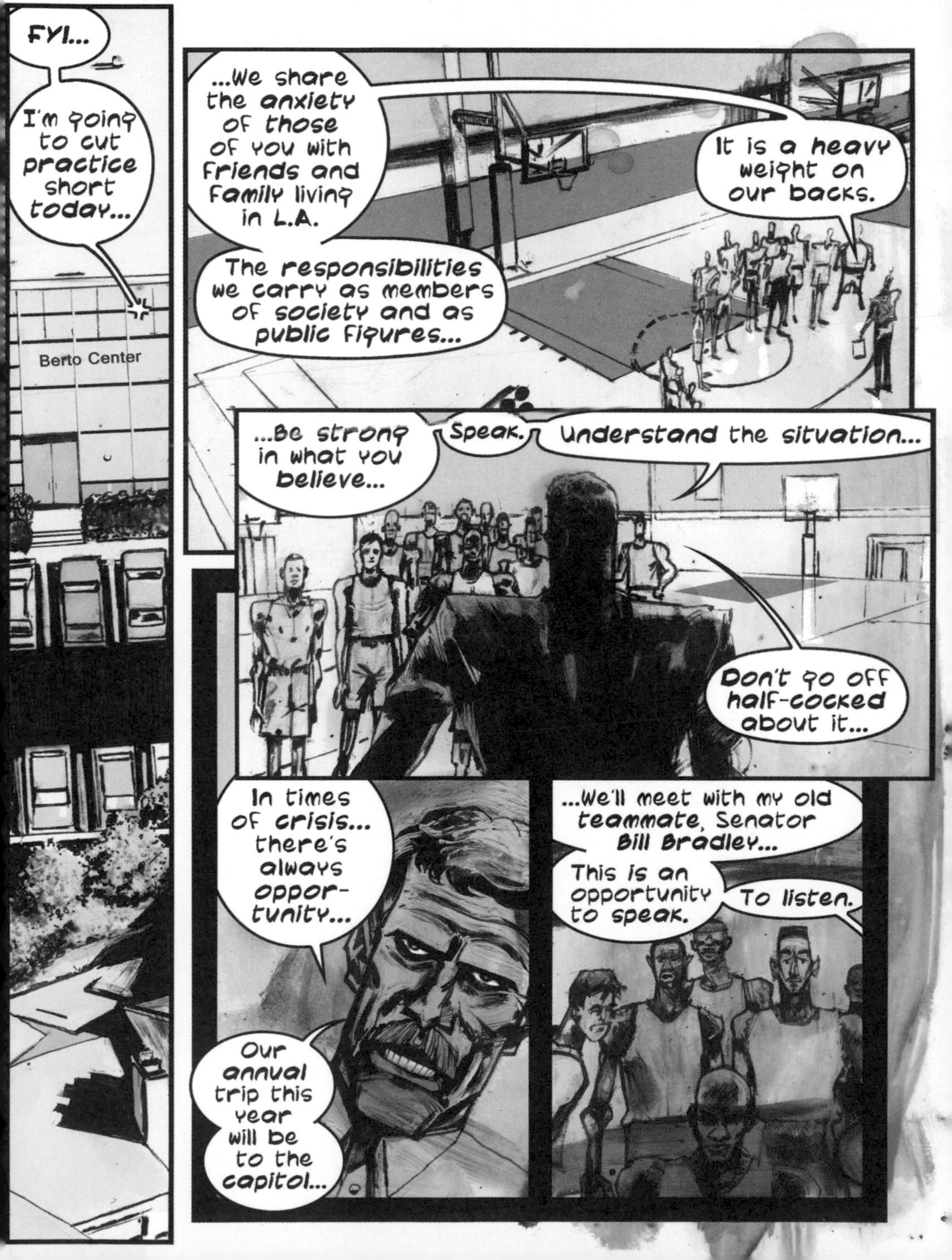
FYI...
I'm going to cut practice short today...
Berto Center
...We share the anxiety of those of you with friends and family living in L.A.
The responsibilities we carry as members of society and as public figures...
It is a heavy weight on our backs.
...Be strong in what you believe...
Speak.
Understand the situation...
Don't go off half-cocked about it...
In times of crisis... there's always oppor-tunity...
Our annual trip this year will be to the capitol...
...We'll meet with my old teammate, Senator Bill Bradley...
This is an opportunity to speak.
To listen.

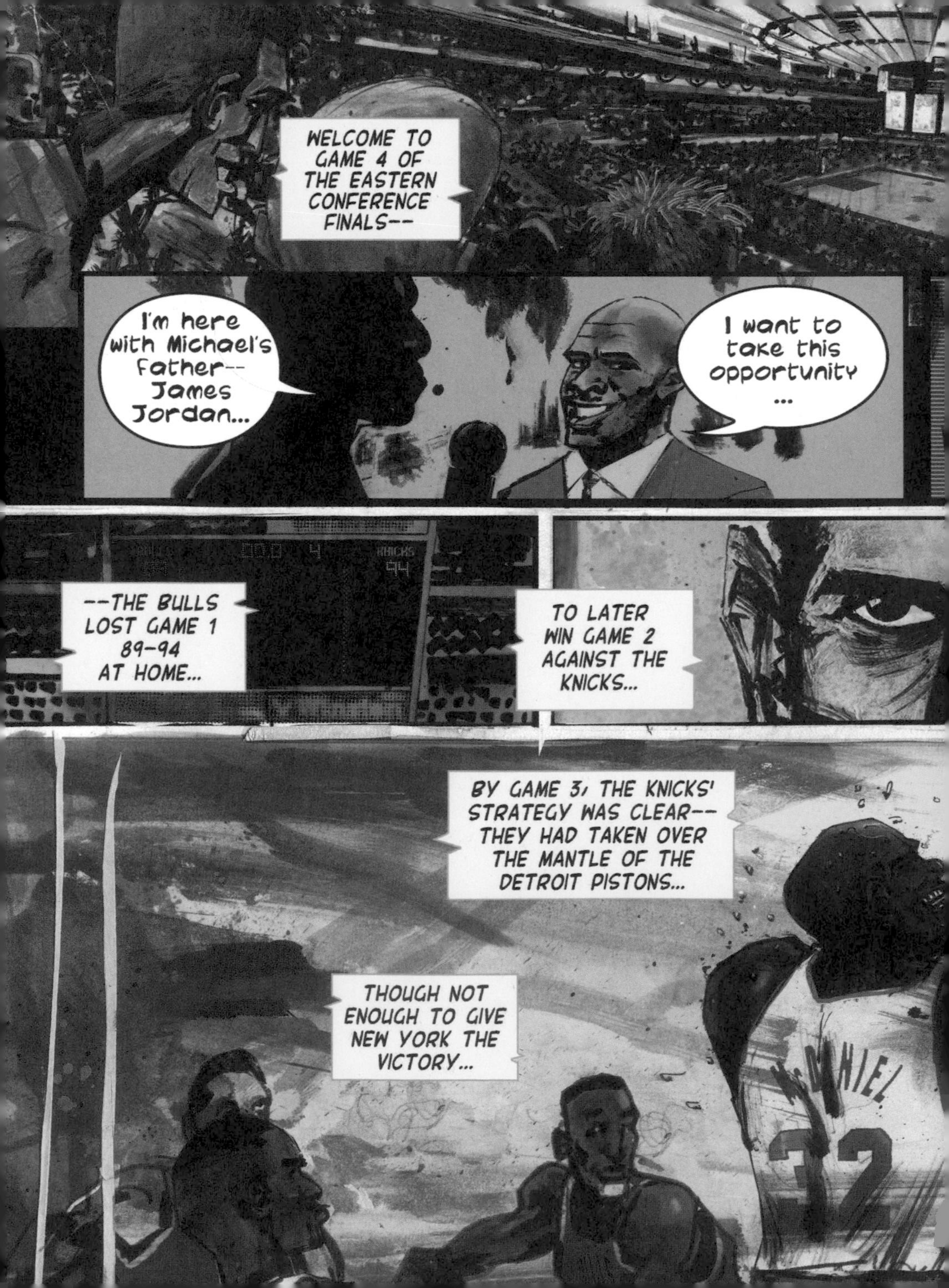

WELCOME TO GAME 4 OF THE EASTERN CONFERENCE FINALS--
I'm here with Michael's father-- James Jordan...
I want to take this opportunity ...
--THE BULLS LOST GAME 1 89-94 AT HOME...
TO LATER WIN GAME 2 AGAINST THE KNICKS...
BY GAME 3, THE KNICKS' STRATEGY WAS CLEAR-- THEY HAD TAKEN OVER THE MANTLE OF THE DETROIT PISTONS...
THOUGH NOT ENOUGH TO GIVE NEW YORK THE VICTORY...

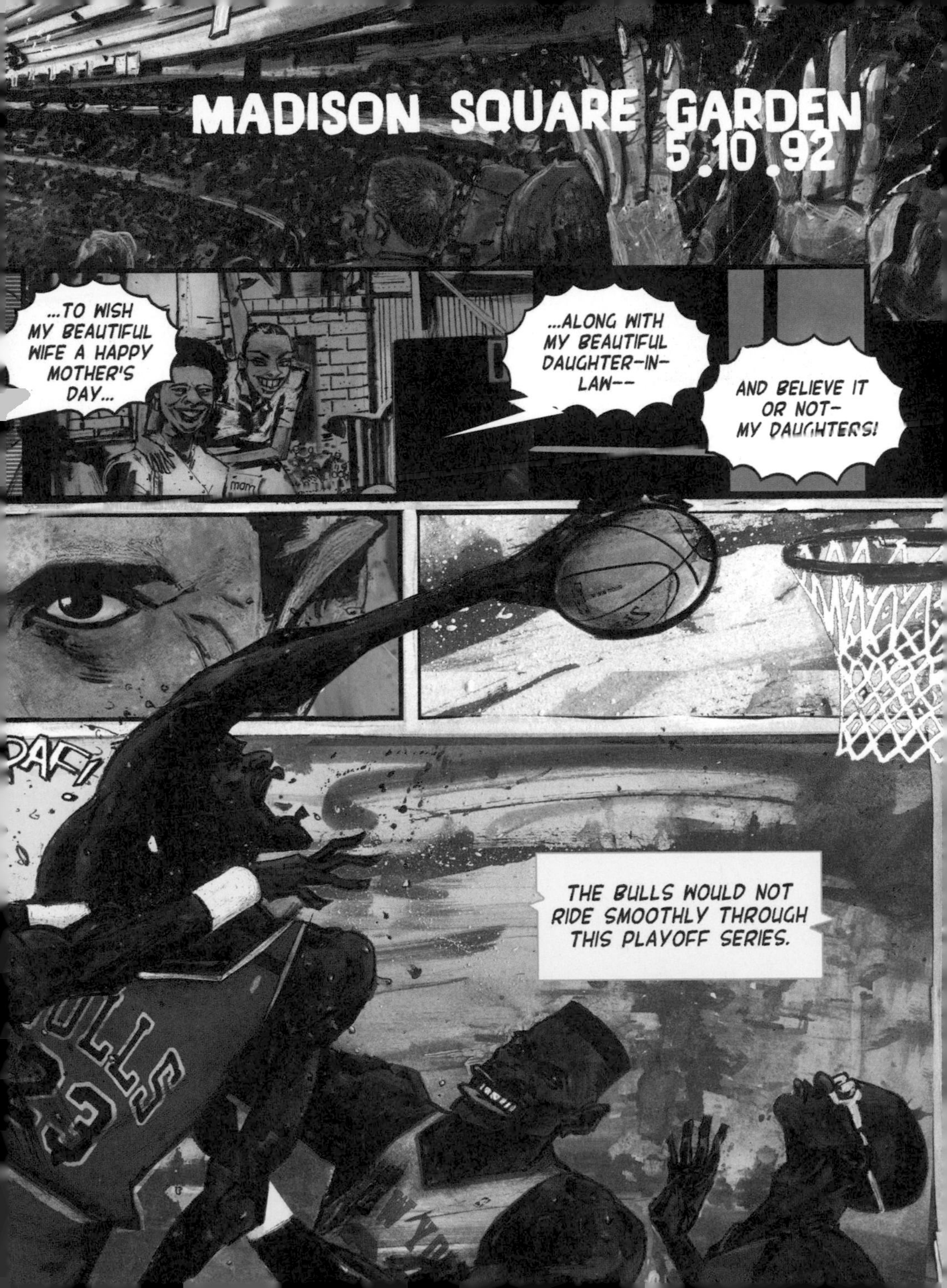
MADISON SQUARE GARDEN
5.10.92
...TO WISH MY BEAUTIFUL WIFE A HAPPY MOTHER'S DAY...
...ALONG WITH MY BEAUTIFUL DAUGHTER-IN-LAW--
AND BELIEVE IT OR NOT- MY DAUGHTERS!
THE BULLS WOULD NOT RIDE SMOOTHLY THROUGH THIS PLAYOFF SERIES.

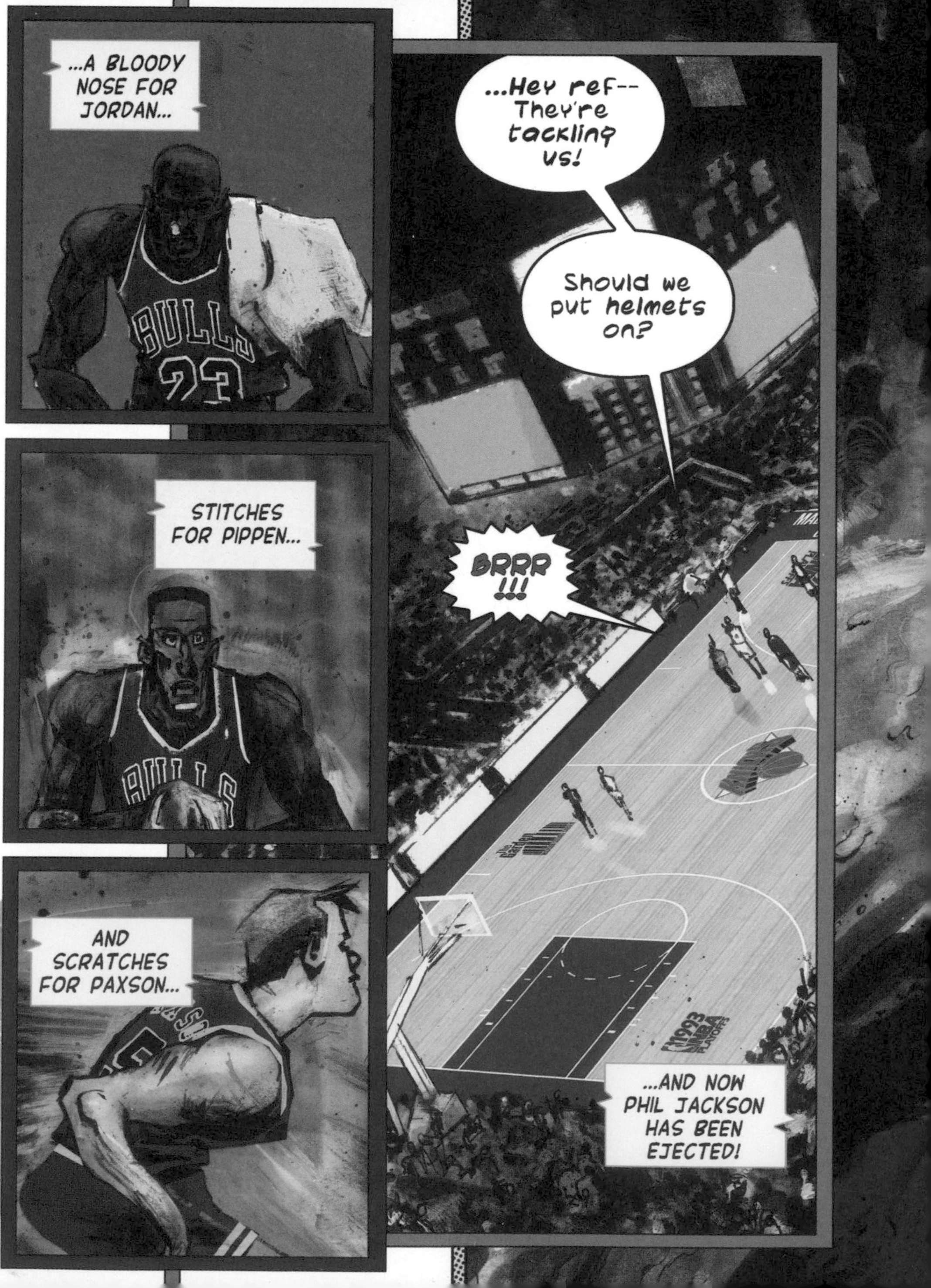
...A BLOODY NOSE FOR JORDAN...
STITCHES FOR PIPPEN...
AND SCRATCHES FOR PAXSON...
...Hey ref-- They're tackling us!
Should we put helmets on?
BRRR !!!
...AND NOW PHIL JACKSON HAS BEEN EJECTED!

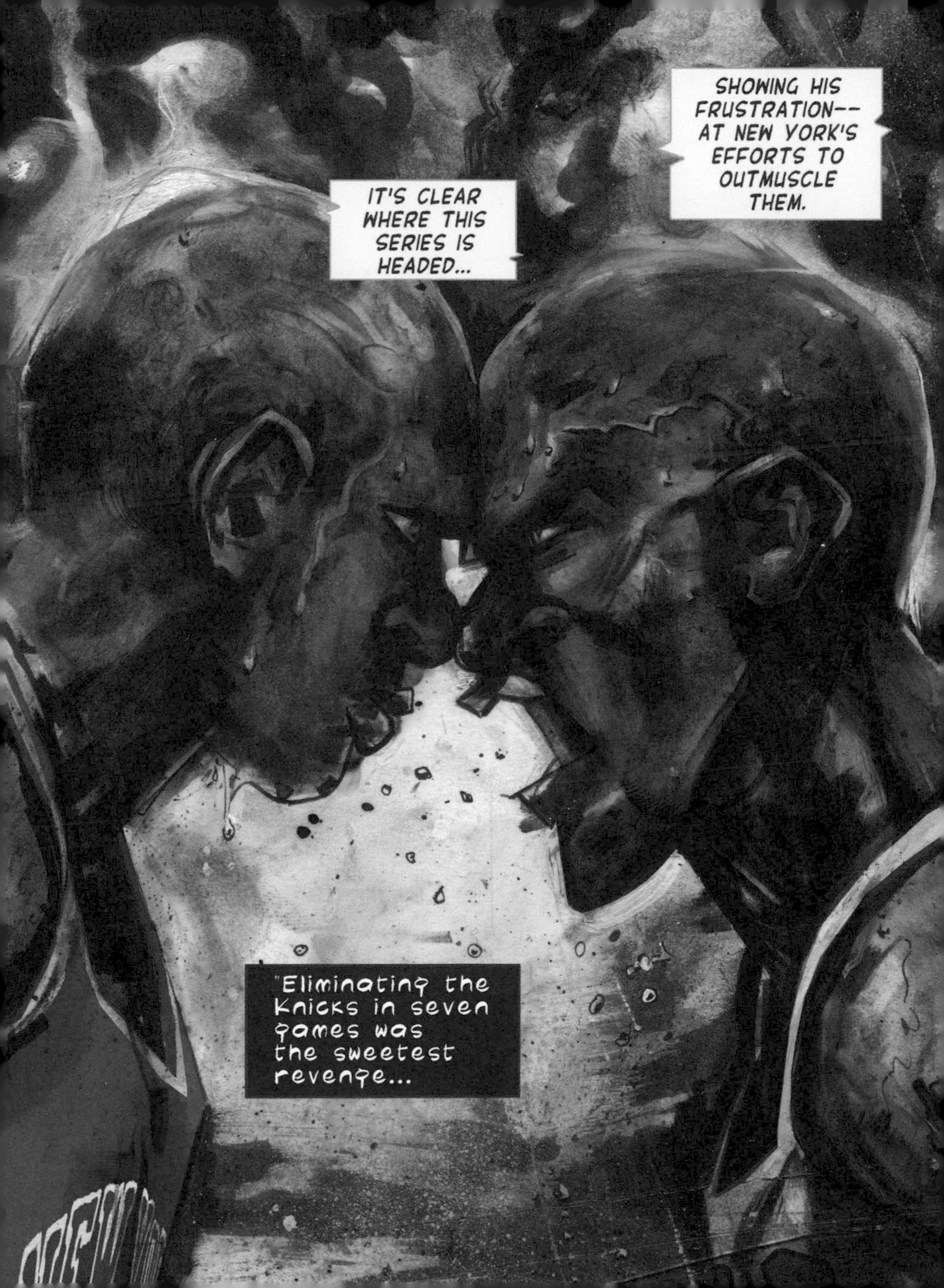
IT'S CLEAR WHERE THIS SERIES IS HEADED...
SHOWING HIS FRUSTRATION-- AT NEW YORK'S EFFORTS TO OUTMUSCLE THEM.
"Eliminating the Knicks in seven games was the sweetest revenge...

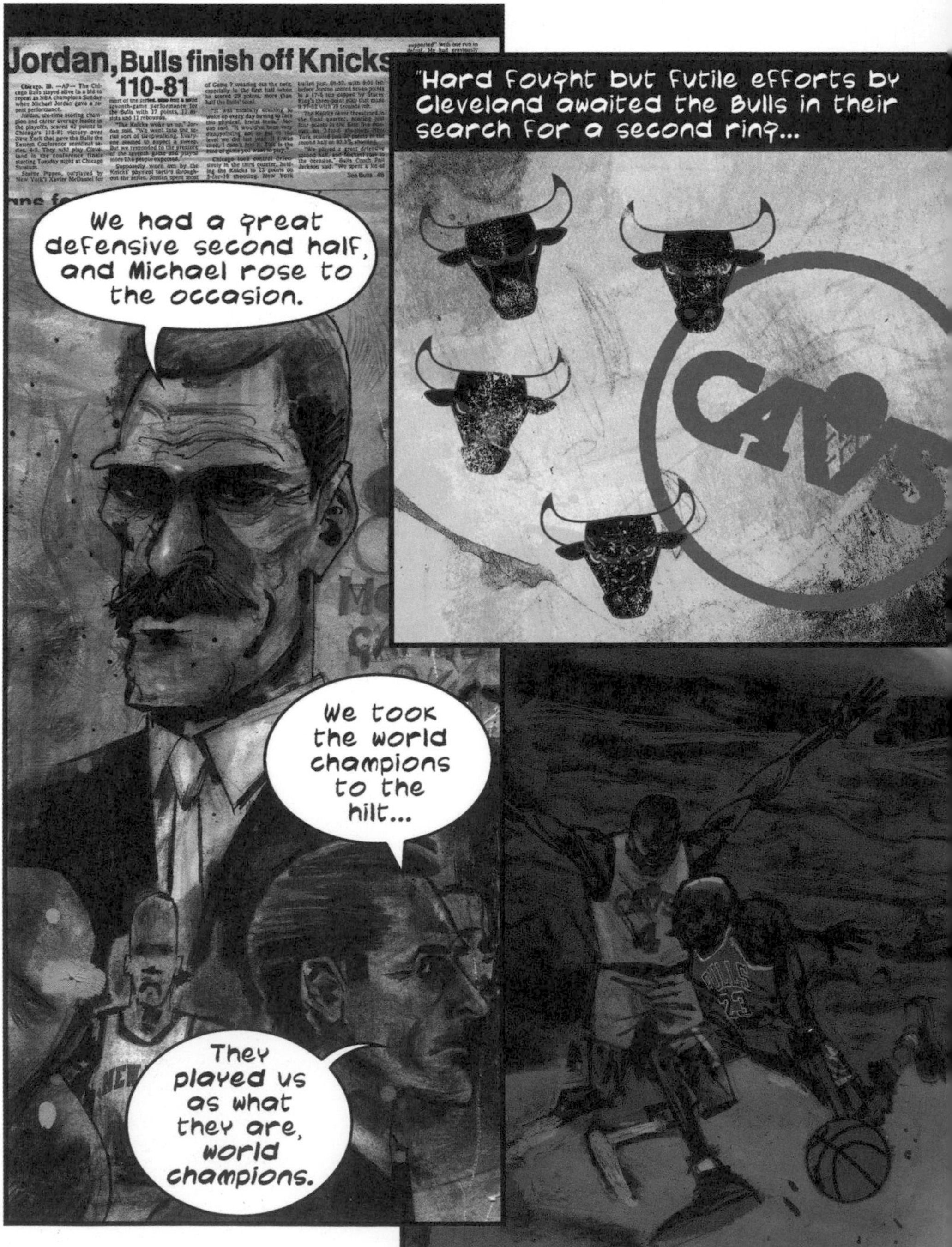

Jordan, Bulls finish off Knicks 110-81
We had a great defensive second half, and Michael rose to the occasion.
We took the world champions to the hilt...
They played us as what they are, world champions.
"Hard fought but futile efforts by Cleveland awaited the Bulls in their search for a second ring...
CAVS

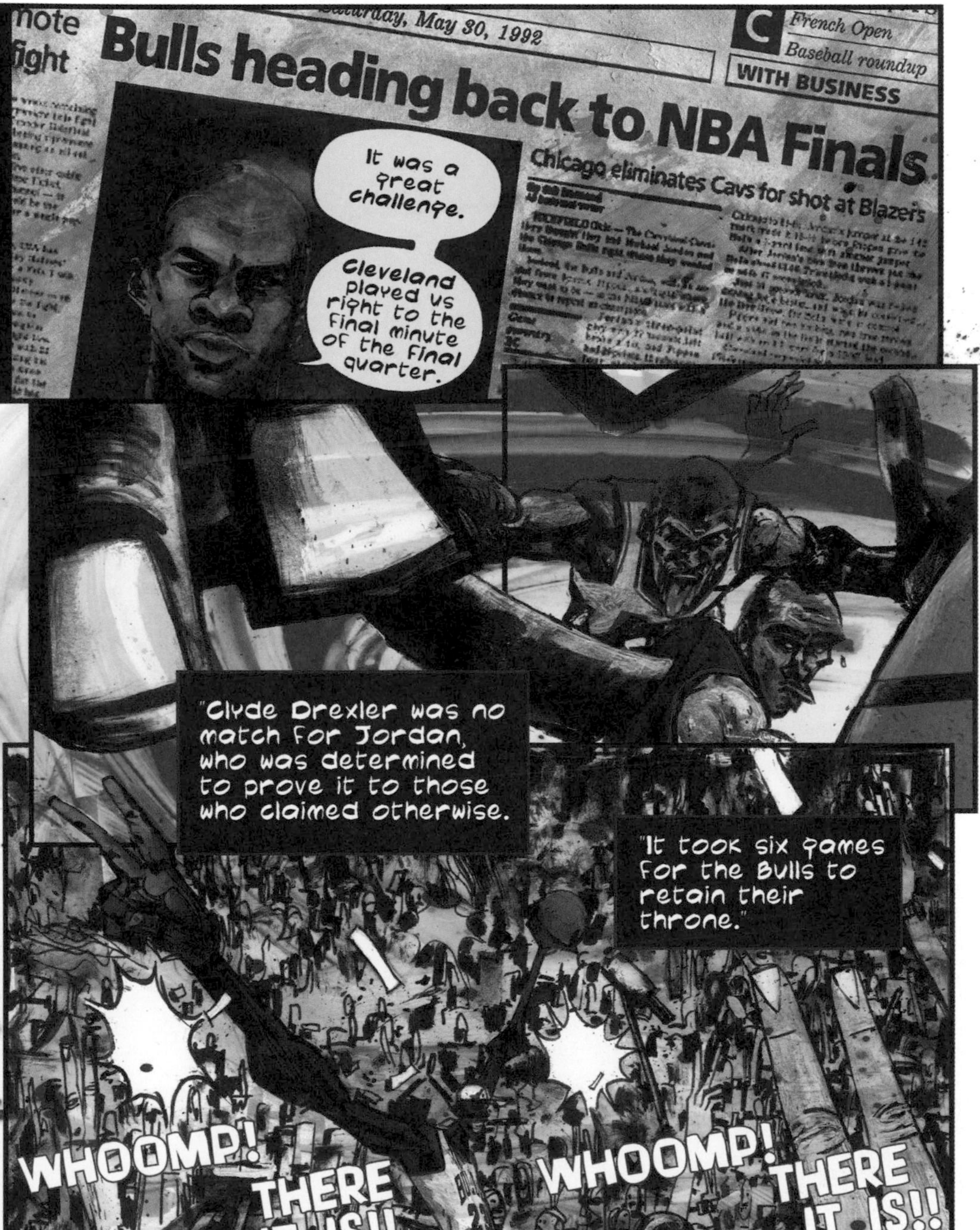
Saturday, May 30, 1992
Bulls heading back to NBA Finals
Chicago eliminates Cavs for shot at Blazers
C
French Open
Baseball roundup
WITH BUSINESS
It was a great challenge.
Cleveland played us right to the final minute of the final quarter.
"Clyde Drexler was no match for Jordan, who was determined to prove it to those who claimed otherwise.
"It took six games for the Bulls to retain their throne."
WHOOMP! THERE IT IS!!
WHOOMP! THERE IT IS!!

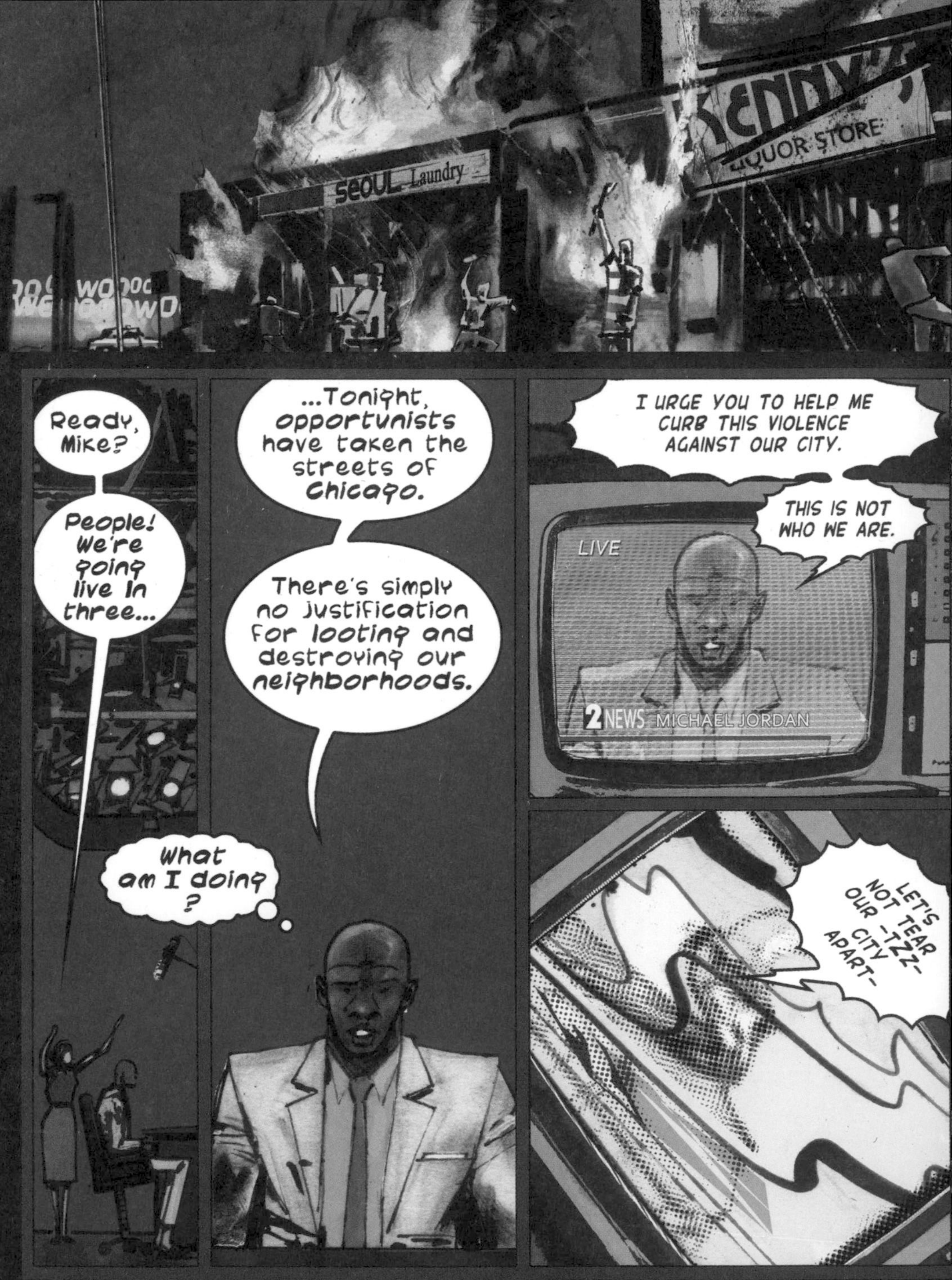

SEOUL Laundry
KENNY'S LIQUOR STORE
Ready, Mike?
People! We're going live in three...
...Tonight, opportunists have taken the streets of Chicago.
There's simply no justification for looting and destroying our neighborhoods.
What am I doing?
I URGE YOU TO HELP ME CURB THIS VIOLENCE AGAINST OUR CITY.
THIS IS NOT WHO WE ARE.
LIVE
2NEWS MICHAEL JORDAN
LET'S NOT TEAR OUR -TZZ- CITY APART-

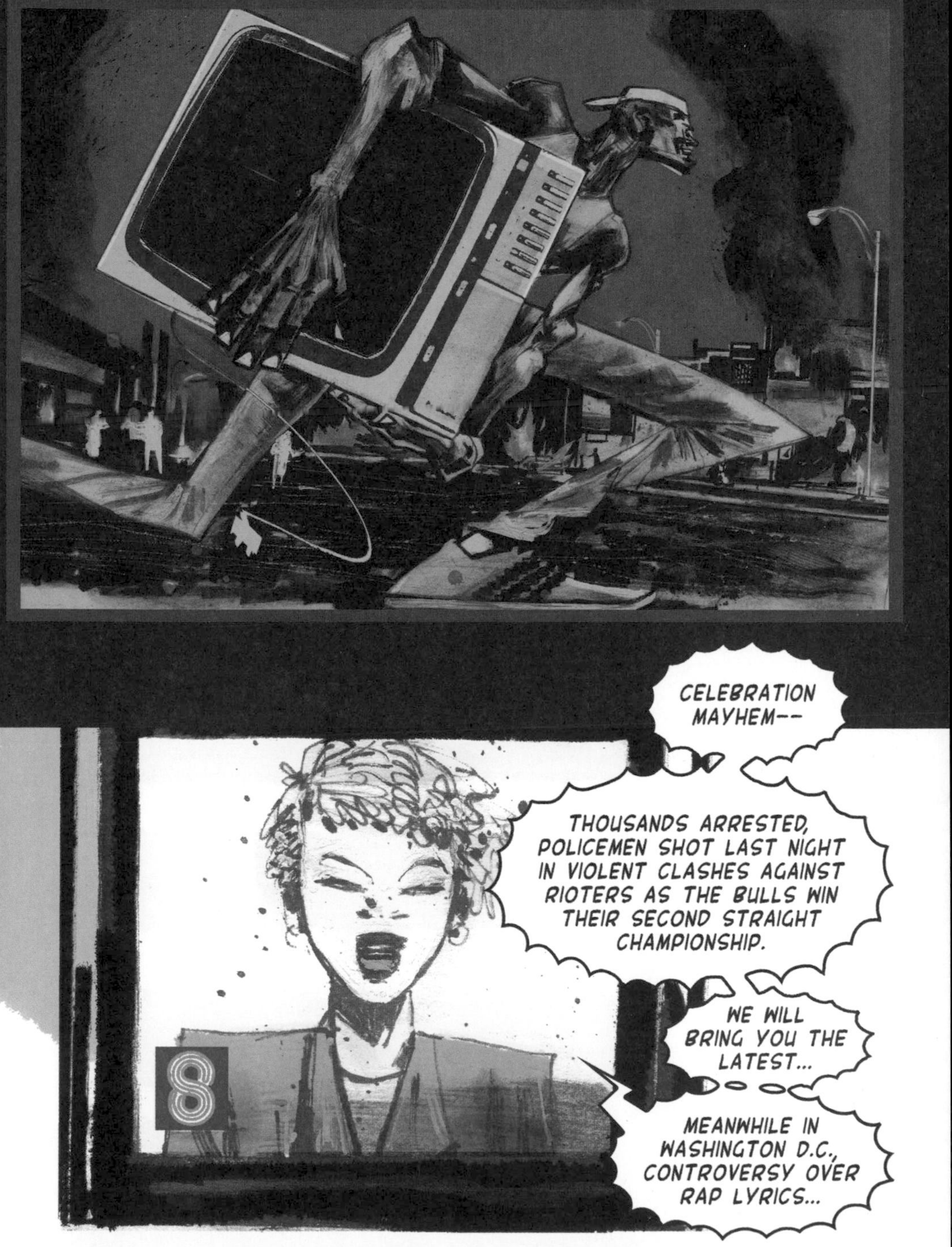
CELEBRATION MAYHEM--
THOUSANDS ARRESTED, POLICEMEN SHOT LAST NIGHT IN VIOLENT CLASHES AGAINST RIOTERS AS THE BULLS WIN THEIR SECOND STRAIGHT CHAMPIONSHIP.
WE WILL BRING YOU THE LATEST...
MEANWHILE IN WASHINGTON D.C., CONTROVERSY OVER RAP LYRICS...
8

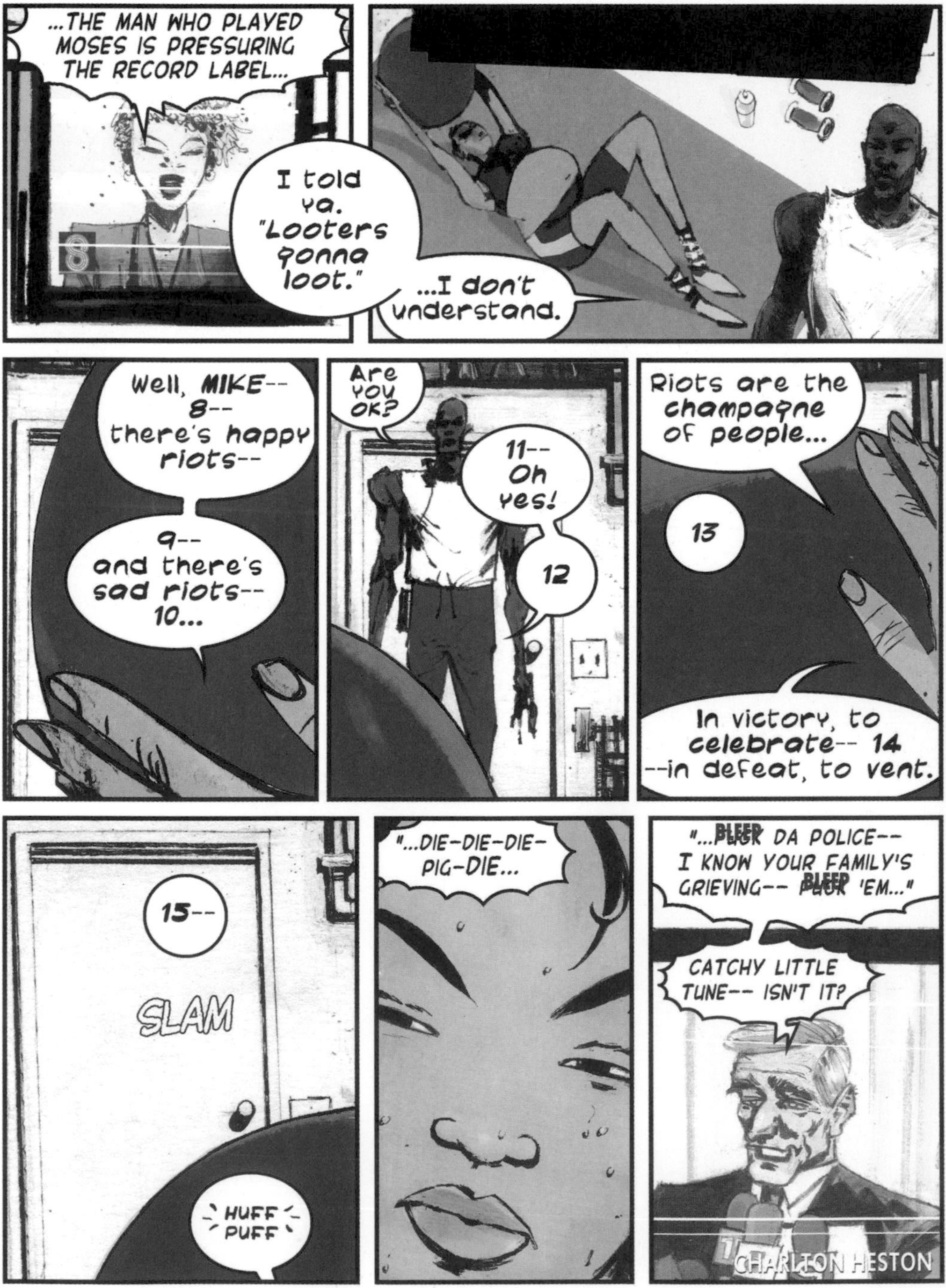

...THE MAN WHO PLAYED MOSES IS PRESSURING THE RECORD LABEL...
I told ya. "Looters gonna loot."
...I don't understand.
Well, MIKE-- 8-- there's happy riots--
9-- and there's sad riots-- 10...
Are you OK?
11-- Oh yes!
12
Riots are the champagne of people...
13
In victory, to celebrate-- 14 --in defeat, to vent.
15--
SLAM
HUFF PUFF
"...DIE-DIE-DIE-PIG-DIE...
"...BLEEP DA POLICE-- I KNOW YOUR FAMILY'S GRIEVING-- BLEEP 'EM..."
CATCHY LITTLE TUNE-- ISN'T IT?
CHARLTON HESTON

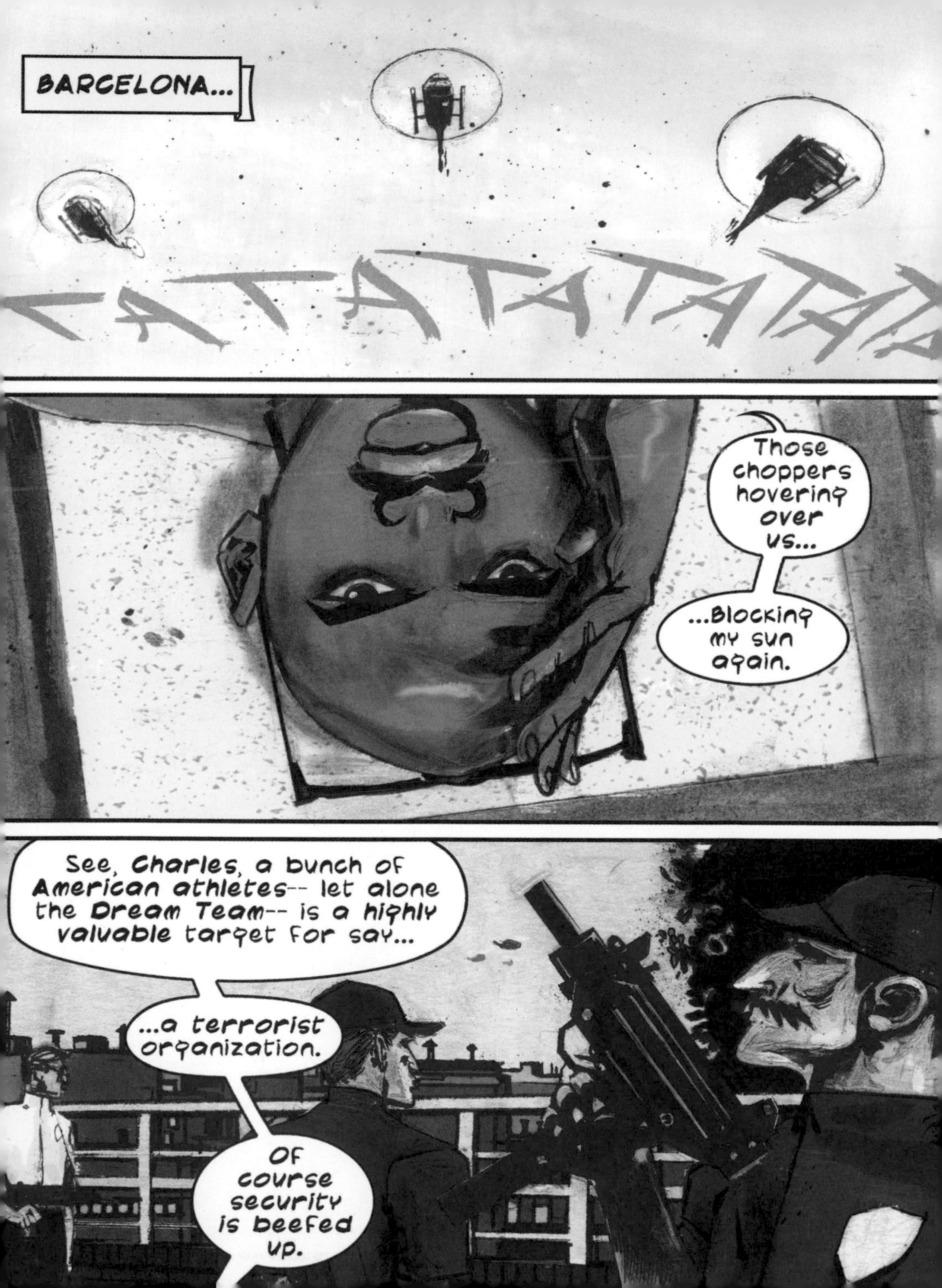
BARCELONA...
Those choppers hovering over us...
...Blocking my sun again.
See, Charles, a bunch of American athletes-- let alone the Dream Team-- is a highly valuable target for say...
...a terrorist organization.
Of course security is beefed up.

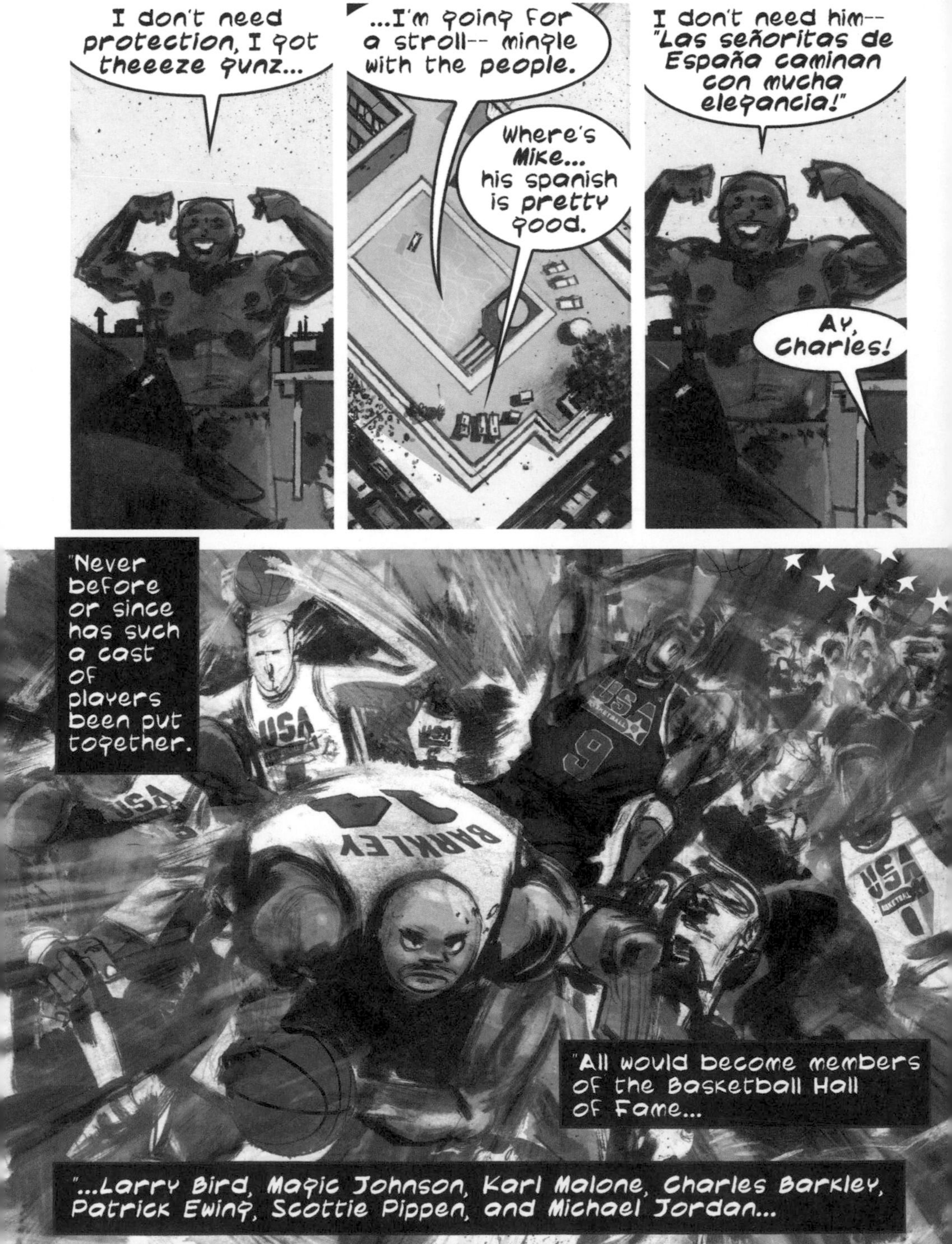
I don't need protection, I got theeeze gunz...
...I'm going for a stroll-- mingle with the people.
Where's Mike... his spanish is pretty good.
I don't need him-- "Las señoritas de España caminan con mucha elegancia!"
Ay, Charles!
"Never before or since has such a cast of players been put together.
USA
BARKLEY
14
USA
9
"All would become members of the Basketball Hall of Fame...
"...Larry Bird, Magic Johnson, Karl Malone, Charles Barkley, Patrick Ewing, Scottie Pippen, and Michael Jordan...

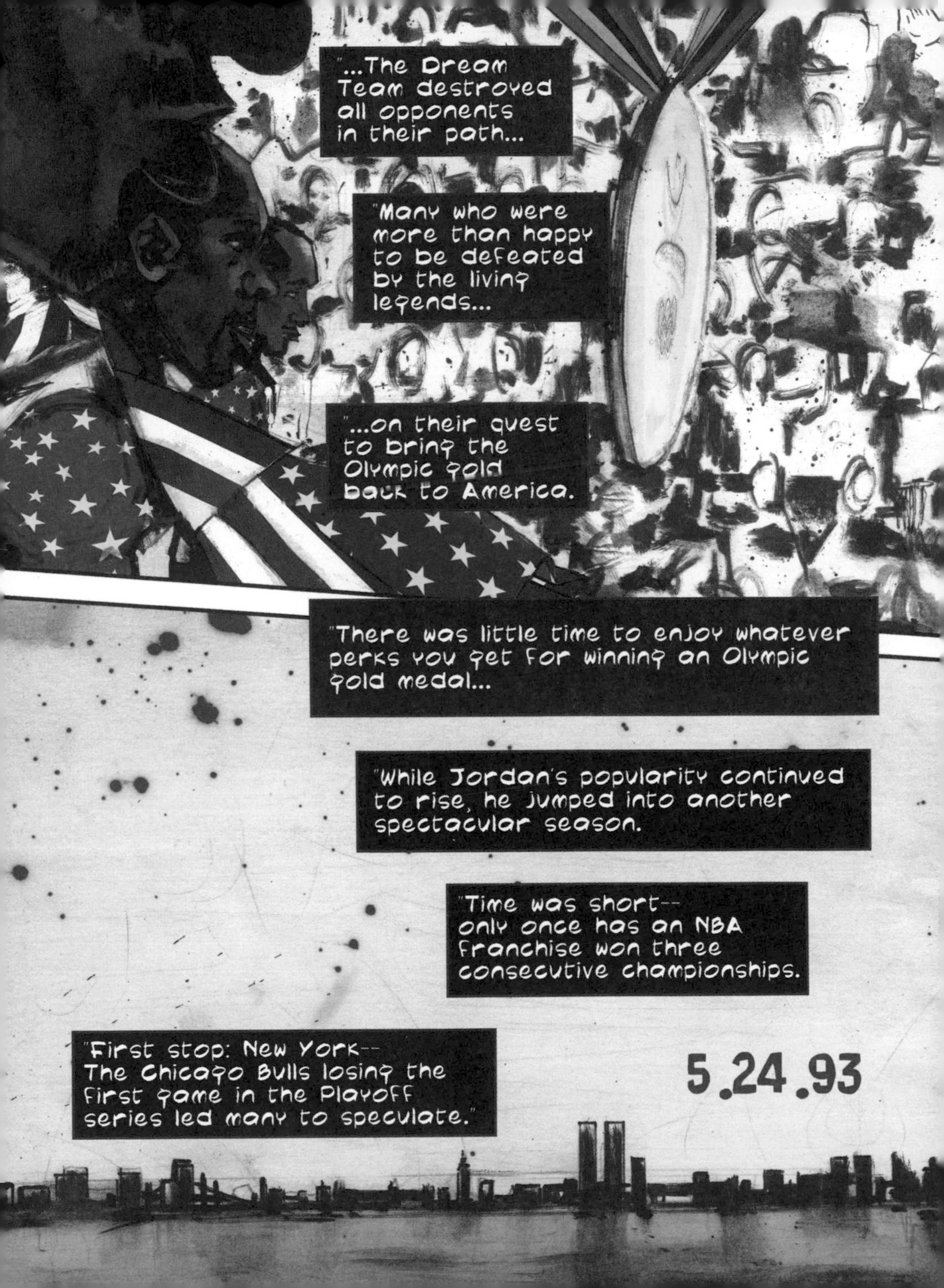
"...The Dream Team destroyed all opponents in their path...
"Many who were more than happy to be defeated by the living legends...
"...on their quest to bring the Olympic gold back to America.
"There was little time to enjoy whatever perks you get for winning an Olympic gold medal...
"While Jordan's popularity continued to rise, he jumped into another spectacular season.
"Time was short-- only once has an NBA franchise won three consecutive championships.
"First stop: New York-- The Chicago Bulls losing the first game in the playoff series led many to speculate."
5.24.93

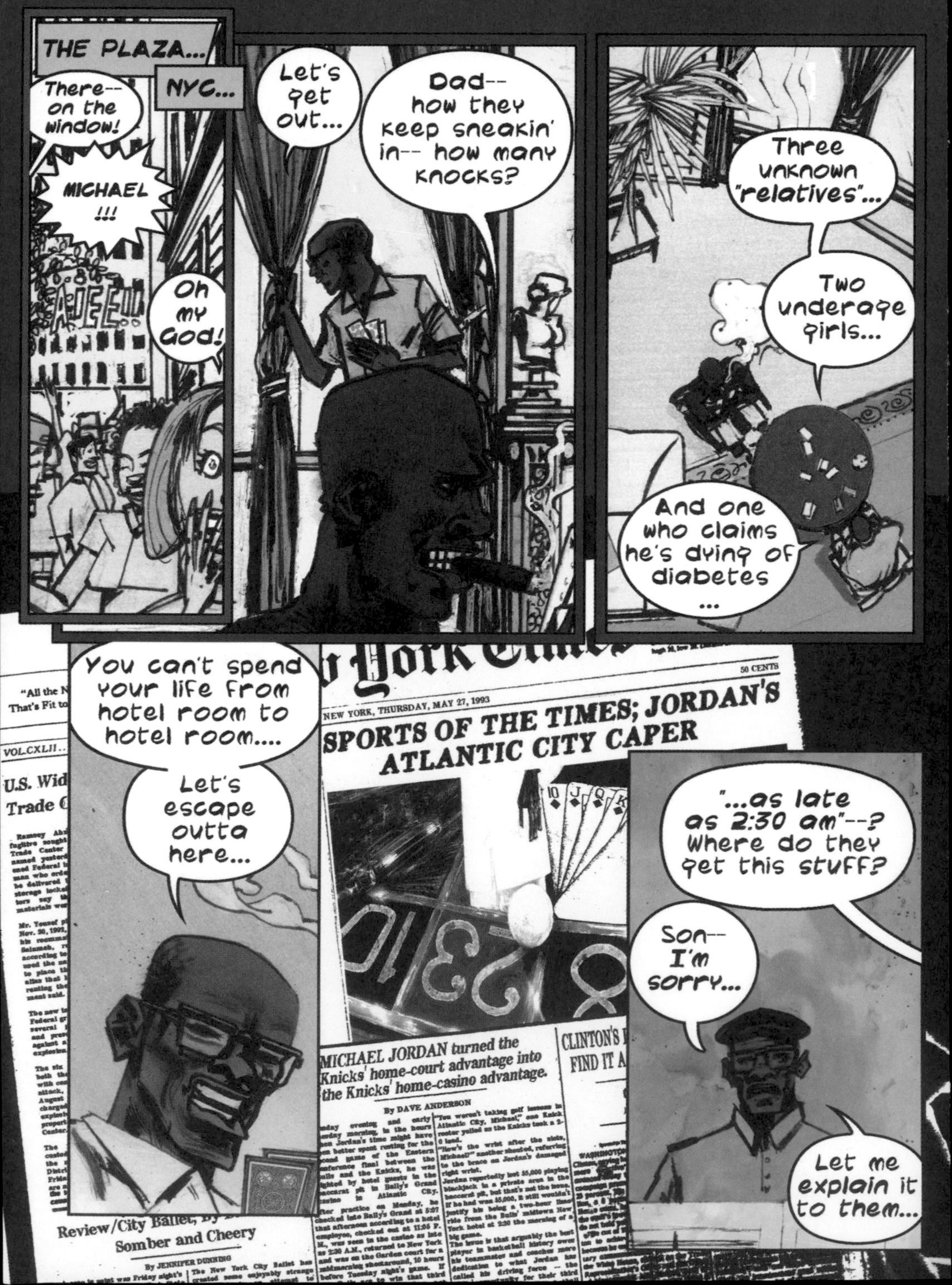
THE PLAZA...
NYC...
There-- on the window!
MICHAEL !!!
Oh my God!
Let's get out...
Dad-- how they keep sneakin' in-- how many knocks?
Three unknown "relatives"...
Two underage girls...
And one who claims he's dying of diabetes ...
You can't spend your life from hotel room to hotel room....
Let's escape outta here...
NEW YORK, THURSDAY, MAY 27, 1993
50 CENTS
SPORTS OF THE TIMES; JORDAN'S ATLANTIC CITY CAPER
MICHAEL JORDAN turned the Knicks' home-court advantage into the Knicks' home-casino advantage.
By DAVE ANDERSON
Review/City Ballet, By
Somber and Cheery
"...as late as 2:30 am"--? Where do they get this stuff?
Son-- I'm sorry...
Let me explain it to them...

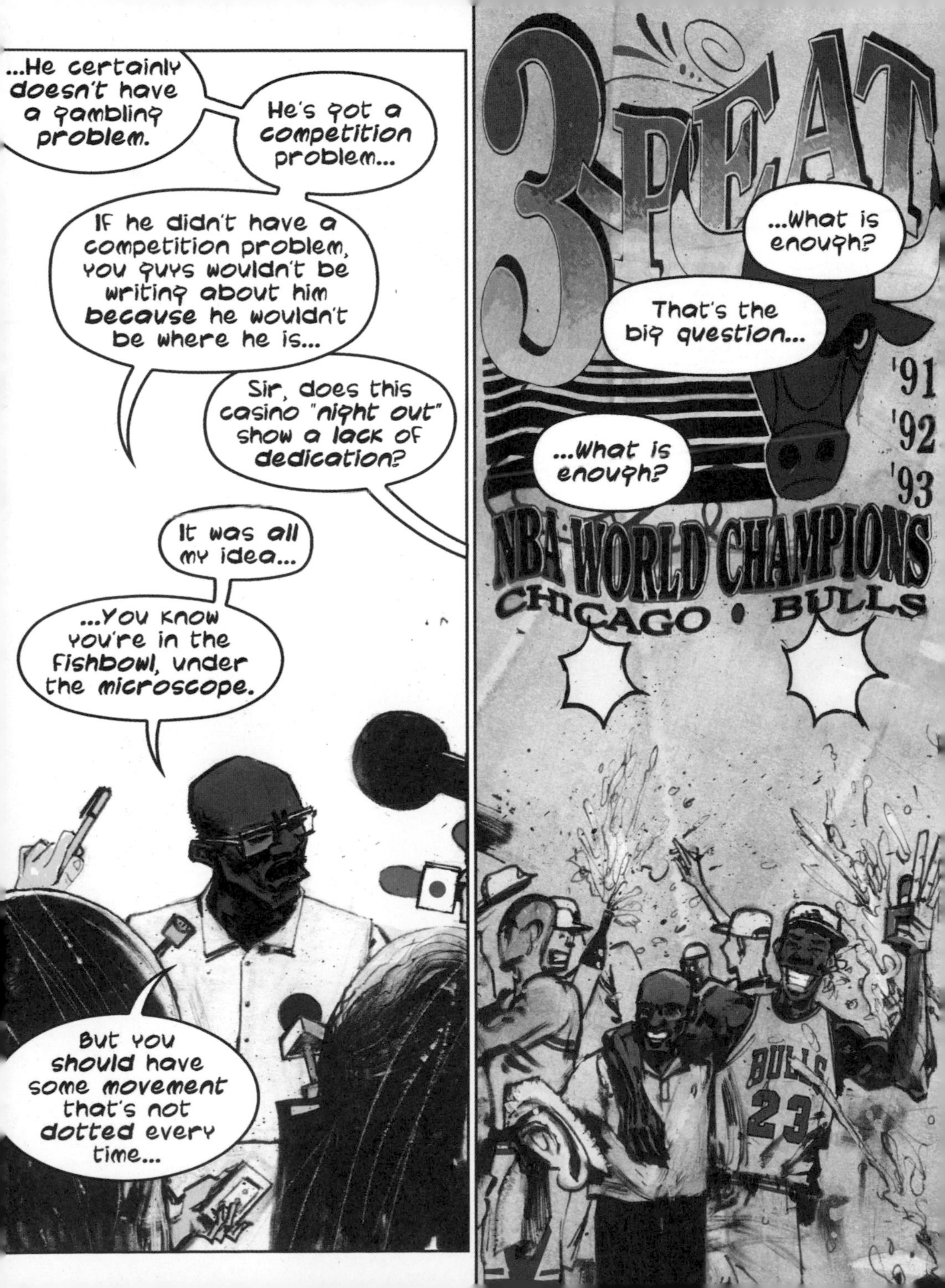
...He certainly doesn't have a gambling problem.
He's got a competition problem...
If he didn't have a competition problem, you guys wouldn't be writing about him because he wouldn't be where he is...
Sir, does this casino "night out" show a lack of dedication?
It was all my idea...
...You know you're in the fishbowl, under the microscope.
But you should have some movement that's not dotted every time...
3-PEAT
...What is enough?
That's the big question...
'91
'92
'93
...What is enough?
NBA WORLD CHAMPIONS
CHICAGO • BULLS
BULLS
23

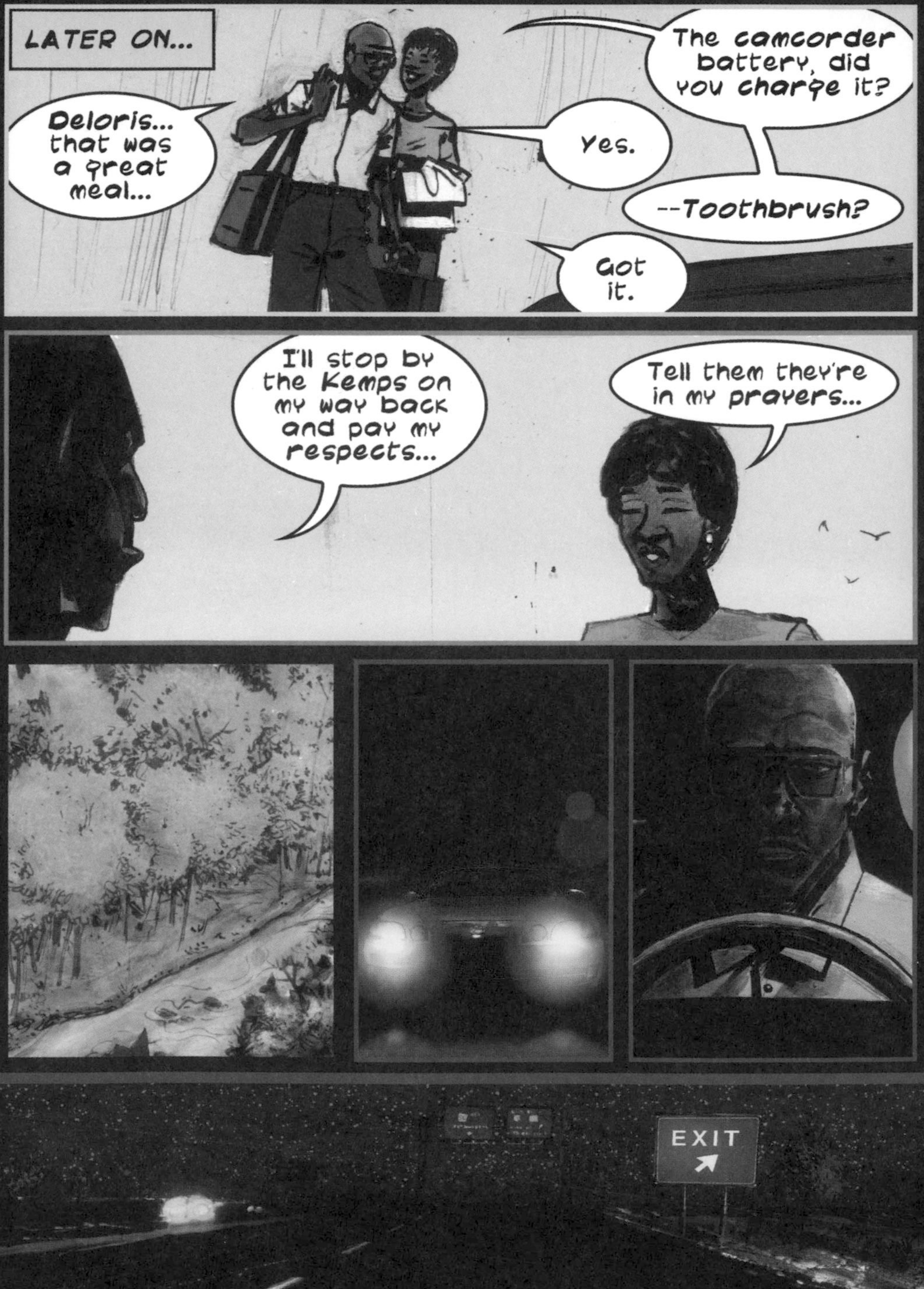
LATER ON...
Deloris... that was a great meal...
The camcorder battery, did you charge it?
Yes.
--Toothbrush?
Got it.
I'll stop by the Kemps on my way back and pay my respects...
Tell them they're in my prayers...
EXIT

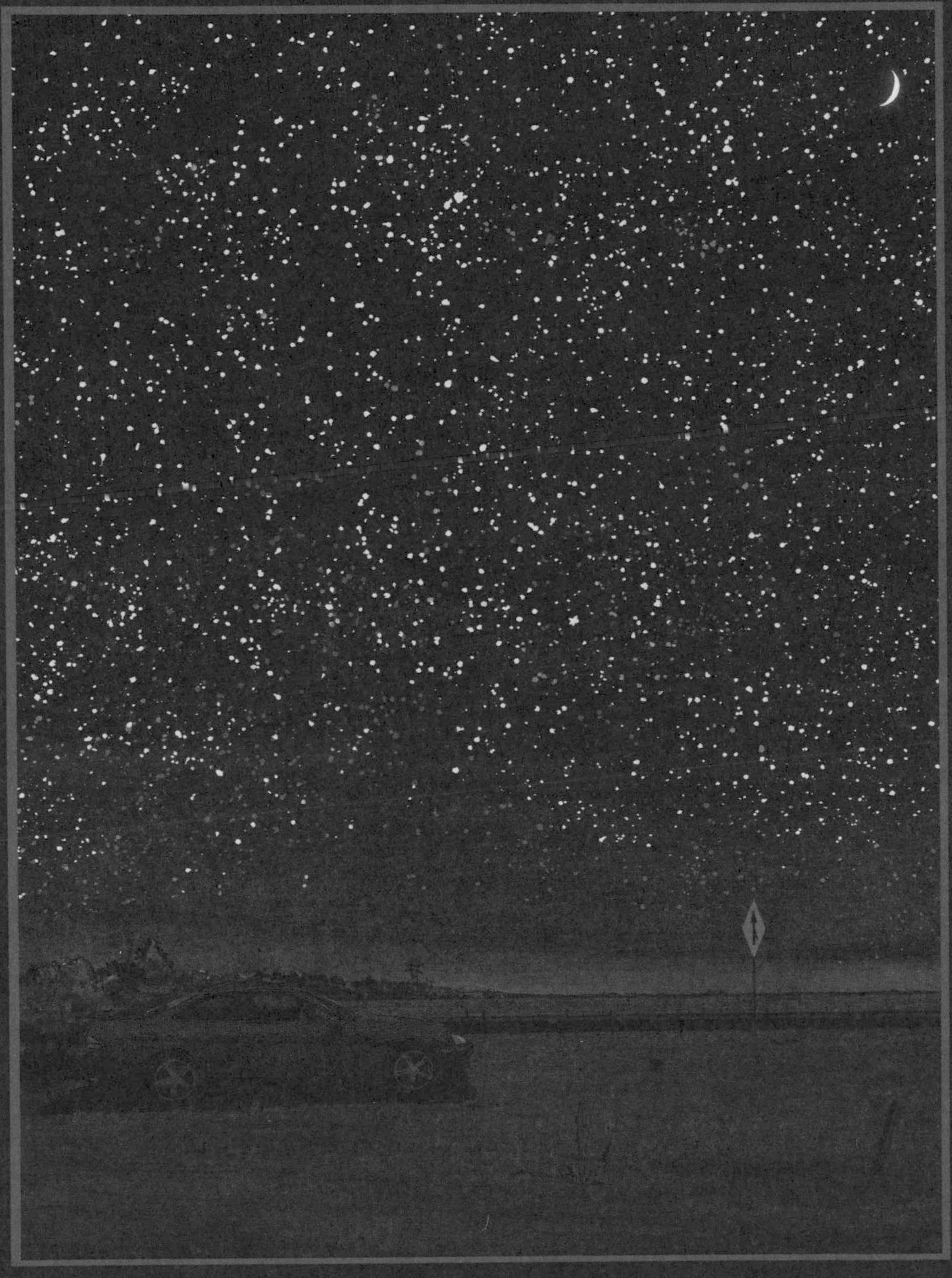

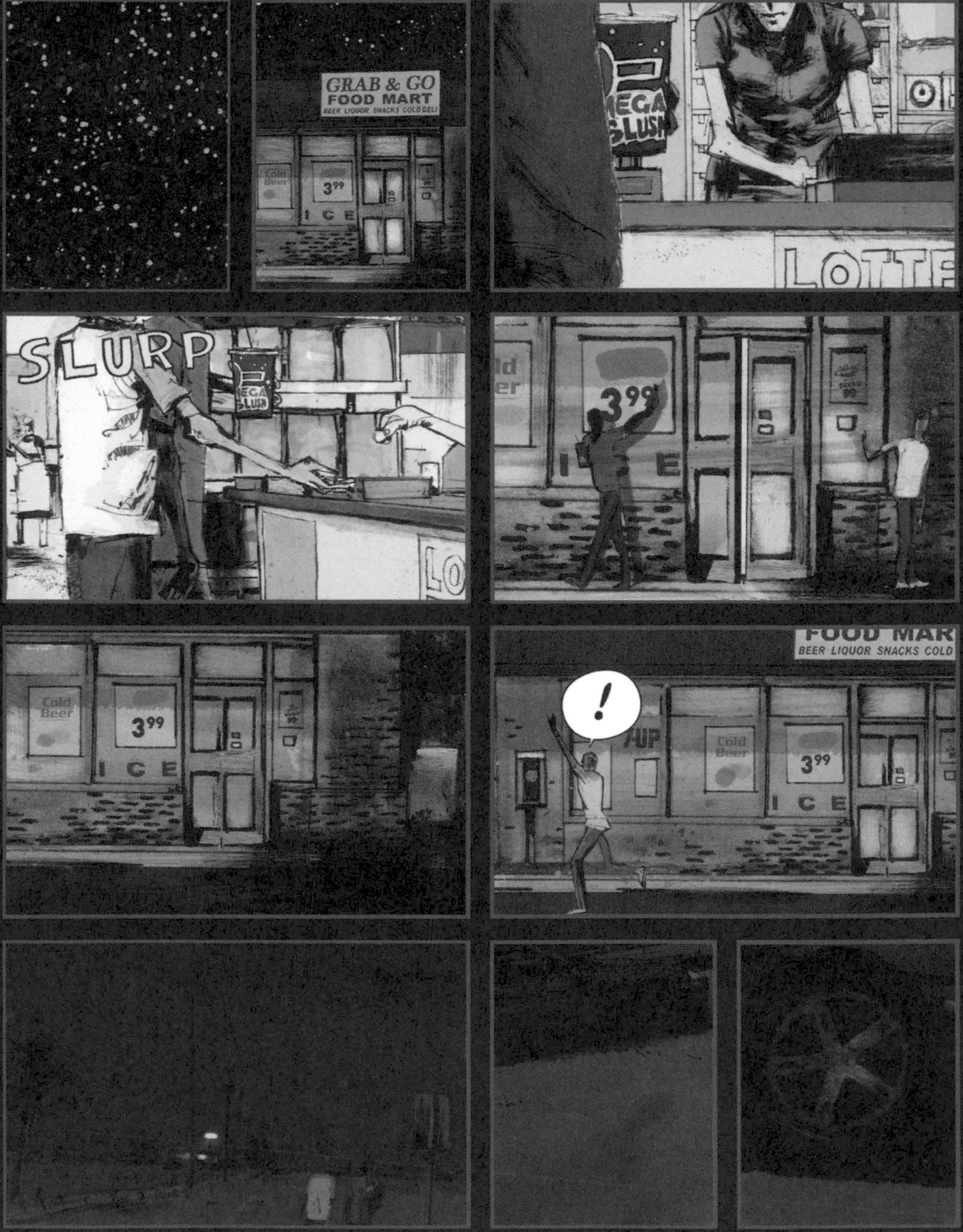
GRAB & GO
FOOD MART
BEER LIQUOR SNACKS COLD DELI
Cold Beer
3.99
ICE
MEGA SLUSH
LOTTE
SLURP
MEGA SLUSH
LO
3.99
ICE
BREAD
Cold Beer
3.99
ICE
FOOD MAR
BEER LIQUOR SNACKS COLD
!
7UP
Cold Beer
3.99
ICE

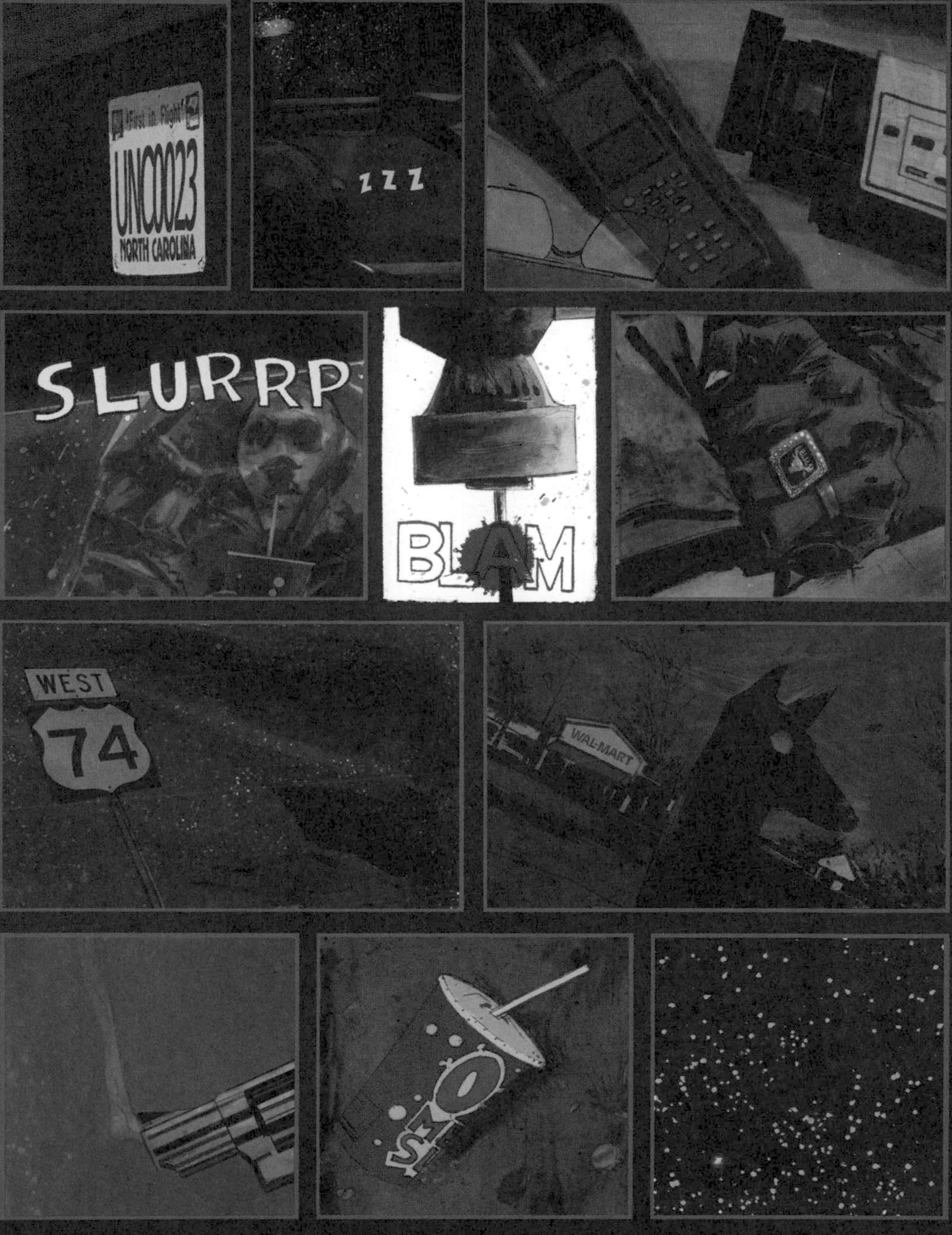
First in Flight
UNC0023
NORTH CAROLINA
Z Z Z
SLURRP
BLAM
WEST
74
WAL-MART

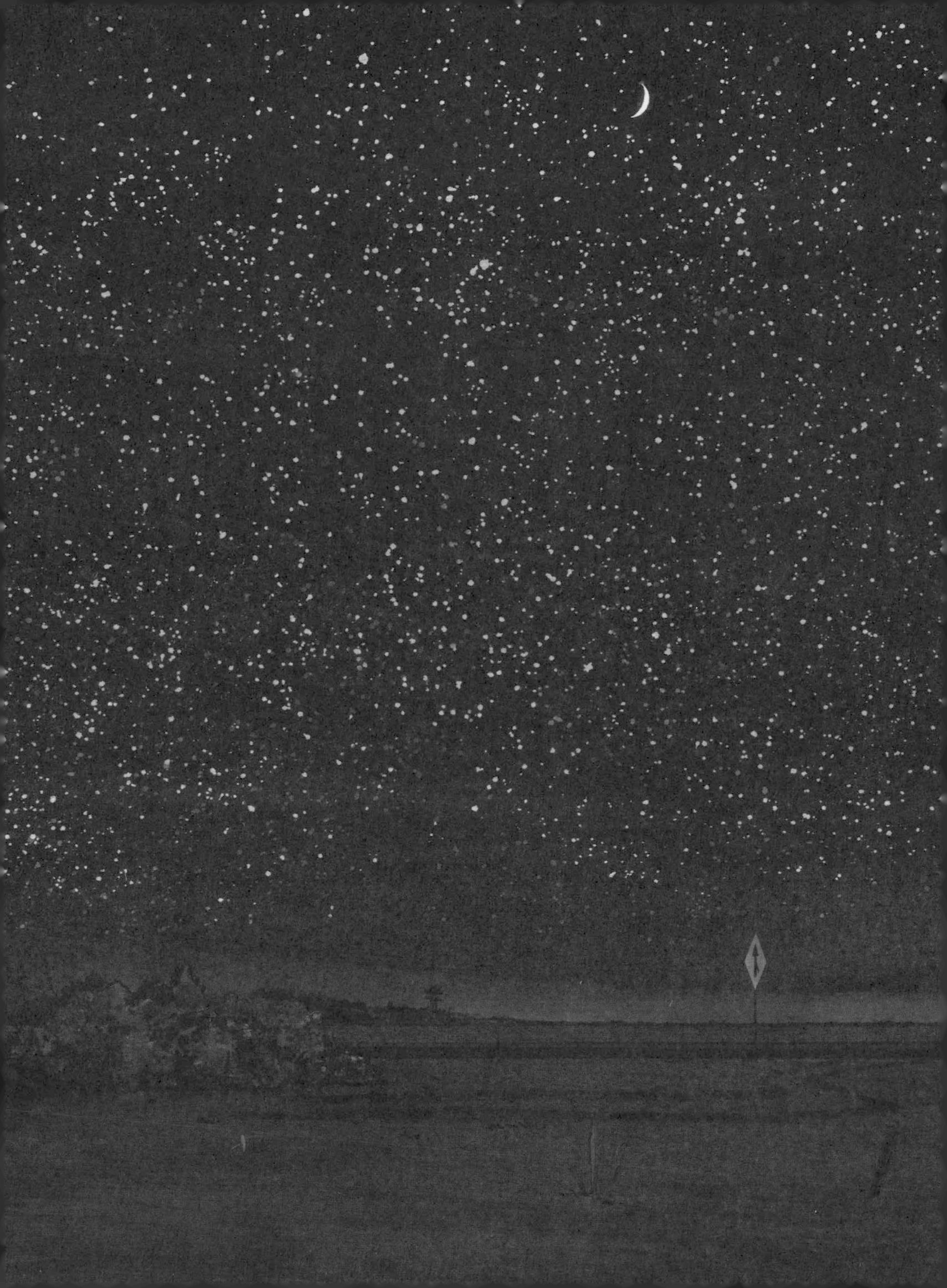

ONE FINE AFTERNOON IN A CHICAGO SUBURB

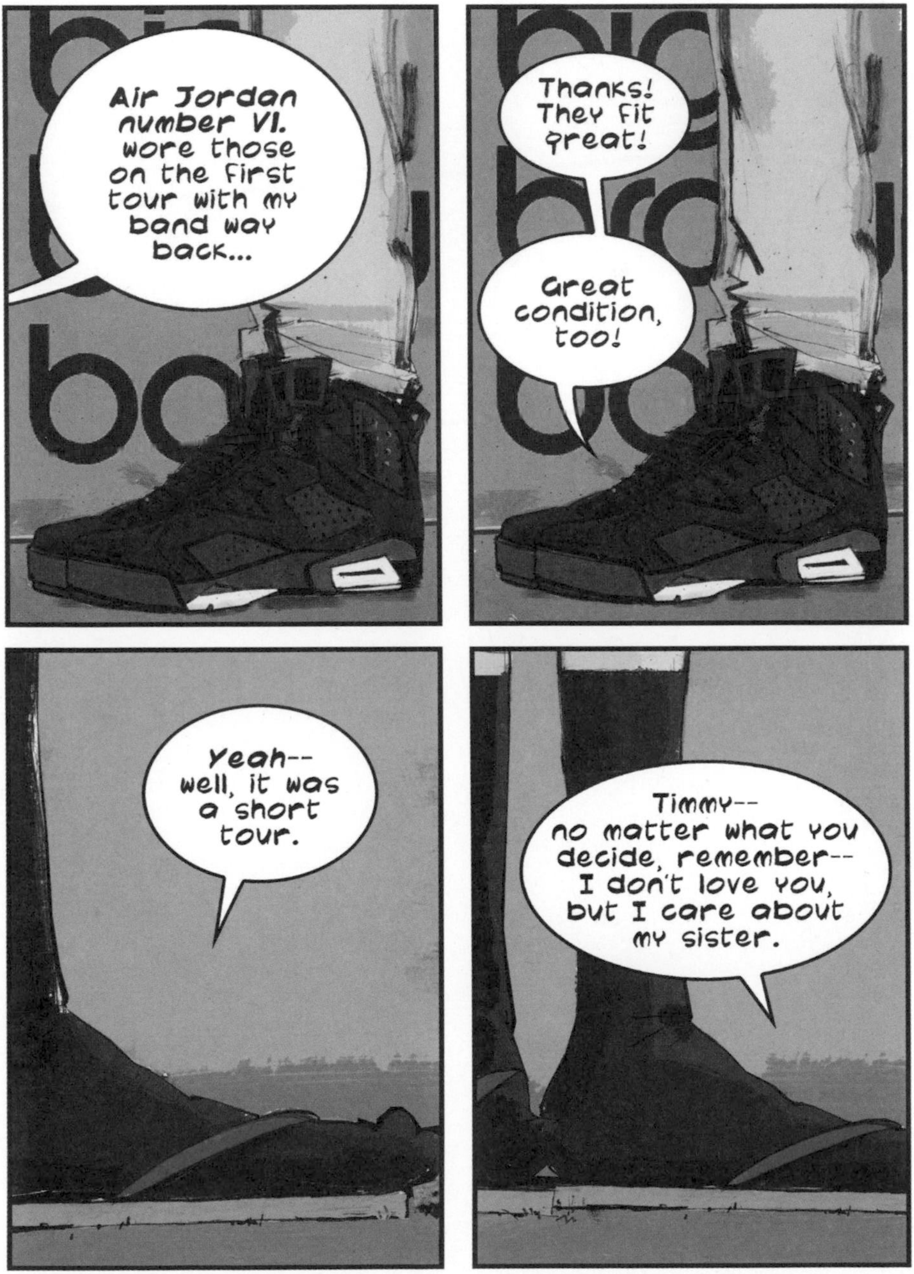

Air Jordan number VI. wore those on the first tour with my band way back...
Thanks! They fit great!
Great condition, too!
Yeah-- well, it was a short tour.
Timmy-- no matter what you decide, remember-- I don't love you, but I care about my sister.

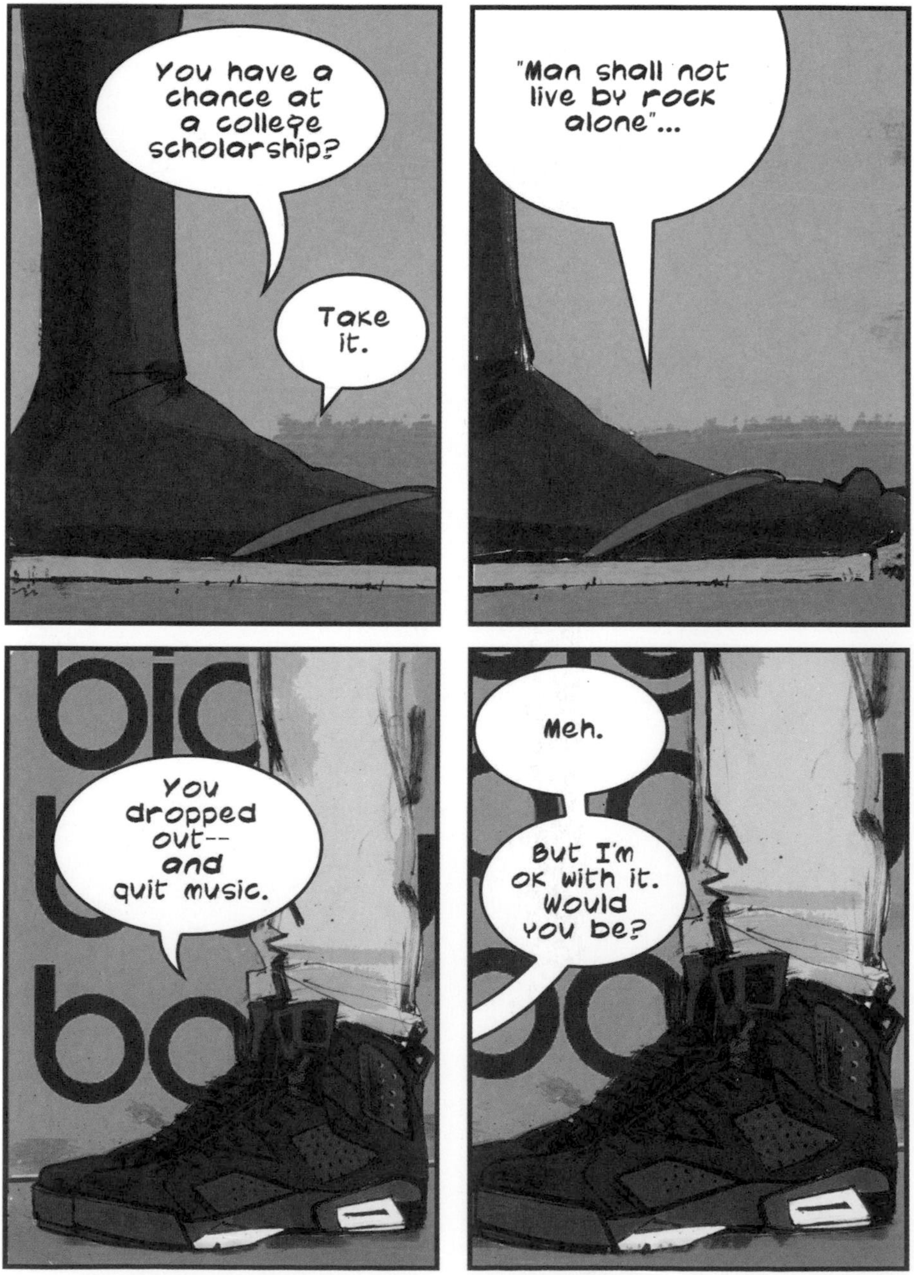
You have a chance at a college scholarship?
Take it.
"Man shall not live by rock alone"...
big
You dropped out-- and quit music.
Meh.
But I'm ok with it. Would you be?

4:
Things Done Changed

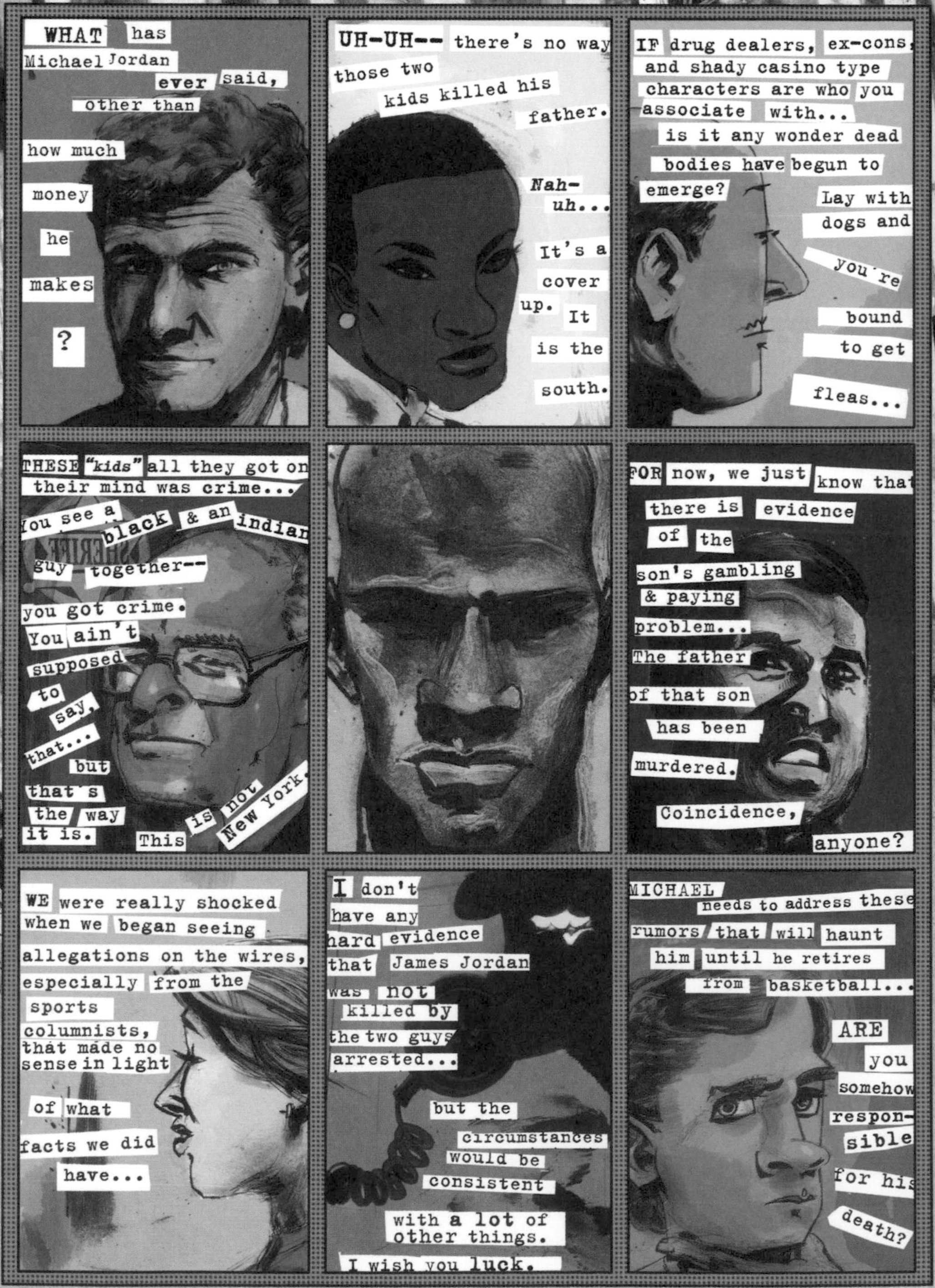
WHAT has Michael Jordan ever said, other than how much money he makes ?
UH-UH-- there's no way those two kids killed his father.
Nah-uh...
It's a cover up. It is the south.
IF drug dealers, ex-cons, and shady casino type characters are who you associate with... is it any wonder dead bodies have begun to emerge?
Lay with dogs and you're bound to get fleas...
THESE "kids" all they got on their mind was crime...
You see a black & an indian guy together--
you got crime. You ain't supposed to say, that... but that's the way it is.
This is not New York.
FOR now, we just know that there is evidence of the son's gambling & paying problem... The father of that son has been murdered.
Coincidence, anyone?
WE were really shocked when we began seeing allegations on the wires, especially from the sports columnists, that made no sense in light of what facts we did have...
I don't have any hard evidence that James Jordan was not killed by the two guys arrested...
but the circumstances would be consistent with a lot of other things.
I wish you luck.
MICHAEL needs to address these rumors that will haunt him until he retires from basketball...
ARE you somehow responsible for his death?

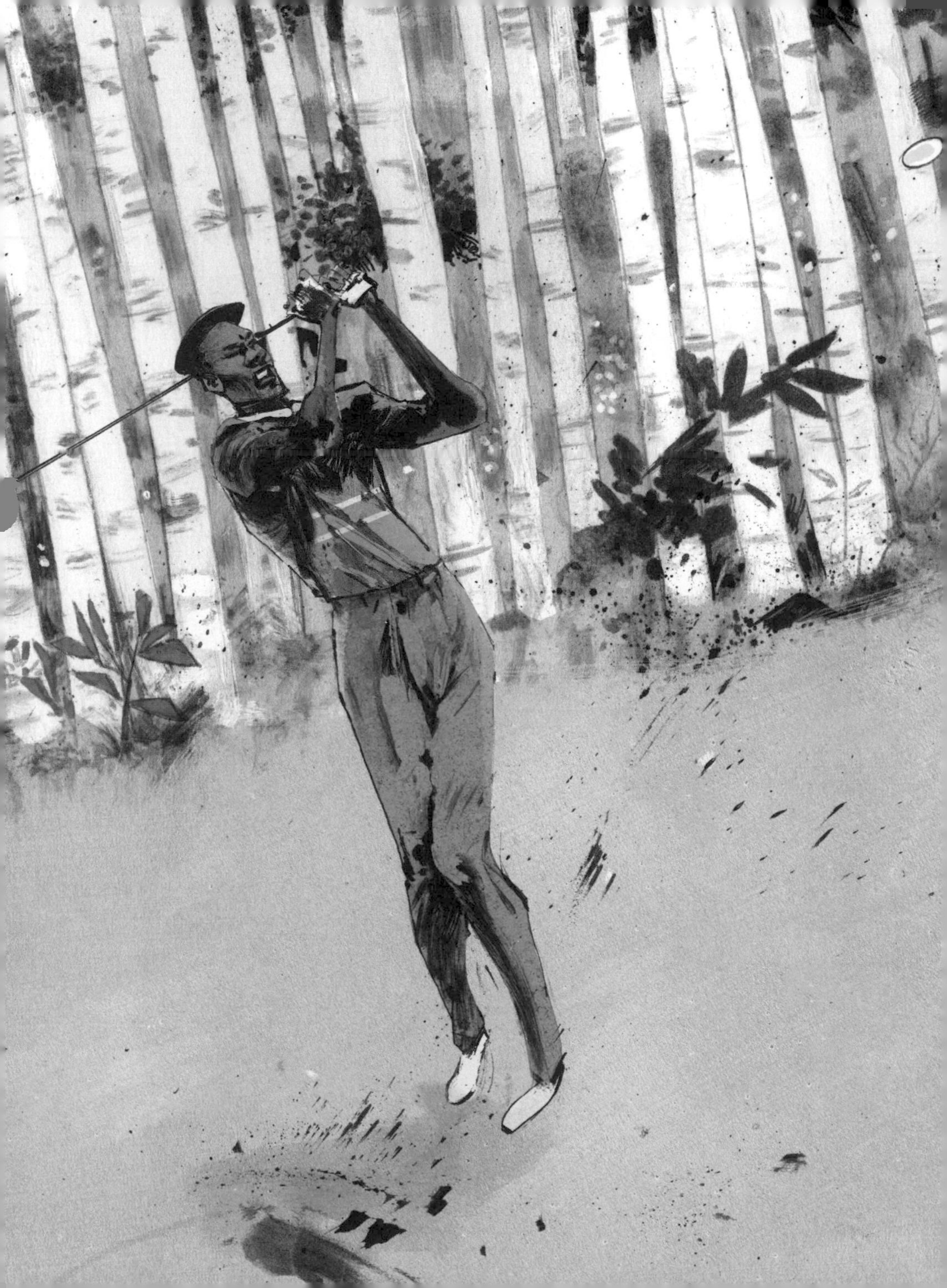

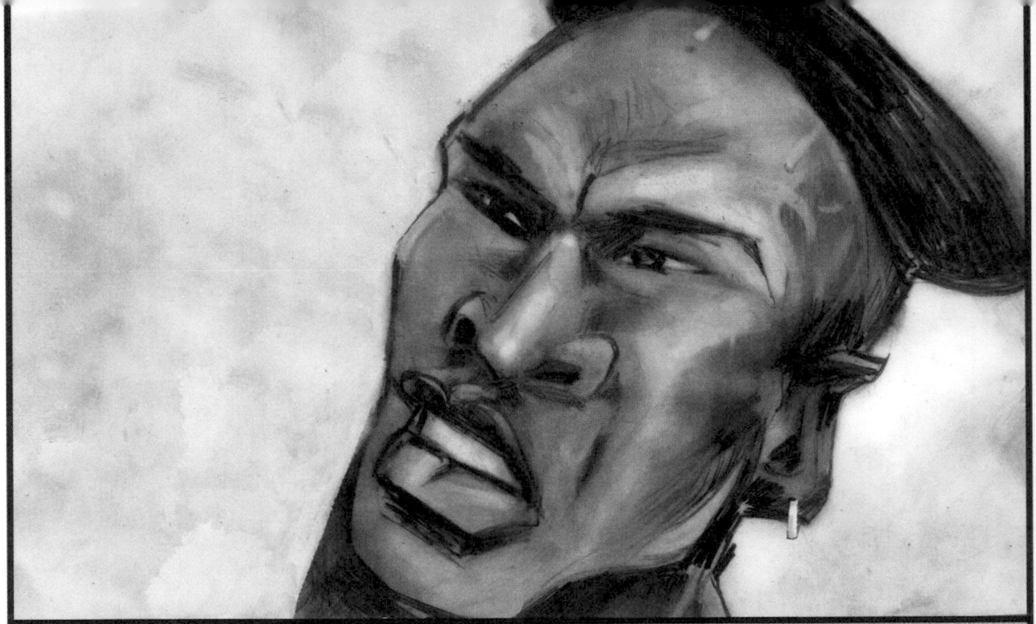
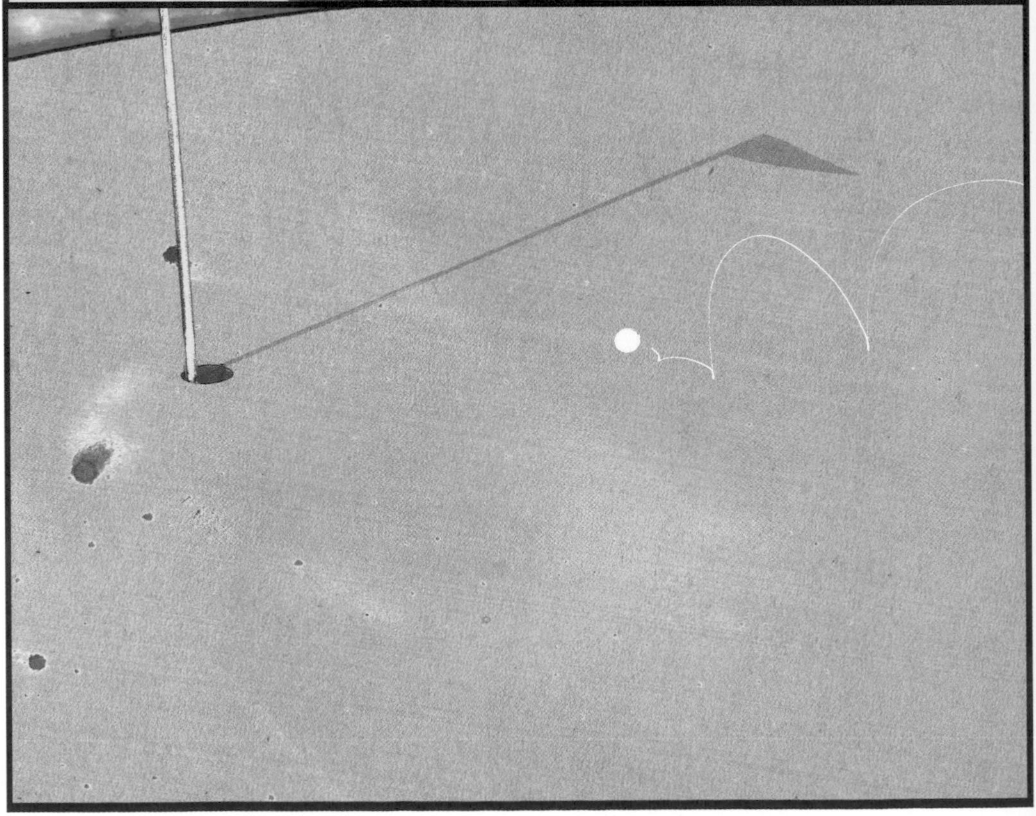

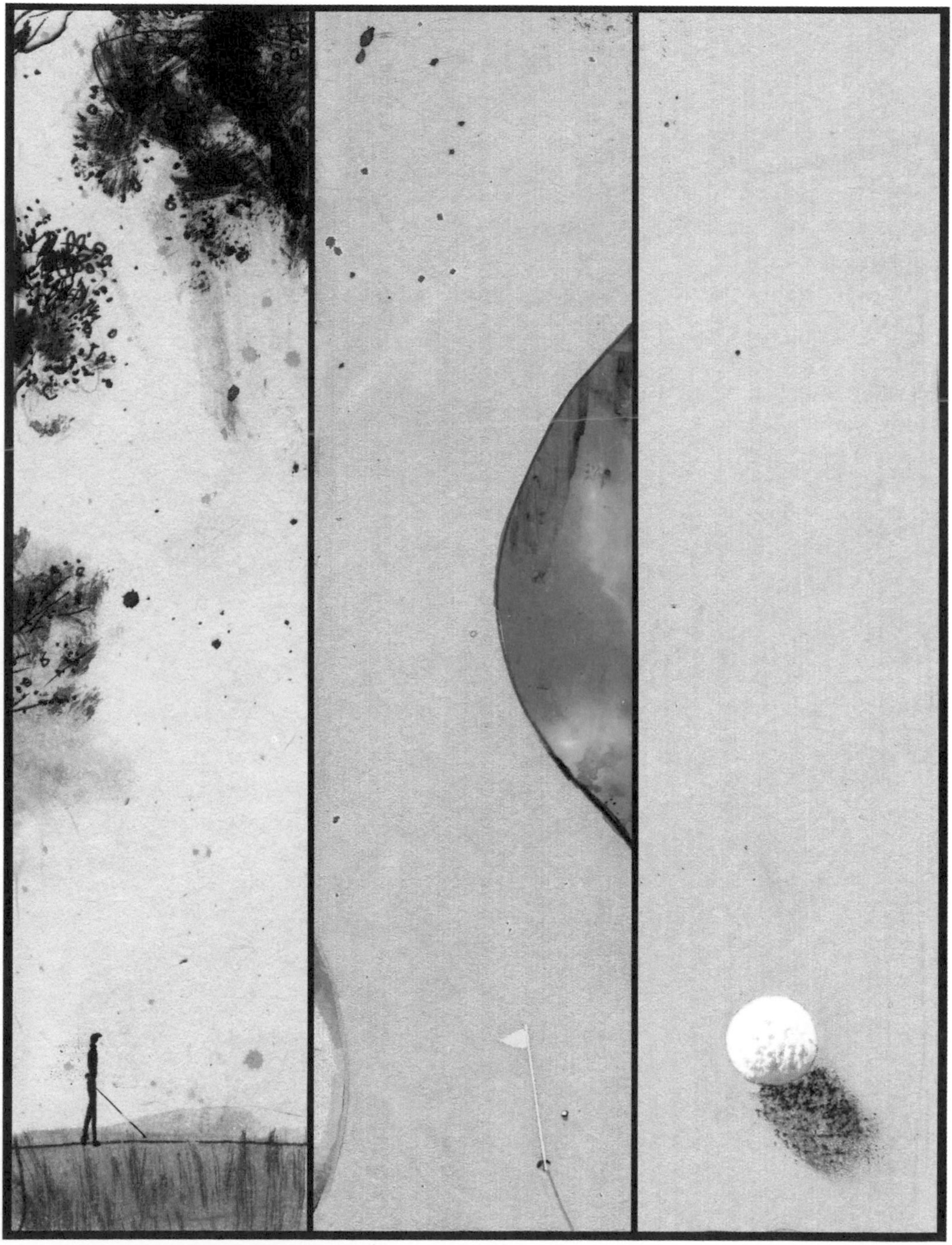

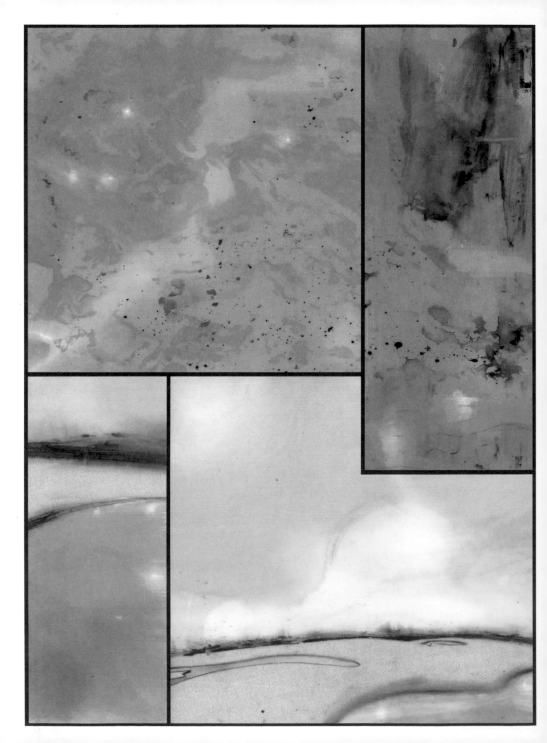

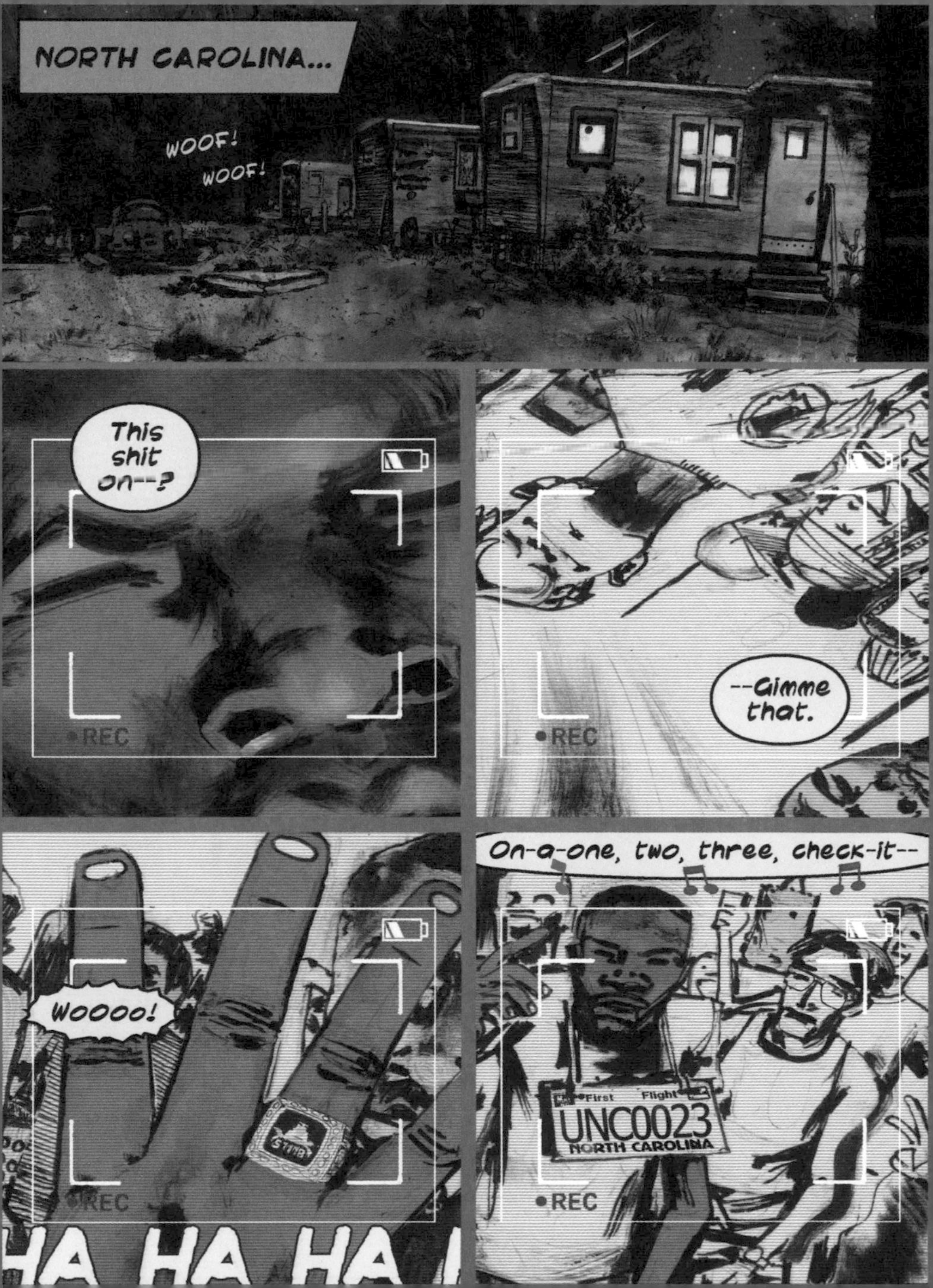
NORTH CAROLINA...
WOOF!
WOOF!
This shit on--?
REC
--Gimme that.
REC
WOOOO!
REC
HA HA HA
On-a-one, two, three, check-it--
First Flight
UNC0023
NORTH CAROLINA
REC

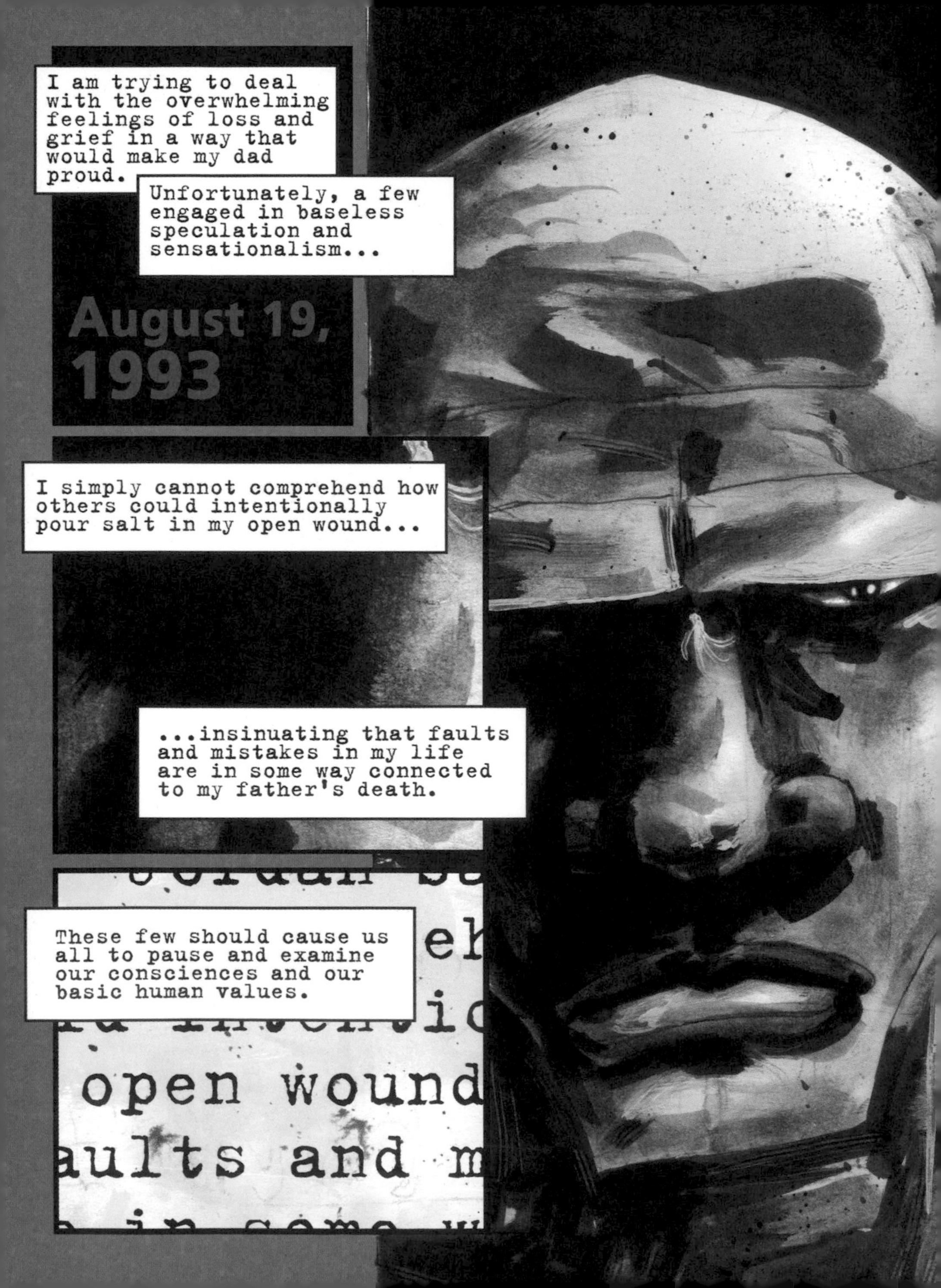

I am trying to deal with the overwhelming feelings of loss and grief in a way that would make my dad proud.

Unfortunately, a few engaged in baseless speculation and sensationalism...

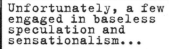

August 19, 1993

I simply cannot comprehend how others could intentionally pour salt in my open wound...

...insinuating that faults and mistakes in my life are in some way connected to my father's death.

These few should cause us all to pause and examine our consciences and our basic human values.

7

THE STATEMENT ISSUED
BY JORDAN'S AGENT,
DAVID FALK, COMES AS
TWO TEENAGERS ARE
ACCUSED OF FATALLY
SHOOTING JAMES JORDAN,
FATHER OF THE BASKET-
BALL STAR, IN WHAT
APPEARS TO BE A
RANDOM ACT OF VIOLENCE.

7

THE APPARENT MOTIVE
WAS ROBBERY. AUTHORI-
TIES TRACED THE VICTIM'S
ELECTRONIC FOOTPRINT
TO THE TWO JUVENILES,
WHO HAD HIS CELLPHONE
AMONG OTHER ITEMS,
IN THEIR POSSESSION.

7

MEANWHILE CRITICISM IS
MOUNTING REGARDING THE
CORONER'S DECISION TO
CREMATE THE BODY WITHIN
THREE DAYS WITHOUT
PROPERLY IDENTIFYING IT.
THE IDENTITY OF THE BODY
FOUND IN THE SWAMP IN
BENNETTSVILLE, SOUTH
CAROLINA WAS CONFIRMED
LAST WEEK THROUGH
DENTAL RECORDS.

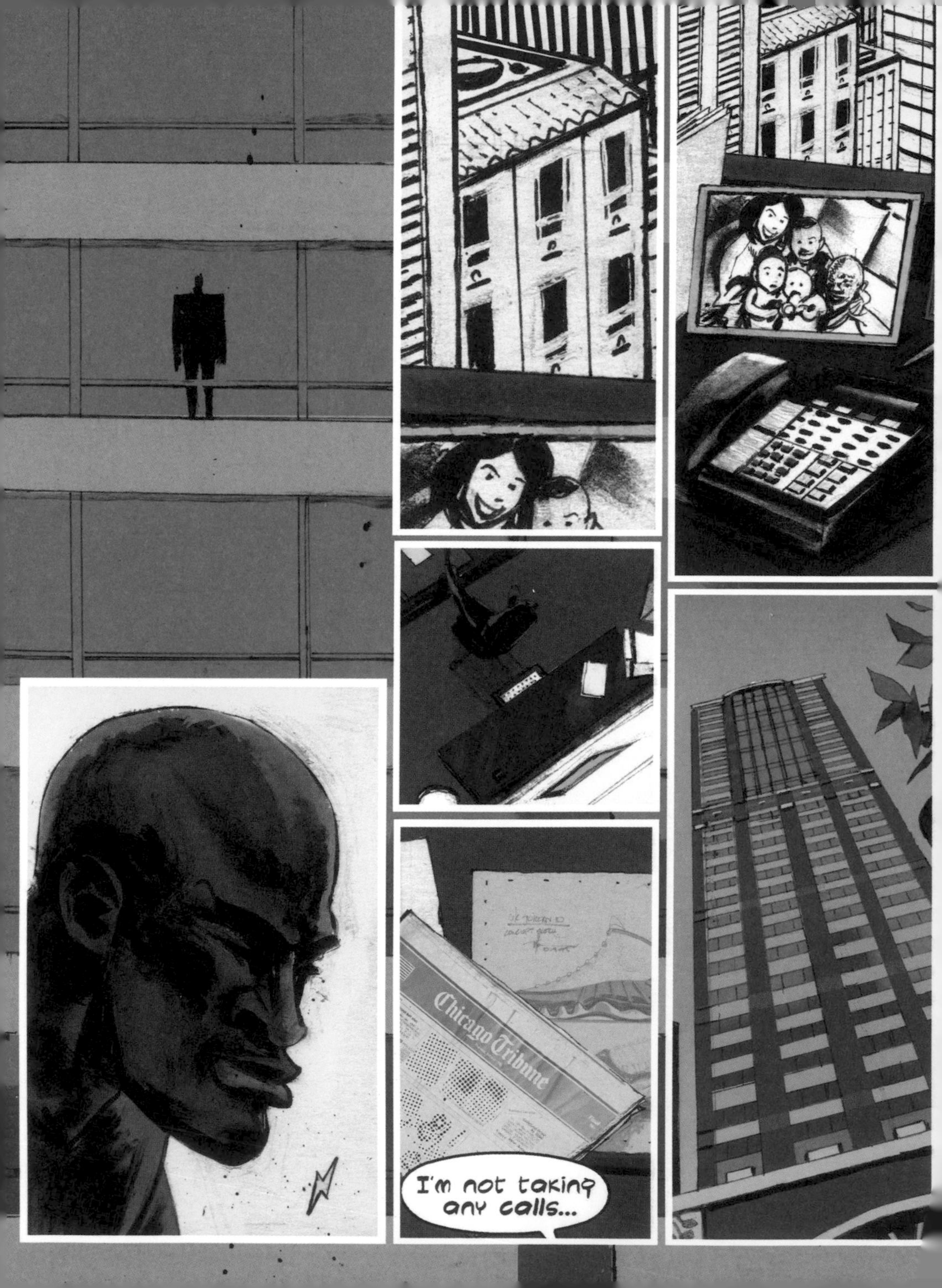
Chicago Tribune
I'm not taking any calls...

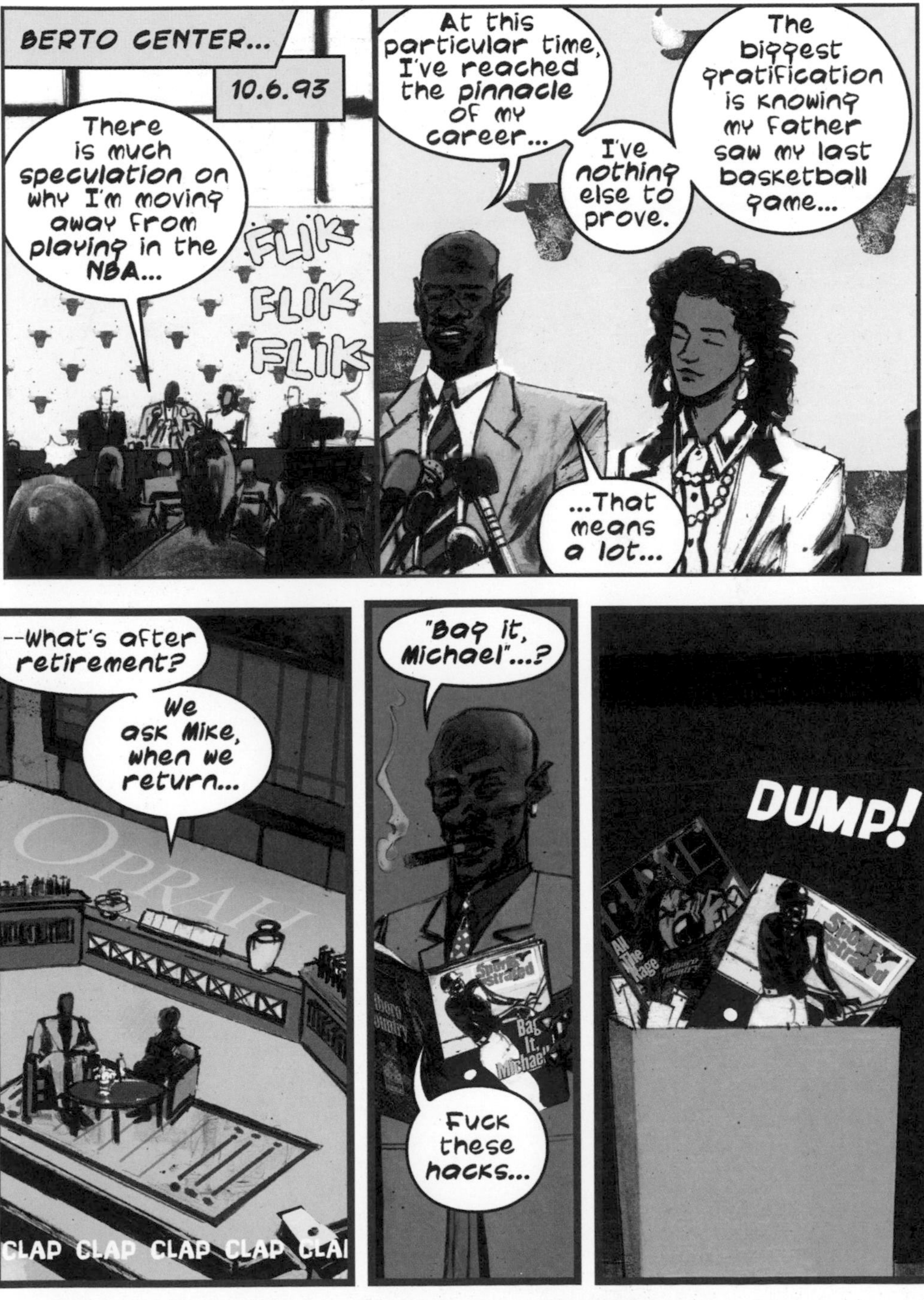
BERTO CENTER...
10.6.93
There is much speculation on why I'm moving away from playing in the NBA...
FLIK
FLIK
FLIK
At this particular time, I've reached the pinnacle of my career...
I've nothing else to prove.
The biggest gratification is knowing my father saw my last basketball game...
...That means a lot...
--What's after retirement?
We ask Mike, when we return...
OPRAH
CLAP CLAP CLAP CLAP CLA
"Bag it, Michael"...?
Bag It, Michael
Fuck these hacks...
DUMP!

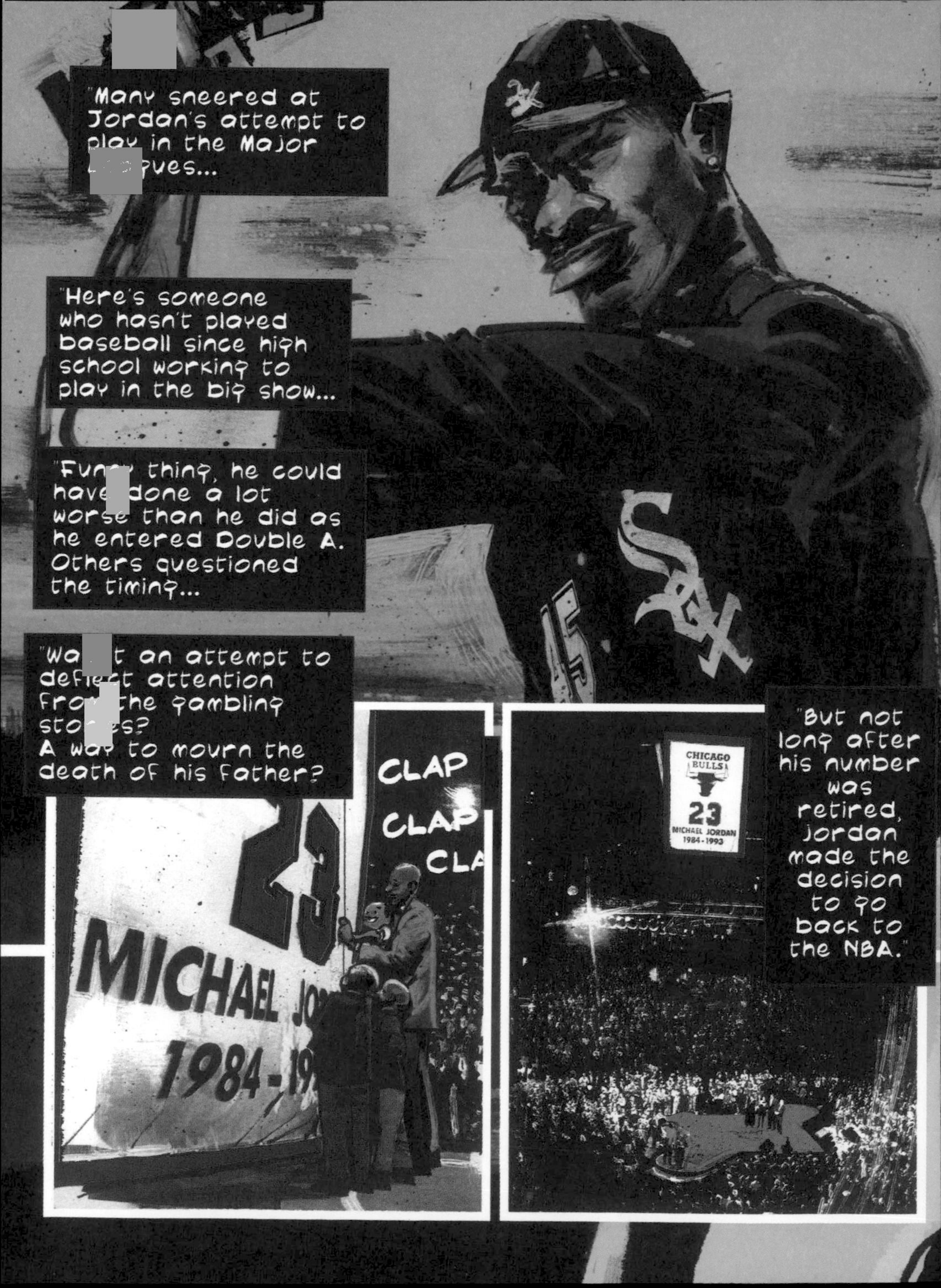
"Many sneered at Jordan's attempt to play in the Major Leagues...
"Here's someone who hasn't played baseball since high school working to play in the big show...
"Funny thing, he could have done a lot worse than he did as he entered Double A. Others questioned the timing...
"Was it an attempt to deflect attention from the gambling stories? A way to mourn the death of his father?
SOX
CLAP
CLAP
CLA
23
MICHAEL JO
1984-19
"But not long after his number was retired, Jordan made the decision to go back to the NBA."
CHICAGO BULLS
23
MICHAEL JORDAN
1984-1993

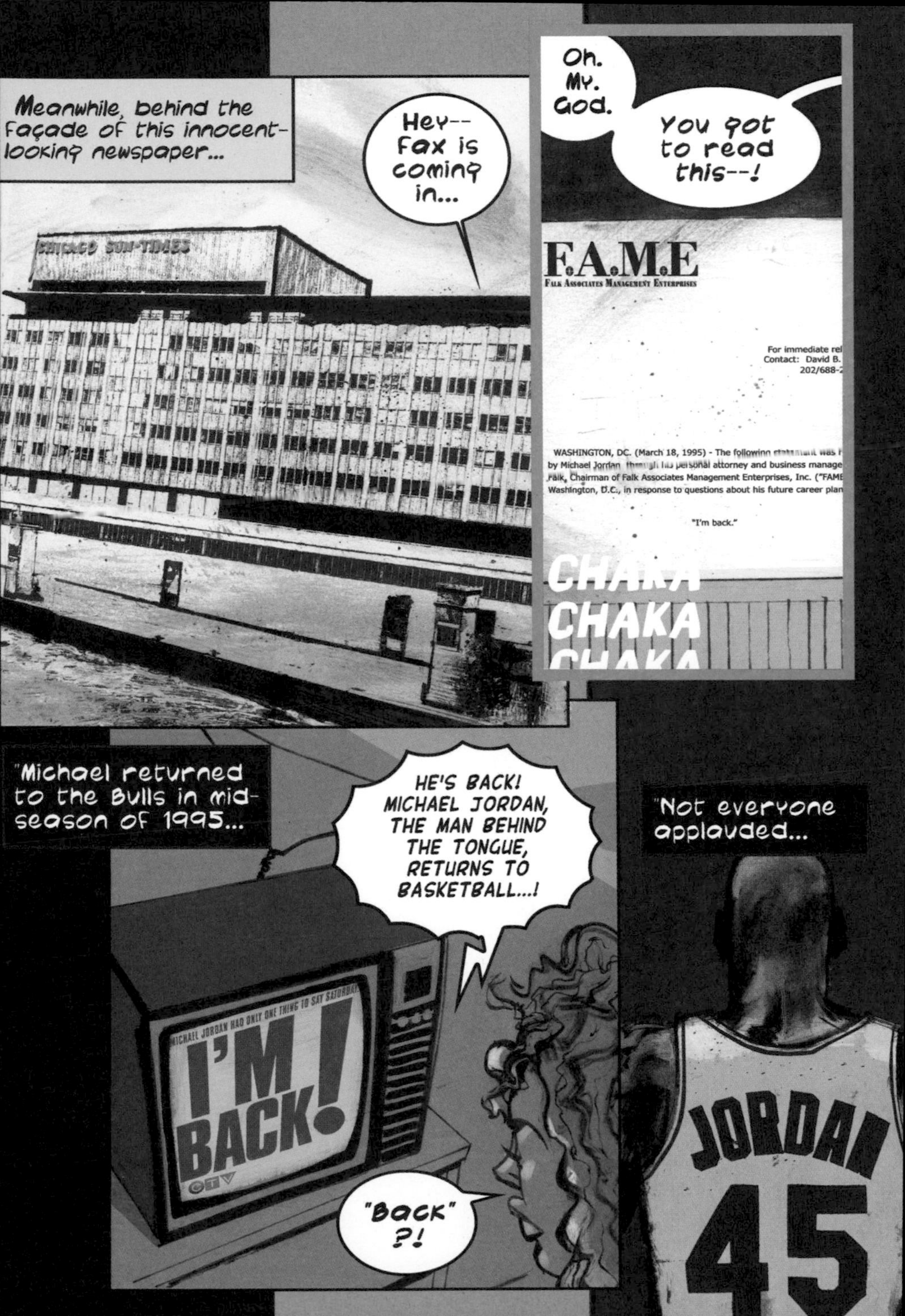
Meanwhile, behind the façade of this innocent-looking newspaper...
CHICAGO SUN-TIMES
Hey-- Fax is coming in...
Oh. My. God.
You got to read this--!
F.A.M.E
FALK ASSOCIATES MANAGEMENT ENTERPRISES
For immediate rel
Contact: David B.
202/688-
WASHINGTON, DC. (March 18, 1995) - The following
by Michael Jordan personal attorney and business manage
Falk, Chairman of Falk Associates Management Enterprises, Inc. ("FAME
Washington, D.C., in response to questions about his future career plan
"I'm back."
CHAKA
CHAKA
"Michael returned to the Bulls in mid-season of 1995...
HE'S BACK! MICHAEL JORDAN, THE MAN BEHIND THE TONGUE, RETURNS TO BASKETBALL...!
MICHAEL JORDAN HAD ONLY ONE THING TO SAY SATURDAY
I'M BACK!
"Back" ?!
"Not everyone applauded...
JORDAN
45

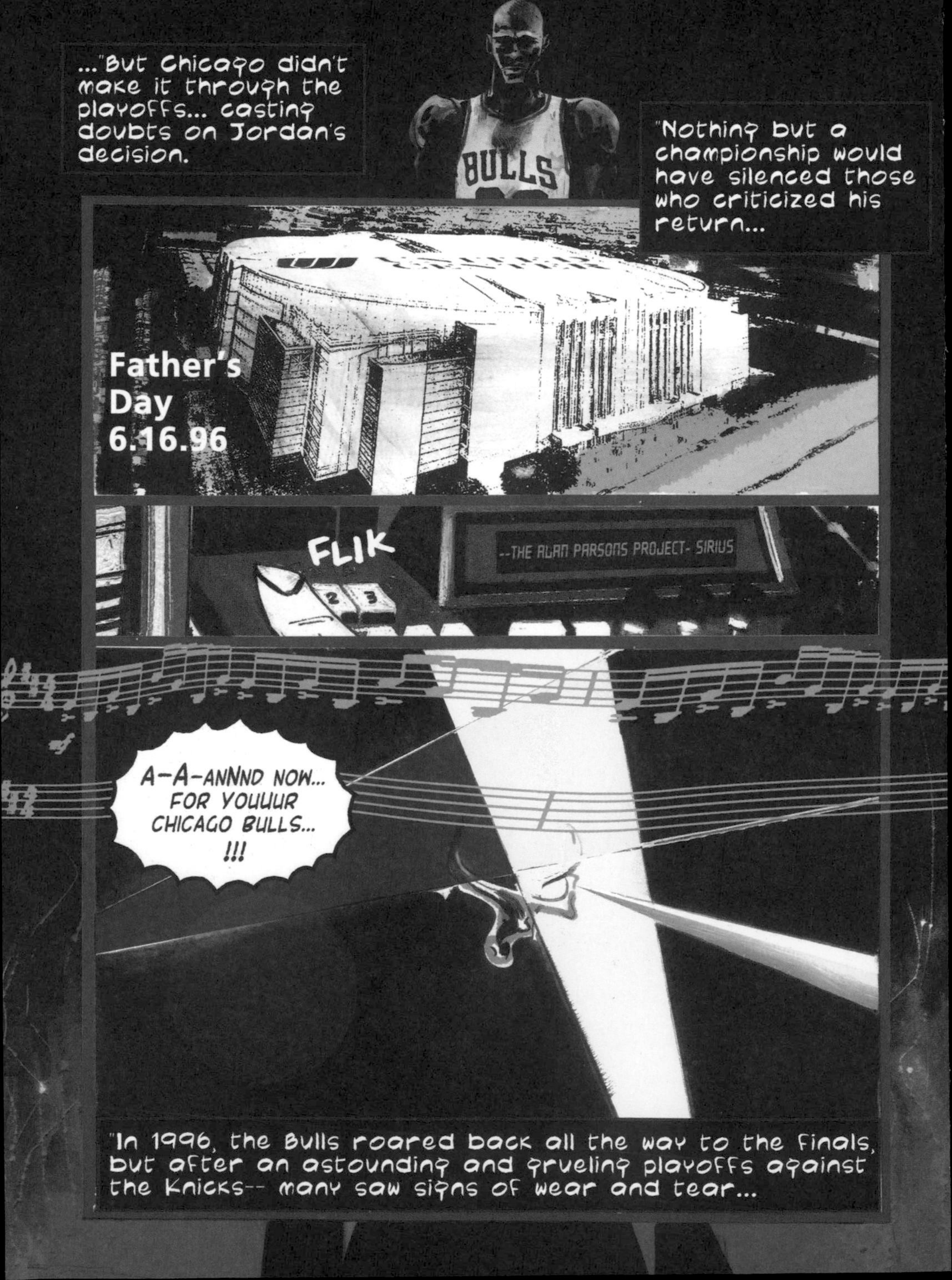
..."But Chicago didn't make it through the playoffs... casting doubts on Jordan's decision.
"Nothing but a championship would have silenced those who criticized his return...
Father's Day 6.16.96
FLIK
--THE ALAN PARSONS PROJECT- SIRIUS
A-A-ANNND NOW... FOR YOUUUR CHICAGO BULLS... !!!
"In 1996, the Bulls roared back all the way to the finals, but after an astounding and grueling playoffs against the Knicks-- many saw signs of wear and tear...

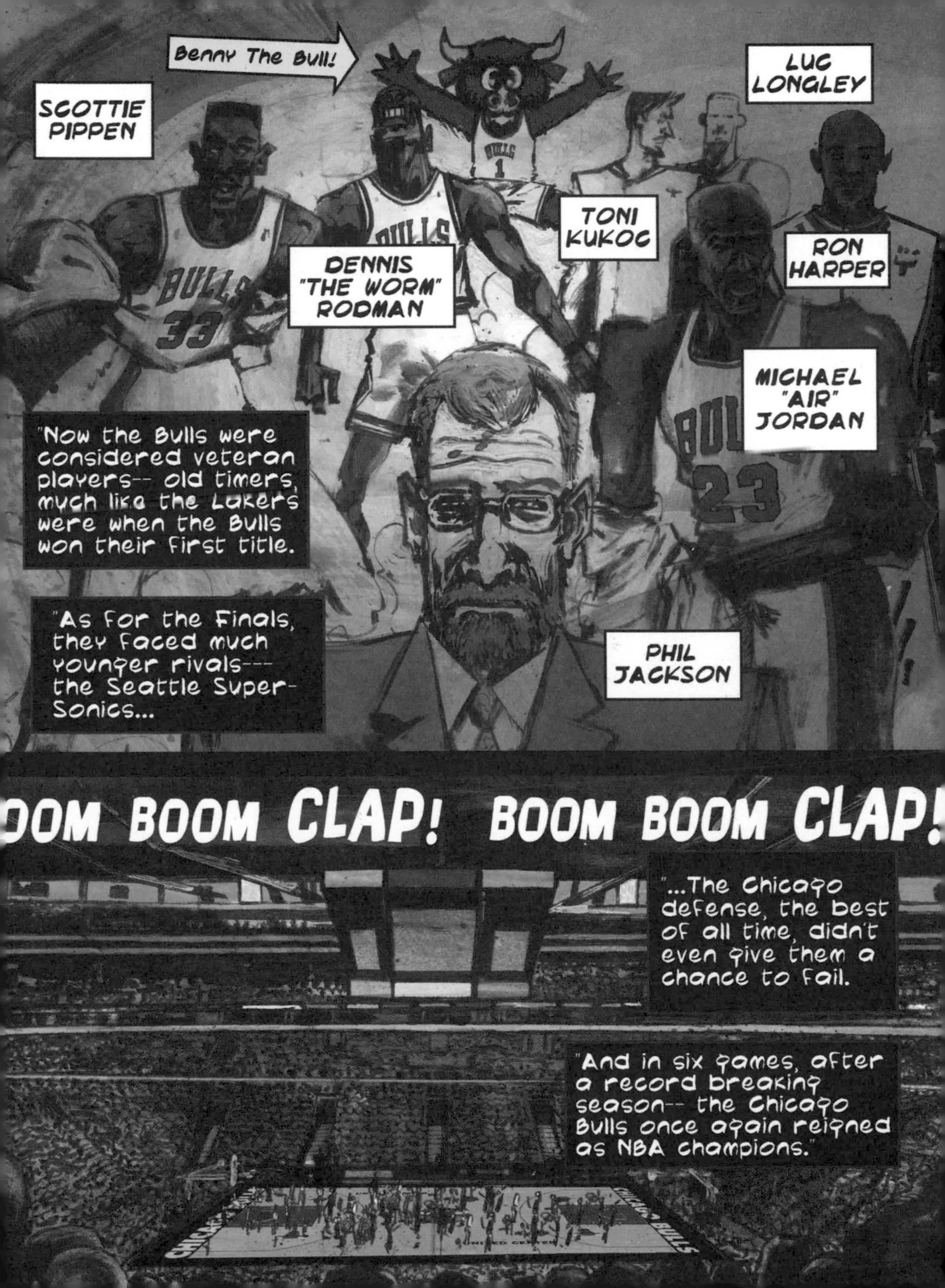
Benny The Bull!
SCOTTIE PIPPEN
LUC LONGLEY
TONI KUKOC
RON HARPER
DENNIS "THE WORM" RODMAN
MICHAEL "AIR" JORDAN
"Now the Bulls were considered veteran players-- old timers, much like the Lakers were when the Bulls won their first title.
"As for the Finals, they faced much younger rivals--- the Seattle Super-Sonics...
PHIL JACKSON
OOM BOOM CLAP! BOOM BOOM CLAP!
"...The Chicago defense, the best of all time, didn't even give them a chance to fail.
"And in six games, after a record breaking season-- the Chicago Bulls once again reigned as NBA champions."

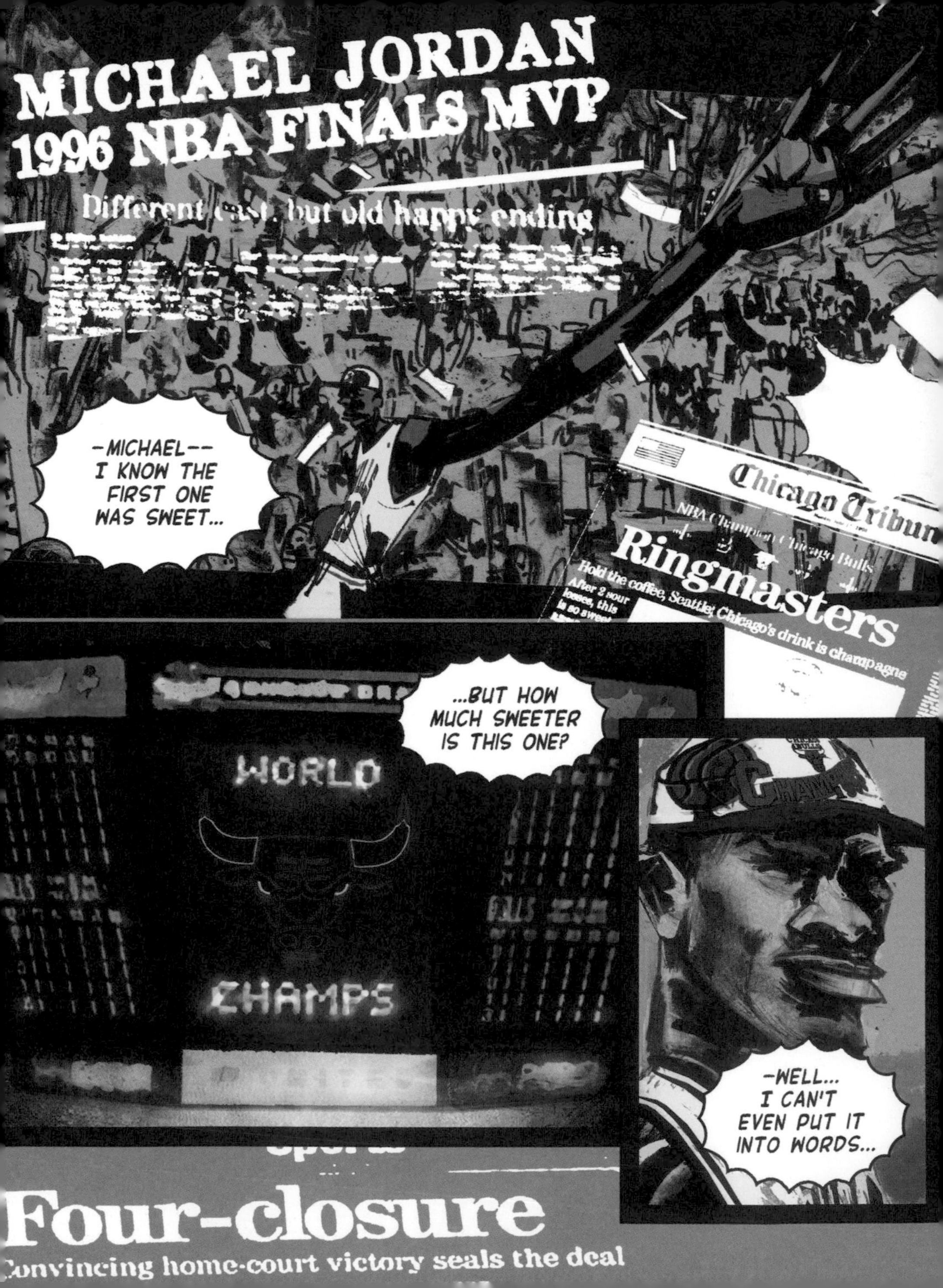
MICHAEL JORDAN
1996 NBA FINALS MVP
Different cast, but old happy ending
-MICHAEL--
I KNOW THE
FIRST ONE
WAS SWEET...
Chicago Tribune
NBA Champion Chicago Bulls
Ringmasters
Hold the coffee, Seattle; Chicago's drink is champagne
After 2 sour losses, this is so sweet
...BUT HOW
MUCH SWEETER
IS THIS ONE?
WORLD
CHAMPS
-WELL...
I CAN'T
EVEN PUT IT
INTO WORDS...
Four-closure
Convincing home-court victory seals the deal

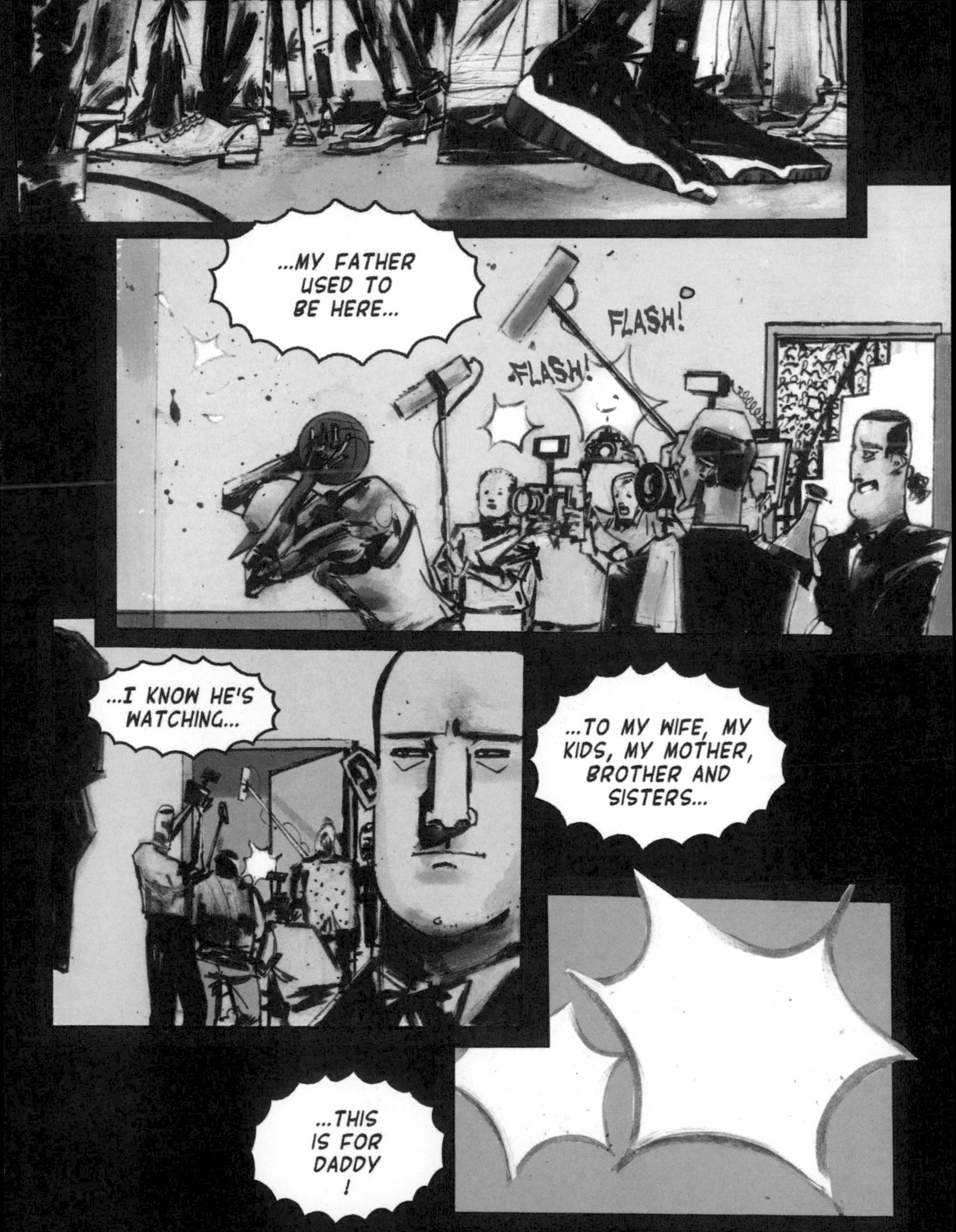
...MY FATHER USED TO BE HERE...
FLASH!
FLASH!
...I KNOW HE'S WATCHING...
...TO MY WIFE, MY KIDS, MY MOTHER, BROTHER AND SISTERS...
...THIS IS FOR DADDY !

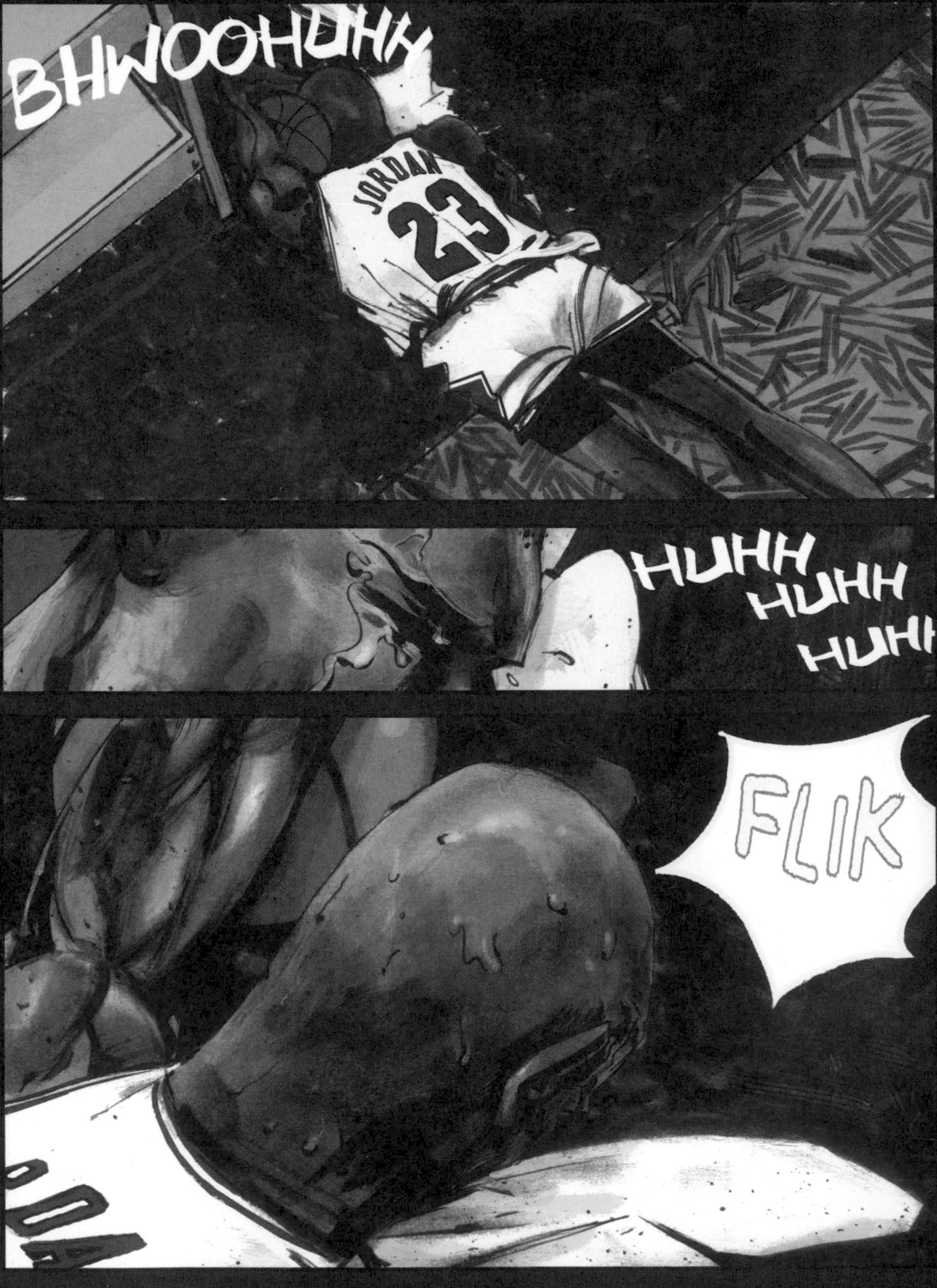
BHWOOHUHH
JORDAN
23
HUHH
HUHH
HUH
FLIK

ONE FINE NIGHT IN A CHICAGO SUBURB

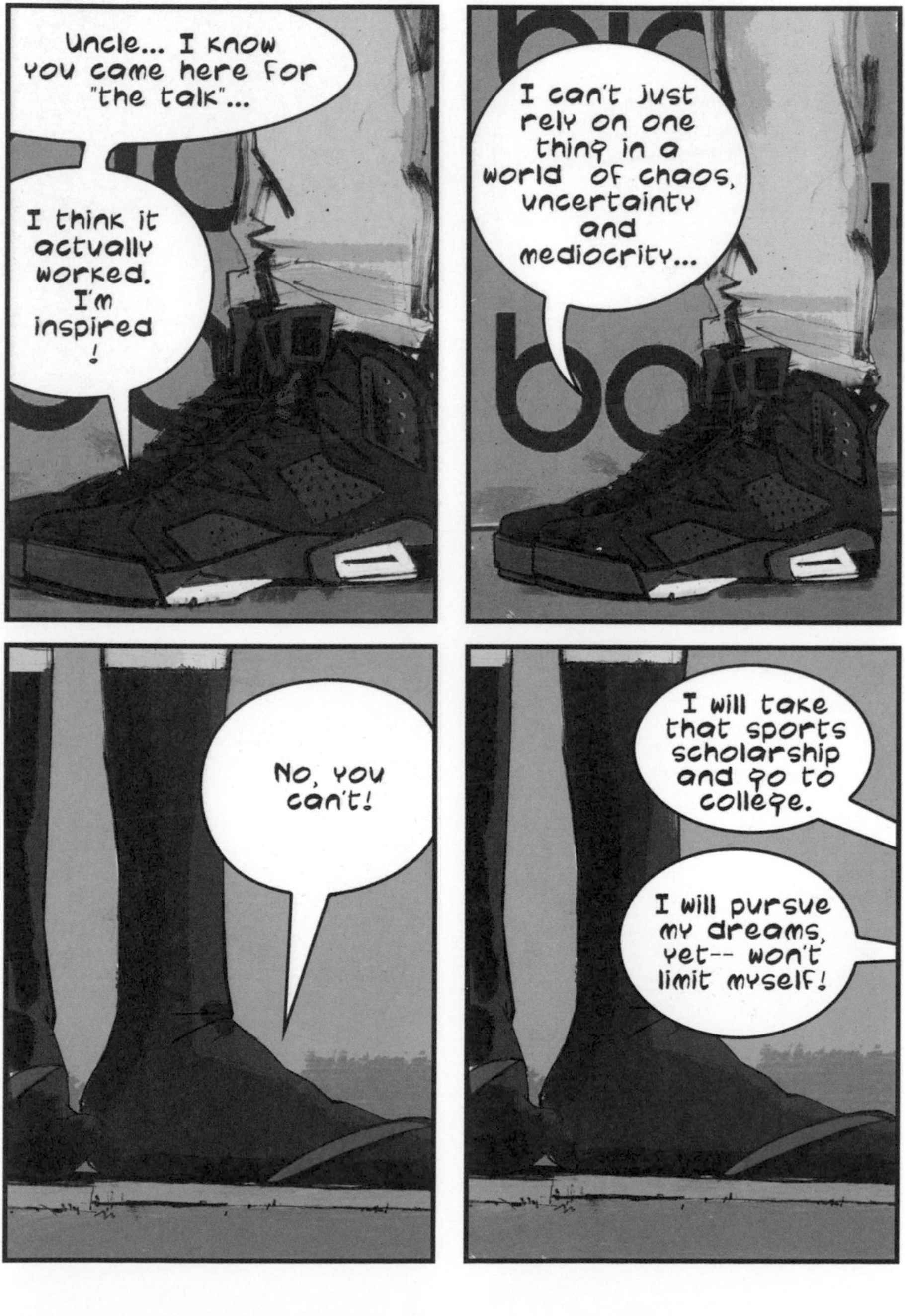
Uncle... I know you came here for "the talk"...
I think it actually worked. I'm inspired!
I can't just rely on one thing in a world of chaos, uncertainty and mediocrity...
No, you can't!
I will take that sports scholarship and go to college.
I will pursue my dreams, yet-- won't limit myself!

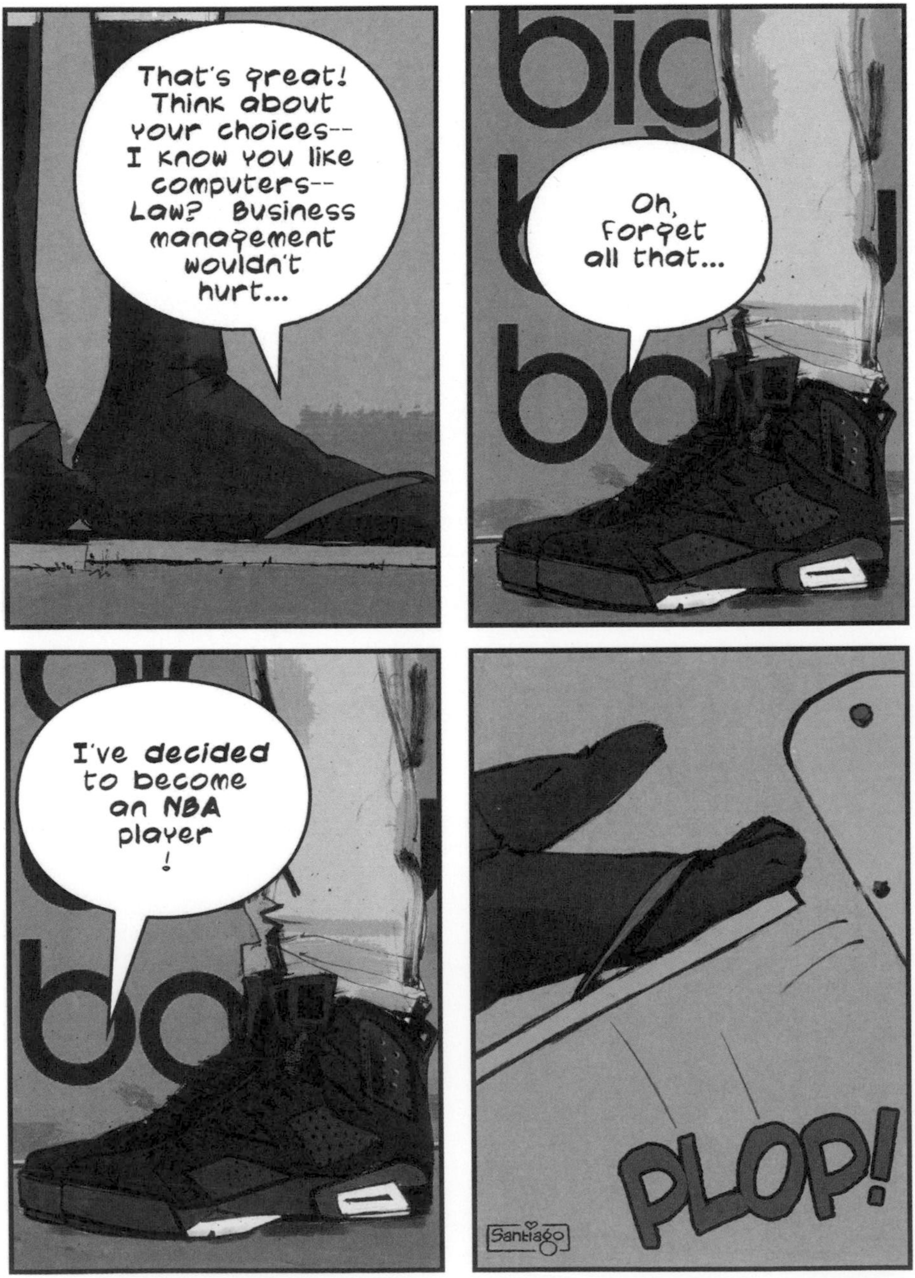
That's great! Think about your choices-- I know you like computers-- Law? Business management wouldn't hurt...
big
Oh, forget all that...
I've decided to become an NBA player !
PLOP!
Santiago

5:
Bitter Sweet Symphony

"When Michael Jordan came out of retirement back in '95, I used to work in a hotel before hustlin' Bulls tickets. That season I used the moneys to build a studio from scratch, cut a few tracks with my homes, printed promo t-shirts and all. I began making so much dough scalpin' the whole music idea got sidetracked.

Bulls tickets flew out of my hands no matter how much I asked. I made tens of thousands of moneys each season, no sweat. I felt like the Michael Jordan of scalping, son!

By the time Jordan and the Bulls won their fourth, then their fifth championship ring against the Utah Jazz, I wuz getting ticket requests from Japan, Denmark, Germany, you name it.

Cops?

Hahahaha...I had no worries with the law. They got their tickets, then looked the other way. My clients got more sophisticated though. Sold tickets fast to all kinds of people. Lawyers, doctors, politicians, hoop hoes, Wall Street types. I really went to town on the Wall Streets when it came to price. It's one of those situations where you know, in any other circumstance cats would have never bothered to address you eye to eye. But yeah, it didn't matter, they abided with sincere glazed-eye joy no matter the price. Strictly business, right? Jordan returning to Chicago left the city ecstatic, like when you wake up and realize it was just a nightmare.

Chicago, the Windy City, some called it the Second City, the Murder Capitol to those who really try to be mean. That's just ignorant. But 'The Second City'? –Fuck that, we got Jordan. That was my attitude. The idea is New York City is number one, right? This wuz back in the days when everyone in the world had mad love for the Big Apple, before New York bashing became a thing. New York had everything going on at the time, the money, the glitz, the music, the scene– whatever, everyone wanted to be there. *Ahh,* it had everything but Michael Jordan! And all the money in the world wasn't going to change that. Jordan had built roots in Chicago. Sweet irony is he was actually born in Brooklyn. *Ha!* New York would've given up their first borns if it meant Jordan would've joined their Knicks.

The money I made? The money went fast, I mean, Jordan kept getting better, Bulls kept winning, I wuz a young buck flying high... I didn't think about when or what wuz gonna end or being more disciplined with my music.

Yeah... right now I'm homeless, yes... Tryin' to get my act together– I mean, I've done it before.

I got out of the life soon after Jordan retired the second time. I've been living on the north side for a few years now. Tried to kickstart the music career a few times... I dunno, it was just a whole different scene, but no regrets.

There wuz game 5 in the 1997 Finals, Jordan played against the Utah Jazz while sick as shit, but it was irrelevant, everyone went through the motions and he still spanked that Jazz ass, who lost the game. Mike simply by the end of the the fourth quarter almost single-handedly created the key plays and scores to send the Jazz packing. Then he went on to win his fifth ring the game after.

I could've been in Salt Lake City for game 5 but I sold them tickets. That's my only regret. Saw it on TV though. That game to me was what Jordan was all about. Air Jordan, flying under the weather, with a pathological resilience to win. And he did...

Nah, no more music for me. The other day I headed to the Salvation Army, right after my AA meeting to grab some things, pants, a couple of shirts– and one of them had an Air Jordan image. As I headed to check out– *true story,* right then and there I read the front of the other t-shirt: 'T-Rex Unda Pendant Hip-Hop Trax'.

I wuz holding in my hand the very same promo t-shirt I printed more than a decade ago!"

-Eustace Stanford, 37

Thomas Parks (2008) "The Music Business: A Contact Sport"
Sociology of Music Journal, *Vol. 9, Nr. 6: 628-659*

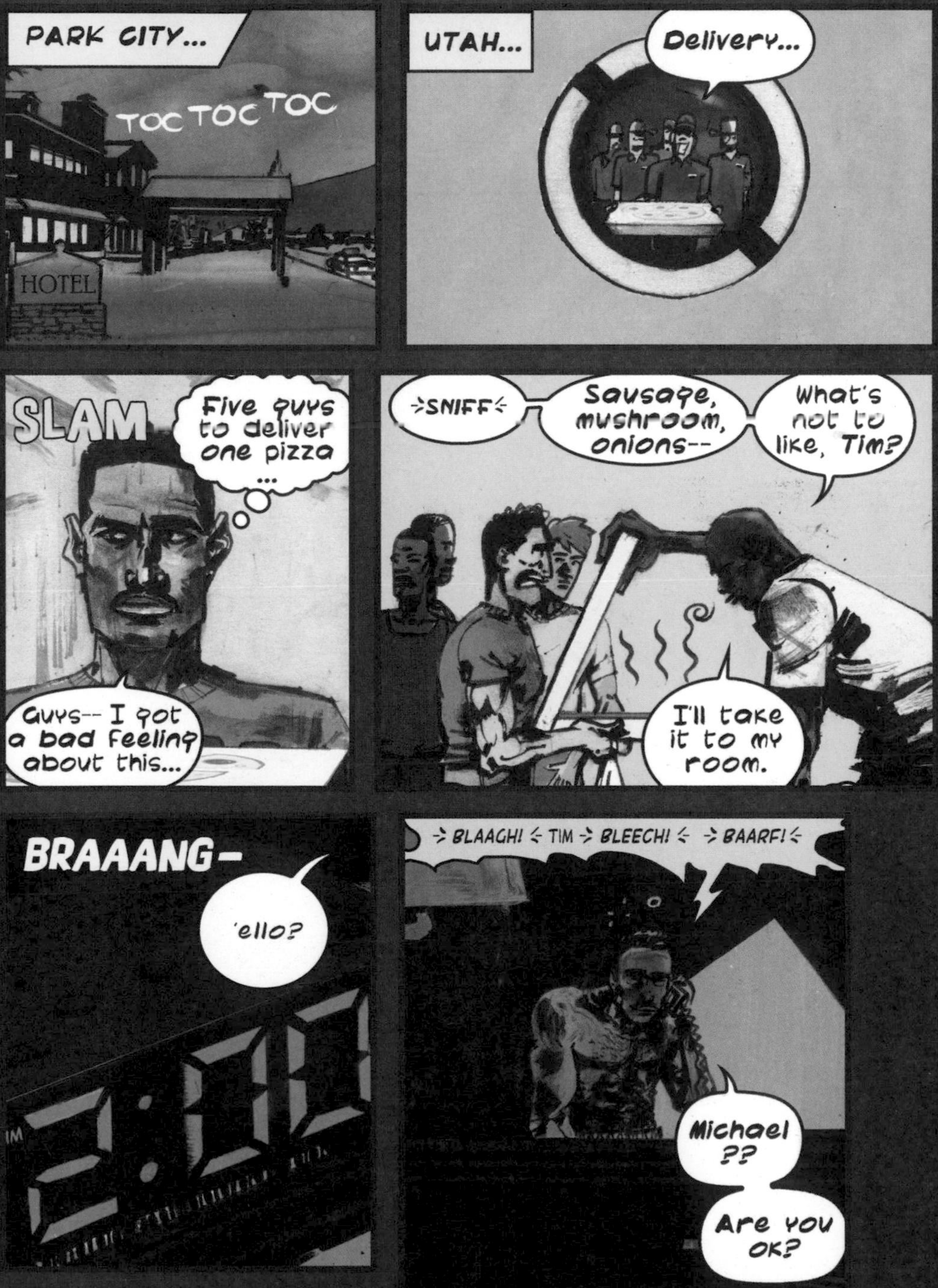
PARK CITY...
TOC TOC TOC
HOTEL
UTAH...
Delivery...
SLAM
Five guys to deliver one pizza ...
Guys-- I got a bad feeling about this...
SNIFF
Sausage, mushroom, onions--
What's not to like, Tim?
I'll take it to my room.
BRAAANG-
'ello?
BLAAGH! TIM BLEECH! BAARF!
Michael ??
Are you OK?

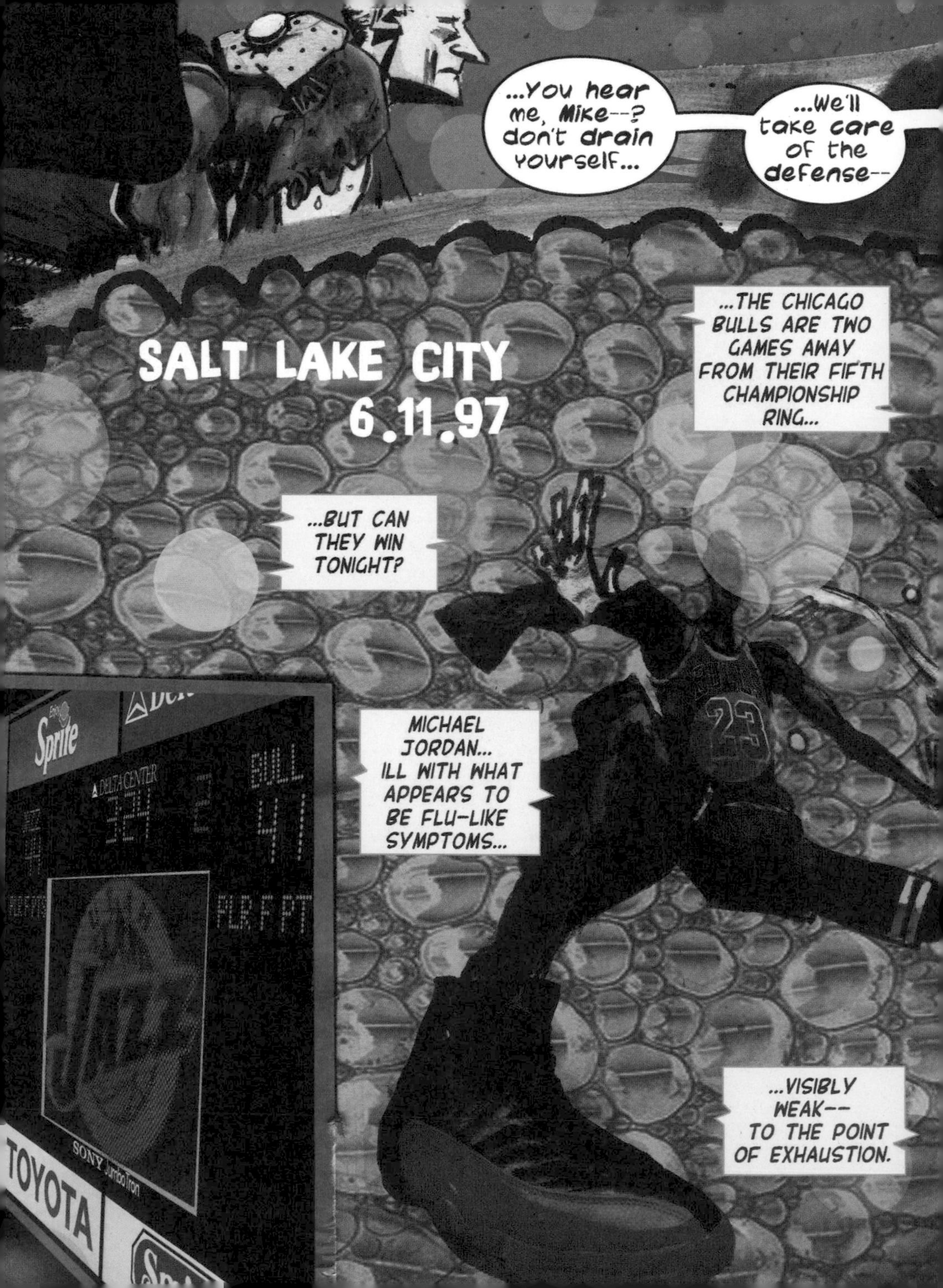
...You hear me, Mike--? don't drain yourself...
...We'll take care of the defense--
SALT LAKE CITY 6.11.97
...THE CHICAGO BULLS ARE TWO GAMES AWAY FROM THEIR FIFTH CHAMPIONSHIP RING...
...BUT CAN THEY WIN TONIGHT?
MICHAEL JORDAN... ILL WITH WHAT APPEARS TO BE FLU-LIKE SYMPTOMS...
...VISIBLY WEAK-- TO THE POINT OF EXHAUSTION.
Sprite
DELTA CENTER
BULL
SONY JumboTron
TOYOTA

--We'll get you the ball on the other end of the floor where you can score...
You can finish this game off.
THE QUESTION REMAINS...
HOW-LONG WILL-JORDAN-GO?
32

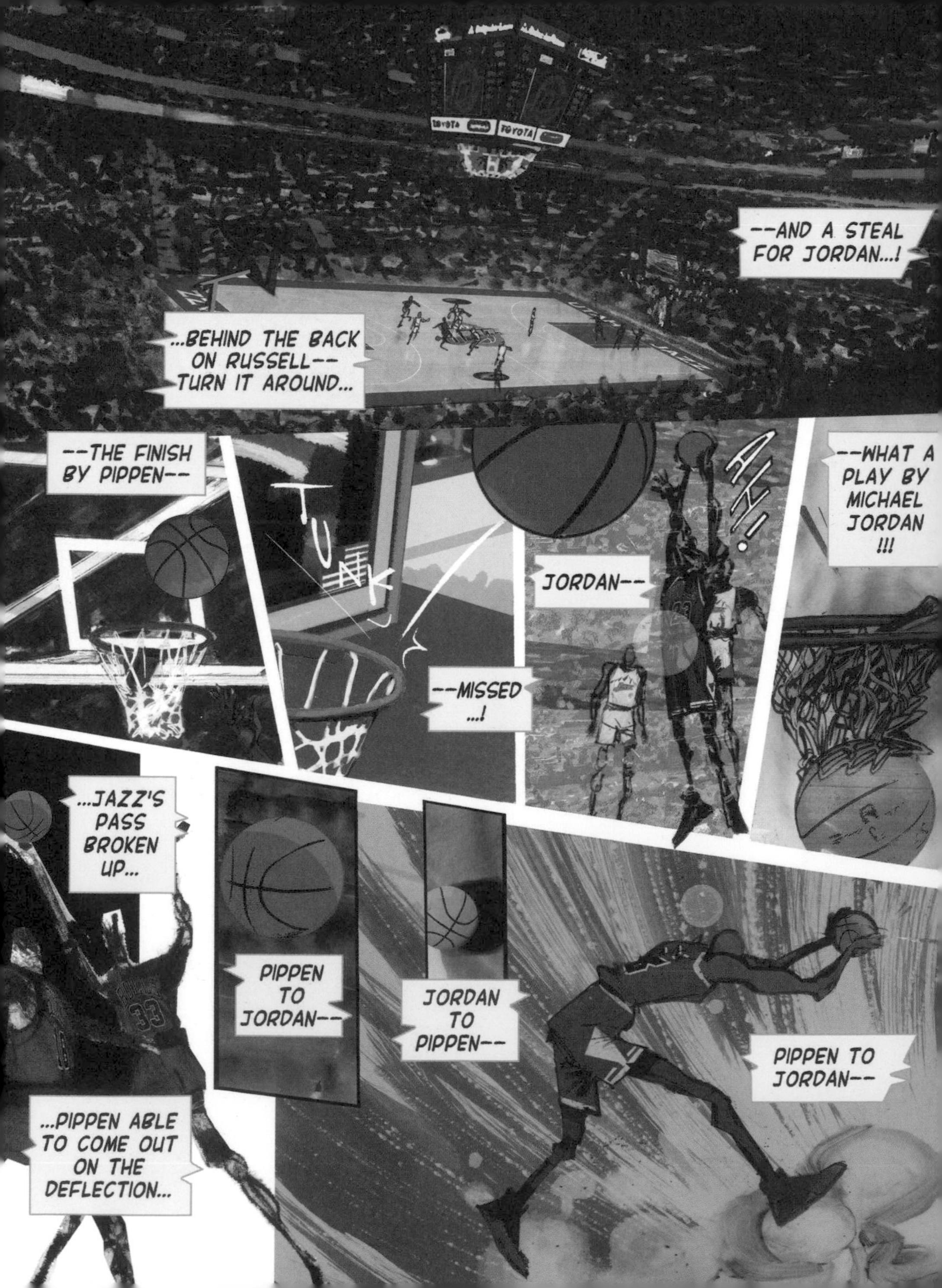
--AND A STEAL FOR JORDAN...!
...BEHIND THE BACK ON RUSSELL-- TURN IT AROUND...
--THE FINISH BY PIPPEN--
TUNK
--MISSED ...!
JORDAN--
AHH!
--WHAT A PLAY BY MICHAEL JORDAN !!!
...JAZZ'S PASS BROKEN UP...
...PIPPEN ABLE TO COME OUT ON THE DEFLECTION...
PIPPEN TO JORDAN--
JORDAN TO PIPPEN--
PIPPEN TO JORDAN--

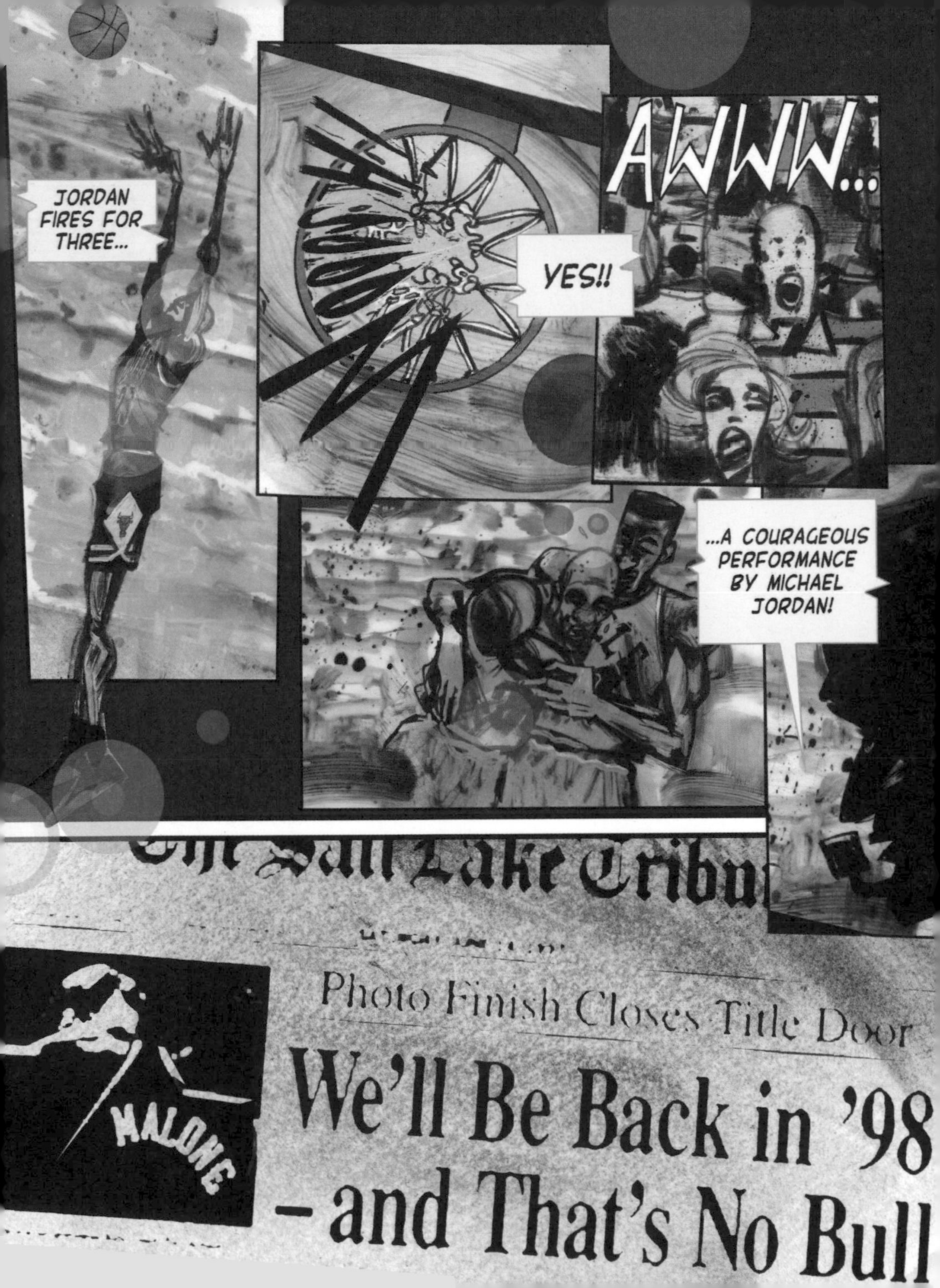
JORDAN FIRES FOR THREE...
YES!!
AWWW...
...A COURAGEOUS PERFORMANCE BY MICHAEL JORDAN!
Photo Finish Closes Title Door
We'll Be Back in '98 – and That's No Bull
MALONE

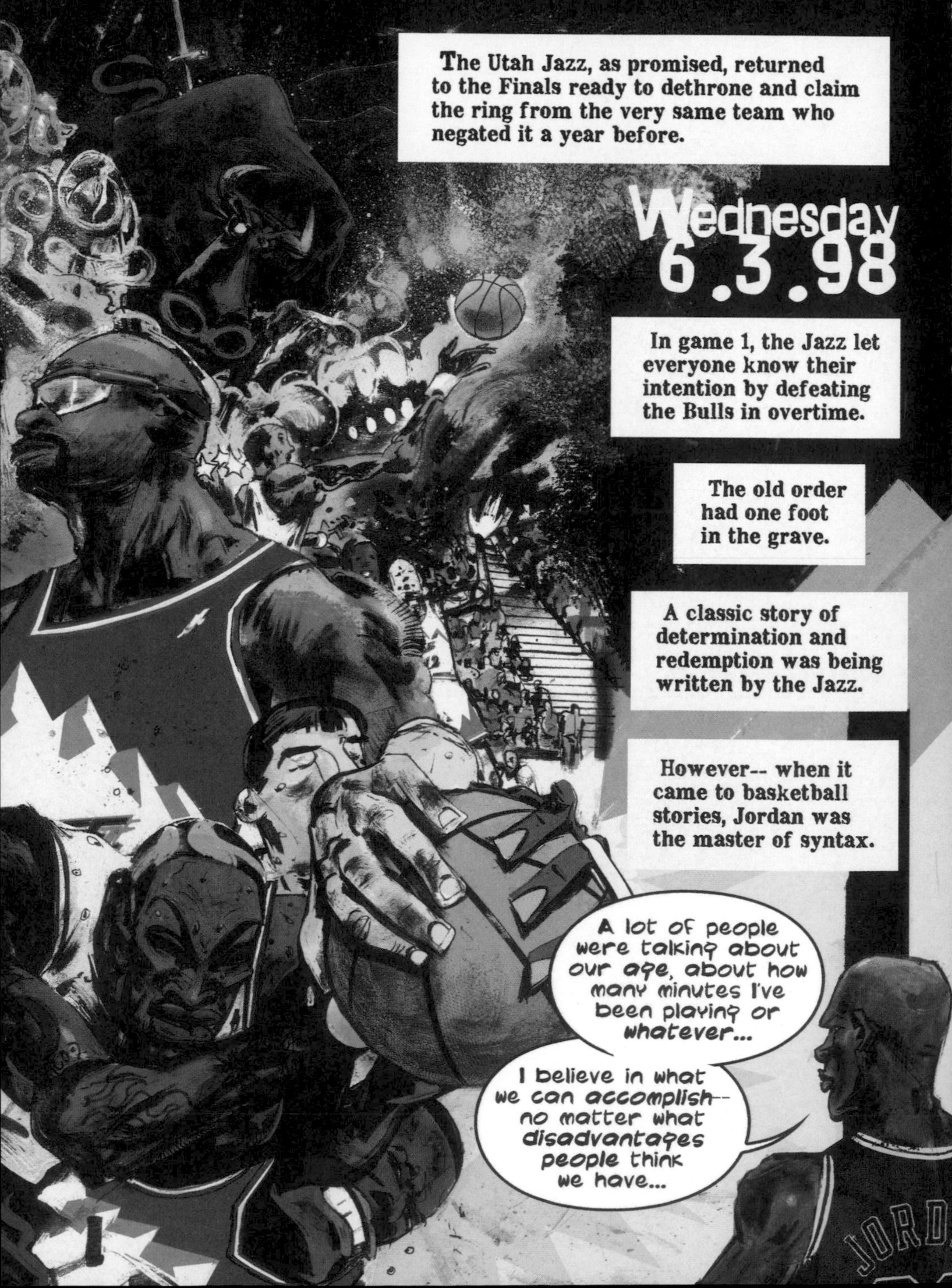

The Utah Jazz, as promised, returned to the Finals ready to dethrone and claim the ring from the very same team who negated it a year before.
Wednesday 6.3.98
In game 1, the Jazz let everyone know their intention by defeating the Bulls in overtime.
The old order had one foot in the grave.
A classic story of determination and redemption was being written by the Jazz.
However-- when it came to basketball stories, Jordan was the master of syntax.
A lot of people were talking about our age, about how many minutes I've been playing or whatever...
I believe in what we can accomplish-- no matter what disadvantages people think we have...
JORD

Enter Utah's weapon-- 6' 9",270 LB human tank, Karl Malone.
The Mailman --
As in, he always delivers on the court.
This time his erratic performance put the Jazz one game away from losing the Finals.
Excluding game 4-- so far Malone had only been handing out junk mail.
Game 6 was the opportunity to show what he had or face defeat.
Sunday
6.14.98
Of course-- everyone knows there's no mail on Sundays.

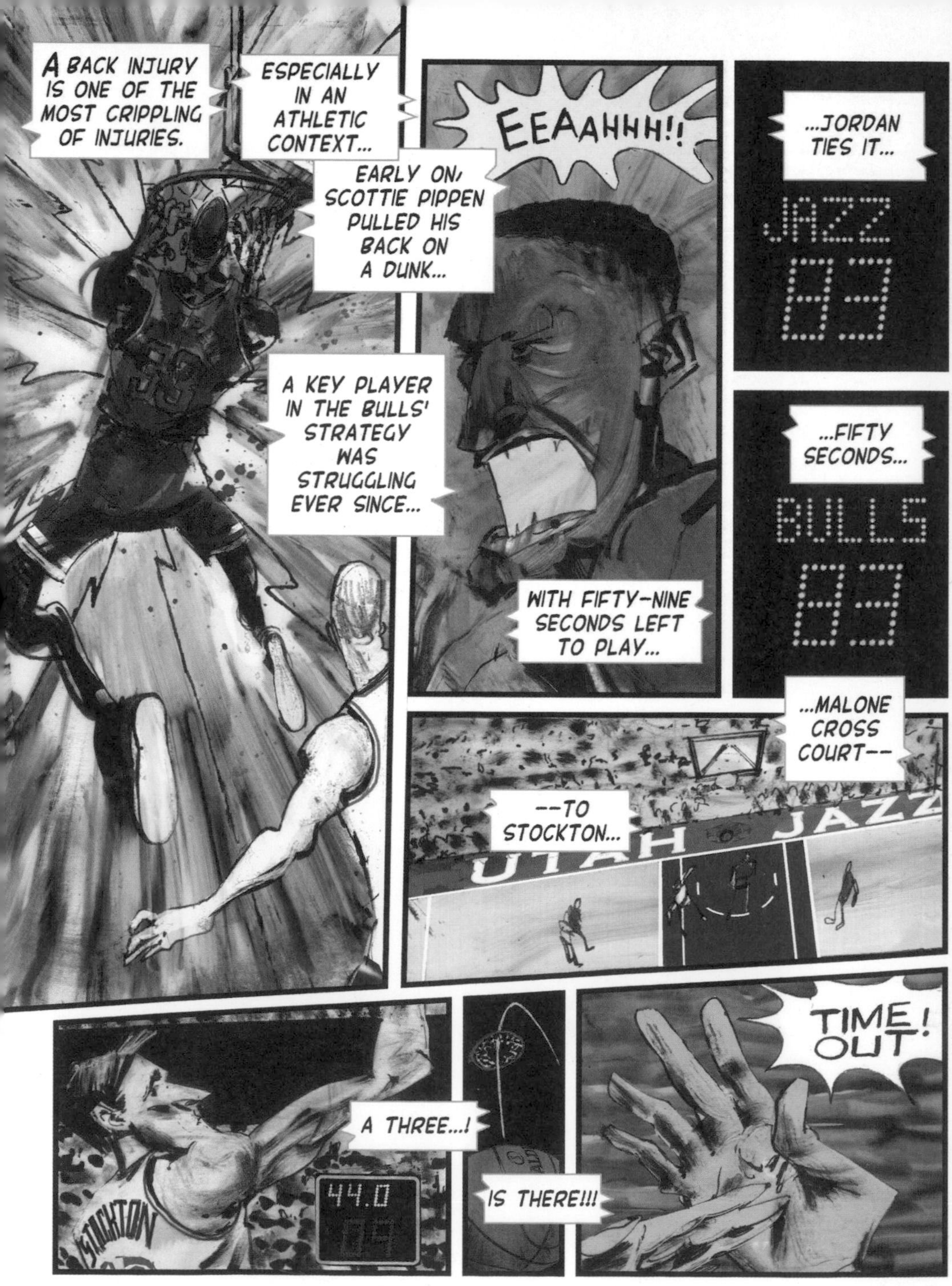
A BACK INJURY IS ONE OF THE MOST CRIPPLING OF INJURIES.
ESPECIALLY IN AN ATHLETIC CONTEXT...
EARLY ON, SCOTTIE PIPPEN PULLED HIS BACK ON A DUNK...
A KEY PLAYER IN THE BULLS' STRATEGY WAS STRUGGLING EVER SINCE...
EEAAHHH!!
WITH FIFTY-NINE SECONDS LEFT TO PLAY...
...JORDAN TIES IT...
JAZZ
83
...FIFTY SECONDS...
BULLS
83
...MALONE CROSS COURT--
--TO STOCKTON...
UTAH JAZZ
A THREE...!
44.0
STOCKTON
IS THERE!!!
TIME! OUT

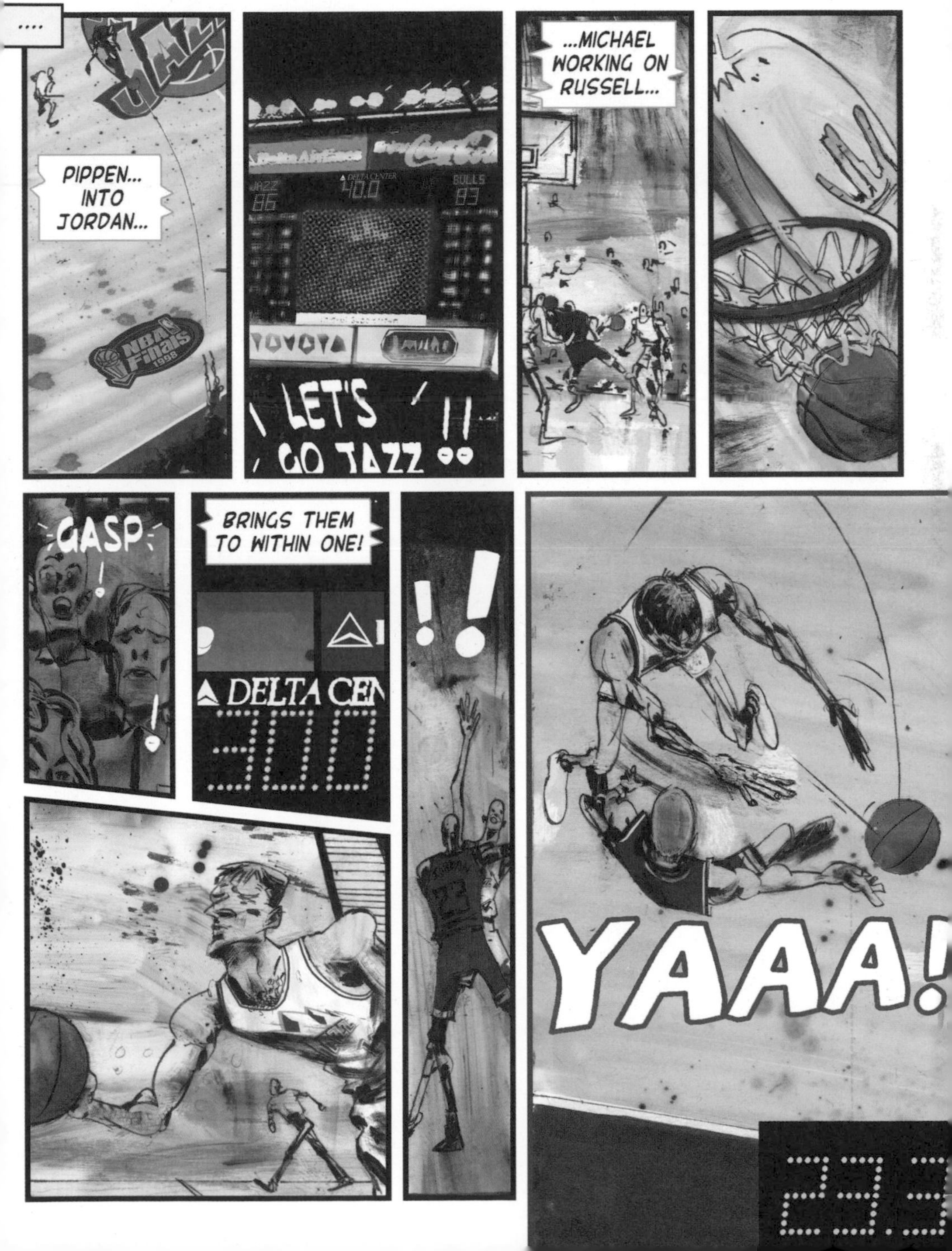
....
PIPPEN... INTO JORDAN...
LET'S GO JAZZ!!
...MICHAEL WORKING ON RUSSELL...
GASP
BRINGS THEM TO WITHIN ONE!
DELTA CEN
!!
YAAA!

23.0

21.0

TAP

MALONE HAS STUMBLED!

SWATTED OUT!!

MARV ALBERT
plead guilty to r
demeanor assau
and battery
charges in a 199
sexual assault tr
He was fired as
sportcaster but
rehired in 2000.
He later scrim-
maged backstag
with rapper 50
Cent's entourag
during a late nig
show appearanc
in 2006.
THUG LIFE.

ID NO.   DATE
974254 05279

ARLINGTON COUNTY POLICE

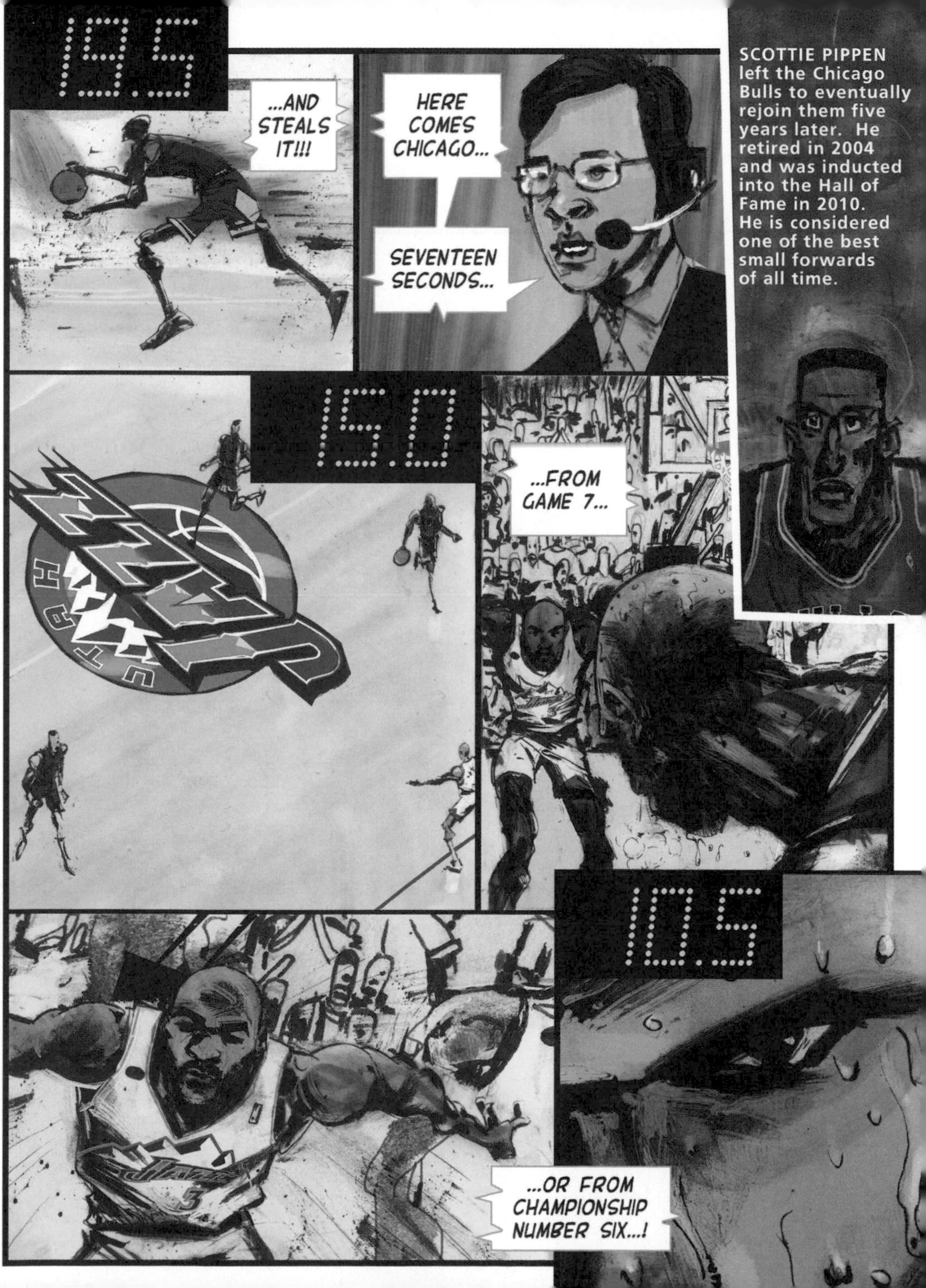
19.5
...AND STEALS IT!!!
HERE COMES CHICAGO...
SEVENTEEN SECONDS...
SCOTTIE PIPPEN left the Chicago Bulls to eventually rejoin them five years later. He retired in 2004 and was inducted into the Hall of Fame in 2010. He is considered one of the best small forwards of all time.
15.0
UTAH
...FROM GAME 7...
10.5
...OR FROM CHAMPIONSHIP NUMBER SIX...!

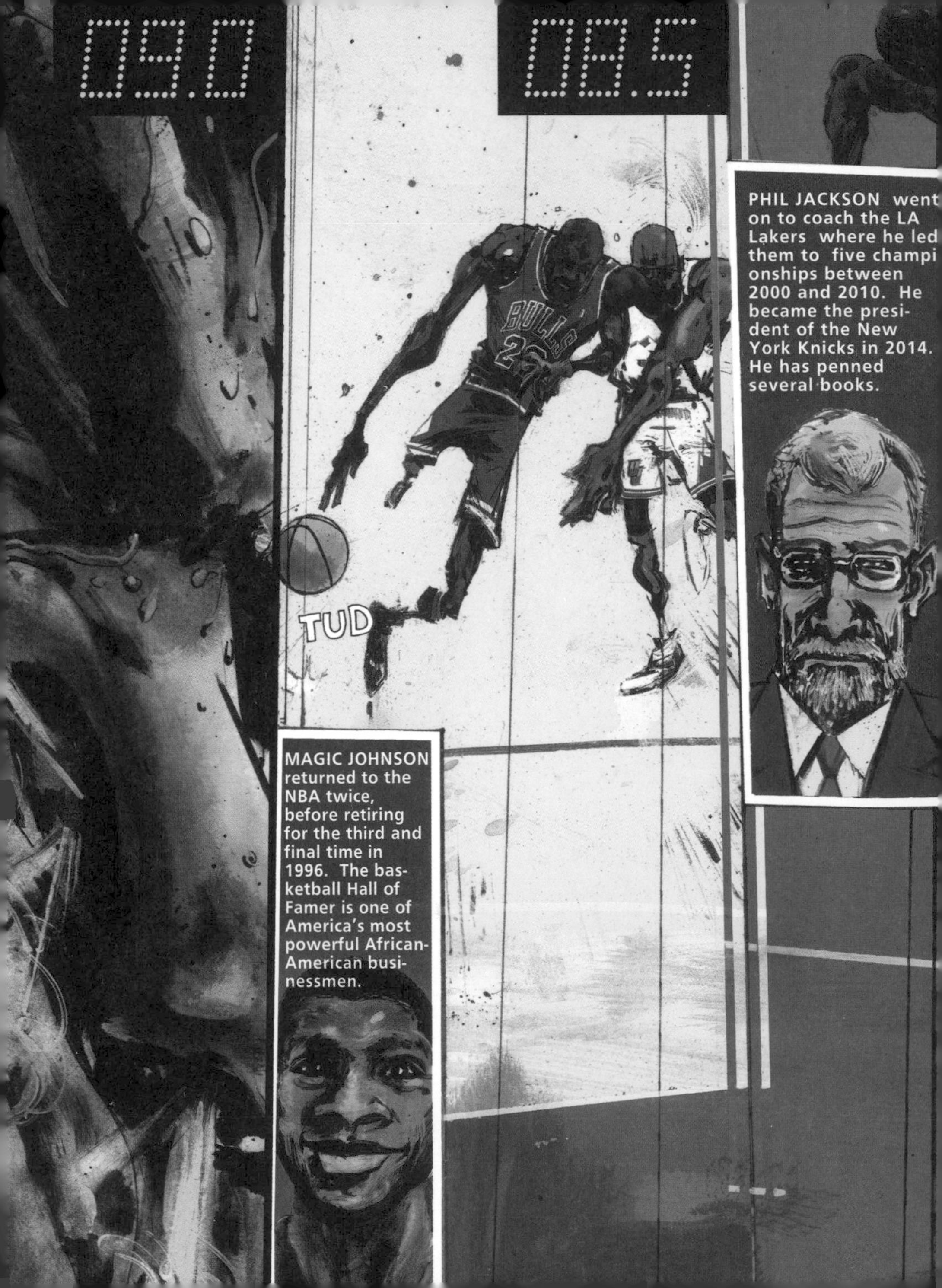
09.0
08.5
PHIL JACKSON went on to coach the LA Lakers where he led them to five championships between 2000 and 2010. He became the president of the New York Knicks in 2014. He has penned several books.
BULLS
TUD
MAGIC JOHNSON returned to the NBA twice, before retiring for the third and final time in 1996. The basketball Hall of Famer is one of America's most powerful African-American businessmen.

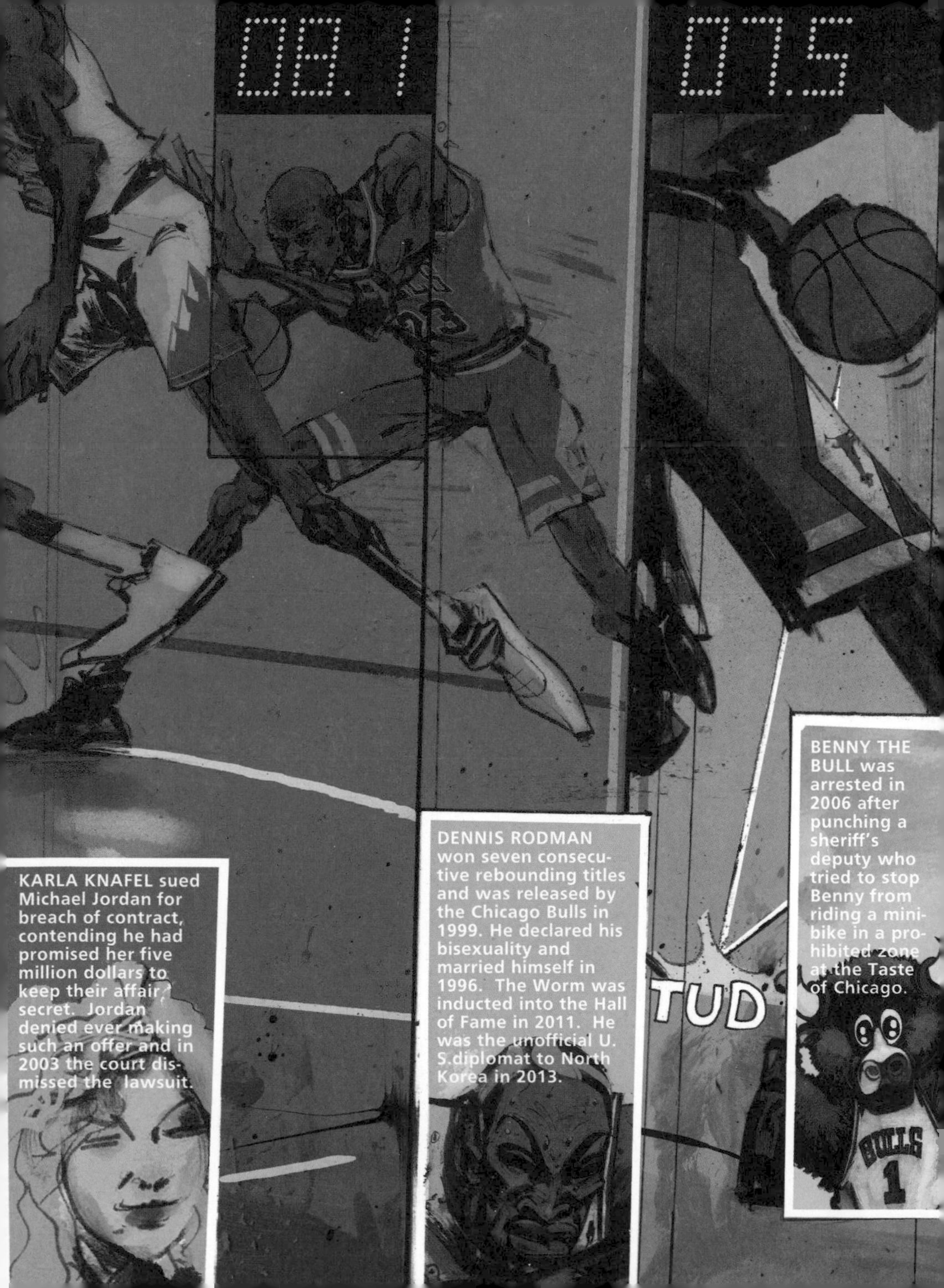
08.1
07.5
KARLA KNAFEL sued Michael Jordan for breach of contract, contending he had promised her five million dollars to keep their affair secret. Jordan denied ever making such an offer and in 2003 the court dismissed the lawsuit.
DENNIS RODMAN won seven consecutive rebounding titles and was released by the Chicago Bulls in 1999. He declared his bisexuality and married himself in 1996. The Worm was inducted into the Hall of Fame in 2011. He was the unofficial U. S.diplomat to North Korea in 2013.
TUD
BENNY THE BULL was arrested in 2006 after punching a sheriff's deputy who tried to stop Benny from riding a mini-bike in a prohibited zone at the Taste of Chicago.
BULLS
1

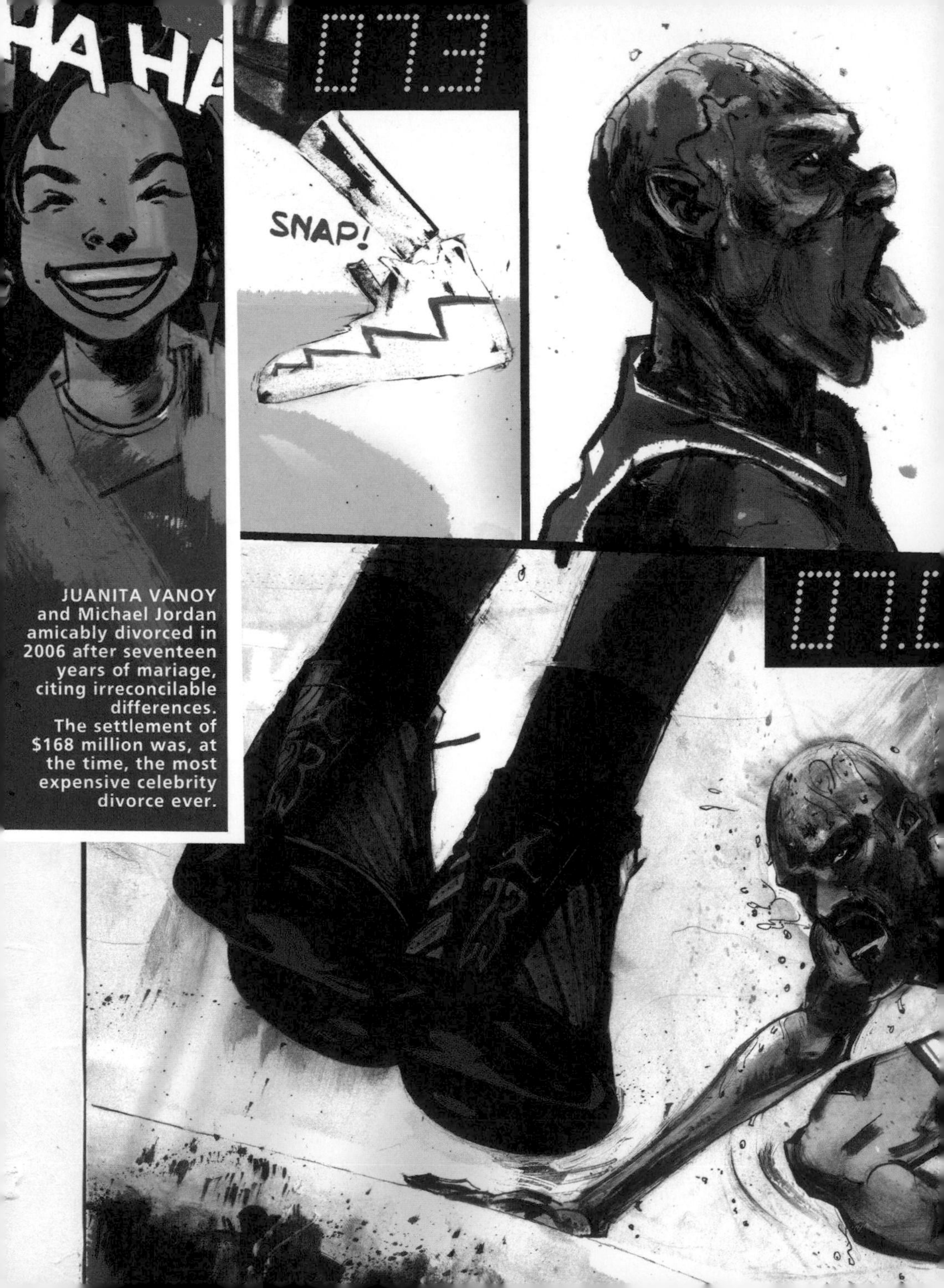
HA HA HA
073
SNAP!
JUANITA VANOY and Michael Jordan amicably divorced in 2006 after seventeen years of mariage, citing irreconcilable differences. The settlement of $168 million was, at the time, the most expensive celebrity divorce ever.

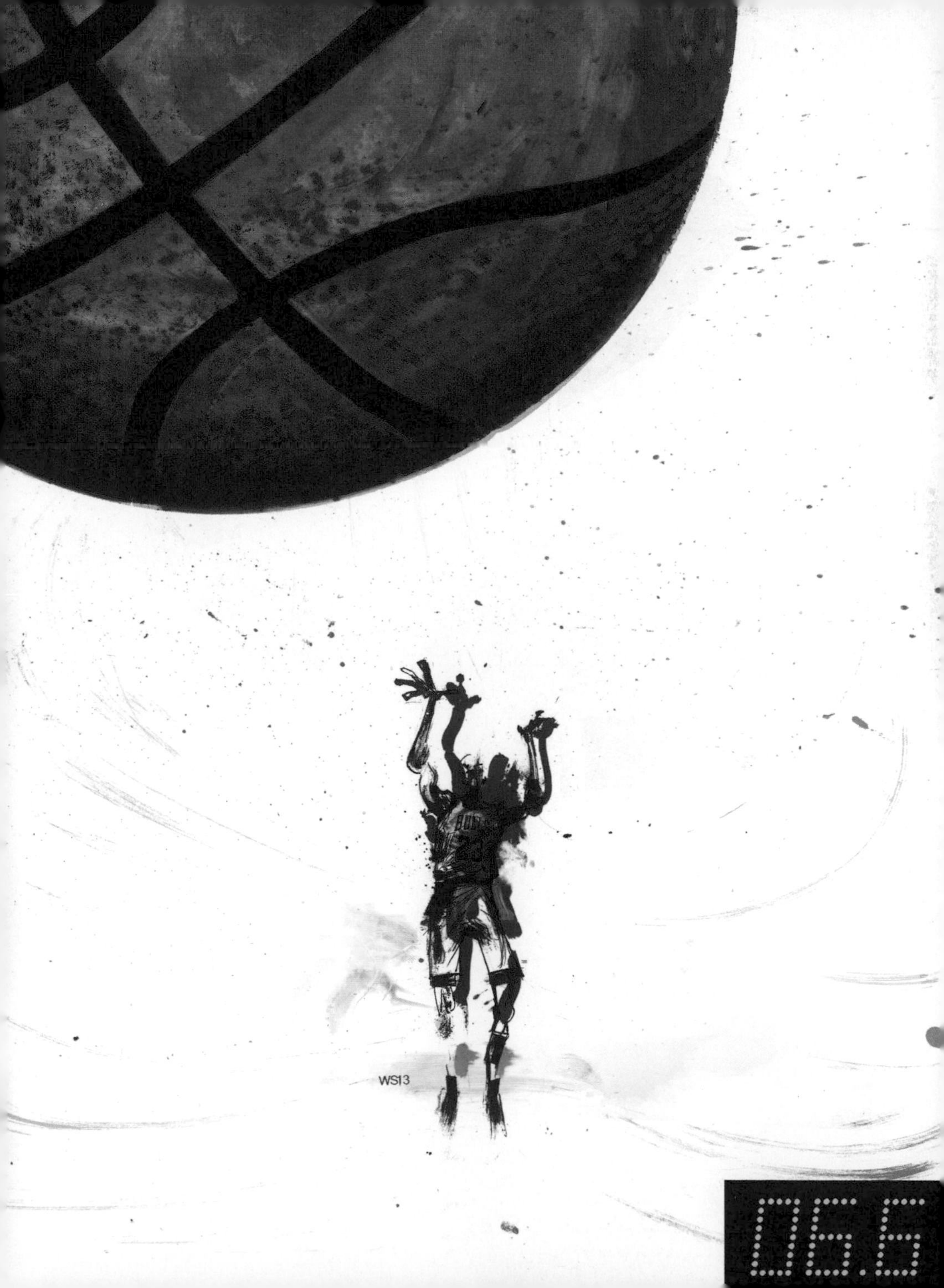
WS13
06.6

MICHAEL JORDAN and the Bulls beat the Utah Jazz 87 - 86 for their sixth championship in 8 years. Michael Jordan was named the Finals M.V.P. He retired only to come back to play for the Washington Wizards before permanently stepping away from the game in 2003. Jordan became the first former player to be a majority owner of an NBA franchise, the Charlotte Hornets, in 2010.

Michael Jordan's current estimated net worth is $1,000,000,000.

He continues to be lauded as the greatest basketball player of all time.

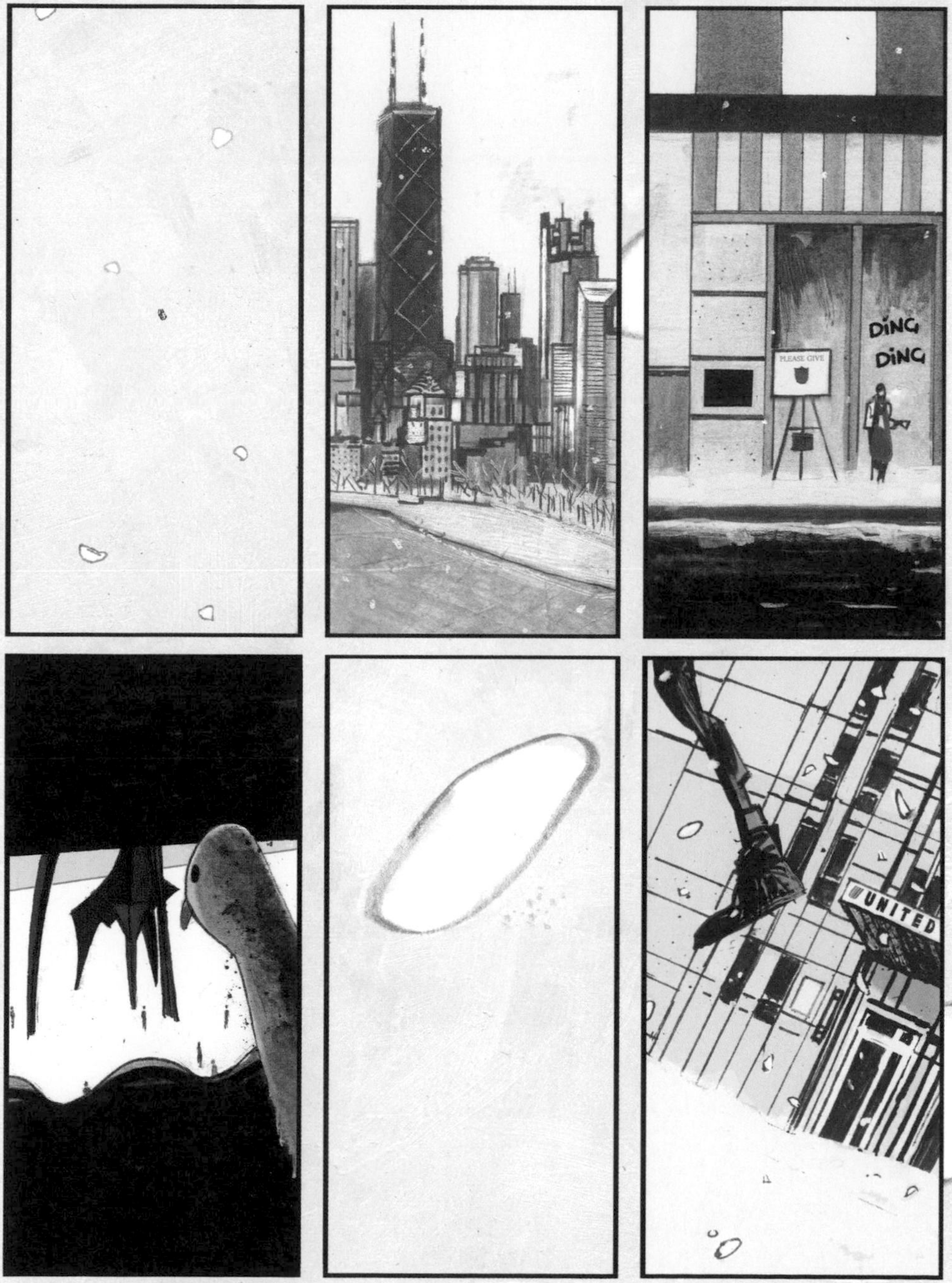
PLEASE GIVE
DING
DING
UNITED

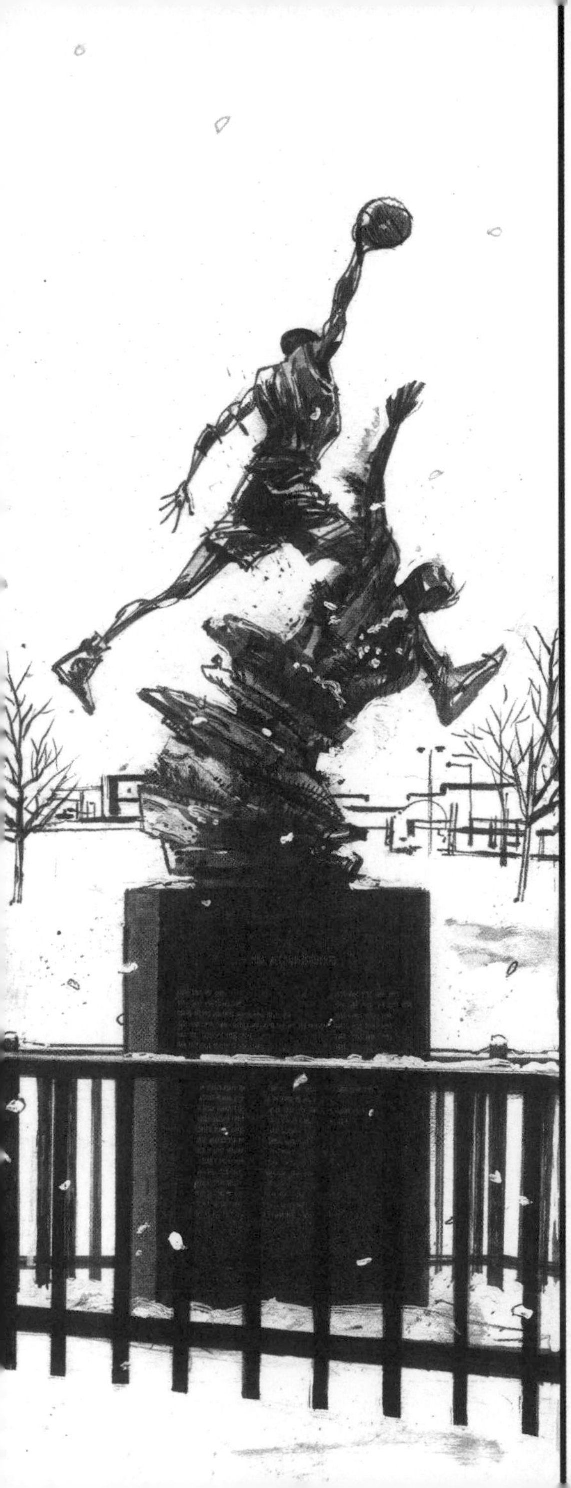

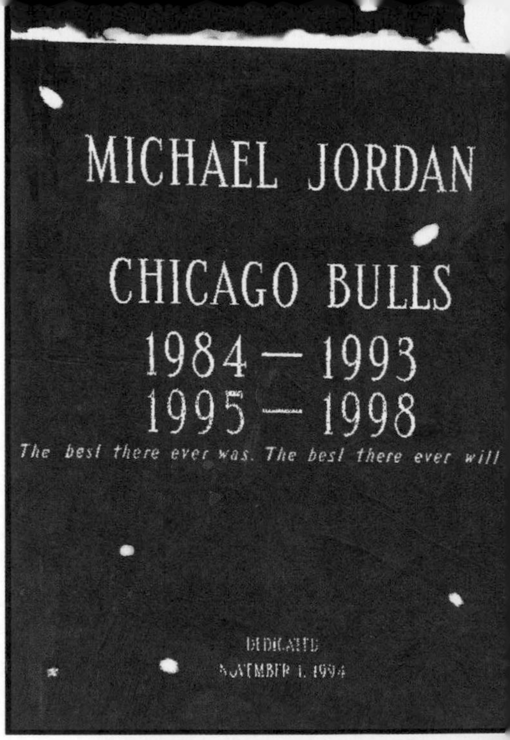
MICHAEL JORDAN
CHICAGO BULLS
1984 — 1993
1995 — 1998
The best there ever was. The best there ever will
DEDICATED
NOVEMBER 1, 1994

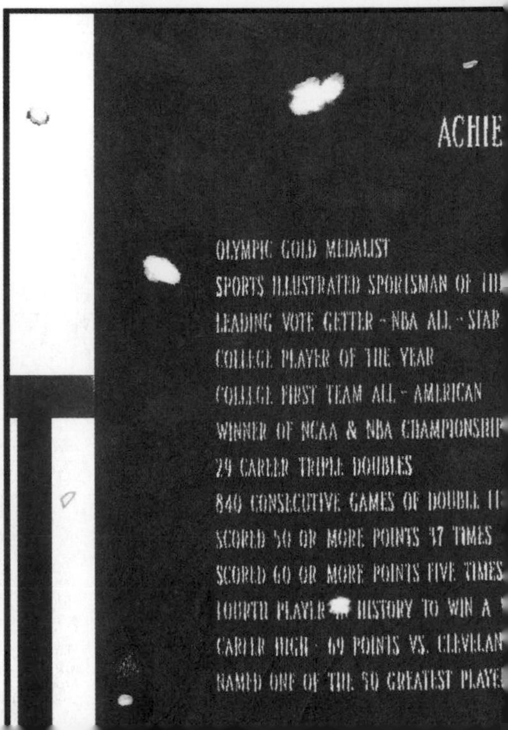
ACHIE
OLYMPIC GOLD MEDALIST
SPORTS ILLUSTRATED SPORTSMAN OF TH
LEADING VOTE GETTER - NBA ALL - STAR
COLLEGE PLAYER OF THE YEAR
COLLEGE FIRST TEAM ALL - AMERICAN
WINNER OF NCAA & NBA CHAMPIONSHIP
24 CAREER TRIPLE DOUBLES
840 CONSECUTIVE GAMES OF DOUBLE
SCORED 50 OR MORE POINTS 37 TIMES
SCORED 60 OR MORE POINTS FIVE TIMES
FOURTH PLAYER HISTORY TO WIN A
CAREER HIGH 69 POINTS VS. CLEVELAN
NAMED ONE OF THE 50 GREATEST PLAYE

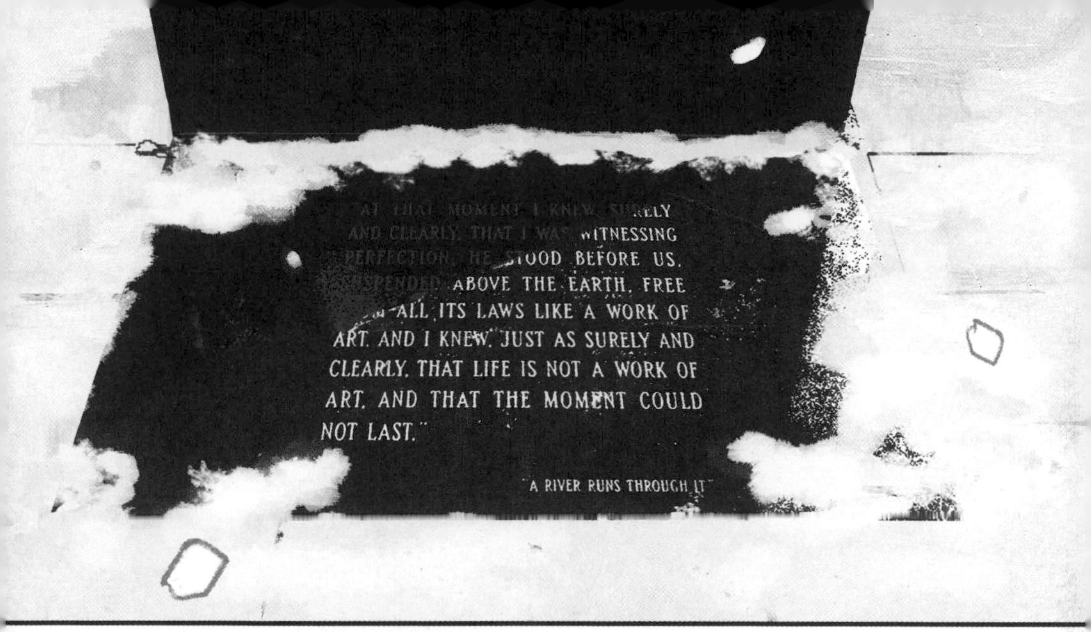

ABOVE THE EARTH, FREE
ALL ITS LAWS LIKE A WORK OF
ART. AND I KNEW, JUST AS SURELY AND
CLEARLY, THAT LIFE IS NOT A WORK OF
ART. AND THAT THE MOMENT COULD
NOT LAST."
"A RIVER RUNS THROUGH IT"

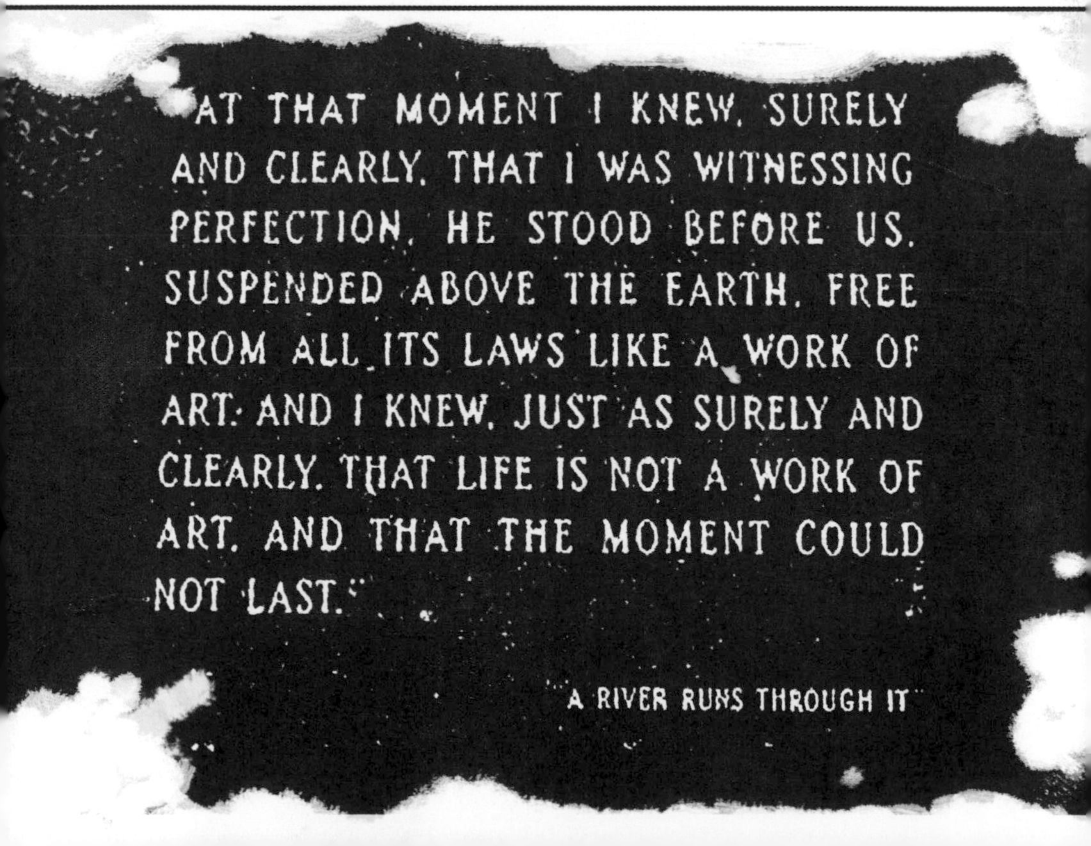

"AT THAT MOMENT I KNEW, SURELY AND CLEARLY, THAT I WAS WITNESSING PERFECTION. HE STOOD BEFORE US, SUSPENDED ABOVE THE EARTH, FREE FROM ALL ITS LAWS LIKE A WORK OF ART. AND I KNEW, JUST AS SURELY AND CLEARLY, THAT LIFE IS NOT A WORK OF ART. AND THAT THE MOMENT COULD NOT LAST."
"A RIVER RUNS THROUGH IT"

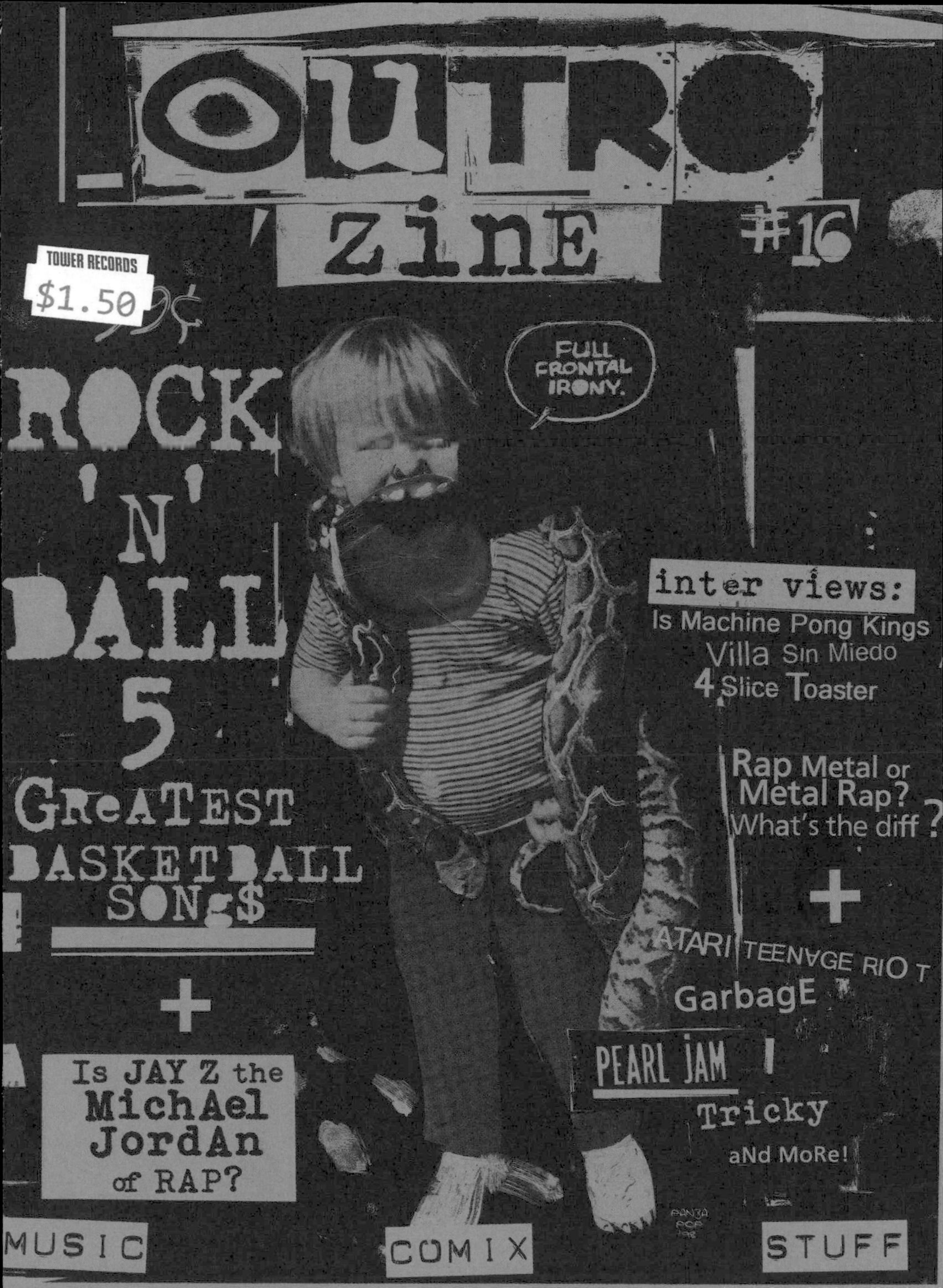
OUTRO
zine
#16
TOWER RECORDS
$1.50
99¢
ROCK 'N' BALL
5 GREATEST BASKETBALL SONG$
+
Is JAY Z the MichAel JordAn of RAP?
FULL FRONTAL IRONY.
inter views:
Is Machine Pong Kings
Villa Sin Miedo
4 Slice Toaster
Rap Metal or Metal Rap? What's the diff ?
+
ATARI TEENAGE RIOT
GarbagE
PEARL JAM
Tricky
aNd MoRe!
MUSIC
COMIX
STUFF

OUTRO #16

Full frontal irony

A Letter From Our PUBLISHER

THIS IS THE END. What started as a side project between bong hits to bring you our passion for music culture in an entertaining and different light is no más. As we discussed over a cold pizza, the logistics of making the move to a full blown glossy magazine, perhaps in a moment of autistic catharsis a thought occurred to me-- "what fucks we doing?" Sure, financially we lost money on every single issue we published, and at least once I had to resort to dubious acts to cover some costs. But these are not the reasons why OUTRO won't be around to indulge, and write about the next sonic morphs of civilization. It's been an interesting decade in music, grunge ate glam metal, rap ate grunge, and from what it looks like, rap will eat itself. Making money was never the goal. For five years putting out the zine was fun, now it's work, a drag, there's no passion to continue it, so it needs to be killed and everybody sent home.

You all out there aren't reading anyway. We have a loyal readership but it's no news people's reading habits have gone to hell for decades so there is no point. Reading is so rare of an activity that Chicago Bulls coach Phil Jackson, an avid reader, a sportsman, who reads, like- books, received them by the hundreds mailed from people fascinated by this rare phenomena. But no one ever wanted to be like Phil Jackson, we all wanted to "Be Like Mike", didn't we?

Tony Asphalt '98

Publisher & Editor - In - Chief
Tony Asphalt

Assistant Editor
Rob Mangles

Art Director
Brenda Sears

Research
Marilyn Wenner

Photography
Rudy Elliott

Art & design
Jeni Shank

Cover
Panza POP

Writers
Larry Young; Jack Diego; Jalapeño Master; Andy Grant; Adriana Davis; Peter Pungent;

Treasurer
Franklyn Delano Romanowski

Sandwiches
Cepillín

CONTENTS

PLUS

- Letters to the Editor
- Demo RevieWz
- Comics
- Have compUters taken oVer?

Also: The Barbi Twins, Dr. Seuss, COOP, Chapulín Colorado, & more!

Doing the right thing is not a strategy.

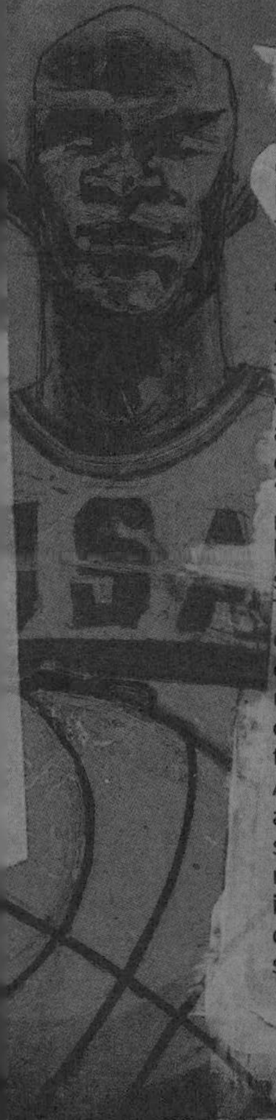

⏭ MICHAEL AIR JORDAN

MICHAEL JORDAN. If you think about Jordan's retirement as the decade nears to an end, it makes sense to revisit the song that made him beyond famous in the beginning of the decade. Sure he was famous, and ring-less, for many years, but 1991 was a game changer-- Jordan got his ring and his first commercial as a spokesperson for Gatorade aired.

'(I Wanna) Be Like Mike", the jingle for the TV spot: you could understand the charm of it, slow motion images of Jordan and children playing b-ball together, friendly, big smile at the camera as he's chugging the drink.

The generic, world music intro enters the screen, then voices of various adults singing and just when you are about to lose interest, voices of children break in to the earworm prone line:

"Like Mike, if I could be like Mike." By the end of the one minute commercial, the woman and the children are all in high pitch frenzy—"I wanna be, I wanna be like Mike" singing to the high heavens.

The "I wanna be like Mike" catch phrase then sprouted out of the mouths of newscasters, politicians, late show guests, everyone took the opportunity to enthusiastically (though unsolicited) voice, "I wanna be like Mike!" to the point of exhaustion. Magazines, comic books, other songs, everything made reference to it, you couldn't escape.

As the commercial went viral, it landed in radio stations, and someone slapped together a "band" to turn the 60 second jingle into the average 3:25 minutes song. That requires a lot of fodder, which you got in the form of the invariable "rap" part. The single cassette by something called "Teknoe" contained three remixes. Three. Of the same song.

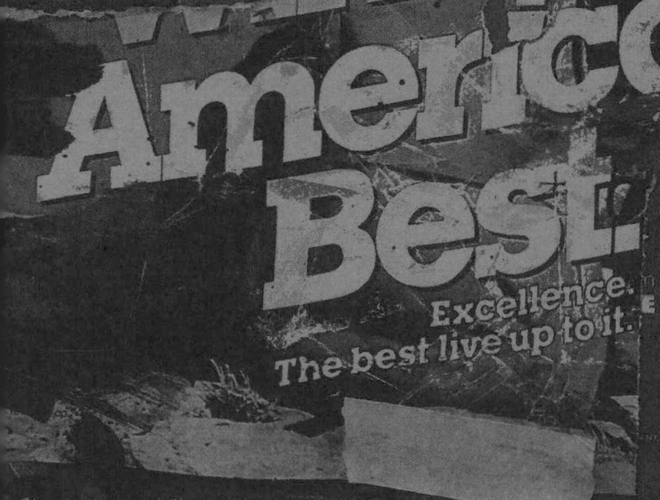
America's
Best.
Excellence.
The best live up to it.

by Jalapeño Master
art: Jeni Shank

"He is the most exciting, awesome player in the game today. I think it's just God disguised as Michael Jordan."
-Larry Bird

For any corporate headquarter, having a product slogan muttered spontaneously amongst the populous is like a band having a #1 hit. As catch phrases go, nothing came close to "Be like Mike" phenomenon.

But what does *"I wanna be like Mike"* even mean?

Does it mean different things to different people?

Sure, children of a certain age believed they can achieve his athletic maneuvering, and dream of it, not long before they understand that no, you won't achieve all your dreams. *"I Wanna…"* carries the self-centered immediacy of what great childhoods are. To *"…Be like Mike"* is metahuman.

Mike the person with all the money imaginable?

Satisfy every whim; what's too much? How do you know when it's enough, when you can have it all? What's the *living dose?* Music has a pool of samples of what's like to get more than what you wished for.
Unlike most musicians, athletes don't go onto the court to be insightful or to get in touch with their feelings; they're there to WIN.
The emotional response of cities depends on it.

Life in the fast lane in music is a cliché for a reason, but in organized sports, as a family spectacle, a certain kind moral conduct, or at least the appearance of it, is expected. That's why anything else would kindle an apology tour.

Realistically, all adults know they will never come close to seeing that amount of money, let alone perform his athletic feats. But the memories of what was once the open land of childhood fantasies and hopes still unspoiled by life forces is comforting, bringing alkaloid-filled joy.

I wanna be like Mike is a triumph in a product and consumer engagement. The perfect combination of hopes wrapped in nostalgia.

Michael Jordan was a role model, you know, for the kids. But most times role models are chosen, a strange expectation when you think about it. What reasonable role models for your child other than yourself is puzzling--unless you consider it a transfer of responsibility.Never mind all the unscrupulous stuff that goes on behind organized sports, nobody cares to protest these systems where so many young people don't make it.
But symbols are powerful.

Full flavor to match the best of times

Change perspective and you will change perception.

Did you rage against the machine and boycott Jordan products because of child labor scandal? And where do you stop? Will you stop listening to your favorite artist if allegations come out? Will you unlike their music?

You've come a long way, baby.

Not watch their movies? What would be your breaking point? Infidelity? Gay life? Necrophilia? If you look deep you can figure that if you reject everything that came from a point of origin adverse to your ethics or moral views, you will soon end up naked, shoeless, with no transportation, homeless and will end up starved, for the reality is that's how the system was set long before our births.

So if you can't change it or overthrow it, and if you are not working towards those ends, as you enjoy all the goods it brings, then step aside.
Be like Mike could have been an ad for a cologne, soap, or mouthwash. It would have been as impactful by default of Jordan's game. It became the definition of excellence, the cream of the crop. Had his game collapsed and his team not started piling up rings, the whole thing would have faded away in months.

Instead "Be like Mike" morphed into something you can actually aspire to. To be the best at whatever an individual aspires to.
With no secret code for how to get there, but the basic understanding that excellence is directly proportionate to the time dedicated to practice. No short cuts. No guarantees.

The best at washing cars?

Then you are the Michael Jordan of car washing. The best at flipping burgers? Then you are the Michael Jordan of grills; Eddie Van Halen is the Jordan of guitar; De Niro of acting, Ron Jeremy is the Jordan of porn, and so forth. MJ is the bar which those like him are measured by.
You could argue about his politics or lack of it, his business practices, but at this point very few would stand and refute Jordan's status as the best basketball player to ever live. The proof is in the pudding.

He entered the stage as a performer. To win and leave those who love the sport in awe with remarkable, fast food-like consistency. And that's the product. That's what you're buying. He plays basketball, and he was the best at it. Anything else is fluff.

"Consequences, schmonsequences-- as long as I'm rich." -Daffy Duck

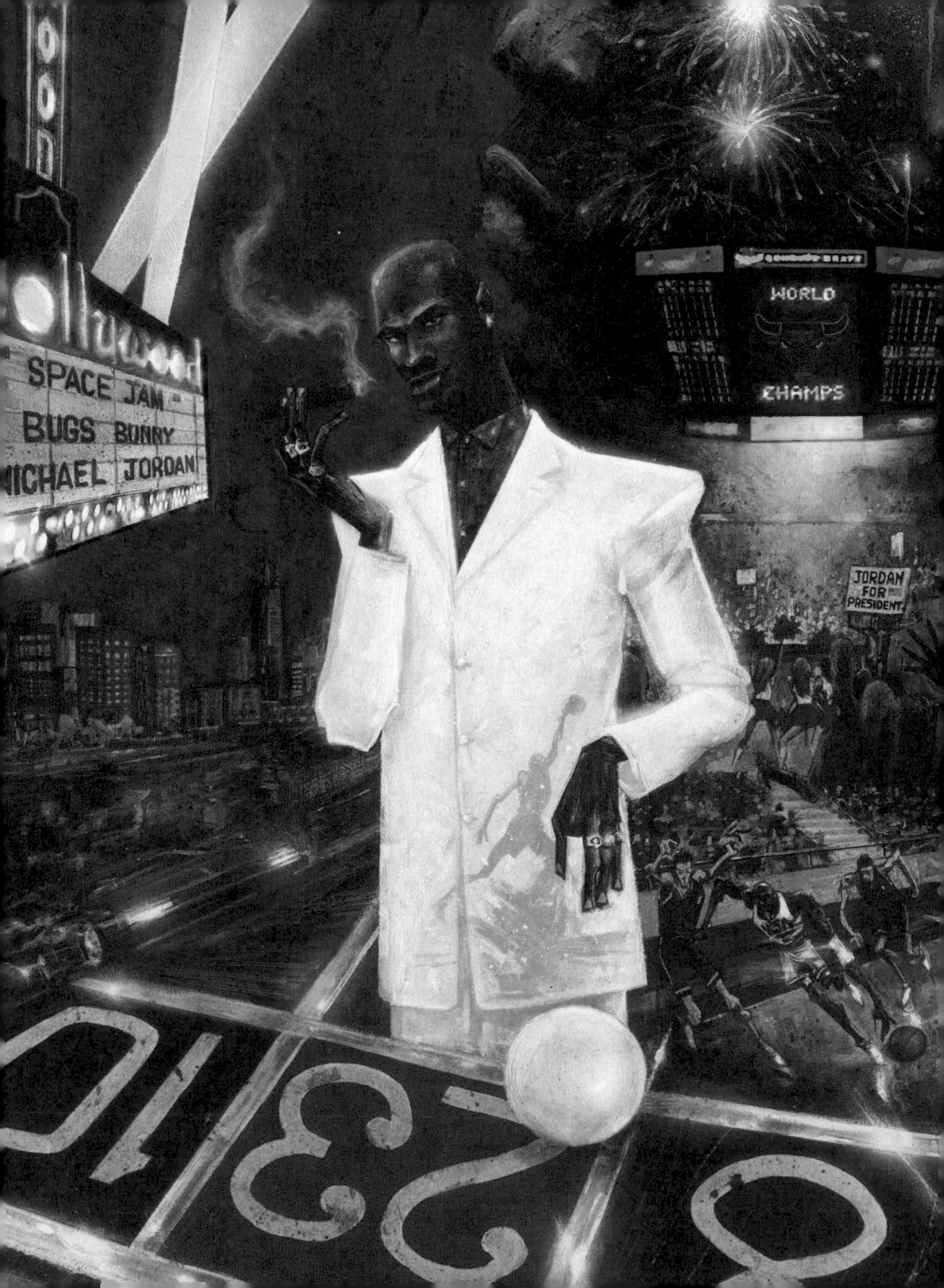
SPACE JAM
BUGS BUNNY
ICHAEL JORDAN
WORLD
CHAMPS
JORDAN
FOR
PRESIDENT

fin

WWW.FANTAGRAPHICS.COM

MICHAEL JORDAN BOP

Fantagraphics Books INC.
7563 Lake City Way N.E. Seattle WA, USA 98115

SANLIDA CHENG
editor

ERIC REYNOLDS
editorial liaison &
associate publisher

GARY GROTH
publisher

Additional Jacket design Keeli McCarthy
ART + TEXT by Wilfred Santiago,

FIRST EDITION 2014

ISBN: 978-1-60699-711-6

SUMMARY>> The astonishing journey of the greatest basketball star to ever play in the NBA and his evolution into the biggest icon of the 20th century.

Printed In The People's Republic of CHINA

10 9 8 7 6 5 4 3 2 1

N●TE AB●UT THE F●NT:
is graphic novel is mostly set in Doo Doo Brown, a typeface produced by ENGBOT & released in 2010. Designed by Wilfred Santiago, Doo Doo Brown nbines the classic characteristics of old style penmanship with the urban ight & aesthetic of the modern font.

Acknowledgments

For their critique, assistance, or inspiration while undertaking this endeavor, my gratitude to Gary Groth, Eric Reynolds, Keeli McCarthy, Jacquelene Cohen, Jen Vaughn, Janice Headley and Mike Baehr at Fantagraphics. To the Cheng family, Christopher Borrelli, Julie Deramos, Alex Cotto, and the city of Chicago.

And to my lady whom I dedicate this book, your endless patience, love and excellence is what made this graphic novel into a reality.

SOURCES:

WWW

AJR.ORG * BASKETBALL-REFERENCE.COM * CHICAGOTRIBUNE.COM * DEADSPIN.COM * ESPN.COM
NBA.COM * NYT.COM * SI.COM * THESMOKINGGUN.COM * UCLA.EDU * YOUTUBE.COM

NEWSPAPERS

CHICAGO TRIBUNE> June 10, 1991; May 2, 1992; May 10, 1992; May 11, 1992; September 10, 2009. DAILY
NEWS> November 5, 1991. DESERET NEWS> September 25, 1991. LOS ANGELES TIMES> June 10, 1991;
April 30, 1992; May 1, 1992; May 2, 1992; August 22, 1993; September 26, 1997; MILWAUKEE SENTINEL>
June 3, 1991; June 6, 1991. WILMINGTON MORNING STAR> February 17, 1979; May 28, 1993. ORLANDO
SENTINEL> August 14, 1993. SALT LAKE TRIBUNE> June 14, 1997. SUN TIMES> November 11, 1991. THE
GUARDIAN> July 9, 2012. THE NEW YORK TIMES> March 29, 1992; March 31, 1992; July 16, 1992; May 27,
1993; August 14, 1993. THE PHILADELPHIA INQUIRER> May 31, 1993.

MAGAZINES

AMERICAN JOURNALISM REVIEW> October 1993. CIGAR AFICIONADO> July 2005. EBONY> November
1991. ESPN> March 14, 2013. GQ> March 1994. HOOP> Summer 1991. JET> August 30, 1993. LA
WEEKLY> May 8, 1992. NIEMAN REPORTS> Fall 1999. ROLLING STONE> August 20, 1992; December 10,
1992; December 26, 1996. SPORTS ILLUSTRATED> July 1, 1968; November 28, 1983; December 10, 1984;
May 14, 1990; August 5, 1991; December 23, 1991; June 15, 1998; June 22, 1998; January 16, 2012.

BOOKS

DRIVEN FROM WITHIN> By Michael Jordan, Edited by Mark Vancil, Atria Books, 2005
ELEVEN RINGS: The Soul of Success> By Phil Jackson & Hugh Delehanty, Penguin Press, 2013
FIRST IN THIRST> By Darren Rovell, Amacon Books, 2006
FOR THE LOVE OF THE GAME> By Michael Jordan, Edited by Mark Vancil, New Line Books, 2001
HANG TIME> By Bob Greene, Bantam Doubleday, 1992
PLAYING FOR KEEPS> By David Halberstam, Random House, 1999
RARE AIR> By Michael Jordan, Mark Vancil, Walter Iooss, Jr., Collins Pub San Francisco, 1993
RELENTLESS> By Tim S. Grover, Scribner Publishing, 2013
SACRED HOOPS> By Phil Jackson, Hyperion, 1995
TALES FROM THE BULLS HARDWOOD> By Bill Wennington & Kent McDill, Sports Publishing, 2004
THE BALD TRUTH> By David Falk, Gallery Books, 2009
THE JORDAN RULES> By Sam Smith, Simon & Schuster, Inc., 1992

OTHERS

COME FLY WITH ME> Fox Home Entertainment, 1989
LEARNING TO FLY> Warner Home Video, 2006
THE OPRAH WINFREY SHOW> November 5, 1993

For Sanlida

WILFRED SANTIAGO

MJBOP

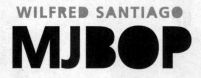